1918

1918

Babe Ruth and the World Champion Boston Red Sox

Allan Wood

Writers Club Press
San Jose New York Lincoln Shanghai

1918
Babe Ruth and the World Champion Boston Red Sox

Writers Club Press
an imprint of iUniverse.com, Inc.

For information address:
iUniverse.com, Inc.
5220 S 16th, Ste. 200
Lincoln, NE 68512
www.iuniverse.com

The author has made every effort to locate and credit owners of copyrighted photographs.

ISBN: 0-595-14826-3

Printed in the United States of America

FEB 2004

To Laura

Of course it is possible that some year will yet
see a Boston team losing a world's championship.

Boston Herald and Journal, September 13, 1918

CONTENTS

PREFACE

The scenes in this book were obtained from many sources, including players' descendants and friends, newspapers, books and magazines. No scene was invented. I have, however, edited dialogue to make it sound more natural.

When there were discrepancies among several sources, I attempted to resolve them to the best of my ability. Any distortions or errors are solely my responsibility.

Sportswriters, players and fans in 1918 referred to the World Series as the "World's Series"; with a few exceptions, I have used the modern term.

Readers who want more information on principal sources are invited to email me at: "ajw@1918redsox.com".

ACKNOWLEDGEMENTS

The author wishes to acknowledge the following people for their research assistance: Debbie Matson of the Boston Red Sox, Scot Mondore, Timothy Wiles, Bill Burdick and Leigh Connor of the National Baseball Hall of Fame Library, the staff of the New York Public Library and the New York Library of the Performing Arts, Greg Schwalenberg and Michael Gibbons of The Babe Ruth Birthplace and Baseball Center, Dick Johnson of the New England Sports Museum, Mary Beth Dunhouse, Curator of the Boston Tradition in Sports Collection at the Boston Public Library, Patricia Maurer of The Bostonian Society, Mary Ellen Kollar, Sue Klem and Michael Sparrol of the Cleveland Public Library, Diane Palmer of Marietta College, Marietta, Ohio, and the Society for American Baseball Research (SABR).

Thanks also to Robert Creamer, John Royster of *Baseball America*, Peter Koukounas of Corbis, Mark Rucker of Transcendental Graphics, Susan Brearley of The Brearley Collection, Tom Congalton of Between the Covers Rare Books and Joe Nathan and Steve Gietschier of *The Sporting News*.

The author wishes to acknowledge the individual assistance of: Charles Alexander, Howard Ballard, Rev. Gerald Beirne, Phil Bergen, Robert Bluthardt, Bill Carle, Frank Contey, Jeff Devine, Jack DeVries, Donald Duren, James Floto, Wes Goforth, Eddie Gold, Peter

Golenbock, Barry Halper, Inez Klein, Franz Lidz, Ed Linn, Norman Macht, Frank McMillian, Ed Nixon, Larry Ritter, Patrick Rock, Jim Sargent, Gabriel Schechter, Tom Shieber, David Shiner, Mike Sowell, Glenn Stout, Dick Thompson, Mike Vogel, David Voigt, Kal Wagenheim, Ed Walton, J. Vincent Watchorn and Paul Zingg.

Heartfelt thanks to the relatives of the 1918 Red Sox players: Allen Agnew, Elizabeth Mays Barker, Maurice Dubuc, Jeanne Fahey, John Hooper, Ethel Koneman, Eileen Littlefield, Dave Shean Jr., Julia Ruth Stevens, Robert Thomas, Susan Constance Thomas, Warren Thomas and William Wagner.

Special thanks to Thomas Foley and his daughter Mary McNiff, and to Ralph Sheridan.

Thanks to Ned Martin and Jim Woods (Red Sox radio), Peter Gammons (*Boston Globe*) and Steve Simels (*Stereo Review*) for early inspiration.

Thanks to Chris Corrigan for proofreading and Kate Robison for website tips.

Thanks to friends who offered encouragement, lodging and sympathetic ears: Tom Adelman, Larry Cahn, Barry Crimmins, Frederick Curry, Abby Evans, Joan Gilbert, Matt Hopkins, Connie Kaminker, Alan Kissane, Ray Parizo, Anthony Scarzafava, Jane Schwartz and Mary Wood. Thanks also for the unceasing joy and desk-side companionship provided by the most wonderful dogs in the world: Gypsy, Clyde, Cody and Buster.

And a ticker-tape parade to my partner Laura Kaminker (a Yankees fan) for her unflagging support, encouragement, patience, editing and organization skills. Her periodic swift kicks were a large reason this project moved beyond a pile of research notes and microfilm printouts.

I

VICTORY

It was a fastball, a waste pitch left too far out over the plate. As soon as it left George Tyler's left hand, Babe Ruth picked up the ball's rotation, and his eyes lit up.

With a sharp intake of breath, the young Boston Red Sox slugger stepped into the pitch. In his mind, the crowd at Fenway Park—20,000 fans, staring, howling, imploring—fell away to silence as he cut the air with a ferocious swing. All he heard was hard wood hitting old leather.

It sounded like a rifle shot. The ball went screaming over the second baseman's head, not rising more than 10 feet off the ground. In right field, Max Flack of the Chicago Cubs took one step in—then suddenly realized his mistake. He turned his back to the infield and started running as fast as he could. He leapt, but the ball sailed over his glove, bounced once and banged up against the bleacher fence.

Fenway Park erupted. Straw hats sailed through the air. Scorecards and bags of peanuts flew skyward. Men slapped each other on the back and cheered their hero with lusty, proprietary roars. On the field, everyone was in motion: Flack chasing the ball to deep right field, Dode

Paskert sprinting over from center, Charlie Pick coming out from second base to relay the outfielder's throw, Charlie Deal straddling third base, watching the action unfold. Boston runners George Whiteman and Stuffy McInnis crossed the plate, both turning to watch Ruth tearing around second, dead set on third.

Babe slid hard into the bag—SAFE! Deal tossed the ball back to Tyler. The crowd yelled even louder. Ruth stood on the bag, hands on his hips, the ovation echoing in his ears. What a remarkable season it had been for the 23-year-old Boston pitcher. His dreams of playing every day finally had been taken seriously and he had thrived. His name had begun appearing in newspaper headlines around the country and hundreds of people came out to games for no other reason than to see him in uniform. For seven weeks in July and August, he achieved a streak of sustained excellence unmatched in baseball history. It was fitting that Ruth's first World Series hit was a triple, because deep in his heart, Babe knew that *nothing* felt better than smacking a three-bagger with men on base.

As Tyler walked slowly back to the center of the diamond with his head down, the triple was replayed in 20,000 minds and its importance began to sink in. The Red Sox now held a 2-0 lead in Game Four of the 1918 World Series. Boston would go on to win the game 3-2, widening its lead over Chicago to three games to one.

Two days later, on September 11, the Red Sox won their third World Series championship in four years, their fourth in seven seasons, and became the first team ever to win five World Series titles. Of course, none of the 15,238 people in Fenway Park that Wednesday afternoon could have known the significance that Game Six victory would eventually hold. If they had, they might not have filed out so quietly afterwards, their overcoats buttoned against the early autumn chill. If any of those fans could have foreseen the future, they might have lingered a little longer, tried to burn a stronger imprint of the game into their minds.

Exactly two months later, the Great War in Europe would come to an end. No one could imagine that after that beleaguered 1918 season—a summer in which the eventual champions battled clubhouse dissensions, threats of a players' strike, the bumbling ineffectiveness of the game's ruling body, a possible shut-down of the game by the government, and a tragic, untimely death—Red Sox fans would wait and wait and wait—now 82 years and counting—for another World Series title.

2

"BASEBALL IS IN GREATER DANGER NOW THAN EVER BEFORE"

Harry Hooper tugged his white cap snugly down on his head, walked the length of the Boston dugout and stepped up into the bright April sunshine.

One week ago, Hooper and his Red Sox teammates had been riding a train through Louisiana and Alabama, passing blossoming magnolias and lily-filled ponds, heading north after their spring training tour with the Brooklyn Dodgers. The team arrived in Boston on Friday, April 12, expecting to work out at Fenway Park before Monday's season-opening game, and were shocked at the frigid temperatures and slush-covered sidewalks. A fierce storm of freezing rain and snow had caused tremendous damage along the coastline, and the Red Sox players, having shipped their overcoats with the equipment trunks, shivered as they headed to their various apartments, boarding houses and hotel rooms.

"I'm gloomy," manager Ed Barrow said. "To come home and find the ground covered with snow is enough to sadden anyone. The players feel the same way. They're anxious to get started. I had hoped to have the men practice at Fenway tomorrow, but that's out of the question now."

Jerome Kelley and his grounds crew worked all day Sunday and Monday morning getting the field ready for the first game of the American League's 19th season and the Red Sox's seventh year at Fenway Park. One of the men out shoveling snow was Red Sox owner and president Harry Frazee. Sections of the grandstands had been completely overhauled in the off-season and thanks to the grounds crew and a warm weekend, the field was in good shape. Only scattered portions of the outfield remained soggy.

Hooper warmed up along the first base line, slow-tossing with a teammate, and when a few fans behind the home dugout called out his name, he turned and waved. He was beginning his 10th season with the Red Sox, an anniversary he never would have imagined back in 1907 at St. Mary's College in California. Hooper had played baseball in college, but it was strictly recreational. After graduating with a degree in civil engineering, the only reason he signed up with Sacramento in the Pacific Coast League was because the team arranged a job for him, surveying for the Western Pacific Railroad.

After Hooper batted .347 in 1908, John Taylor, the owner of the Red Sox, offered the talented outfielder a $2,800 contract. Hooper decided his engineering career could wait a few years. Now, at age 30, his skills remained sharp. He was one of the best outfielders in either league, with a strong, accurate arm, and the undisputed master of Fenway's spacious right field. When the park was built in 1911, Taylor made sure the setting afternoon sun would not bother either the pitcher or the batter. Instead, it shone directly in the right fielder's eyes. Yet Hooper rarely misplayed a ball. After Fred Clarke of the Pittsburgh Pirates fastened sunglasses under the bill of his cap in 1916, enabling him to flip them down when tracking a fly ball, Hooper became one of the first American Leaguers to adopt the practice.

His remarkable bare-handed catch of Larry Doyle's long blast in the eighth game of the 1912 World Series, made while falling backwards over a temporary fence in deep right field, remained clear in the minds of the 17,000 people who were at Fenway that afternoon. Other fans still talked about a catch Hooper made against the Tigers in 1916. Bobby Veach had slammed the ball towards the right field corner, a triple certainly, perhaps an inside-the-park home run, but suddenly there was Hooper, running like a deer, grabbing the ball out of the air with—again—his bare hand.

Hooper had perfected a type of sliding catch that helped him snare or block sinking line drives. Rather than diving face first and landing on his belly as a lot of players did—and taking the chance the ball might bounce past him—Hooper would slide towards the ball, his left leg folded under him. This allowed him to bounce back up into a standing position, ready to throw. He was also an efficient and speedy leadoff man, with quick reflexes and a habit of leisurely moving the bat back and forth while waiting for the pitch, like a cat swishing its tail.

In recent years, Hooper had freely offered suggestions and opinions on strategy to player-managers Bill Carrigan and Jack Barry. Ed Barrow was Boston's third manager in as many years and because he had held several front office positions, including president of the International League, he hadn't managed a major league game in nearly 15 years. Hooper's consistent good sense, and his status as senior member of the Red Sox, prompted Barrow to enlist him as "co-manager." It was strictly an advisory position. Hooper sat beside Barrow on the bench and was in charge of the team on the field. The added responsibility was reflected in an additional $1,000 in Hooper's contract, an agreement which took the better part of a week during spring training to iron out.

As fans entered Fenway Park from Jersey Street, they might have noticed the military service flag over the main entrance. It featured 13 yellow stars, one for each Red Sox player lending his energies to the Great War in Europe. Every major league club had lost players to the draft, enlistment or war-related work, but the Red Sox had been hit harder than most. Hooper and shortstop Everett Scott were the only two position players still in the lineup from 1917.

Left fielder Duffy Lewis had enlisted over the winter and was now stationed at the Mare Island Navy Yard near San Francisco. Several other players, including Jack Barry and Ernie Shore, were working at the Boston Naval Yard; later in the spring, they formed a baseball team known as the Wild Waves.

Lewis's absence gave 35-year-old minor league journeyman George Whiteman a chance to win the left field job. The bandy-legged Whiteman was coming off of a fantastic season in which he batted .342 for the Toronto Maple Leafs, the 1917 International League champions. He had two cups of coffee with the Red Sox (in 1907) and the Yankees (in 1913), but had never played in Fenway Park.

There was uncertainty as to exactly which players would be available when training camps opened in March. Many owners were reluctant to restructure their rosters several months in advance, but Red Sox president Harry Frazee was one of the most active magnates during the winter. He believed the war would be over by opening day: he had a $2,000 wager on it. But even if he was wrong, Frazee wanted a contender by mid-April and was prepared to spend the necessary cash.

On December 11, 1917, Frazee sent three players and $60,000 to the Philadelphia Athletics for pitcher Joe Bush, catcher Wally Schang and center fielder Amos Strunk. Schang and Strunk had apparently been on the trading block for awhile, after they had battled Athletics manager Connie Mack regarding salaries in spring training, and Bush had been suspended after a late-season argument with Mack in Cleveland. The Red Sox were suddenly serious pennant contenders. "What will the Old

Roman say when he hears about this?" Frazee cackled amid the buzz of activity in the Red Sox offices. The Old Roman was Charles Comiskey, owner of the defending world champion Chicago White Sox, and he would not be pleased.

But Frazee wasn't finished. Shortly after Christmas, he began dropping hints that another trade was brewing. "This new man is a star who has always had a big following in Boston," he teased. "It will be the equivalent to clinching the pennant for us, I am positive." Many fans thought he was referring to Stuffy McInnis, the top-notch first baseman of the Athletics, the last remaining star still chafing under Mack's penny-pinching. No one was too surprised when the trade was announced on January 5.

Two weeks later, McInnis, who lived outside Boston in Gloucester, married Elise Dow. McInnis was the eighth member of the Athletics sent to Boston in less than three years, and for awhile, there was even talk of Mack managing the Red Sox. Paul Shannon, writing in the *Boston Post*, called the idea "utterly ridiculous.... Mack has just about as much chance to manage the Boston team this year as Babe Ruth has." The three players Frazee sent to Philadelphia to complete the deal were not agreed upon until the end of February.

The *New York Times* accused Frazee of trying to buy the pennant. An editorial expressed disgust at the "disorganizing effect" the Red Sox president, along with Chicago Cubs' president Charlie Weeghman, was having on the national game by "offering all sorts of money for star ballplayers.... The club owners are not content to wait for a few seasons while their managers develop a pennant winner, but have undertaken to accomplish in one year what other clubs have waited years to achieve." Weeghman, who made his fortune with a chain of lunch counters and restaurants in Chicago, had spent roughly $60,000 for the Philadelphia Phillies' superb battery of pitcher Grover Alexander and catcher Bill Killefer, and said he would shell out another $100,000 for Cardinals shortstop Rogers Hornsby.

Frazee scoffed at the criticism, calling it sour grapes and pointing out that Mack had initially approached Yankees owner "Colonel" Jacob Ruppert with the disgruntled players. "The men were there for Ruppert, for me and for anyone else who wanted them," Frazee said. "If the Colonel didn't succeed in buying any of them, it's no one's fault but his own." Ruppert's only response was, "I am not going to throw my money away."

Frazee compared running the Red Sox to operating one of his many theatrical productions. "You can't fill a theater with a poor attraction and you can't interest the fans with a losing ball club," he said. "Boston has been educated to expect winners. I had to act or play to empty benches."

"Not more than six major league teams have made money in the last four years and baseball is in greater danger now than ever before," wrote Joe Vila in the February 28, 1918, issue of *The Sporting News*. The *Chicago Daily Tribune* reported that only 7 of the 16 teams had made any money at all in 1917. Vila railed against players who were holding out against salary cuts, saying they showed a "gross negligence for the national pastime.... [They] care nothing for their employers or the fans who make baseball salaries possible." Another columnist demanded that bonuses be eliminated: "The players, many of whom have no regard for the welfare of the club owners, should be made to deliver the goods without receiving additional inducements."

Before the 1918 season, Connie Mack suggested something he called "cooperative baseball": if his players accepted salary cuts, he would share any profits with them. "If we make $10,000," he said, "we will gladly share it with the players, but it is up to them to do their share. The salaries have not been cut because I want to cut them, but because I have to." Washington's manager Clark Griffith favored cutting the salaries of "players who are drawing very large stipends, as a war measure, and for the duration of the war only."

In Boston, Harry Frazee was singing a different tune. "Last year was a big financial success for our league," he said. "The Red Sox club was on velvet by September 1. We made money; we made lots of it. We'll make money this season. The howling of some baseball men is beyond me. They made millions in the game. Some of them may have been pinched a little last season, but why screech about it?"

The first Red Sox player to sign his 1918 contract was Babe Ruth, who arrived at the club's Dexter Building offices on January 11 wearing a coonskin coat. One of the secretaries pointed out that the protective cover of his left shoe was missing; it had probably slipped off somewhere on the slushy downtown streets. Babe grabbed the cover off his right shoe, said, "I guess I won't be needing this anymore," and threw it out the seventh-story window. Then he met with Frazee for a few hours and signed a one-year contract for $7,000.* "Babe was not unreasonable exactly," the *Boston Post* reported, "but it took a long time before owner and player came to terms."

The contract called for a bonus if Ruth won 30 games. Babe's record in 1917 had been 24-13. In 9 of his 13 losses, he allowed three runs or less, and Boston was either shutout or scored only one run. With a few timely rallies, Ruth's record could easily have been 29-8.

Despite Frazee's off-season acquisitions, the Red Sox still had several question marks. In the infield, only shortstop Everett Scott was a sure thing. First baseman Dick Hoblitzell arrived late to camp and promptly announced he had enlisted in the Army's Dental Corps and could be called up very soon. Jack Barry was in the Navy and long-time third baseman Larry Gardner had been sent to Philadelphia in the McInnis swap. Bench players Del Gainer, Chick Shorten, Mike McNally and Hal Janvrin were all in the service.

---

* Other salaries for the 1918 Red Sox include Harry Hooper, $6,000-$8,000; Stuffy McInnis, $5,000; Everett Scott, $4,500; and Sam Agnew, $4,000.

Harry Hooper was still in right field and Amos Strunk would replace Tilly Walker in center, but left field was up for grabs. The likely candidate was George Whiteman, who was from Harry Frazee's hometown of Peoria, Illinois. Whiteman hadn't played professional baseball until he was 23. He had originally been a high diver, touring the country with a partner, diving from a portable platform into a shallow tank of water. When his partner was killed in an unsuccessful dive, Whiteman quit the business and turned to baseball.

Whiteman joined the Texas League in 1905 and was sold to Boston two years later, but only after the Red Sox agreed to also sign a fellow outfielder named Tris Speaker. Whiteman appeared in only three games with Boston before going back to Texas. He played all over the minors, except for 11 games with the 1913 Yankees, in which he batted .344. He was a man of many nicknames—in addition to "Whitey," "Chief" and "Bandit Pete," he was also called "Lucky" because he had played on six minor league championship teams in 11 years.

Schang would probably be the starting catcher, since he was a much better hitter than either Sam "Slam" Agnew or Wally Mayer, the former lithographer who had caught a handful of games for Boston in 1917.

The Red Sox's strength—its starting pitchers—had survived the winter nearly intact. Carl Mays, Babe Ruth and Dutch Leonard were still in the fold, and "Bullet" Joe Bush filled the spot vacated by Ernie Shore. Rube Foster was at home after refusing to sign his contract and second-stringers Herb Pennock and Lore Bader had both enlisted.

Bush was only 25 years old, but had already logged six big league seasons. Having come up with Philadelphia at age 19, Bush was still six weeks shy of his 21st birthday when he pitched a five-hit victory in the 1913 World Series. Despite his great fastball and biting curve, Bush often needed to throw a shutout to earn a victory with the run-starved Athletics.

On the eve of the new season, no one knew quite what to expect from the Red Sox. "What an experiment the Boston team is going to be this season," *The Sporting News* reported. "In no club in the league...has there been such a revolution." The weekly newspaper's predictions placed the top four teams in the American League in the order they had finished the year before: Chicago White Sox, Boston, Cleveland Indians and Detroit Tigers. The New York Yankees, St. Louis Browns, Washington Senators and Philadelphia Athletics occupied the bottom four spots, or "second division." For the National League, the editors picked the New York Giants to repeat as champions, with the Chicago Cubs (who finished fifth in 1917) second, followed by the St. Louis Cardinals, Cincinnati Reds, Pittsburgh Pirates, Brooklyn Dodgers, Boston Braves and Philadelphia Phillies.

"The men all looked good in the South," Frazee said, "but we need a stronger bench, men who can fill in and at the same time have the club maintain a high level of efficiency." Manager Ed Barrow announced, "I won't predict the pennant, but I will say I've got a powerful team. I'm going to give it my best efforts and I think the boys will be with me all the way."

The Opening Day crowd trickled in. The low murmur of voices blended with the warm pop of balls smacking into leather gloves, the shouts of vendors and the two brass bands playing patriotic songs and popular standards. A group of fiercely loyal fans known as the Royal Rooters marched in the outfield with homemade banners and noisemakers.

Fenway Park, the home of the Red Sox for the past six seasons, had been modeled in part on Philadelphia's Shibe Park, the first concrete and steel ballpark, which opened in 1909. Boston fans considered the modern red brick structure a good luck charm. In 1912, the park's inaugural season, the team had gone 57-20, tying a record for the most home victories in one season.

Fenway Park's most striking feature was the steep dirt embankment which ran from the left field foul line to deep center field, 488 feet from home plate. Serving as both a warning track for outfielders and seating space for overflow crowds, it was nicknamed "Duffy's Cliff" and "the Lewis Mound" in honor of the Boston left fielder who had skillfully negotiated the slope for many years. The wall behind the embankment was only 10 feet high when the park opened, but it now rose to 37 feet and held baseball's first electric scoreboard (Fenway also had the first screen backstop behind home plate). The big wall was covered with advertisements for whiskey, chocolates, local clothing stores, insurance, 10¢ cigars and various taxi services.

Roughly 30 minutes before the game's 3:15 start, Pop Connelly walked to a spot behind home plate. Facing the crowd, holding a megaphone to his mouth, he called out the lineups for both teams. As tradition dictated, the fans razzed Connelly, acting as if they couldn't hear him, shouting "Whoooo?" after each name. Connelly announced the Boston lineup:

Harry Hooper, right field
Dave Shean, second base
Amos Strunk, center field
Dick Hoblitzell, first base
Stuffy McInnis, third base
George Whiteman, left field
Everett Scott, shortstop
Sam Agnew, catcher
Babe Ruth, pitcher

Then Connelly walked down the first base line to the cheaper pavilion seats and repeated the lineups. He walked counter-clockwise around the perimeter of the field, making his announcements at the right field pole, in front of the centerfield bleachers and at the third base grandstand.

Next, both teams lined up along the foul lines and with a small musical contingent between them, marched to the flagpole in center field.

Trailing the players was one of the Red Sox's batboys, who was about 10 years old, dressed in a Boston uniform and holding a flag urging fans to "Buy Liberty Bonds." The team captains, Hoblitzell and Philadelphia's Rube Oldring, raised the American flag and led the crowd in singing "The Star-Spangled Banner." Back at home plate, Boston mayor Andrew Peters presented Hoblitzell and Frazee with a horseshoe floral arrangement, and then threw out the first ball of the season.

In January, a fan had written in an open letter to Harry Frazee:

> As a great admirer of the Boston Red Sox, I would like to have a slight suggestion carried out this season. I suggest that the Sox have some kind of lettering on the shirtfront of their play-at-home uniforms this season instead of nothing at all, as it is at present.

> I think a great many fans from out of town, happening to see the Sox play for the first time, would hardly know the home team if they appeared on the field first. Another thing I notice is that the Sox are the only team in the league without some kind of lettering on their shirtfront.... I suppose I'll get a good bit of criticism for making a suggestion as foolish as this appears to be, but I'll wager a good many fans would like to see the Sox uniforms lettered, at that....

> Hoping that the Red Sox win the flag this year, and that you will not be bored reading this, I remain,

> Yours truly,

> Joseph E. Kelley

The suggestion was not used. For 1918, the Red Sox home uniforms remained white, with thin blue pinstripes; their caps were also white. Only their gray road uniforms had "RED SOX" written in red across the chest. Players didn't wear uniform numbers—if you couldn't identify every player by sight, you weren't much of a fan—although they were each assigned a number in the scorecard, which was used to identify them when they came up to bat.

The home team took the field and all eyes were on the pitcher's mound as Babe Ruth completed his warm-up tosses. This was his fourth full season in Boston and with a career record of 67-34 and an ERA (earned run average) of 2.07, Ruth was one of the best pitchers in the game. In 1917, he established himself as the top left-hander in the American League with a 24-13 record, a 2.01 ERA, a league-leading 35 complete games and a record (for southpaws) of nine shutouts. His batting average was a team-best .325.

When the Red Sox began spring training in Hot Springs, Arkansas, the roster was in such disarray that Ruth felt bold enough to mention his desire for increased playing time. He had talked about it the previous summer, and the Boston sportswriters occasionally tossed around the idea, usually whenever Ruth had a big game at the plate. Because he was pitching so well, however, no one took him seriously.

With the club so short handed, Ruth had played first base in intrasquad games and in the first few exhibitions against Brooklyn, and had thoroughly enjoyed himself. After handling six chances without an error in his first game, he couldn't keep quiet. "Eddie, admit it," he bragged to Barrow, "if you didn't know any different, you'd think I was the regular out there. It was great. I felt like I'd been out there for a couple of years." Babe paused for a moment. "That's the job I'm going after if the old soupbone ever goes wrong."

In that same game, Ruth had cracked two long home runs, the second sailing out of the park, across the street and landing in the outdoor pens of the Arkansas Alligator Farm.* In batting practice the next day, Ruth slammed two more over the fence. Sitting in the stands, Harry

---

* Before the Red Sox left Hot Springs, Ruth bought a small alligator to take with him on the road. The Boston papers do not report whatever happened to Babe's pet.

Frazee squinted in the direction of the second disappearing baseball and said, "That's ten bucks in balls you've lost on me, Babe."

"I can't help it," Ruth called back, smiling, "they oughta make these fucking parks bigger."

"Hey, Ed," Frazee said to Barrow. "Charge those balls to Ruth."

Five minutes later, Ruth broke his bat. "More expense!" Frazee moaned. "The next thing you know he'll be tearing his uniform."

A week later at Hot Springs's Whittington Park, Ruth smacked Al Mamaux's first pitch over the right field fence—but foul. Then he drilled the next pitch so far that one observer feared the ball might "knock the trolley car off the tracks on the street outside the park, except the motorman saw it coming and turned on the juice."

When the Red Sox and Dodgers left Hot Springs for a two-week exhibition tour through Texas, Louisiana and Alabama, Barrow told Ruth that from then on, he would use him only as a pitcher. Fooling around in practice was one thing; playing games that counted in the standings was another. In Dallas, Ruth struck out against Rube Marquard and flung his bat halfway to right field in frustration. On his next time up, he turned around and batted right-handed—and struck out again.

While the teams were in Texas, Frazee announced that he had acquired second baseman Dave Shean from the Cincinnati Reds. At 34 years old, Shean was out of draft range, and had a lot of minor league experience. In 1914, he had played second base for the Providence Grays and won the International League batting title; one of his teammates that year was 19-year-old Babe Ruth. Shean had also managed the Grays in 1915 and 1916. Like Stuffy McInnis, Shean lived in the Boston area; his family ran a wholesale food business in Arlington.

Once Shean joined the Red Sox, Barrow used that week's games to sort out his batting order. Hooper would be the leadoff man as he had been in previous years. Everett Scott had been the number two hitter; now Shean was in that spot and Scott was moved down to seventh.

Barrow tried various combinations of Strunk, McInnis and Whiteman in the 3-4-5 spots. And as was the custom, the catcher batted eighth and the pitcher hit ninth.

Back in Boston, Red Sox team secretary Larry Graver was preparing the club's offices for the season. Graver had been the assistant treasurer of the Cort Theater in Chicago, which Frazee financed in 1907, and when Frazee bought the Red Sox, he brought Graver along. "The boys were in grand condition when I left," Graver said. "Red Sox fans think they have seen Babe Ruth hit them far in the past, but this spring he's getting even greater distance and less height with his drives, which means if he straightens them out at Fenway Park as he has been doing in the South, it'll be necessary to repair the fences quite often."

In the first inning of the new season, Babe Ruth retired the Athletics in order, including a called third strike on ex-Sox Larry Gardner, who was warmly greeted by the crowd. Babe wobbled in the second, walking two men, committing a throwing error and allowing one run. Boston answered with two runs of its own and Ruth's single put the Red Sox ahead 2-1. After that, the burly six-foot, two-inch pitcher, dubbed "The Colossus" by sportswriter Burt Whitman, allowed only five men to reach base, and none of them advanced to second. Boston added single runs in the third and fourth and tacked on three more in the sixth. Ruth finished with a four-hitter and an easy 7-1 win, his third consecutive opening day victory.

Carl Mays, the team's other ace, got the ball on Tuesday. His pitching style was an unusual submarine motion he picked up from "Iron Man" Joe McGinnity. As he whipped the ball towards the plate, his knuckles occasionally scraping the ground, Mays looked like a cross between an octopus and a bowler. Many of Mays's throws came high and tight for a low-ball pitcher, and his reputation for brushback pitches and intimidation was well known. Right-handed hitters often stepped backwards, away from an inside pitch, only to see it break down across the edge of the plate.

Mays, 26 years old, had the same broad shoulders and rugged physique as Ruth, but was a few inches shorter, with short blond hair and a beakish nose. In many ways, Mays was the anti-Babe. His father had been a traveling preacher who died when Carl was 10 years old. Mays never wavered from his strict upbringing. No matter where he played—town teams in the Midwest, Providence, Rhode Island, Boston—he was treated like an outcast, often hated by his own team-mates, described as sulky and antagonistic, a man with a permanent toothache. By the time Mays arrived in Boston, he'd grown accustomed to that opinion. He never shied away from voicing his opinion in the clubhouse, and he was fiercely independent. "I have been told I lack tact," he once said, "which is probably true, but that is no crime."

That afternoon against Philadelphia, Mays looked in mid-season form, allowing no hits through seven innings. Scott Perry held a similar mastery over the Red Sox, conceding only four hits and no runs. With one out in the Philadelphia eighth, Joe Dugan's hot grounder skidded towards right field. Dave Shean darted to his left and tried grabbing the ball with both hands, but slipped on the outfield grass and couldn't make the throw to first. Dugan was given a single.

Mays was always highly critical of his own performance and he expected perfection from everyone around him; he saw nothing wrong with berating a teammate from the mound after a botched fielding play. But five outs away from a no-hitter and the $100 bonus that accompa-nied it, the pitcher held his tongue.

In the Red Sox eighth, Mays led off with a walk. Harry Hooper tapped back to the mound and Perry threw to second. Dugan took the throw and stepped on the bag for the force, an instant before Mays crashed into him, knocking the ball out of his glove. Mays was out, but the collision gave him a bit of quick revenge. Stuffy McInnis's double, and singles from George Whiteman and Everett Scott, gave Mays the ninth inning run he needed for a 1-0 shutout. The slick-fielding Scott was usually called "the Deacon," but some teammates also called him "Scitchy."

Mays finished with a one-hitter and, with his heavy pitches being pounded into the ground, there were only two fly balls to the outfield. Harry Frazee complained about the scorer's decision. "That was an error for sure," he said in the clubhouse. Ed Barrow disagreed. "It looked like a hit from the dugout. Shean did well to knock it down."

The movie star Mary Pickford was at Fenway before Wednesday's game, walking through the stands with about 100 other women from the Liberty Loan Drive, collecting donations for the soldiers at nearby Camp Devens. Several other Hollywood stars, including actors Douglas Fairbanks and Theda Bara, and singer Enrico Caruso, were raising money for war bonds. But not even Pickford's luminous presence could distract the fans from the Red Sox, who overcame ghastly fielding from left fielder George Whiteman and pitcher Dutch Leonard to grab another ninth-inning victory.

Leonard's rough start, coming one day after his 26th birthday, continued an exasperating spring. The left-hander, who had shone so brightly in 1914 with a microscopic 0.96 ERA, arrived in camp from his 90-acre vineyard in Fresno, California, late and overweight. Weeks passed before he appeared in a game and when he did, Brooklyn's Jimmy Johnston smacked his first pitch for a home run. Leonard's only other outing led to the firing of newly hired coach Johnny Evers.

"This victory showed my team has a fighting spirit," Barrow said after the ugly 5-4 win. "We aren't going to wait for the breaks to come to us, but intend to make the breaks ourselves. Today's game was one in which it was up to the manager to stir things up a little. I drove the club when things looked bad and the boys responded beautifully."

There was a difference between "driving" and "abusing" a team, Barrow explained: "You can get results without abuse. If you have hard things to say to a player, the place to say them is off in a corner. That way, the player's spirit isn't broken and his feelings aren't hurt."

It may have been a good philosophy, but Edward Grant Barrow didn't always practice what he preached. Born on a hemp plantation in Springfield, Illinois, in 1868, Barrow was named for Civil War General Ulysses S. Grant, under whom his father had served. His own baseball career had been scuttled after an arm injury as a teenager, but Barrow became involved in nearly every other aspect of professional baseball. He sold hot dogs and scorecards at Pittsburgh's Exposition Park in 1894 with concessionaire Harry Stevens. Three years later, Barrow discovered and signed the legendary shortstop Honus Wagner. Barrow managed teams in both the minor and major leagues and served for seven years as the International League president until internal conflicts led to his resignation after the 1917 season.

Barrow was a large, barrel-shaped man, with huge bushy eyebrows, very little sense of humor, and absolutely no sympathy for slumping ballplayers. His temper was well known. In 1900, while managing Toronto in the Eastern League, he kept his team at the hotel because, as he later claimed, one of the opposing team's owners had said the game would be rained out. Actually, there was no rain and Barrow forfeited the game. When the opposing manager, Al Buckenberger, informed Barrow of this, Barrow punched him repeatedly in the face. He was fined $25. Three years later, during his stint as manager of the Detroit Tigers, Barrow spent a night in a Nashville jail after throwing a bucket of water on some jeering fans at an exhibition game.

When Barrow got angry, his face and neck turned fiery red. Pitcher Sam Jones was fascinated with Barrow's thick eyebrows, which actually seemed to darken with his mood. The Red Sox players called him Simon Legree (after the brutal slave owner in Harriet Beecher Stowe's "Uncle Tom's Cabin"), though not usually to his face. The name stuck. Over time, even Harry Frazee would casually refer to Barrow as "Simon."

In the spring, the disruption with Dutch Leonard came to a boil when Barrow's temper clashed with the cantankerous personality of Johnny Evers. Frazee had signed the once-famous but now-aging infielder in February, thinking Evers might work out as a combination part-time second baseman and bench coach. Evers was often ill and played sluggishly in the field, but that didn't stop him from ranting at other players' errors, poor pitches and lazy at-bats. Evers, known as "the Crab," acted as if every exhibition game was a do-or-die World Series battle.

No one took more of Evers's abuse than Leonard. During an exhibition game in Mobile, Alabama, Leonard reluctantly issued an intentional walk at what he thought was Evers's direction, then walked another batter, which forced in what turned out to be the game-winning run. When Leonard returned to the dugout, he and Evers had to be restrained from brawling with each other. More than a few Boston players were disgusted with Evers and it seemed like the team's morale was crumbling. "Too many managers," captain Dick Hoblitzell confided to a Brooklyn writer.

Once the team was in Boston, Barrow met with Frazee, and Evers was fired the day before the season began. "What happened in Mobile is too childish to be worth considering," said Evers, completely unrepentant. "I've talked like that every day for fifteen seasons."

The New York Yankees and their new manager Miller Huggins arrived in Boston on Thursday, April 18, for a weekend series. Huggins had managed the St. Louis Cardinals for five years before coming to New York and he inherited what many felt was the finest infield in the American League—Wally Pipp at first, Del Pratt at second, Roger Peckinpaugh at shortstop and Frank Baker at third.

The Yankees finished sixth in 1917 and were not expected to improve all that much. The team's weakness was an inexperienced and shaky pitching staff. Veterans Ray Fisher and Bob Shawkey had been drafted and three other pitchers had been traded. George Mogridge, Slim Love and Allan Russell had yet to distinguish themselves, Ray Caldwell was in a two-year slump and Herb Thormahlen was a 21-year-old rookie.

Friday's doubleheader began at 10:30 a.m. in a cold wind. For the fans, including 750 newsboys sitting in the first base pavilion as Harry Frazee's guests, it was worth enduring the chill. Joe Bush's habit (or superstition) of always wearing a heavy red flannel undershirt offered some much-needed insulation. His three-hitter gave Boston a 2-1 win and four Yankee errors helped Babe Ruth take the afternoon contest 9-5. In the second game, Everett Scott tagged and scored from second base on a long sacrifice fly to right field by Ruth.

Ed Barrow paced back and forth in the dugout in his shirt sleeves as the cold weather continued on Saturday. Amos Strunk was hit on the left hand trying to bunt in the first inning and left the game with bruised fingers. George Whiteman moved from left field to center—his box score entry was shortened to "W'n, lf, cf"—and catcher Wally Schang took over in left. Boston won its sixth straight game, something no other Red Sox team had ever done. This unprecedented success had truly been a team effort: eight different players had driven in runs and every victory had been a complete game for the pitcher.

The Red Sox and Yankees had the next day off; Sunday baseball was illegal in Boston. The three other eastern American League cities, Washington, Philadelphia and New York, also prohibited Sunday ball, although Washington would rescind its ban in mid-May 1918. Just before opening day, the New York State Senate voted to legalize games on Sunday after 2:00 p.m., but the bill was rejected by the state's Assembly.

Huggins juggled his lineup on Monday, hoping to shake up his club. Frank Baker moved up two spots in the batting order to third and went 4-4 with two doubles. Wally Pipp, Ping Bodie and Truck Hannah each had two hits. Dutch Leonard couldn't get out of the fourth inning and Barrow went to his bullpen for the first time.

The Red Sox were completely overmatched against lefty George Mogridge, not knocking a base hit out of the infield until the ninth inning. By that time, New York led by nine runs. The final score was 11-4. Mogridge's domination of Boston was nothing new; he had five wins against them in his last eight starts, including a no-hitter on April 24, 1917.

The team's hitting woes continued the next day against Herb Thormahlen, who, like Babe Ruth, was a former pitcher for Baltimore minor league manager Jack Dunn. The lefty Thormahlen was making only the third start of his career. Earlier in the week, he had been handed a 4-0 lead and faced only five batters—he walked three and hit one. But Thormahlen rebounded superbly at Fenway, holding the Red Sox without a hit for eight innings.

Ruth watched from the bench as his teammates grew increasingly frustrated. "Just once I'd like to bat against that guy," he muttered.

The game was still scoreless when Dave Shean flew out in the bottom of the ninth. Amos Strunk, back in the lineup after missing Monday's game, stepped in. Ed Barrow looked down the bench and barked, "Did I hear someone say they want to hit against this fellow?"

Ruth's hand shot out. "Yeah! Who do I hit for?"

"Hobby." Hoblitzell was in a horrible slump—1-28, .036.

"Can I play first base if I get a hit?"

"You sure can," Barrow said.

Strunk ended Thormahlen's no-hitter with a clean single to left. Then Ruth grabbed one of his black bats and walked quickly to the plate. He wasted no time, smacking the first pitch safely into center field. Strunk beat the throw to third with a nifty slide around Frank Baker.

After a brief conference, the Yankees intentionally walked Stuffy McInnis, loading the bases for George Whiteman. With one out, Barrow surprised the Yankees by not calling for a suicide squeeze; it was a play he hated. Whiteman popped the ball up to left; Ping Bodie waited under it and Strunk tagged at third. In his haste to make a quick throw home, Bodie dropped the ball. Strunk scored and Boston had a 1-0 win.

After 8.1 no-hit innings, Thormahlen was the tough-luck loser. Joe Bush allowed only three hits and caught a break in the fifth. Wally Pipp missed second base while running on Bodie's long hit. He was nearly at third before he ran back to touch second; the gaffe cost the Yankees a run. And because Strunk crossed the plate with the winning run, Ruth lost his chance to play first base in the tenth inning.

Ruth had begun pestering Barrow about playing in the field almost as soon as the Red Sox arrived in Hot Springs. It was a tantalizing prospect, since in his limited time at the plate over the last three years, Ruth showed he could hit for average and distance. Unlike almost every other player in the game, Ruth never shortened his grip when the count went to two strikes. He held his bat way down at the end, the knob of the handle wedged into his right palm. The reluctance of Ruth's former managers to play him every day was, besides the fact that he was an excellent pitcher, partly because Babe struck out so much: 68 times in 361 at-bats prior to 1918, an average of one strikeout per 5.3 at-bats. By contrast, Ty Cobb had struck out once every 17.3 at-bats in 1917; Tris Speaker's rate was once every 37.4 at-bats.

In 1915, Ruth's rookie season, *The Sporting Life* called him "one of the hardest wallopers in the big leagues." In morning batting practice, he belted some of the longest drives the Boston sportswriters had ever seen. On July 21 in St. Louis, Ruth's home run sailed over the right field roof of Sportsman's Park and smashed the window of a car dealership across the street. After the game, Babe posed for pictures in front of the damage. Ruth batted .315 and led the Red Sox with four home runs. Braggo Roth led the league with seven, but he had 384 at-bats compared to Babe's 92. Fifteen of Ruth's 29 hits were long (extra-base) hits. Although he didn't have enough at-bats to qualify, his .576 slugging percentage was higher than the official leaders in the American League

(Jack Fournier–.491), the National League (Gavvy Cravath–.510) and the Federal League (Benny Kauff–.509).

"Ruth appears to be one of the best natural sluggers ever in the game," Washington sportswriter Paul Eaton wrote, "and might even be more valuable in some regular position than he is on the slab—a free suggestion for Manager [Bill] Carrigan." Ruth was called "the hardest hitting pitcher in captivity"; the Tigers and the Senators both said that if Ruth was on their rosters, they'd put him in the outfield immediately. The *Boston Post* reported in mid-August that Babe "cherishes the hope that he may someday be the leading slugger of the country…. Babe has not much regard for single base hits, and oftentimes after driving out a two-base clout he comes back to the bench with a downhearted admission that he 'didn't get a good hold on it.'"

When the Red Sox offense sputtered in 1916 after the sale of Tris Speaker, the talk began again. Ruth played center field in spring training, and in June, he tied Ray Caldwell's record with a home run in three consecutive games (June 9, 12 and 13). "Babe is such a great hitter that Bill [Carrigan] wants to have him in the lineup daily if possible," reported the *Boston American* during that five-day power surge. "So fans at home don't be a bit surprised if Ruth soon becomes one of the Red Sox outfielders." Carrigan was reportedly ready to act if his current outfielders didn't come out of their slumps, but it never happened. In fact, less than one month later, Carrigan sent in reserve outfielder Olaf Henrikson, who was also a left-handed batter, to pinch-hit for Babe.

Ruth finished the 1917 season at .325, easily the highest average on the team. Duffy Lewis topped the regulars at .302 and no one else hit above .265. One of Ruth's two home runs was a monstrous blast into Fenway's center field bleachers, the first time anyone had reached those seats during a game. Again, Babe didn't have enough at-bats to qualify, but his .472 slugging percentage would have placed him third in the American League and his batting average fourth best.

The helpless feeling of sitting on the bench for days between pitching assignments gnawed at Ruth throughout 1917. Boston writer Ernest Lanigan remarked, "I believe he would rather play first than eat." That was quite a statement, considering Ruth's gargantuan appetite, which amazed the writers and made his teammates fear for his health. But to Carrigan, Jack Barry and the sportswriters, giving Ruth an everyday job remained nothing more than an entertaining game of "what if."

In their championship seasons of 1915 and 1916, the Red Sox had enjoyed a strong group of reserves who could ably replace an injured starter. The 1918 club was different. When outfielder Paul Smith decided to enlist after not playing in Boston's first nine games, Ed Barrow was left with a 19-man roster and only four non-pitchers on the bench.

"I've talked to Frazee about getting more players," Barrow said. "If any of our regulars gets hurt, we're in trouble. We need another infielder and a couple more pitchers. He told me he's got a couple of deals in the fire, but it's tough. Rosters are tight. No one wants to give up a player without getting someone in return."

Short of conjuring up players from thin air, Barrow could do little but tinker with the lineup. Dick Hoblitzell was dropped to sixth in the batting order. George Whiteman, plagued by a chronic cold and a .194 average, was benched, and Wally Schang, who had experience as an out-fielder, was the new left fielder and clean-up hitter.

Harry Hooper's suggestion was one he had brought up in spring training: "Have you thought any more about putting Babe in the field?"

This wasn't anything Barrow wanted to hear. "How many times are you going to bother me with that?" he shot back. "He's a pitcher, Harry, and a damn good one. We need him on the mound."

"He'd be more valuable if he played more often," said Hooper. "You should trust me, Ed. He wants to play every day."

"He *wants* to? I'm not going to give in to every impulse that big monkey has. Can you imagine if I put the league's best left-hander in the outfield? They'd have me investigated. I'd be the laughing stock of the league. Schang can play the outfield."

"Wally's fine, but he's not the hitter Ruth is," Hooper argued. "You were all set to have Babe at first the other day. You're begging Frazee for more hitters! Here's one who's fallen right into your lap."

But Barrow would not be convinced. "We need him on the mound. Leonard's our only other lefty and that son of a bitch can't get the ball over the plate."

"He doesn't have to quit pitching," Hooper said. "We could use him between starts. No one knows what's going to happen with the war this summer. Getting Ruth in there could put us over the top."

"And what if he gets hurt out there?" Barrow asked. "Then what? I can't do it, Harry. I don't have the nerve."

The sale of Grover Alexander from the Philadelphia Phillies to the Chicago Cubs in December 1917 was one of the biggest transactions in baseball up to that time. Charles Weeghman sent at least $60,000 and two warm bodies to Philadelphia for Alexander and catcher Bill Killefer. Alexander had been superb as soon as he hit the National League, winning 28 games as a rookie in 1911. But in recent years, favoring guile over power, and armed with a great sinker and pinpoint control, he'd been pitching like he was from another planet. In his last three seasons with the Phillies, Alexander won 94 games and threw 36 shutouts, and led the National League in strikeouts and ERA (1.22, 1.55 and 1.83).

The trade boosted the Cubs' chances to dethrone the New York Giants in the National League, especially since the Giants had lost several key players to the draft, including outfielders Benny Kauff and Dave Robertson. But as spring approached, it looked as though the 31-year-old Alexander might also be called. "I'll go and go willingly," he said, despite the fact that he probably could have received an exemption because he supported his mother. "I have no intention of dodging service. My duty to my country is more important than my duty to baseball."

The Phillies-Cubs deal contained a stipulation that if either Alexander or Killefer were drafted at least 30 days before the start of the season, the transaction could be called off. Unfortunately for Weeghman, that didn't happen. Three days before opening day, Alexander learned that he would probably be called by May 1. He pitched in only three games, defeating the Cardinals and Reds on the road and, on April 26, in his only appearance in Chicago, throwing a two-hitter. Alexander was assigned to Camp Funston in Nebraska, where he married his childhood sweetheart, Aimee Marie Arrants, on May 31. He left for France about two weeks later.

The Philadelphia Athletics hosted the Red Sox in their home opener at Shibe Park on April 23. The four former Athletics now with Boston were welcomed back and given gifts before the game—a diamond-studded pin for Joe Bush, a chest of silver for Stuffy McInnis, a bouquet of flowers and a silver-headed cane for Schang and a set of golf clubs for Joe Bush.

Vean Gregg, the sore-armed pitcher Boston traded to the Athletics over the winter, had thrown a three-hitter against Washington the previous week, and was equally sharp against Ruth and the Red Sox. Both pitchers put up zeroes for seven and a half innings. But with one out in the eighth, Ruth walked Merlin Kopp, and Dave Shean booted a slow grounder. Babe tried compensating for the error by blowing the ball past George Burns, but Burns nailed the first pitch and drove it over George Whiteman's head into the left field bleachers. As Burns circled the bases, Ruth felt a twinge in his left arm. That possible strain—which Babe would keep secret for several weeks—would reverberate throughout the season.

Boston lost that game 3-0, but made quick work of the Athletics in the rest of the series. Carl Mays drilled Burns with a pitch the following day on his way to a 6-1 win. Dutch Leonard walked 10 batters, but prevailed 2-1 as Philadelphia stranded 11 men on base. Joe Bush wrapped up the series with a 4-1 victory, giving the Red Sox a 10-2 record.

Most of the regulars went back to Boston while the rest of the team stopped in Bridgeport, Connecticut, for a Sunday exhibition game. Both teams agreed that Red Sox pitcher Dick McCabe, who had started his professional career in Bridgeport, would play for the home team. Halfway through the game, Ruth took over at first base. He had seven putouts, made one error and went 0-1 at the plate. Sam Jones pitched a two-hitter and the Red Sox won 7-0.

In Boston, a cold, rainy mist postponed Monday's game against Washington, but it was not a slow news day. Harry Frazee confessed that he had received an offer of more than $100,000 for Babe Ruth.

3

GREATEST VALUATION IN THE HISTORY OF BASEBALL PLACED ON COLORFUL BABE RUTH

Frazee Rejects $100,000 Offer for Pitcher Ruth

Red Sox Owner Declares He Sooner Would Think of Selling Franchise Than Parting with Big Ace

By Burt Whitman

Since the start of the championship season, Owner Harry Frazee of the Red Sox has been offered more than $100,000 for one ball player, and of course his name is George H. "Babe" Ruth, colossal southpaw pitcher and hitter most extraordinary. The magnate turned down the offer, saying:

"I might as well sell the franchise and the whole club as sell Ruth. The sum named was three times as much as was paid for Tris Speaker, and of course is far and away bigger than any figure that has been used in baseball. But it is ridiculous to talk about it. Ruth is our Big Ace. He's the most talked of, most sought for, most colorful ball player in the game."

Frazee did not care to go into details over the stupendous offer for Ruth. "H. H." was inclined yesterday to belittle the general interest in such an item.... It is a certainty that the offer came from New York or Chicago."

Boston Herald and Journal, April 30, 1918

Late that night, Ruth awoke drenched in sweat, agitated by a nightmare. He dreamt that when he opened his morning newspaper, he discovered he'd been sold by the Red Sox. At Fenway Park the following day, as Ruth warmed up in front of the Boston dugout, Frazee told a group of reporters, "Yes sir, I was offered $150,000 for that Baby, and I would not think of selling him."

The $100,000 figure quoted in the paper had not been attributed to Frazee. If the offer for Ruth was roughly three times the price paid for Speaker, as Frazee had claimed, $150,000 would be the correct amount. One writer told Frazee what Ruth had said about his nightmare. He laughed. "Babe's not the only dreamer."

It was a balmy spring afternoon, warm enough for short sleeves, as Ruth made his fourth start of the season. Burt Shotton lined the game's first pitch into right field for a single, but Babe didn't give up another hit until the sixth inning. He finished with a five-hitter and Boston won 8-1. At the plate, he doubled, stole a base and scored two runs.

In the years 1900–1920, now referred to as the "deadball era," runs were precious commodities. Teams fought for any advantage, psychological or physical, however slight. The style of play—dubbed "inside baseball" or "scientific baseball"—was thick with strategy. The game demanded well-timed teamwork, aggressive base running and a superior talent at making contact, bunting, stealing bases and executing the hit-and-run. "Inside baseball" relied more on brains than on brawn.

As a team's third base coach relayed signs to the batters, the coach at first watched the opposing team's pitcher for clues to his delivery. Without realizing it, a fastball pitcher might alter his motion ever so slightly before throwing a curve, or before throwing a spitball, even though his face was hidden behind his glove, the pitcher's cap might rise a fraction of an inch as he opened his mouth to wet the ball. If a coach could detect a pattern and judge what type of pitch was coming, he'd quickly pass that information to the batter. Boston pitcher Joe Bush, who often coached first base on his days off, had a set of verbal signals: when he shouted encouragement to his teammate at the plate, any sentence with "all right" in it meant a fastball, "come on" signaled a curve, and "get hold of it" meant look out for a spitball.

In the game's cyclical power struggle between pitchers and hitters, this was an era when the men on the mound were kings. Bats were heavy and thick-handled, barely tapered from the barrel down to the handle; some could have probably been gripped effectively at either end. Nearly every hitter would choke up and take a level swing, using his forearms to punch the ball over the infield or drive it between the outfielders. Home runs were often inside-the-park hits that rolled to fences as far as 500 feet away. The home run leaders usually hit about 10 in a season. From 1913 to 1915, National Leaguer Gavvy Cravath hit 19, 19 and 24 home runs, but 52 of those 62 long balls came at his home park, Philadelphia's Baker Bowl, which had a right field pole only 272 feet away. In 1915, Braggo Roth led the American League with 7 and Wally Pipp of the Yankees led the league in 1916 and 1917 with 12 and 9, respectively.

Fenway Park's foul line distances in 1918—321 feet to left and 314 to right—have remained fairly constant throughout the decades. Some measurements give a distance of 550 feet to the right-field side of dead center. This distance has also been measured at 593 feet, but this figure most likely includes the distance to the back wall of the bleachers, which was actually in play, since a ball could conceivably roll past the flag pole and carom sideways behind the stands.

Most parks had very deep center fields: Detroit's Navin Field (later renamed Tiger Stadium) was 467 feet, Philadelphia's Shibe Park was 502 feet, Boston's Braves Field was 520 feet, and at New York's Polo Grounds, it was 550 feet just to the right of center field. When Yankee Stadium opened in 1923, its left-center field fence was 500 feet away and center field was 487; that part of the outfield was known as "Death Valley."*

Team owners were so frugal that one baseball might be used for three or four innings. Any balls hit into the stands were retrieved by club employees or the police, by force if necessary.** After such prolonged use, the ball would soon be covered with scuff marks and little tears; it would get a little soft and be stained as dark as ink from the infield dirt and the tobacco juice the fielders spat into their gloves.

After the introduction of a cork-centered ball in 1911 boosted offense, there was an increase in the discreet use of tobacco juice, licorice, slippery elm, talcum powder and good old saliva to affect the movement of the ball. A pitcher might rub a ball against the jagged edge of his belt buckle, a ring or a piece of sharp metal tucked into his glove; a catcher could scrape it against his shinguards. The covert substances

---

* The deepest part of Yankee Stadium is now only 408 feet. In modern parks, straight away center field is usually about 410 feet away and the alleys are roughly 380 feet. In three parks that opened in 2000 (San Francisco, Houston and Detroit), the distances to the foul poles are so short they are actually in violation of major league rules.

** In 1916, three fans at the Polo Grounds who refused to give up foul balls were arrested for petty larceny. It's not clear who first allowed fans to keep balls hit into the stands. Charles Weeghman of the Cubs is often cited, but Ed Barrow claimed he was the first. In the summer of 1918, fans in Cleveland received great applause when they hid foul balls in their clothing and ran from the ushers.

and the general wear and tear helped pitchers make the ball curve inside or outside, drop straight down or dart in some unanticipated direction.

Russ Ford of the Yankees kept a piece of emery board in his glove. Cubs pitcher Jimmy Lavender tried attaching sandpaper to his uniform, which worked until the umpires wanted to know why he kept scratching himself. One anonymous pitcher kept a mushy banana in his hip pocket; another taped part of a nutmeg grater inside his shirt, so that the points of the grater poked through his uniform and he could scuff the ball when he brought his glove up to his chest.

Carl Mays called White Sox pitcher Eddie Cicotte "a wizard at doctoring a ball. He would rough up one side of the ball and then shine the other on his pants leg where he had a good coat of paraffin wax. He could move the ball either way he wanted by turning the rough side from left to right or the other way—the ball would sail in the direction of the rough side."

The spitball was also effective, but was often denounced as unsportsmanlike—usually by teams that had no good spitballers on their rosters. In December 1917 Harry Frazee demanded the spitball be banned. No Red Sox pitcher threw a spitter, but Eddie Cicotte and Red Faber of the White Sox, expected to be Boston's chief competitor for the 1918 pennant, did. Before the season, the National League started a campaign to abolish the pitch. Brooklyn manager Wilbert Robinson called it "disgusting," C. H. Zuber of the *Cincinnati Times-Star* described it as a freak pitch, "the 'dog-faced boy' of baseball," and veteran manager Ned Hanlon said, "It is not pleasant to see a pitcher slobber all over the ball. It is an unsanitary practice." The spitball was banned in February 1920.

It would be another 30 years before African-American men were allowed to play in the major leagues, but any dark-skinned players, whether they were Cuban or Native American, met with virulent bigotry from fans and teammates alike. In an effort to head off controversy before Cuban players Rafael Almeida and Armando Marsans arrived in Cincinnati, club owner August "Garry" Herrmann asked Victor Muñoz, a noted Cuban sportswriter, to guarantee that the players had only "pure Caucasian blood in their veins." There are tales of managers trying to sneak black players into the big leagues, such as John McGraw's 1901 scheme to pass off second baseman Charlie Grant as a Native American, but no evidence exists that anyone succeeded.

The style of play of any era is reflected by which statistics are printed in the daily newspapers. In 1918, the *Boston Post* printed up-to-date statistics for the two home teams every Monday. Batters' statistics included games played, at-bats, runs scored, hits, stolen bases, sacrifice hits and batting average. Hitters batting over .300 were listed, along with the top 12 run scorers and the top 12 base stealers. Home runs, runs batted in and on-base average were not featured.* For pitchers, it was games played, wins, losses, strikeouts, walks, hits allowed and winning percentage. Earned run averages first appeared in the 1860s, then vanished until the National League resurrected them in 1912 and the American League followed one year later. Most papers didn't use it, though, ranking pitchers by winning percentage instead.

Compared to the statistical tsunami with which baseball begins the 21st Century, the late 1910s were not the Middle Ages—it was cavemen scratching stick-figures on rock walls. The National League kept some statistics that the American League would not recognize as official. In both leagues, individual totals often did not correlate with team totals at the end of the season. It was not uncommon, at least in 1918, for box scores in Boston's various daily newspapers to list different hit and error totals. The first book to contain career statistics and biographical facts about players was the groundbreaking *Who's Who in Baseball*, published in 1912 by *Baseball Magazine* editor John Lawres; it featured games played, batting average and fielding average.

---

* Runs batted in were not counted in any consistent way until 1920; on-base average was not recognized as an official statistic by major league baseball until 1985.

During the 1910s, many observers regarded a 1-0 pitching duel as the closest thing to perfect baseball, while others complained that hitting had become anemic, that the game was "listless" and "monotonous." There were plenty of ideas about how to increase scoring: shrinking the strike zone, reducing a walk to three balls, making a strikeout four strikes, replacing the pitcher in the batting order with a "designated hitter," not calling batters out on fly balls caught in foul territory, and allowing runners left on base to return in the following inning.*

Before spring training began in 1918, St. Louis Cardinals manager Branch Rickey suggested moving the pitcher's mound to the exact center of the diamond, which would place it 63 feet, 6 inches from home plate. "The fans want more batting," Rickey said. "A 10-6 game is more attractive than a 1-0 game. I don't think the pitcher would lose control by giving him three more feet. He could adjust himself by slightly changing his delivery. The extra three feet will give the batter more time to judge the ball delivered by the pitcher. Now we find the ball on top of the batter before he can judge what is in front of him."

On Thursday afternoon, May 2, 1918, Harry Hooper spoke to Ed Barrow in a quiet corner of the Fenway Park clubhouse. "Ed, have you noticed that every time Babe pitches, we have a big crowd?" After 3,365 fans watched Ruth's win on Tuesday, attendance for the next two games dipped to 2,150 and 2,725.

"The fans love him," Hooper said. He knew Barrow had invested money in the Red Sox when he accepted the manager's job and that Barrow had an interest in keeping the turnstiles clicking. "He's been the most popular player here almost from the day he arrived. They like to see him pitch—but they love to see him swing that bat. They even cheer

---

* Most of these ideas were never instituted. In December 1972 the American League voted to adopt the designated hitter rule as a three-year experiment. It is still in effect.

when he strikes out! Now that Whitey's sick, we could really use him for the next few days."

George Whiteman's fever had worsened. When Whiteman arrived at the park that morning, Barrow sent him home and told him he should stay in Boston while the team played in New York and Washington.

"All right, Harry, we'll give it a shot," Barrow finally agreed, more worn down than won over. "But you watch: after the first slump he gets into, he'll be on his knees, begging me to let him pitch again." The Red Sox took their league-leading 11-2 record to New York City that night, flush with confidence. And promptly fell apart.

In 1918, the Yankees and Giants both played at the Polo Grounds in upper Manhattan. (In all five cities that had two major league teams, when one team was home, the other would be on the road.) Joe Bush opened the series in New York on Friday, but never established a comfortable rhythm. He battled into extra innings and even after being hit on the hand by a line drive in the tenth, Bush convinced Barrow to let him stay in the game. One inning later, Bush surrendered three hits and the winning run as the Red Sox lost 3-2.

Ruth didn't play in the first game, but he undoubtedly spent a large part of his Friday night enjoying the excesses of the big city. Yankees manager Miller Huggins heard that Ruth had stumbled back to his hotel around sunrise, and thought he could take advantage of a hungover pitcher. New York scored single runs off Ruth in the first and second innings, and with a runner on in the third, Roger Peckinpaugh pushed a bunt towards the mound. It rolled between Ruth's legs for a hit. Then Frank Baker laid one down. Ruth lunged at it and threw wildly to first base, hitting Baker in the back of the neck. Two runs scored and New York led 4-0. By the end of the afternoon, Ruth handled 13 chances and made two errors.

The Yankees' starter was Allan Russell, a native of Baltimore. He and Ruth had in fact played together in Providence in 1914 and shared a good-natured rivalry. After fanning Ruth early in the game on three pitches, Russell laughed at him.

"Don't get too happy," Ruth called back. "I've got a few more chances today."

In the seventh, Boston trailed 4-1. With one man on and one out, Ruth crushed a ball into the upper deck in right field. It landed about three feet foul. Babe stepped out of the batter's box, tapped some dirt off his spikes with his bat, and turned to home plate umpire Billy Evans. "I'm hitting the next one right back up there," he said flatly, "and it'll be fair this time, no doubt about it."

Ruth stepped back in, his eyes focused on Russell, his hands wringing the end of his bat, waiting for the pitch. He took a huge swing, holding nothing back. As promised, the ball sailed up, up, up, into the top deck, to the left of the foul pole by a wide margin. Ruth tossed his bat aside and went into his first home run trot of the season, taking tiny steps, running on the balls of his feet. When Ruth stepped on the plate, he winked at Evans.

In the ninth inning, many in the crowd of 15,000 were starting for home. It had been a perfect day—the Yankees were ahead 5-3 with one out to go and they'd seen the mighty Ruth belt a home run. But as soon as Sam Agnew doubled, a murmur rippled through the stands. Ruth was next. The mass exit slowed. Russell conferred with his infielders behind the mound and the outfielders took several steps back from their normal positions.

Ruth again pounded the ball into the upper deck—he seemed to do it at will—but he had been too anxious and it curved foul. He hit the next pitch harder than he had hit anything all day. Armando Marsans was standing nearly 380 feet away in right field; the ball went over his head. Agnew scored and Ruth settled for a double. He was itching to score the tying run, but Hooper made the final out.

The Polo Grounds was shaped like a bathtub, with obscenely short foul lines. The left field line was 277 feet from the plate and right field only 256 feet; a photographer's perch in right put the second deck seven feet closer. The rest of the outfield was a spacious meadow, roughly 440 feet to the alleys and nearly 500 feet to straightaway center. Beyond that was a large scoreboard and the teams' clubhouses. Ruth loved hitting in the oblong park and the fans loved seeing him hit; the Boston papers referred to Babe as "the hitting idol of the Polo Grounds." With his home run off Russell, 4 of his 10 career blasts had come in New York.

On the Red Sox's day off, they traveled to Clifton, New Jersey, for an exhibition game against the Doherty Silk Sox. Harry Doherty, the wealthy silk manufacturer, owned a beautiful park (Doherty Oval) and one of the best semi-professional teams in the country. He also promised five dollars to anyone who hit a home run. So when Boston's pitcher-turned-right-fielder-for-a-day John Wyckoff hit Otto Rettig's first pitch over the fence, he circled the bases and then trotted directly to the owner's box. Doherty handed him a five-dollar bill and Wyckoff jogged back to the bench. After a few innings, Ruth replaced Heinie Wagner at first base. He swung from his heels, but managed only a high flyout and a strikeout. Babe earned no extra spending money in Clifton.

Back in New York on Monday, Ruth finished batting practice, grabbed a towel off the bench and wiped the sweat from his face. Barrow came over and sat down.

"How are you feeling today, Babe?"

"Fine, Eddie. I felt good and loose out there." There was still an electric tingle in his shoulders from his last line drive. "How about letting me pinch-hit again today?"

"I may not need a pinch-hitter, but I do need a first baseman."

Ruth perked up. "Really? How come?"

"Hobby's hands are still bothering him and I've got nobody else. Listen, Babe, you know Harry and I have talked about you helping us out in the field. Maybe it's time to try it. You think you're ready?"

"Are you kidding?" Ruth said. "Where'd I throw my mitt?"

So, in his 174th major league game, Babe Ruth played at a position other than pitcher or pinch-hitter and for the first time did not hit at the bottom of the order. He batted sixth and went 2-4, including a two-run home run off George Mogridge in the fourth inning. At first base, Ruth collected four putouts and two assists, one of them on a double play started by Hooper. Ruth took the relay from right field and fired a strike to Sam Agnew, cutting down a runner at the plate.

Yankees owner Jacob Ruppert watched the action from his private box with his friend Harry Frazee. "Say, Harry, that big kid can do it all—pitch, hit, play the field. How much do you want for him?" Frazee just shook his head and laughed.

Ruth had a great afternoon, but the Yankees pounded Carl Mays and Sam Jones 10-3 to complete a three-game sweep. "If Mays got his pitch low, he was tough to hit," Yankee Roger Peckinpaugh said. "If it came in around the knees and then dropped, he was tough to hit. If he got it up higher, it was like most other pitches." Mays's pitches were up, and he had his worst outing ever in New York, surrendering six runs in 4.1 innings. Joe Vila wrote, "The Yankees are hitting so hard that the batting order has been nicknamed 'Murderers Row.'"

The *Boston Globe* compared Ruth to Cleveland's Joe Wood, a former Red Sox pitcher now having a second career as an outfielder. "Ruth's batting, could it be turned to advantage every day, would help the club a lot. Just now it's not likely that Barrow will use Ruth except as an emergency regular, but the Babe's work yesterday suggests that the future holds much in store for him."

When the Red Sox went to Washington, D.C., Ruth remained in the lineup. In fact, Barrow moved him up to the number four spot. Sunday baseball would soon be legal in the nation's capital and Senators manager Clark Griffith was thrilled. "There are about 100,000 extra men and women in Washington because of war activities," he said. "They need relaxation and should support baseball. Then, too, the saloons have been closed [more than half of the country's 48 states were "dry"].

The boys won't be able to stay downtown with their feet on the rail and read the scores on the scoreboards in the saloons. They'll all be out to the park, looking at the games."

Washington had also moved the starting time of its home games from 3:30 to 4:30 p.m., which allowed more workers to attend the games. The wives of those fans were opposed to the change, since it sent their husbands home for dinner at a much later hour.

In the first game, Walter Johnson, the Senators' hard-throwing right-hander, fooled Ruth with off-speed pitches in his first two at-bats. In the sixth, Johnson tried shooting a fastball past him, but Ruth turned on it, sending it over the right field wall into a war garden where it startled a stray dog. The home run—the first one hit in Griffith Stadium that year—earned Ruth a huge ovation. Babe had once again tied Ray Caldwell's record with three home runs in three consecutive games. Oddly enough, Caldwell was also a hard-drinking pitcher who occasionally moonlighted at first base and in the outfield.

But Ruth's heroics couldn't save the Red Sox, who dropped their fourth consecutive game. The 7-2 defeat was particularly tough for Barrow, since Boston had the leadoff man on base in six of the nine innings, but couldn't deliver the punishing blow against Johnson.* There were no home runs the next day, although Ruth did manage to swat a double off the right field scoreboard. It was one of Boston's few highlights. Joe Bush pitched one-hit ball for four innings, then collapsed in the fifth as the first five Senators reached base. Washington scored eight runs in that inning and five more in the next. Carl Mays and John Wyckoff, making his first appearance, mopped up, and the Senators won 14-4.

---

* Dave Shean feared Walter Johnson more than any other pitcher. His plan of attack: "I got the longest bat there was and stood the farthest away from the plate that I could and just tried to hit it down first base."

Washington swept the series by defeating Ruth 4-3 in 10 innings the next day. Boston's sixth straight loss dumped them into second place behind Cleveland, which held a razor-thin .008 edge. Ruth batted fourth and went 5-5 with three doubles, a triple and a single. Ruth desperately wanted to win; after his 10th inning double, he was thrown out trying to steal third.

On the train back to Boston, Barrow wondered if he was doing the right thing. Since he had agreed to play Ruth in the field, the Red Sox were 0-6. In Ruth's first three games as a first baseman, the pitching staff allowed 31 runs. Washington had outscored them 25-9. Was it simply a case of bad timing? Or had moving Ruth upset the balance of the team? The Boston sportswriters were convinced it was a mistake. Melville Webb Jr. of the *Globe* wrote that "putting a pitcher in as an everyday man, no matter how he likes it or how he may hit, is not the sign of strength for a club that aspires to be a real contender."

Yet, assuming the losses were a coincidence, how could anyone argue with the results? Since being in the regular lineup, Ruth had been hitting .563. His season average stood at .500 (16-32) and his 33 total bases gave him an eye-popping 1.031 slugging percentage. He was pounding the stuffing out of the ball. Only a fool would put him back on the bench.

"We played some poor ball last week," Harry Hooper told his teammates in the clubhouse before the start of an 18-game home stand. "But I think a lot of that was dumb luck—so many of those hits were off the end of the bat or fought off the handle. Now, don't think about the losses. Get fired up out there. We're home now and we need to play tough. Battle for everything, raise a fuss about every umpire's call. I'll be yelling from the outfield on plays I can't even see."

The pep talk seemed to work. After two infield hits led to a first inning for St. Louis, Carl Mays permitted only three base runners the rest of the way, rebounding from his two dreadful outings with a five-hitter. Seven Red Sox players hit safely and Boston won 4-1. The Browns managed only five fly balls to the outfield and none of them went to left field, where Ruth was making his debut.

"It's lonesome in the outfield," Ruth said glumly as he jogged into the dugout after the eighth inning, Dick Hoblitzell having reclaimed his spot at first base. "It's hard to stay awake with nothing to do." For the first time in more than three weeks, Ruth went hitless, snapping a 10-game hitting streak.

St. Louis Browns owner Phil Ball had traded away half of his infield over the winter after second baseman Del Pratt and shortstop Doc Lavan each filed a $50,000 lawsuit against Ball, charging him with libel. In September 1917 Ball told a sportswriter that the two players and pitcher Bert Shotton were "laying down on the job"—a euphemism for consciously playing below their abilities, if not intentionally throwing games.

On January 22, 1918, Pratt was sent to New York where he asked for a guaranteed contract as protection against being run out of the game if his suit was successful; Lavan and Shotton were traded to the Senators. The St. Louis sportswriters gleefully reported that Ball had crushed "the Bolsheviki [sic] rebellion," referring to the players as "Lenine Pratt and Krylenko Shotton." Depositions were taken from several players and a trial date was set, but thanks to the intercession of American League president Ban Johnson and Washington manager Clark Griffith, both players settled out of court. Ball later explained that by "laying down," he meant only that the players weren't showing the spirit and pep he expected from them.

Ed Barrow consulted with Harry Hooper and they juggled the lineup almost daily, trying to seize on a winning combination. Dave Shean was suffering from neuralgia (nerve pain), which acted up whenever he ran. No sooner had Dick Hoblitzell returned to the lineup when he was hit on the elbow by a pitch. Two days later, Hoblitzell, a dentist in Cincinnati in the off-season, learned he had been named as a first lieutenant in the Army's Dental Corps by President Wilson and that a call-up was imminent. Rookie Fred Thomas had a bruised right hand, and coach Heinie Wagner, who could conceivably fill in during an emergency (although he hadn't played regularly since 1915) had a severe cold.

Harry Frazee hoped that Frank Truesdale, a switch-hitting second baseman, could help patch up the wounded infield. Truesdale, 34 years old, had played with the 1910 Browns and the 1914 Yankees, and he had been a teammate of George Whiteman in Toronto in 1917. Boston's interest in Truesdale had been percolating since opening day and Frazee finally tracked him down at a mining camp in New Mexico. Truesdale joined the club during the St. Louis series, but the local press was not impressed. "Frank never could hit his weight," sniffed the *Globe*.

With Hoblitzell sidelined again, Ruth returned to first base, where he continued performing with surprising agility for a novice. The fans loved the effect he had on the opposition. Each time he came to the plate, the infielders played back and the outfielders retreated toward the fence. Then, every once in a while, Babe would drop a bunt down and easily beat it out. "He's a great hitter," Browns manager Fielder Jones said after Ruth hit a double and two singles in a losing effort. "But, you know, there are stretches of play during which a batter can hit anyone at any time, and then a few days later he finds he can't hit anyone at all. I'm not ready to rank Ruth up with the greatest batters of all time on what I have seen of him in the two games so far this season."

The following day, May 13, Ruth lost his infield job when Stuffy McInnis was moved from third base, across the diamond, to the position he had starred in for seven years in Philadelphia. Fred Thomas made his debut at third and George Whiteman was in left field. But the lineup was still shifting. After a rainout, Ruth took his turn on the mound and beat Detroit 5-4. Then he was back in left field.

Up in Fenway Park's rooftop press box, the writers joked about Ruth, who shouted loudly while chasing down balls in the outfield. They questioned his ability to negotiate Duffy's Cliff; a betting pool formed on exactly when the unrestrained outfielder would get conked on the head by a fly ball. In a more serious moment, Edward Martin of the *Boston Globe* worried that long throws from the outfield might damage Ruth's golden arm.

But for the Red Sox, every one of Barrow's moves worked. Two weeks after being benched, a healthy Whiteman rebounded, boosting his average from .194 to .269. McInnis had done a wonderful job at third base, a position he hadn't played since 1910. He committed only one error in 23 games, but his hitting suffered. His .284 average was 30 points below his usual high standard, and it was causing him great worry. Back at first base, he quickly put together a six-game hitting streak and batted safely in 15 of his next 19 games.

Fred Thomas's constant hustle at third base earned him the nickname "Rabbit." Thomas had begun his career in the 1911 Milwaukee City League while still in high school, playing under the alias "John Wallace." In Boston, he made the most of his opportunity, hitting .321 after one week.

The Red Sox won two out of three games against St. Louis, then swept four straight from the Tigers. In the first game, Ty Cobb didn't hit the ball out of the infield in four at-bats against Ruth. Harry Hooper hit the season's first home run at Fenway in the second game when his line drive took an ugly bounce past right fielder Harry Heilmann and rolled to the fence.

Barrow and Frazee kept brainstorming on where to find additional players, especially infielders and pitchers. "It's easy to say we're going to get the extra players," Barrow admitted, "but a different matter to actually do it. There are many we'd like, but either they're not on the market or we have no men to trade." Dutch Leonard was the focus of trade rumors after he frittered away a 7-0 lead against Detroit, and even though Boston rallied to win 11-8, Barrow would have gladly gotten rid of him. But what team would give up players for the slumping pitcher?

The weak bench remained a cause for concern, but by mid-May Barrow felt he had a regular line-up that could carry the team through the summer. Since returning to Fenway, Boston had won six of seven games. On May 18, the team was in first place, the weather was beautiful and 10,230, the largest crowd of the season, came out for the final game against Detroit. When the first pitch was thrown, there were still long lines of fans filing in.

Both the bigger crowds and the evolving lineup were due largely to Ruth. Since his infield debut in New York, he had moved effortlessly into the cleanup spot in the order and played three positions equally well. In one three-game span, he pitched, played left field and first base, and went 8-for-12 at the plate. Ruth was absolutely untroubled and unconcerned about which position Barrow would tell him to play—after all, he was also experienced at shortstop, third base and catcher. If anyone asked, his preference was first base, but as long as he was in the lineup, he was happy. Anywhere was better than the bench.

Before Ruth began playing every day, he was batting .438. Two weeks later, his average had climbed to .476. "Ruth is the large rumble in the Red Sox family," Burt Whitman wrote in the *Boston Herald and Journal*. "That $150,000 valuation placed on the Big Fellow which owner Harry Frazee passed up without batting an eye does not seem far fetched. Ruth's proving to be worth his weight in gold." Already the most popular player in Boston, Ruth assumed a near-mythical status as a Baseball God.

4

"A Loose-Jointed, Dirty-Faced Kid"

He chewed tobacco at age five. He cursed with gusto, skipped school whenever possible and drained the beer and whiskey from the many glasses in his father's saloon. "I was a bum when I was a kid," he said. "Looking back, I honestly don't remember being aware of the difference between right and wrong."

George Herman Ruth was born on February 6, 1895, the first child of George and Catherine Ruth of Baltimore, Maryland. It was one of the coldest days of the winter and a neighborhood midwife named Minnie Graf assisted with the delivery in the second floor bedroom of Catherine's parents' home at 216 Emory Street.

George Ruth listed his occupation on his son's birth certificate as "lightning rod worker." He and his older brother, John Ruth Jr., constructed, sold and installed rods on barns, schools and farmhouses. Before marrying Catherine Schamberger, Ruth worked periodically as a horse-and-buggy driver, a butcher, a harness salesman and a cable car gripman.

At about the same time his young wife was expecting their first child, George Ruth started his own business, opening a bar-and-grill on West Camden Street. A dark, smoke-filled room with a pressed tin ceiling, it was the first of several saloons he would operate in the waterfront neighborhood, often under the name Union Bar, though sometimes called Ruth's Cafe. At 23, he was a rough, heavy-set man, reportedly barely literate and possessed of a volatile temper. All four of his grandparents had emigrated to the United States from Prussia, in northern Germany, around 1840. George Ruth was born on New Year's Day in 1871.

Catherine "Katie" Schamberger was also a child of German immigrants. Born in July 1874, she was the youngest of Pius and Johanna Schamberger's five children. Pius worked as an upholster and was the vice president of Woodworkers Local No. 6. Katie was a few weeks shy of her 20th birthday, and roughly two months pregnant, when she married George Ruth on June 25, 1894, in Baltimore's Fulton Street Baptist Church.

Katie Ruth was a small woman, barely five feet tall. Overworked and frequently sick, she suffered from poor physical and emotional health all of her life. Besides the son who would become the Babe, Katie gave birth to six other children, including two sets of twins, but only one daughter—Mary "Mamie" Ruth, born in 1900—survived. Although she married outside her religion (the Ruths were Lutheran, the Schambergers, Catholic), Katie had her first child baptized at St. Peter the Apostle Roman Catholic Church, a predominately German congregation, when he was less than one month old. Katie's sister, Lena Fell, was the child's godparent.

"I hardly knew my parents," Ruth admitted as an adult. Despite the enormous amount of attention he would receive during his life, very little is known about either of his parents and the information that is available is often vague, confusing and contradictory. Few photographs exist. The Ruths were merely another family trying to earn a living along the Baltimore waterfront.

When George Ruth opened his first bar, Baltimore was still reeling from the Depression of 1893, which forced the closing of hundreds of banks and 15,000 businesses nationwide. Nearly half of the city's industrial workers were unemployed and those fortunate to hold jobs worked 10 hours a day, 6 days a week, for an average of $10 a week. Running a saloon in turn-of-the-century Baltimore was an extremely competitive proposition. As the sixth largest city in the U.S., Baltimore boasted the highest ratio of bars to people—one saloon for every 105 residents. The harbor bustled with activity and there were many factories nearby. The longshoremen, stevedores, factory workers and waterfront bums washed down Katie's German cooking with lots of beer. When money was scarce, the Ruths simply worked longer hours, sometimes as many as 100 in a single week.

When Ruth looked back, he remembered his family as being "very poor. There were times when we never knew where the next meal was coming from." The Ruths certainly had some rough times, but they didn't live in the city's worst slums and probably would not be considered poverty-stricken by today's standards. Still, with his business dependent upon people who were themselves often financially unstable, there is no doubt George Ruth found it difficult to rely on a steady income.

Like most of the working-class kids living near the waterfront, Little George, as the family called him, led an unstructured and unsupervised existence. The "loose-jointed, gangling, dirty-faced kid in knee pants" spent a lot of time in his father's smoky bar, wandering among the tables, overhearing and repeating the rough talk of the men. He and his friends formed gangs, squared off against each other in mock battles in the filthy, congested streets and on the docks.

The boys stole vegetables from sidewalk pushcarts and threw their pilfered produce at passing horse-and-buggies, then scattered to avoid capture by either the storekeepers or the police. The tale of Ruth's ability to throw a curveball with a potato at age six is undoubtedly apocryphal, but he did wonder if his youthful vandalism served as early pitching training, since "tossing overripe apples or aged eggs at a truck driver's head is mighty good practice."

Life in the apartment above the bar was unstable. Katie was often pregnant, though almost all of her children died soon after birth. She was "a pleasant woman, but apparently not a particularly devoted mother.... Mainly she left the boy to shift for himself."

As the family's financial worries grew, George Sr.'s mean streak emerged. A neighbor once saw him beat his son with a billiard cue. "Daddy used to whip him something terrible," Mary Moberly, Babe's sister, recalled. "He wouldn't mind Daddy, that was the problem. That's part of the reason he was sent off to that school.... Once, Babe went out the kitchen door and looked back and said, 'You S.O.B.' Oh, it was terrible. If Daddy had heard him, he'd have killed him."

Shortly after his seventh birthday, George and Katie Ruth decided they could no longer control Little George. The courts declared him "incorrigible" and his parents arranged for him to live in what would now be called a reform school or a juvenile detention facility. On June 13, 1902, George Ruth packed a battered suitcase and he and his son rode the streetcar four miles to the outskirts of the city. They got off at the corner of Caton and Wilkens Avenues in front of a huge brick structure called St. Mary's Industrial School for Orphans, Delinquent, Incorrigible, and Wayward Boys.

The Brotherhood of St. Francis Xavier had founded St. Mary's in 1866 for Civil War orphans and as a haven for German and Irish Catholic children who were victims of bigotry and discrimination. The Xaverian Brothers accepted the "young unfortunates" of the city: orphans, homeless or abused children, petty thieves sent by the courts, even a few boarders whose families paid tuition. In keeping with all institutions of the time, it was racially segregated, open only to whites. In 1890, St. Mary's was cited as a model institution of its kind. The school, or "moral hospital," quickly reached its limit of 700 boys, and eventually expanded to six buildings and several acres of land.

That June afternoon must have been traumatic for Little George. He screamed and cried, but his tears did not dissuade his father or the Xaverian Brothers. When his father said goodbye and walked out the front gate, George Jr. had no idea when or if he would ever see any member of his family again. Though he started out as one of the youngest boys in the home, Ruth would remain at St. Mary's until he reached legal majority at 21. Of course, the sniffling seven-year-old could not have known that this apparent act of abandonment would have an enormously beneficial effect on his life. All he knew was that he had been cut off from the only life he had ever known.

Ruth claimed that he was never completely certain why he was sent away. His sister said he simply would not go to school. "The truant officer would keep coming," she remembered. "He was out at our house, I think, more than at his own house. 'What's wrong with him that he won't show up for school?' And my father would say, 'I don't think anything's wrong with him. He just doesn't want to go.'" An old story from the 1940s states that the police were called to the bar one night after a neighbor heard gunfire. "There's a young kid living there," the neighbor said. "It's no place for him."

It's worth noting that in 1902, the year Ruth was sent to St. Mary's, Baltimore passed a compulsory schooling law for children between the ages of 8 and 12, and for unemployed children between 12 and 16. Although the school year didn't start until the fall, perhaps this was the most expedient way for the Ruths to get some relief from their recalcitrant son and comply with the law.

George stayed at St. Mary's for only four weeks before he was taken home for the first of several attempted reconciliations. If the one-month stay was meant to shock the boy into good behavior, it failed. He still drank, refused to go to school and stole money from his father. As an adult, Ruth remembers the bottles behind the bar: "When he wasn't looking, the stuff was free." Once after he caught his son buying ice cream for his friends with money swiped from the bar, George Ruth whipped his son with a riding crop. After four months of chaos, his parents brought him back to St. Mary's in November.

That was also a short stay. According to John Ruth, Babe's uncle, "His mother missed him when he was in the Home and she would cry and ask her husband to get him out. Then when he came home she'd have trouble with him and hit him, and his father would put him back in again." One of Katie's cousins said, "When the boy was home, she used to strike him over the head and otherwise abuse him."

At Christmas time, the Ruths moved and George was again released. He spent most of 1903 with his family. There were at least five occasions of Ruth being "paroled" from St. Mary's, for anywhere from one month up to a year. His long-term residence at St. Mary's actually began in 1904, when he was nine years old.

At first the rigid structure and discipline of St. Mary's drove the youngster crazy. "I missed the crowds, and the dirt, and the noise of the street," Ruth recalled. He was so homesick that he even grew wistful for getting smacked around by the shopkeepers who caught him stealing. But St. Mary's was more of a boarding school than a prison. When the Brothers meted out punishment for various infractions, it was more often a suspension of privileges than beatings.

For the first time, Ruth's life had some semblance of order. The boys would wake up each morning at 6:00, attend Mass, eat breakfast, make their beds and attend school for three hours. After lunch and some free time, the younger boys would return to class for the afternoon, while boys 14 and older would have three hours of vocational training. Each student was expected to learn a trade; printing, shoemaking, electrical work, baking and carpentry were among the options. George Ruth worked as a tailor and a shirtmaker. Roughly 90 "inmates," as the boys called themselves, worked in the third-floor shop in one of the main buildings, sewing pairs of blue overalls (the school's traditional uniform), as well as the outfits for the band, choir and baseball teams. The boys also did work contracted to St. Mary's by private companies in Baltimore, making inexpensive blue and gray cotton shirts. On the floor below, other boys turned out a seemingly endless supply of underwear and stockings.

Lawton Stenersen, nicknamed "Scoffer" because of his large appetite, worked alongside Ruth. "I was a joiner and he put the collars on," Stenersen recalled. "We got six cents a shirt from the Oppenheim Shirt Company." Ruth stitched together the shirt parts on an electric sewing machine. He was quite dexterous and claimed he could sew a shirt in under 15 minutes. It was a skill he never lost; as an adult, he insisted on fixing his frayed collars himself.

Every afternoon, the boys were turned loose to burn off their youthful energy on St. Mary's two athletic fields. They played many sports—handball, soccer, football, basketball, boxing, wrestling—but baseball was the most popular. Ruth took to baseball immediately, spending all his available time on the diamond, playing in all kinds of weather. One Christmas morning, Ruth brushed snow off the base paths and rounded up enough boys for a game. Baseball boosted his self-confidence. He was at home anywhere on the field and he projected a keen sense of bravado. When one of the Brothers saw Ruth wearing only a thin undershirt and asked if he was cold, he said, "Not me, Brother. I'm too tough." Ruth would run around the yard, blowing on the fingers of shivering boys and rubbing their gloveless hands to keep them warm.

Brother Herman, who supervised St. Mary's recreation program, described the adolescent Ruth as "pretty big for his age, on the wiry side. He was full of mischief, nothing timid about him; an aggressive, shouting boy, always wrestling around with the others." Although much bigger and stronger than his peers, Ruth was not a bully; in fact, he was just the opposite. Ruth was protective of younger or smaller boys, tolerating no harassment when he was around. He often worked extra hours in the tailor shop to earn credit at the school store. After dinner, Ruth would fill up a cap with sweets and make the rounds, paying special attention to the boys who had no relatives or visitors. His generosity and kindness made him loved and admired among his fellow inmates. As adults, many men remembered their childhood at the Home as a social stigma—where the "bad boys" had come from. Ruth never felt that way; he loved St. Mary's and often returned to visit. Any story he told about the Brothers, the boys and the Home was one of mutual support, community and family.

Mamie Ruth said she and her mother rode the trolley out to St. Mary's every month, often bringing packages of food; there is no evidence that George Ruth ever went to see his son. Ruth never mentioned family visits of any kind. "I'm too big and ugly for anyone to come see me," the teenaged Ruth once told a friend. A fire in 1919 destroyed much of St. Mary's, including any records that could have shed light on the subject. Ruth's feelings for his parents are similarly unclear. In 1948, Ruth biographer Bob Considine wrote, "He was never close to his parents. He told me during the course of our work on his book that he actively disliked them, but he admitted that the feeling, or lack of it, might have been mutual."

Katie Ruth was living with her sister when she died on August 11, 1912, at age 38. Her death certificate states she died of tuberculosis and exhaustion. She is listed as a widow, which is incorrect, but could mean that she and her husband had separated. It is unclear whether young George, then 17, was released from St. Mary's while his mother was ill (he might have been needed to work at the bar) or if he was allowed to leave for her funeral.

If any moment can be pinpointed as pivotal in George Ruth's life, it would be the summer afternoon in 1902 when he first saw Brother Matthias playing baseball in the Big Yard. Matthias was a huge, pear-shaped man; at 6 feet, 4 inches and 225 pounds, he was known as "Big

Matt" or "The Boss." He had a stern face and imposing manner, but his equally strong sense of fairness commanded total respect from the boys.

Matthias was born Martin L. Boutlier on Cape Breton Island, Nova Scotia, in 1872 and moved to the U.S. after joining the Xaverian Order. "He taught me to read and write," Ruth said, "and he taught me the difference between right and wrong. He was the father I needed and the greatest man I've ever known."

How George Ruth first discovered baseball is lost to history. The boys at St. Mary's played a game called "potemkis" or "pokem," in which one player bats until he strikes out, then he, the pitcher and the fielders all rotate positions. He may have played makeshift games on the waterfront's cobblestone streets. One thing is certain: after he saw Brother Matthias with a bat in his hands, Ruth was never the same. Big Matt spent many afternoons tossing a worn-out baseball in the air and hitting it out to the boys, sometimes driving the lumpy sphere 350 feet away. "I would stand there and watch him, bug-eyed," Ruth remembered. "I had never seen anything like that in my life. I think I was born as a hitter the first day I ever saw him hit a baseball."

The impressionable youngster imitated Matthias's hitting style— gripping the bat tightly down at the knobbed end, taking a big swing at the ball—as well as his way of running with quick, tiny steps. Ruth said Matthias worked with him by the hour, bunting balls and honing his fielding skills, "correcting the mistakes I made with my hands and feet," and tutoring him in the finer points of the game. "He singled me out when I first came to St. Mary's. It wasn't that I was his 'pet.' But he concentrated on me, probably because I needed it."

Since by 1907 the population at St. Mary's had grown to 1100 and Matthias also had many administrative duties, it seems unlikely that any one boy could have received so much individual attention. But for Ruth, St. Mary's functioned almost like a private baseball academy. "When most boys were spending their leisure in the movies or standing around corners smoking cigarettes," Brother Gilbert noted, "Babe

Ruth was getting ten hours rest every night and from two to three hours batting practice every afternoon for at least ten months out of the year."

Evidence of Ruth's baseball achievements date back to 1911, when he was 16 years old. He was a catcher and usually played with boys two or three years older than himself. Inadequate equipment at the Home meant the left-handed Ruth had to use a right-hander's mitt. He quickly devised and mastered a strategy for dealing with this handicap: he would catch a pitch in his gloved left hand, flip the ball in the air, drop the glove or tuck it under his right arm, catch the ball with his now-bare left hand and throw. His arm was powerful and accurate; players knew if they crept too far off the bag, they'd get picked off.

Louis Leisman arrived at the Home in July 1909, just after his 11th birthday. His father had died and his mother, unable to support four children, sent two of her sons to St. Mary's. Leisman first heard about Ruth's baseball prowess from some boys buzzing about an upcoming game. The Number 2 Dormitory (15- to 19-year-olds) was playing the Number 3 Dormitory (8- to 15-year-olds), and as a boost to the younger boys, "Nigger Lips is going to catch for Number 3!" As a teenager, Ruth had an olive-colored complexion, full lips and a flat, broad nose on his round moon face; the kids called him "Nig" or "Nigger" for short.

In 1912, Ruth was the catcher on St. Mary's championship team, coincidentally nicknamed the Red Sox. In the team photo, he is instantly recognizable, taller than the other boys, wearing his chest protector and holding his mitt and mask across his broad chest. Ruth's pitching career began after he razzed a teammate named Congo Kirby. "We were playing an outside club and our pitchers were getting belted all over the lot," Ruth said. "Somehow that struck me as ridiculous. I roared and Brother Matthias came over and asked 'What seems to be so funny?'

"I told him that the way our hurlers were getting shellacked was a big joke. He said, 'You apparently know more about pitching than the pitchers. So you go in and pitch.'

"I thought he was kidding. But he wasn't."

Ruth had no idea how to pitch, how to throw a curve, how to toe the rubber. But he dutifully trudged out to the center of the diamond. As soon as he got there, "I felt a strange relationship with the pitcher's mound. It was as if I'd been born out there. Pitching felt like the most natural thing in the world."

Asked about his St. Mary's baseball experience in a 1918 interview, Ruth said he had little difficulty anywhere on the field. "Sometimes I pitched. Sometimes I caught, and frequently I played the outfield and infield. It was all the same to me. All I wanted was to play. I didn't care much where."

On June 8, 1913, the *Baltimore American* published a brief note about a game at St. Mary's—the first mention of Ruth outside the school newspaper. The Stars (so named because they were the Home's top players), led by their catcher, Ruth, topped the White Sox 10-3. One week later, the *American* reported that "Roth, the speed boy," a pitcher for the St. Patrick's Catholic Club, threw a one-hitter against Northwestern A.C., with 12 strikeouts. According to Ruth biographer Robert Creamer, the Brothers had begun allowing Ruth to suit up with local amateur and semipro teams on the weekends. Creamer believed "Roth" was a misprint: it was actually 17-year-old George Ruth. A week after the St. Patrick's victory, "Roth" struck out 14 men in a 4-3 loss, and after one more victory, he disappeared from the sports pages.

Only a few weeks later, on August 3, George Ruth caught both games of a doubleheader and banged out three hits for a team known as the Bayonnes. Late in the month, he played left field for the same team in a 18-2 rout of the Sparrows Point Marines, going 4-4 with two doubles and a home run. After belting another homer in September, Ruth was dubbed "the Bayonne fence buster."

Around this time, Ruth was transferred to the Saint James Home, another Xaverian institution in Baltimore, where young men were allowed more freedom to better prepare them for the outside world. After only two months, he was transferred back to St. Mary's for unknown reasons. Leisman remembers the day Ruth returned: "He was dressed in a grey suit and was wearing a black baseball cap.... [As he entered the Big Yard,] he walked very slowly with his head down and did not seem to hear the voices of the three or four hundred boys who were screaming, 'Welcome back, Nigger Lips!'"

During the summer of 1913, Ruth batted .537 and never lost a game on the mound. In one game, he caught, played third base and pitched, struck out six men, batted leadoff and collected a double, triple and home run. During doubleheaders, Ruth would often pitch one game and catch the other.

No one man propelled George Ruth from reform school phenomenon to the major leagues, but much of the credit goes to Brother Alban, an English man in his late 20's, who worked in the St. Mary's print shop. Alban also played first base for the school's Red Sox and at some point in 1913, he mentioned his exceptional teammate to Brother Gilbert, the baseball coach at nearby Mount St. Joseph's College and a respected judge of diamond talent. After Gilbert watched Ruth in action, he described him as "a tall, powerful, well-knit, dark-skinned, carefree boy of 18 years, without a tight muscle in his body."

In a well-hyped match-up between St. Mary's and the MSJ freshman team—the misfits against the upper-class kids, destitute Davids taking on the wealthy Goliaths—Ruth outpitched highly-touted Bill Morrisette. St. Mary's won the game 6-0 or 8-0 (reports vary). Ruth struck out as many as 22 batters, but no fewer than 14, and collected four hits himself. The *St. Mary's Evening Star* of September 20, 1913, mentions a game in which Ruth pitched a one-hitter, struck out 22 men, walked one and got four hits, but doesn't give the name of the opposing team.

In Baltimore baseball circles, most roads led to Jack Dunn. A former big league pitcher himself, Dunn earned the nickname "Handyman" by playing every position except catcher and first base. He won a career-high 23 games for the 1899 National League pennant-winning Brooklyn Superbas and had been a back-up third baseman on John McGraw's Baltimore Orioles in 1901.

In 1913, Dunn was the owner and manager of the minor league Baltimore Orioles in the International League. In mid-September, traveling on a train from Baltimore to Washington, he ran into Washington Senators pitcher Joe Engel, an MSJ alumnus. Engel told Dunn he had just seen a few games the day before and "some orphan asylum played in the first game and they had a young left-handed kid pitching for them who's got real stuff."

Engel was impressed not only with Ruth's prowess on the mound, but with his haircut. Ruth's jet black hair was clipped close on both sides and "roached" on top, the locks brushed straight back off his forehead. It was a style worn by bartenders in the 1890s and the most mature haircut Engel had ever seen on a kid. He added that Ruth played in the post-game marching band, still in his uniform, sitting in the stands, beating the life out of a bass drum. He was hard to miss.

Dunn, always on the lookout for talent, had also received a tip on Ruth from Brother Gilbert. On a chilly Valentine's Day morning in 1914, Dunn and Gilbert drove out to St. Mary's to take a look at George Ruth. Fritz Maisel, a New York Yankees infielder and Baltimore native, went along for the ride. The three men found Brother Matthias and explained why they had come.

"Ruth can hit," Matthias said matter-of-factly.

Dunn didn't really need any more hitters. "Can he pitch?"

"Sure, he can do anything."

Matthias called for Ruth to be sent down to the Yard. Word about the visitors quickly circulated and a small group of boys hovered nearby, keeping a respectful distance from Dunn and Maisel. Ruth came charging outside, sliding on some stray patches of ice. His blue overalls were pulled tight across his chest and he wore three shiny metal rings on the fingers of his left hand.

"There's our victim," Gilbert whispered to Dunn.

Dunn let out a low whistle. "Wow, he's a regular Rube Waddell in the rough," he said, referring to the eccentric left-handed pitching star of the Philadelphia Athletics.* Ruth chatted with the men briefly before changing into his uniform. Ruth remembered that Dunn "had me pitch to him for about a half hour, talking to me all the time, and telling me not to strain and not to try too hard."

After the try-out, Brother Gilbert asked, "What do you think, John?"

Dunn wanted to sign Ruth on the spot, but didn't know how to proceed. "What do you want for him, Brother?"

"What do I want for him?" Brother Gilbert repeated. "John, he's not mine to sell. All I want for him is a good home, proper care and the chance for him to make somebody of himself in the world, no more and no less." Gilbert told Dunn that because Ruth was a minor, he would have to assume guardianship of the young man. That was fine with Dunn. (Ruth's father was apparently not involved in these discussions.) When Ruth was told he'd be paid $100 a month—$600 for the season— to play the game he loved, he was stunned.

"The Oriole magnate signed another local player," the *Baltimore Sun* reported. "The new Bird is George H. Ruth, a pitcher who played with teams out the Frederick Road. Ruth is six feet tall and fanned 22 men in an amateur game last season. He is regarded as a very hard hitter, so Dunn will try him out down south."

---

* Waddell's best pitching years were 1902–1907. At the time of Ruth's tryout, he was dying of tuberculosis; he passed away on April 1, 1914, at age 37.

Ruth signed his first professional contract on February 22, 1914, and officially left St. Mary's five days later. He spent a weekend with his father and before he left, he returned to St. Mary's and said goodbye to his friends.

"Lefty, you're a great fellow and a corker ballplayer," said "Keyhole" Smith. "Just don't choke up down there. I hate like hell—I'll miss you, but I'm pullin' for you to make good."

"You fellows are one bunch of swell guys," Ruth said, tears welling in his eyes. "We've had lots of fun together and there isn't one squawker in the whole bunch of you. I sure do wish that some of you were going with me, then I know I'd make good. And hey, when I come back to Baltimore, I'll come back and tell you guys all about it."

Brother Paul drove Ruth to the train station.

"We forgot my baseball uniform, Brother. I can't play in these clothes."

"The Orioles will give you a uniform, George. They have their own uniforms."

"Where will I live when I'm down there?"

"You'll stay with the team at the hotel. Now remember, your main job is to do as you're told. Keep your ears open and your mouth shut."

Ruth was chewing his gum furiously when Jack Dunn met them at the station. "Hello, Brother," said Dunn, shaking Brother Paul's hand. "This kid looks good." He eyed his newest recruit. "Boy, I know I'm going to like you. Work out slowly until I get to camp. I don't want you to get a sore arm."

"I won't, Mr. Dunn. Since I signed with you, I've played eight games."

"You what?"

"Yes sir, I played eight games. I pitched two games, caught two games, played shortstop for two games and played first base in one game. The other game, I played one inning at each position. Brother Matthias told me to do that so I'd be ready for any position you want me to play."

"And your arm isn't sore?" Dunn asked.

"No, sir," Ruth said. "My arm doesn't get sore."

Dunn was pleased. "Well, Brother, one thing about this mustang: he's no alibi artist. Most beginners sob a swan song, but this kid has frog legs, he's ready to go."

Before Ruth boarded the train, Dunn told him he'd join him and the rest of the team in a week, and slipped five dollars into Ruth's coat pocket. The youngster could barely contain his excitement. It was the first train ride of his life.

5

"You're a Ballplayer, not a Circus Act!"

When George Ruth stepped off the train in North Carolina, he was surprised that the weather was warmer in Fayetteville than in snowy Baltimore. At the Lafayette Hotel, he bribed the elevator operator into letting him work the controls. On his first attempt, mesmerized by the contraption, his head was outside the door and he nearly decapitated himself when the cab began to rise. After one of the veterans told him the club paid for meals at the hotel—"Order anything you want, kid"—he packed away three huge helpings of ham and wheatcakes, chewing loudly and drawing stares. He was the greenest of rookies, the quintessential country bumpkin.

But on the ballfield at the Cape Fear Fairgrounds, Ruth was supremely confident. In the Orioles' first intrasquad match, Ruth started at shortstop and pitched the final inning of his team's 15-9 win. Batting in the seventh inning, Ruth "landed on a fastball and circled the bases before Billy Morrisette had picked it up in deep right field."

This was the same Morrisette from Ruth's MSJ duel; Dunn had signed him, too.

Under the headline "Homer by Ruth Feature of Game," the *Baltimore Sun* reported, "George Ruth, a pitcher Jack Dunn picked off the lots of Baltimore, is credited with making the longest hit ever seen by Fayetteville fans." The local record had been set by 1912 Olympic decathlon star and part-time New York Giants outfielder Jim Thorpe. Ruth's drive carried about 60 feet further than Thorpe's. A modern marker puts the distance at 405 feet.

Dunn initially dismissed the stories about Ruth in the papers that first week as "wild tales," but once he got to camp, he realized the writers were not exaggerating. "He hits like a fiend," Dunn said, "and seems to be at home in any position." Ruth was making news every day: four strikeouts in each of two three-inning appearances on the mound, then five assists and a double play in another game at shortstop. One article described him as a switch-hitter.

"Ruth looks like one of the best pitchers I have ever laid my eyes on," Dunn said. "He possesses every quality of what I term a major leaguer. He is strong, has speed and can hit the ball. He needs developing and within a year's time I may be able to spring another big surprise on the baseball world."

Ruth wrote several letters to the Xaverian brothers at St. Mary's.

Dear Brother Alban:

I am making good in everything that they have down here—basketball, baseball and running. Get Brother Gilbert to send down some more boys from the school.

Yours Truly,
Geo. Ruth

P.S. On rainy days, the squad plays a little basketball in the armory....

In a letter to Brother Gilbert, Ruth wrote, "There are about six more fellows at school that could make this team. Try to help them."

After practice, Fayetteville was Ruth's personal amusement park. He made friends with several boys who hung around the field and often borrowed their bicycles in the afternoons. One evening, Ruth sped past the hotel, yelling "Look at me! Look at me!" Dunn watched in horror as Ruth slammed into the back of a hay wagon, flew a few feet in the air and landed on his back. "You wanna go back to that school?" Dunn shouted. "You're a ballplayer, not a goddamn circus act!"

After another accident, Orioles scout Sam Steinman remarked to sportswriter Roger Pippen, "If Dunn doesn't shackle that new babe of his, he won't be a Rube Waddell in the rough, he'll be a babe Ruth in the cemetery." In his next article, which appeared in the March 19, 1914, *Baltimore American*, Pippen referred to the "young fledgling" as "Babe Ruth"—the first use of the nickname in print.[*]

On March 18, less than three weeks after leaving St. Mary's, Ruth faced major league hitters for the first time, appearing in relief against the Philadelphia Phillies. He was shaky at first, but pitched three solid innings. The next day, Ruth came out of the pen in the sixth inning. He balked on his first pitch when he forgot there was a runner on base, but then struck out two batters to retire the side and allowed only two singles over three innings. In his two appearances, he faced 29 batters, surrendering only six hits and two unearned runs.

---

[*] There are numerous stories of how Ruth got his nickname. This story was taken from Brother Gilbert's book about St. Mary's. In another story, after Ruth had been heckled by the Oriole veterans, Steinman told the players, "Stop being so rough with the boy. He's Dunnie's babe and if Jack got wind of the rough-housing, he wouldn't like it." Jesse Linthicum, a Baltimore sportswriter, said the nickname came from Ruth crying so often at St. Mary's. New York sportswriter Fred Lieb said Ruth had told him a similar story years later.

"That Ruth is a comer," said Phillies coach Pat Moran. "He has the build, the speed and curves and can hit quite a bit himself. You can't expect anymore of a pitcher, can you?"

Ruth got a starting assignment one week later against the Philadelphia Athletics, winners of three of the last four World Series. "Hey Dunnie, who's that big stiff at third base?" Ruth asked midway through the game. "I can't seem to get him out." The "stiff" was Frank Baker, the four-time American League home run champion and World Series hero. Despite Baker's four hits, Ruth threw a complete game, winning 6-2. Several Athletics said Ruth was one of the best youngsters they'd seen in a long time.

Over the next two weeks, Ruth beat the Brooklyn Dodgers 10-6, lost to the Yankees 4-0, and lost to the Giants 3-2 (the *New York World* called him "Baby" Ruth). "That young left-hander looked awfully good," Giants manager John McGraw told Dunn. "Whenever you're ready to put him on the market, I want you to give me first crack at him." McGraw insisted that Dunn had agreed and never forgave him for breaking his promise. According to former Red Sox owner Joe Lannin, Babe nearly became a member of the New York Giants. Lannin said that the day after he purchased Ruth, Ernie Shore and Ben Egan, McGraw made a considerably better offer. "Just a day of delay," he said, "and Babe Ruth would have gone into the National League."

Ruth's first International League start was a 6-0 shutout of Buffalo before a tiny crowd of 200 fans. He went 2-4 at the plate and banged a pinch-hit triple the following day. His performances ran hot and cold; he went from impressive to erratic. By the end of June, Ruth's record was 11-7. At the plate, he was batting only .195, but when he connected, it was often for a long hit—he had four singles, a double and three triples.

One day early in the season, Newark pitcher Al Schacht was walking towards the players' entrance of the Orioles' park when someone plowed into him on a bicycle. He looked up from the ground and saw a "gangling, moon-faced kid" clutching a handful of hot dogs.

"Why the hell don't you watch where you're going, Rube?" Schacht yelled.

"Sorry, mister, I almost dropped a hot dog and my hand slipped."

The kid stuck a brown cap on his head and pushed his bicycle to the other side of the park while stuffing hot dogs in his mouth.

That hayseed, Schacht thought, he's probably seeing his first ball game. Later that day, Schacht was doubly surprised when he saw the kid on the field, wearing a Baltimore uniform.

One month into the season, Dunn doubled Ruth's salary to $1,200, then upped it again, to $1,800, a rate comparable to the team's veterans. Dunn thought highly of Ruth's talent, but the raises were also intended to keep him away from the Federal League agents who were hanging around the park.

The Federal League was one of the bigger headaches for organized baseball during the 1910s. Since it operated outside the authority of the rules and agreements that governed the major leagues and most of the many minor leagues, it was known as an "outlaw" league.

The league began in 1913 with six teams—St. Louis, Pittsburgh, Cincinnati, Chicago, Indianapolis and Cleveland—and hoped to attract enough talent to gain acceptance as a third established major league. The Federal League expanded into three eastern cities—Baltimore, Buffalo and Brooklyn—in 1914. The teams initially respected major league rosters, but the case of Phillies catcher Bill Killefer changed that. In 12 days during January 1914, Killefer left the Phillies, signed a contract with the Chicago Whales, then went back to the Phillies for a new contract. Philadelphia was awarded custody of Killefer and from that point on, the Feds reasoned that since organized baseball had ignored the validity of their contract with Killefer, they would ignore organized baseball contracts altogether. The Feds also filed an anti-trust suit and the player raids began.

Federal League agents visited spring training camps and ballparks during the 1914 season. Years later, Babe Ruth admitted that the Baltimore Terrapins offered him $10,000 per season plus a $10,000 signing bonus. It was an outrageous amount of money for a rookie and only the fear of being blacklisted from the American and National Leagues caused Ruth to turn it down. Hal Chase, Claude Hendrix, Armando Marsans, Russ Ford and Cy Falkenberg all crossed over, as did pitcher Walter Johnson.

After a magnificent 36-7 season with a 1.09 ERA and only 38 walks in 346 innings, Johnson asked for a raise—and was rebuffed. Senators owner Clark Griffith offered Johnson the same salary he had paid him the previous year, and so Johnson signed a lucrative deal with the Chicago Whales. Fans were dumbstruck that the upstanding Johnson had yielded to the temptation of the dollar and derided him as an incurably greedy man. In a personal visit to Johnson's home in Kansas, Griffith convinced Johnson to break his Whales contract and return to Washington. Johnson's $6,000 signing bonus was paid back, but who paid it is unclear. Griffith purportedly convinced Charles Comiskey to write a check, arguing that it was in his best interests to keep Johnson off the Whales and out of Chicago where he could draw fans away from the White Sox.

The Federal League raids threw the formerly monopolistic American and National Leagues into a bidding war. With outsiders enticing the same players, salaries went up, approaching the players' true worth. In 1911 to 1913, Detroit's Ty Cobb batted .420, .409 and .390, but his annual salary remained at $9,000. "You will play for what I am offering," Tigers owner Frank Navin told him, "or you will not play at all." But facing a reported Federal League offer to Cobb of $100,000, Navin bumped his outfielder's pay to $20,000. In Boston, Red Sox owner Joe Lannin doubled Tris Speaker's salary from $9,000 to $18,000. Other players used the threat of a "jump" to the Feds to negotiate a better contract; these included Rabbit Maranville, whose salary increased from

$1,800 to $6,000, Jack Daubert, $5,000 to $9,000, and Ray Caldwell, $2,400 to $8,000. The National Commission scrapped the rules governing roster size so teams could keep an unlimited number of players under contract and away from the Feds.*

The Federal League had been in precarious financial condition from its beginning, and after offering generous contracts, defending itself in court and building new ballparks, it eventually crumbled under the weight of its many debts. In December 1915 a settlement agreement was reached with organized baseball. Players coming back to the majors were offered salaries at pre-Fed levels; the Pittsburgh Pirates cut Honus Wagner's salary from $10,000 to $5,400; in Boston, Tris Speaker was offered his usual $9,000.

The relationship between baseball players and the men who own the teams has always been uneasy at best. But despite any similarities between baseball in the 1910s and the modern game, the labor landscape of those times was radically different. Free agency was more than half a century away. There was no players' union and no agents. Radio broadcasts of games were years away and there was no revenue from television or merchandising. Most players worked in the off-season as farmers, laborers or craftsmen. Athletes, many of whom were uneducated and unsophisticated, negotiated their contracts with shrewd businessmen without the benefit of representation.

Management paid the players as little as possible. Most contracts were for one year, and salaries could be reduced for any number of reasons, from a drop in performance to an owner's whim. An outfielder earning $7,000 might receive $5,000 as salary, plus a $2,000 signing bonus; regardless of his performance, negotiations for the next season

---

* The three-member National Commission—the two league presidents and a chairman chosen by them, Cincinnati Reds owner Garry Herrmann—acted as the major leagues' governing body until it was replaced by a Commissioner in 1921.

would begin at $5,000. During negotiations, a player had two options: sign the contract or retire. A player who balked at a pay cut was often sent to the minor leagues. If two owners were interested in the same player, they avoided a bidding war by reaching an agreement. Such "gentlemen's agreements" were common and the rules were as elastic as was necessary to suit the owners' needs. Collusion was another word for doing business.*

Nearly every decision about a player's career was unilaterally decided by management. The club that signed a player was that player's employer for his entire baseball career—or until the club decided to trade or release him. Every contract included the now-illegal "reserve clause" that gave the team the exclusive right to the player's services for the following year. In other words, when a player signed for one year, he automatically bound himself to that team for the following year.

Judge Kenesaw Mountain Landis of the District Court of Northern Illinois presided over the Federal League's anti-trust suit. Although the league had been encouraged by Landis's reputation as a trustbuster (in 1907, he fined Standard Oil $29 million for monopolistic practices), they didn't count on the judge being a baseball fanatic with very definite ideas about how the game should be run. To avoid ruling against the National Commission, Landis delayed his decision for nearly a year, until the Federal League had conveniently gone out of business. Major league owners selected Landis as the sport's first commissioner in January 1921.

In Baltimore, the Federal League Terrapins played directly across the street from Jack Dunn's Orioles and most fans flocked to the new team. Some days there were only a few dozen customers, and Dunn, out of

---

* Donald Fehr of the Players' Association said in 1991, "Go through *The Sporting News* of the last 100 years, and you will find two things are always true. You never have enough pitchers and nobody ever made money."

funds, worried he might have to move the Orioles to Virginia. In mid-June, Dunn announced that everyone on his roster was available. He rejected an offer from the Chicago White Sox for six players, including Ruth; a week later, he turned down the Yankees' offer of $25,000 for Ruth and three others. Some writers thought the Philadelphia Athletics held an inside track on the top Orioles because Connie Mack had helped Dunn out financially. But Mack was also having financial difficulties and would start dumping his own stars after the season.

Red Sox owner Joe Lannin had passed on several Orioles earlier in the season, but he was now willing to do business. On July 3, while the Red Sox were playing a series against the Senators, Dunn and his coach Freddie Parent went to Washington to meet with Boston manager Bill Carrigan. "If you can get Ruth and [Ernie] Shore, you'll win the pennant," Parent said. "Shore's ready to win in the majors right now. Ruth is still very crude, but he can't miss with a little more experience." That was good enough for Carrigan, who trusted Parent, a former teammate.*

Ruth pitched for the Orioles on July 4, then asked for the afternoon off to play a pick-up game and visit his old friends at St. Mary's. A few days later, when Dunn told him about the sale, Babe was heartbroken. With tears in his eyes, Ruth told Dunn how much he hated to "leave home, the school and you." Going to Boston meant nothing to Ruth; he had only begun to feel comfortable in his new situation and now he had to move on.

Ruth played two more games for the Orioles, both in left field, then on the night of July 10, Ruth, Shore and Egan boarded the Federal

---

* At the time, the deal was reported as $20,000, $25,000, $27,000 and $30,000. In later years, Lannin said he had offered $15,000 for Shore and Ruth and Dunn's counteroffer was $18,000 for the two pitchers and catcher Ben Egan. Carrigan claimed in 1943 that the price was $18,000. In 1919, however, Dunn said $12,500 of the total price was for Ruth, which would bring Shore's portion of the price down to about $3,000, which is ridiculously low considering the two pitchers' respective talents.

Express for Boston. Lannin greeted them at the Back Bay Station early Saturday morning, took them to the club's offices and then to Fenway Park. There, his new manager told Ruth he would pitch that afternoon against the last-place Cleveland Indians. "Don't be nervous, kid," Carrigan said. "I'll be catching. Just throw what I tell you."

A few hours later, Ruth made his way onto the field, walking with short, cautious steps. But right away, he exhibited coolness under pressure. In the first inning, Ruth prevented a runner from advancing by cutting off a throw from the outfield, and he picked Joe Jackson off first base. His pitches had plenty of movement, although every so often he threw a fat one down the middle. In the seventh inning, he was pulled for a pinch-hitter, and when the Red Sox rallied for a 4-3 win, Ruth had his first major league victory.

The *Boston Herald* announced Ruth's arrival as "easily the best twirler uncovered in the minor league ranks this season.... a big, powerful fellow with a heart like a child...Ruth can catch, play the outfield or hold down first base almost as well as he can pitch. And he can hit.... He is a husky, hardened boy of outdoors, standing more than six feet and weighing 180 pounds in his present splendid condition. He simply loves baseball and will play all day if permitted."

Ruth's journey from the St. Mary's dormitory to the pitcher's mound at Fenway Park had taken only four and a half months.

If Ruth was sad to leave the Orioles, no one on the Red Sox was overly happy to see him arrive. He was a newcomer, a teenager, a nobody. In those days, veterans rarely showed any kindness to rookies—why help someone who could steal your job? The day after his debut, Ruth spied a ball that had gotten away from pitcher Joe Wood during warmups. Ruth grabbed it and tossed it back, but Wood wasn't paying attention and the ball struck him in the back. Furious, Wood whipped the ball back as hard as he could, hitting Babe in the leg.

When Ruth tried taking batting practice with the regulars, the harsh treatment intensified. "A rookie doesn't do that," said Ernie Shore, "much less a rookie pitcher. But he pushed himself in whenever he could." One day Ruth arrived at the park to find all his bats neatly sawed in half. "They thought I was a fresh kid who didn't have much respect for big baseball reputations," he remembered. "I did talk back, but not because I was fresh. I just wanted to show them I was as good as any of the other pitchers."

After he was hit hard in his second start by the Detroit Tigers, Ruth stayed on the bench. Boston's rotation was the best in the league and already included left-handers Ray Collins and Dutch Leonard, who was on his way to a record 0.96 ERA. The team would soon add Vean Gregg, another talented lefty. There was simply no room for the new kid. Babe won two mid-August exhibition games and was then sent to the minor leagues. Red Sox owner Joe Lannin wanted Ruth to help the pennant chances of the Providence Grays, the International League club he had recently purchased. There were snags getting Ruth through waivers— Cincinnati, Washington and Brooklyn all put in a claim—but after Lannin explained that he wasn't actually dumping Ruth, the other teams relented.

Lannin claimed to have a soft spot for Providence—"The first ball games I ever saw were the hair-raising contests between Boston and Providence in the early 1880s"—but legend has it that he bought the Grays (also known as the Clamdiggers) for one reason: to acquire a talented submarine pitcher named Carl Mays.

Ruth joined the Grays just in time for a four-game showdown with first-place Rochester. Babe won his first game, helping his cause with a ninth-inning triple. Among the people in the crowd that day was International League president Ed Barrow. Ruth's best outing with the Grays came in Toronto on September 5, when he threw a one-hitter and clubbed his only minor league home run.

Lannin's move worked: the Grays won the league pennant. With the race over, the last game of the season was a virtual circus. Both managers pitched and the teams combined for 56 hits. Eight home runs were hit, including five by various pitchers, though none by Ruth, who played the entire game in right field. He collected two singles and a triple, stole two bases and scored three runs. The Grays won 23-19.

The Chicago Cubs, in Boston for a series with the Braves, traveled to Warwick, Rhode Island, for a Sunday exhibition against Providence. Ruth pitched a complete game, winning 8-7, and hit a home run. Facing a lefty late in the game, Ruth turned around and batted right-handed, but grounded out.

On September 28, Ruth and Mays boarded a train to Boston to spend the final week of the season with the Red Sox. A few minutes into their 40-mile trip, Ruth elbowed his teammate. "Say, that's a pretty hot lookin' chick down the corner there that just come in the car," he said, pointing with his cigar.

"Babe, it's only 8:30 in the morning."

"So what? 8:30 is just as good as any other time."

In Boston, Ruth signaled for a cab and when they arrived at the hotel, Mays was shocked at the 90¢ fare. "Listen, kid," Babe said with authority, "You're in the big time now. You got to do things big time."

Mays didn't play at all that week. Ruth pitched a complete game victory over the Yankees and got his first major league hit, a double off King Cole of the Yankees. Three days later, as a pinch-hitter, he struck out against Washington's Walter Johnson. On the last day of the season, Ruth pitched three innings in relief, and singled in his only at-bat. 1914 had been an extraordinary year for the 19-year-old Ruth. Even with a month spent on the Red Sox bench, Babe finished with a combined record—Baltimore, Providence and Boston—of 28-9.

The Red Sox ended the year 91-62, second to the Philadelphia Athletics. But that summer the city of Boston belonged to its National League team, the Braves. After a dismal 4-18 start and an embarrassing exhibition loss to a team of soap factory workers, the Braves found themselves mired in last place by mid-July. Then the misery turned into a miracle. Led by pitchers Bill James and Dick Rudolph and infielders Johnny Evers and Rabbit Maranville, the Braves won 52 of their remaining 66 games, took over first place on August 25 and won the pennant by 10½ games. They went on to sweep the heavily-favored Athletics in the World Series.

One day in October, before leaving Boston for the winter, Ruth stopped by Landers' Coffee Shop on Dartmouth Avenue, across the street from the Back Bay train station. He had been dating 17-year-old Helen Woodford, a private-school student and waitress in the diner, for a few months. How Babe and Helen first met is unclear. The most common story is that Helen served Babe breakfast on his first day in Boston in July. It is also possible that Helen's brother, a big Red Sox fan, met Ruth after his first game in Boston and introduced the two teenagers.

Myrtle Durant, one of Helen's co-workers at the diner, described Ruth as "a big, lummockin' sort of fella." Durant and her boyfriend Parker Hatch often double-dated with Babe and Helen, going to the movies, ice skating or dancing. Helen liked Babe a lot—they called each other "Hon"—and was flattered when he would take the train from Providence to Boston to see her on his days off. Once he hired a cab to drive him the entire 40 miles.

At the diner, Babe got straight to the point. He told Helen he hoped she would return to Baltimore with him and they would get married. She thought for a minute, then accepted his proposal. Because Ruth was not yet 21, he needed his father's permission. George Ruth Sr. gave his blessing and the couple was wed on October 17 in the Baltimore suburb of Ellicott City. Although her parents had been born in Newfoundland, Canada, Helen was described in the Boston papers as "the daughter of a

prominent Texas rancher, a man of wealth and influence in his community." The newlyweds spent the winter with Ruth's father in the apartment above the Conway Street saloon. Babe planned to work as an
"automobile demonstrator."

6

"THERE IS NO GOOD BUYING ANYTHING BUT THE BEST"

Babe Ruth was about twenty pounds overweight when he reported to Hot Springs, Arkansas, for spring training in 1915. Manager Bill Carrigan had him shagging fly balls in the outfield to work off the winter flab. Ruth was still considered an extra pitcher in camp, but he showed unbridled enthusiasm. Usually the first player out of the hotel each morning, by the time the rest of the squad arrived, Ruth could be found pitching to the groundskeeper. When he wasn't on the mound, he was knocking out fungoes to the outfielders.

Trimmed down, Ruth had a broad chest, powerful shoulders and a small waist—built "like a bale of cotton" was one description. "He was a striking-looking guy, big and homely," said Herb Pennock, who joined the Boston pitching staff that season. "His features were heavy, his hair thick and black, his eyes brown." At 6 feet, 2 inches and 190 pounds, Ruth was 4 inches taller and 25 pounds heavier than the average major leaguer. Sportswriters soon began calling him "the Big Fellow."

Ruth spent many hours in the Hot Springs casinos, and also found time for golf, fishing and horseback riding. He bowled both left-handed and right-handed and was the best bowler on the team. He was much less successful at poker. "He might as well give his money away," said Joe Devine, a rookie catcher in camp. "Why doesn't he just leave a deposit and go see a movie?"

It didn't take long for Carrigan to discover Ruth's rambunctious side. When Babe was found wandering around town at 4:00 one morning, Carrigan demanded to know why he hadn't obeyed the midnight curfew. "But I did," Ruth explained. "I got to my room by midnight and went out at a quarter past."

Ruth's fellow pitcher Dutch Leonard, who was stocky and dark-complexioned like the Babe, turned out to be nearly as wild as Ruth, too. The two became fast friends. Since they were playing only every fourth day, the two pitchers had the luxury of staying out late, knowing they could recover on the bench the following day. "They were more interested in good times than their jobs," Carrigan admitted.

Leonard loved starting arguments with anyone he could and while Carrigan and coach Heinie Wagner were smart enough to ignore him, the less worldly Ruth fell for the bait time and time again. "Then the fun would begin," Carrigan said. "Many times, Heinie and I had to hold them apart to keep them from springing at each other's throat."

That soon became the manager's part-time job. "I have a ball club to run," Carrigan complained. "I can't let these guys go out and get drunk every night." For a while, Carrigan insisted that both Leonard and Ruth room with him, before Ruth roomed with Wagner, and Carrigan and Leonard took an adjoining suite. "Babe was forever trying to think up schemes to get away from us," Carrigan said. "One night, I turned my back just long enough to look in a mirror to put on a tie. When I turned around, the Babe had disappeared."

Ruth was clearly an overgrown adolescent. Only a few months past his 20th birthday, he wore checked suits with rainbow-hued ties and sometimes sported yellow shoes. "He had never been anywhere," Harry Hooper said. "He didn't know anything about manners or how to behave among people. And Lord, he ate too much. When we were traveling, he'd stop and order half a dozen hot dogs and as many bottles of soda pop, stuff them in, one after the other, and then give a few big belches. That would hold him for a couple of hours."

Even while sitting on the bench, Ruth would ask an usher to slip him a hot dog, a bag of peanuts or an ice cream cone. Carrigan eventually banned all food from the dugout. The Boston sportswriters were also amazed by Ruth's appetite. "According to Mrs. Ruth, and she ought to know," the *Boston Post* reported, "the Babe will eat two-and-a-half pounds of rare beefsteak for dinner any day excepting Friday. And at every such meal he consumes, unaided, an entire bottle of chili sauce."

If Ruth was invited to someone's house for dinner, his hosts were usually left shaking their heads. One night in 1917, Ruth visited manager Jack Barry's home in Worcester and Barry's wife was preparing hamburgers. Ruth told her, "Don't bother cooking mine, I'll just eat it raw"—then proceeded to shove the uncooked meat into his mouth.

Ruth's behavior was crude even by ballplayers' standards. Off the field, his instincts were wrong more often than not, but if he appeared selfish or boorish, it was more likely awkwardness and a lack of social skills. Even so, his habit of blurting out whatever popped into his head didn't win him many friends. "He was foul-mouthed, a show-off, very distasteful to have around," said Margaret Gardner, the wife of Boston's third baseman. "The kind of person you would never dream of having over to dinner." Another player's wife said, "He used so many swear words it embarrassed you, and believe me, I don't embarrass easy."

Ruth's cursing got him, Harry Hooper and catcher Chet Thomas thrown off several golf courses around Boston. Sportswriter Fred Lieb claimed that Ruth "couldn't say five words without three of them being vulgar." When anyone casually asked him how things were going, instead of "Pretty good, pretty good," Babe's standard response was, "Pussy good, pussy good." After suspending Ruth for some infraction, American League president Ban Johnson remarked, "He has the mind of a 15-year-old."

Ruth's teammates and their spouses may have found his naiveté amusing or disgusting, but his lack of manners rarely, if ever, impeded his romantic success. Such was the lure of a big league ballplayer. "I don't know if the Babe had ever been with a woman before he joined the Red Sox," one friend said, "but after he found out what it was all about, why, he was a *bear*." A friend said Ruth would "stick it in anything that had hair"; an unfortunate roommate described him as "the noisiest fucker in North America."

Larry Gardner remembered walking in on Ruth and "the guy was lying on the floor being screwed by a prostitute. He was smoking a cigar and eating peanuts, and this woman was working on him." Ernie Shore roomed with Ruth at first, but threatened to quit the team unless he was given a different roommate. The family version of the story says that Ruth kept using Shore's toothbrush. "So what?" Ruth supposedly replied, "he's welcome to use mine anytime." Other sources say Ruth never flushed the toilet and kept Shore up at nights bringing women into the room.

With his nights free and his wallet full, Ruth was like a kid in a candy store when it came to his seemingly unquenchable sexual appetite. He had telephone numbers of women in all the American League cities and was no stranger to the red-light districts. The "sporting girls" on Boston's Aberdeen Street and Hemenway Street, both a short distance from Fenway Park, probably knew Ruth well—as did the women on Lower Tremont Street, Shawmut Avenue and West Canton Street. In those early years, Ruth was often found passed out on the streets, his pockets long since emptied by whomever he had been running around with the night before. Whenever a search party was dispatched to find the pitcher, the boys who hung around outside the hotel would join the fun, treating it like a contest to see who could find Ruth first.

Ruth's impulsive behavior caused his manager to put him on an allowance. "He had no idea whatsoever of money," Carrigan said. "He didn't seem to think it would ever run out. I'd draw Babe's pay and give him a little every day to spend. That generally lasted about five minutes." Babe's rule was to stay out as long as there was money in his wallet. As he said years later, "I never spent dough in those days, I shot it out of a cannon."

The Red Sox clubhouse was rowdy and chaotic, and Ruth was right at home in the middle of it, entertaining his teammates with details of his sexual escapades. "What an ass on her," he'd say, stripping off his street clothes in the locker room. "And her skin—not a mark on it!" He'd pantomime the whole act, thrusting his hips, waving his arms, grunting and moaning. "The ladies of Boston," he'd bellow from the shower, "they'd recognize this cock anywhere."

"You'd see Babe only at game time," infielder Chick Shorten said. "As soon as it was over he'd take off for a party and have more fun. There was a saying among the Sox that 'He does everything right on the ballfield and everything wrong off it.'"

As might be expected from the impulsive, carefree way he gamboled through the rest of his life, Babe Ruth was not especially careful or attentive when behind the wheel of an automobile. His driver's license was revoked after an accident in 1914, and according to one report the following year, he "struck pedestrians while going at a speedy clip." Red lights meant nothing to him; he often drove right through them. He once abandoned a car in traffic to chase a teammate who razzed him from the sidewalk. Ruth's erratic driving once resulted in a hay wagon being overturned, spilling its contents all over a country road, but once the police saw who was to blame for the mess, "everyone enjoyed a hearty laugh." No doubt *The Sporting News* had drivers like Ruth in mind when it counseled ballplayers to forgo the "extravagance" of owning a "machine" and called on club owners to "forbid this fad" which was "a result of players' natural craving for speed and undue risk."

Babe was involved in another accident in November 1917, such a common occurrence by then that the brief report was headlined:

"Ruth's Annual Auto Affair." Babe had tried driving between two trolley cars at a crossing near Fenway Park in the wee hours of the morning. His car got caught and was twisted and smashed into a "shapeless mess." Ruth had remained behind the wheel and escaped injury, but his unidentified female companion (apparently not his wife Helen) was taken away in an ambulance.

Ruth loved to play practical jokes. One of his favorites was slipping a piece of scorecard or a bit of gauze into a teammate's sandwich, then watching from a corner of the room while his victim bit into his lunch. Ruth also dropped lighted cigars down teammates' pant legs as they got dressed. Because of the baggy, bloomer-style uniforms of the time, it might take a few minutes before the player realized his clothing was on fire. Some players sought revenge. After Larry Gardner learned Ruth was terrified of bugs and snakes, he could put Babe in a panic by producing nothing more dangerous than a caterpillar. For awhile, Ruth thought butterflies were bad luck and would chase them across the field, throwing his cap and glove at them.

Ruth's inability to remember faces and names was also becoming legend. In 1916, a few hours after Babe had defeated Philadelphia, Stuffy McInnis, then the Athletics' first baseman, spotted Ruth in the hotel lobby. "Babe, that was a hell of a fine game you pitched this afternoon," said Stuffy. Ruth looked at him. "Thanks, kid, that's very nice of you. Glad you were able to come out and watch us play." Whenever McInnis told the story, he'd always shake his head. "He didn't know me. He didn't even know I was a ballplayer."

The Red Sox clubhouse in the mid-1910s was sharply divided into two groups, split along religious lines. The Catholic contingent included card players and bar hoppers such as Carrigan, Wagner and Duffy Lewis; the more conservative Protestants and Masons were led by Tris Speaker, Joe Wood and Gardner. Ruth was in the Catholic camp, possibly in loyalty to his Xaverian guardians or out of his respect for, and need to stay on the good side of, his manager.

When outfielder Lewis joined the Red Sox in 1910, he rebelled against the pecking order of veterans and rookies, and his swaggering, confrontational attitude annoyed Speaker. Any pretense of civility between the two was destroyed four years later when Speaker embarrassed Lewis during warmups at Fenway; Lewis threw his bat at Speaker's shins and Speaker needed help walking off the field. Harry Hooper suspected that Speaker deliberately fouled off pitches to sabotage Hooper's stolen base attempts. Hooper's wife, Esther, believed Speaker thought of Hooper as an assistant in the outfield—when the center fielder caught the final out of an inning, he often flipped the ball to right fielder Hooper before jogging to the dugout.

Speaker and Joe Wood were best friends and both hated Ruth. During the 1½ seasons they all played together in Boston, they mocked Ruth as "the Big Pig," "the Big Baboon" and "Tarzan the Ape Man." In quieter moments in the locker room, one of them would bellow, "Baboon!" It drove Ruth nearly to tears.

Babe actually liked being called "Tarzan" until he learned what the name meant. He certainly knew by January 1918, when the first movie made from Edgar Rice Burroughs's best-selling stories opened. The *New York Times* described the film, "Tarzan of the Apes," as "the story of a primeval man—or, rather, of a man brought up among apes and endowed with many of their abilities." After Joe Bush saw the movie, he would provoke Ruth by singing, "Big Babe Ruth was picking his tooth/With the limb of a coconut tree." The old taunt of "Nigger Lips" resurfaced as players noticed Ruth's olive complexion and his broad, flat nose. Many players, not only on the Red Sox, thought Ruth had racially mixed ancestry.*

---

* Ty Cobb apparently believed Ruth was African-American. In the 1920s, they were assigned sleeping space at the same hunting lodge in Brunswick, Georgia. Cobb objected: "I have never slept under the same roof with a nigger and I'm not going to start here in my native state of Georgia."

Early in 1915, with so much off-the-field activity, Ruth struggled on the mound. In his first game, he walked four consecutive batters and lasted only four innings. He won his first start at Fenway on April 26, a rainy 9-2 victory over Philadelphia, but that was the exception. On May 11 against Detroit, Ruth allowed nine hits and eight walks in 5.2 innings; 11 days later in Chicago, he self-destructed in the first inning, giving up three hits and three walks, throwing a wild pitch and committing an error on a double-play ball. By the end of May, his record was 1-5. Ruth wasn't the only Boston player in a slump. As the Red Sox hobbled through May near .500, Tris Speaker and Joe Wood were criticized in the papers for poor performance, and Dutch Leonard was suspended for not staying in shape.

Ruth's one bright spot of the month came on May 6, when he hit his first major league home run in his first game at the Polo Grounds. It came in the third inning off Yankee Jack Warhop; the ball traveled so far, the *Boston Post* stated, "the ushers never made any attempt to recover it." When Boston concluded its month-long road trip back in New York on June 2, Ruth hit another long home run, again off Warhop. "When he hit one, you could hear it all over the park," said Larry Gardner. "That's really the first thing I can remember about him—the sound when he'd get a hold of one." Another observer said it sounded like two billiard balls colliding. Ruth was walked intentionally twice in that game and kicked the bench in frustration, breaking his toe and missing the next two weeks.

When he returned, he started winning. Over nine days in late June, Ruth won three complete games, one against the Senators and two against the Yankees. He pitched his first shutout on July 5, a 6-0 whitewash of Washington. Between June 1 and September 2, 1915, Ruth was 13-1, with three no-decisions. He finished the season with an 18-8 record (10-2 at Fenway) and a 2.44 ERA. Ruth allowed 6.86 hits per nine innings, second only to Dutch Leonard's mark of 6.38. Leonard and

Ruth also finished first and second in lowest opponents batting average: .208 and .212, respectively.

The Red Sox outlasted the Tigers for the 1915 pennant and then defeated the Philadelphia Phillies in the World Series, four games to one. Boston played its home games of the 1915 and 1916 Series at brand new Braves Field because of its larger seating capacity. Ruth didn't pitch in the 1915 Series, though he did pinch-hit once. At the time, it was thought Carrigan kept Ruth on the bench to blunt his ego, to show him that the Red Sox could win without him. Years later, Carrigan denied this, saying that he had many good pitchers and simply did not need to use Ruth.

After the World Series, Ruth went back to Baltimore, where he played in an exhibition game at Mount St. Joseph's College. After pitching three innings, Ruth went behind the plate and caught the rest of the game. His World Series share of $3,825 was more than his annual salary, and after conferring with the Brothers at St. Mary's, Ruth helped his father establish a new saloon, located at 38 South Eutaw Street, across the street from what became known as the Bromo-Seltzer Tower.

Babe and Helen lived upstairs from the saloon, while Ruth worked alongside his father and managed a private back room where men could work out with a punching bag. Babe thought it would be his last winter in Baltimore. "I began looking around for a home near Boston, for it had become my hometown and I fully expected to spend the next twenty years there, pitching for the Red Sox."

Now that the Federal League was out of business, and American and National League owners were slashing salaries, in Boston Joe Lannin's main targets were Tris Speaker and Joe Wood. Speaker's salary was cut nearly in half, and Wood, who led the league with a 1.49 ERA, was offered $5,000, down from $7,500. Neither player reported for spring training. Carrigan played Ruth in center field and told anyone who would listen that he was more than willing to begin the season without

Speaker. In late March, Speaker showed up, saying he'd consider a compromise of $12,000 and hoping a good performance would influence Lannin. But two days before the season began, Speaker was sent to the Cleveland Indians for $55,000 and two bench players, Sam Jones and Fred Thomas.

It was a shocking trade. Speaker, only 28, had anchored the Red Sox lineup for seven years. His career batting average at the time was .337, and even if he hadn't been on good terms with Duffy Lewis and Harry Hooper, the three men were baseball's best defensive outfield. Furious at Lannin's stinginess and the sale of his best friend, Wood sat out the entire season.

On Opening Day 1916, Ruth edged Philadelphia 2-1; five days later he beat Walter Johnson 5-1. When he again struggled in May, Paul Shannon of the *Boston Post* noted that Babe was "more than a little overweight." Shannon called attention to Ruth's "increased waistline" and said the pitcher would return to form only "when he gets rid of that surplus poundage."

On May 20, Ruth lost a chance at a no-hitter against St. Louis when he was pulled in the sixth inning after walking his seventh batter. In August, Ruth became dizzy and unsteady on the mound and was taken out of the game. It looked like he was bothered by the heat, but the *Post* mentioned "a sudden attack of heart trouble." Angry at the implication that he was an "invalid," Babe explained he had merely wrenched a muscle near his ribs.

Ruth went 6-0 in September, finishing with 23 wins and a league-leading 1.75 ERA. He set a new record for lefties with nine shutouts, two of which were 1-0 victories over Walter Johnson (one of those going 13 innings).* Ruth allowed the fewest hits per nine innings (opponents batted .199 against him), was second in winning percentage and third in

---

* Ruth's shutout record still stands; it was tied by Ron Guidry of the New York Yankees in 1978.

wins, innings pitched and strikeouts. Carl Mays and Dutch Leonard each won 18 games, Ernie Shore won 16 and Rube Foster added 14. The Red Sox threw a league-leading 24 shutouts and allowed the fewest runs in the league; only one other team walked fewer batters. The club also committed the fewest errors. Boston won their second straight pennant and met the Brooklyn Dodgers in the World Series.

Dark clouds hung over Braves Field before Game Two on October 9, 1916, as 41,373 fans watched one of the greatest battles in World Series history. It was Ruth's first World Series start and the crowd was roaring from the first pitch. Hy Myers hit an inside-the-park home run in the first inning, but Boston tied the game in the third when Everett Scott tripled and scored on Ruth's ground ball. Brooklyn's Sherry Smith struggled as the game went on, but Boston couldn't break the 1-1 tie.

In the fifth, Chet Thomas was awarded third base on a hotly contested interference call against Brooklyn shortstop Ivy Olson. Batting with two outs, Ruth looked at strike one, then whiffed on the next two. Babe kept the game scoreless in the eighth by covering home plate during a rundown and sustained a bloody nose after a collision with Dodger Mike Mowrey. Then Ruth retired the next batter by leaping straight up to snare a high bouncer and throwing to first.

Ruth retired the Dodgers in order in the ninth. He gave up a two-out walk in the tenth, and was perfect in the eleventh and twelfth innings. A Brooklyn runner reached base on an error to open the thirteenth, but was stranded at first. In the fourteenth, the Dodgers went down on only nine pitches and when Boston finally scored a run in the bottom half, Ruth completed the marathon, throwing 147 pitches for a 2-1 win. Over the final seven innings, Ruth allowed no hits and only one walk. The game is still the longest World Series contest by innings.

Boston split the next two games in Brooklyn, then returned home, where Ernie Shore's three-hitter gave the Red Sox its second straight championship. New York sportswriter Hugh Fullerton suggested that since the American League had won six of the last seven titles, the World

Series should be abolished, as the National League was too weak. Ruth used his post-season earnings as a down payment on a farmhouse in Sudbury, 20 miles west of Boston. He also invested in a small cigar factory, which introduced the Babe Ruth cigar—five cents apiece with the pitcher's round face on the wrapper. "I smoked them until I was blue in the face," he said.

Joe Lannin had won consecutive World Series titles, but attendance at Fenway had been modest at best. Lannin had assumed full control of the Red Sox just as the Federal League wars were heating up and he was tired of the salary battles. In 1916, Lannin had been criticized for trading Tris Speaker, had accused an umpire of conspiring against the Red Sox (and was forced to publicly apologize), and had quarreled with Brooklyn's Charles Ebbets over World Series tickets. After the Series, manager Bill Carrigan retired. "I'm too much of a fan to own a ball club," Lannin admitted. "It's had me on edge all summer, which has accounted for my outbursts from time to time."

When Harry Frazee, a 36-year-old New York theater producer, heard that Lannin was selling, he jumped at the opportunity. Lannin met with three separate parties, but only Frazee and his two partners, Hugh J. Ward and G. M. Anderson, were willing to meet the asking price, reportedly $675,000. "We wanted champions," Ward said when the deal was completed on November 1, 1916. "That is why we bought the Boston club. There is no good buying anything but the best, and when we saw the Red Sox clean up Brooklyn in the recent World Series, we decided that was the club we wanted." Lannin called the new owners "good sportsmen and great lovers of the game. It is up to them to keep the champions at the top."

"Now I'll have a chance to show what I know about handling a ball club," Frazee said. "By giving the public a first-class team, I'm bound to hold their support. And this goes double for Boston, by all odds the greatest ball town on earth."

7

"EITHER THE GAMBLERS GO OR FRAZEE GOES!"

Harrison Herbert Frazee was born in Peoria, Illinois, on June 29, 1880. Although he loved baseball, his first passion was the theater. After graduating from high school, Frazee became the assistant treasurer of the Grand Opera House in his hometown. He worked as an advertising agent and advance agent for several houses before taking his first production on the road at age 22.

"I go in entirely for light shows, farces and musical comedies," Frazee once said. "My theory is that people attend the theater to be amused, for diversion, and I try to give them what they want. There are enough undertakers' announcements in the papers. Gaiety and life are in popular demand."

Frazee was also involved in boxing. A promotional tour with Frank Gotch and heavyweight champion Jim Jeffries was expected to be a disaster, but Frazee had confidence in his instincts. The venture netted him $48,000. "No one ever made any money in this world unless he took a chance," he said. "I was never afraid to play my one best bet for all I had after that."

In his late-twenties, Frazee yearned to break into major league baseball. "Baseball is the greatest amusement in the world, because it gives one complete relaxation," he said. "You forget everything else in the world when you are watching a game. That's why it has such a hold on people. I'm a great fan and I think the game is only in its infancy. Ten years ago, they were building ballparks to accommodate 10,000 people. Now they are building them to seat 50,000 and in ten years from now, ballparks will have to hold 100,000."

Frazee had an opportunity to buy the Chicago Cubs in 1905, but couldn't raise enough money. In March 1911 *The Sporting News* reported that Frazee had placed a bid on the Boston Braves. The Braves' owner denied the report, but said Frazee might have purchased a few shares in the team. Frazee and a partner offered John Brush $1,000,000 for the New York Giants that same year, but were turned down.

Frazee rated the Cubs, White Sox, Giants and Red Sox as the most desirable teams; he said he bought the Red Sox "because I had the chance." The deal between Lannin and Frazee was the first time a transfer of an American League club had been negotiated without league president Ban Johnson's knowledge. That, combined with Frazee's independent nature, led to years of hostility between the two men.

During his first months as the team's owner, Frazee dropped hints that he was trying to land stars like Ty Cobb and Walter Johnson. When he heard a rumor that the Senators would sell Johnson for $50,000, Frazee said he'd pay $60,000. He also tried to persuade Bill Carrigan to come out of retirement to manage the 1917 team, but Carrigan refused.

In the early months of the year, as the United States inched closer to involvement in the Great War, Ban Johnson announced that "extravagances, especially salaries, must be reduced." Payrolls were cut by as much as 25% while ticket prices were increased. Harry Frazee was not particularly harsh when he mailed out his contracts. There were several hold-outs, such as Carl Mays, who wanted an additional $1,400, but most players eventually re-signed for the same salary as the previous year. Babe Ruth was one of the few players who was given a raise, from $3,500 to $5,000.

But Frazee was not adverse to cutting costs in other ways. When his ushers worked doubleheaders, they were paid for one-and-a-half games. Twinbills were often played on national holidays like Memorial Day and the Fourth of July; they were sometimes also scheduled on short notice when a team needed additional travel time. But the owners never thought they were a good idea. As Johnson commented before the 1918 season began, "Playing two games for one admission cheapens the sport and creates in the minds of the fans the belief that they are not getting their money's worth out of a single game of nine innings. Doubleheaders have done more to injure professional baseball than any other one thing."

Frazee required the Red Sox players to put down a deposit on their uniforms and other club-owned clothing to stop the loss of sweaters and other items that had occurred in past seasons. The deposits would be returned at the end of the season when the clothing was turned in.

In 1917, his third year with Boston, Ruth's patience with the umpires was wearing thin. He would argue balls and strikes by showboating and gesturing out on the mound. "His head swelled up like a balloon the minute he became a star," Harry Hooper said. Dan Howley, one of the Red Sox coaches, started calling Ruth "Two-Head." But Ruth backed up his cockiness by winning his first eight decisions.

Before a June 23 start against the Senators, Ruth's record was 12-4. After staying out late the night before, he chatted with some friends in the stands instead of properly warming up. When his first two pitches to Ray Morgan, Washington's leadoff hitter, missed the strike zone, Babe made several noises directed at home plate umpire Brick Owens. Ruth's third pitch was high and he walked off the hill and barked a little louder. "Keep your eyes open!"

"Get back there and pitch," Owens said. "It's too early for you to kick."

When Ruth's next pitch was called "ball four," Morgan jogged to first and Babe ran towards the plate. "Are you drunk?" he screamed at Owens. "Come on! Call 'em right!"

The umpire stepped out in front of the plate. "Get back to the mound or you'll be out of here in a minute."

"If I'm out of here, you'll get a punch in the jaw."

"That's enough. You're through."

Ruth lunged at Owens. Catcher Chet Thomas tried holding him back, but Babe landed a glancing punch behind Owens's left ear. After a brief scuffle, Ruth was led off the field. Thomas was also ejected.

Boston manager Jack Barry spied Ernie Shore sitting at the end of the dugout. The lanky right-hander had pitched in New York two days before and was looking forward to a lazy afternoon, but when Barry asked if he could pitch an inning until someone got ready, Shore agreed. Morgan took off for second base on Shore's first pitch, but Sam Agnew, the new catcher, threw him out. The next two hitters grounded out and Shore returned to the dugout. Barry said, "If you feel like pitching a little more…"

Shore's overhand fastball was dipping sharply that day and the Senators kept pounding the ball into the ground. Inning after inning went by and so far no one had reached first base. Washington had gone down in order in the first four innings—then five innings—then six— and seven—now eight.

Boston led 4-0 and the crowd was buzzing. Howard Shanks was an easy out to start the ninth. Then John Henry smoked a line drive to left, the only well-hit drive off Shore all afternoon. Duffy Lewis played it perfectly and caught it for the second out. Mike Menosky, batting for the pitcher, tried pushing a bunt past the mound. Barry charged in from second, grabbed the ball and flipped it to first for the final out. On what was supposed to be his day off, Ernie Shore had pitched a no-hitter. While not technically a perfect game, Shore was on the mound for 27 outs and had not allowed a base runner. Babe Ruth, for his part, achieved the rare distinction of getting co-credit for a no-hitter and punching an umpire in the same game.

Ban Johnson suspended Ruth indefinitely, but the punishment was later scaled back to 10 days and a $100 fine. The Ruth-Owens incident came only two weeks after New York Giants manager John McGraw had slugged umpire Bill Byron and was fined $500 and suspended for 16 days. After McGraw mouthed off to a writer about the deficiencies of the umpires and league president John Tener, then signed a statement denying he said what was printed, Tener raised the fine to $1,500.

Boston battled the White Sox for first place through July, but the Red Sox slumped in August and the White Sox pulled away, winning the 1917 American League pennant by nine games.

On September 15, Ruth put on a show for his New York fans. He hit a mammoth home run in the ninth inning, as well as a towering foul ball that disappeared over the right field roof. Going into the last of the ninth, he had a two-hitter and an 8-0 lead, so Babe decided to have some fun. He started lobbing his pitches, laughing heartily as the New York players hit safely. The crowd loved it. Ruth let the Yankees close the gap to 8-3 and put two men on base before bearing down again. He finished the game and walked off the field to a standing ovation.

Ruth's record that season was 24-13; only Chicago's Eddie Cicotte won more games. Ruth completed 35 of 38 starts, threw six shutouts and had an ERA of 2.01. Without that final comedic inning in New York, his ERA would have been under 2.00 for the second straight season.

At that time, every major league park had its congregations of bettors—and there were periodic crackdowns and arrests, but now Ban Johnson was threatening club owners with the loss of their franchises if the illegal behavior continued. Fenway Park was "infested" with gamblers; Chicago sportswriter James Crusinberry wrote, "There is no other city where it is allowed to flourish so openly."

An incident in Boston on June 16, 1917, got Johnson's blood boiling. It was raining and the Red Sox were trailing Chicago 2-0; the game would become official as soon as the White Sox finished batting in the top of the fifth. But if the White Sox couldn't complete their turn at bat, the game might be washed out. After two quick outs, a group of fans from the center field bleachers jumped the short fence and ran across the field to the covered area of the first base grandstand. The police calmed the crowd, but then at least 300 fans from the grandstand and pavilion swarmed onto the infield in an attempt to protect their bets. The mob was eventually broken up, the game continued and Chicago won 7-2. As he left the field, White Sox infielder Buck Weaver was punched in the jaw by a Red Sox fan.

It wasn't the first time gamblers had disrupted play at Fenway. "Either the gamblers go or Frazee goes!" Johnson thundered, and he had detectives roam through the Fenway stands and arrest bettors. Frazee defiantly asserted that what went on in his ballpark was his own business, although he made a small concession by having signs painted on the outfield fence and on the back wall of the grandstand for the 1918 season: "No Betting Permitted" and "No Gambling Allowed."

8

"BRING THE WHOLE GANG"

Babe and Helen Ruth spent the winter of 1917–18 at their farmhouse in Sudbury, Massachusetts. They often took a horse and buggy into the nearby town of Maynard, where Helen would shop and Babe would buy cigars and play pool at the Maynard Smoke Shop, which was owned by Frank and Joe Sheridan. The owners' younger brother, 19-year-old Ralph, had followed the Red Sox since 1908, and he recognized Ruth the first time he walked into the store.

Several times that winter, Ruth invited young men and kids from the area out to his house. Ralph Sheridan worked in a nearby woolen mill and on the weekends, he and some friends, all teenagers, would walk from Maynard about one mile, across Willis Lake to Ruth's farm.

That winter was very cold and snowy for Massachusetts and the rest of New England. Babe and Helen were often out playing in the snow when Sheridan and his friends came by. One Saturday they arrived with skis, and Babe, not wanting to be left out, grabbed a pair.

"You ought to try them on the flat ground first," Sheridan suggested, "to get the feel of them."

Ruth shrugged him off—"If you kids can do it, I can do it"—and off he went.

The boys had constructed a jump at the bottom of a nearby hill, banking the snow in front of a low stone wall. Babe started his run down the hill, his skis often moving in opposite directions, unsteady but never completely losing his balance. Ruth hit the jump and went sailing over the wall, ripping his dungarees and catching his underwear on a stick. He rolled in the snow and finally came to a stop, laughing, with his rear end exposed.

Out on the pond on another weekend, Ruth laced up an old pair of skates he had found in a closet and tried to join the boys in a hockey game. Because of his minimal skating ability, Ruth was a goalie. During a scramble in front of the net, he lost his balance and fell. Moaning that his hip was sore, Ruth refused to get up and walk home. He told the boys to run back to the house and ask Helen for a sled. When they returned, Ruth climbed onto the sled and the boys dragged him home.

At the end of the day, everyone would go inside the house for hot chocolate. Helen would play the piano while Babe led the young men in a singalong. Once it grew dark and everyone's clothes were dry, the boys would head home. "Come on over again, kids," Ruth would call after them. "Bring the whole gang."

Generosity came as naturally to Ruth as hitting a baseball. Before winter set in, he often arranged for a busload of boys from a Roxbury orphanage to come to his farm, where the kids could fish in the pond, play with the animals—and play baseball. Ruth would stand in an open field and hit golf balls with a bat—just as Brother Matthias had done back at St. Mary's—while the kids, hundreds of feet away, would scamper around trying to track the balls down. They would have a big cookout and Helen would take care of any cuts and bruises. And before the boys boarded the bus at the end of the day, Ruth would bring out a canvas-covered wagon and give each boy a bat, a glove and an autographed baseball.

In Boston, Ruth, Fred Thomas and Everett Scott often went to an amusement park on their days off. Babe fit right in with the kids, running around, overeating, trying all sorts of games. He'd buy candy for virtually every kid he saw, spending every cent he had and then borrowing money from Thomas or Scott to get back to the city.

On Saturday mornings when the Red Sox were home during the 1918 season, Ruth would hurry to Fenway Park and go straight to the large storage area off the players' locker room, where the peanut vendors would be preparing their goods for the next few games. Ruth would often help them bag the peanuts. It wasn't that he liked the work; he loved the company—the vendors were neighborhood boys, mostly poor Irish-American kids.

During the week, the boys raced from school to the ballpark and arrived shortly before the first pitch. But on Saturdays, the young men needed to bag enough peanuts for the upcoming week, then work the game that afternoon. They would show up around 8:00 in the morning, and a little later, Ruth would saunter in, the only player in the park. Dressed in his street clothes, he'd sit down at the big table, grab a brown paper bag and shoot the breeze as everyone filled bags with warm peanuts.

Ruth talked a blue streak, laughing and telling stories. While he worked, he would occasionally toss a dollar bill or some coins on the table. A group of boys would lunge forward and some lucky kids would stuff the loot in their pockets. The boys peppered Ruth with questions about the game and the Red Sox.

"Hey, Babe, how come you're not pitching as much?"

"Gotta help the team. We need more hitting these days."

"Which do you like better—playing first base or pitching?"

"I'd like to go through an entire season playing every day, in some position like first base," he'd say. "You're right in the action, you know, involved on nearly every play. Not like the outfield. I'm yawning all day long out there. Like this guy." Ruth skimmed a peanut across the table, where it plunked off the chest of a boy who hadn't been doing much work.

"I'd rather make one home run than six singles," he said. "Put a lot of beef into my swing and watch it sail. It's a circus to watch the other fellows chasing that ball."

Babe outlined his recipe for success: "If you guys practice real hard and get lots of sleep, you can hit just like me. Any player can hit if they take the time and trouble to learn. There's no reason why not." It was what he had always said: He came from tough circumstances, and if he could do it, these kids could do it, too. The boys didn't really buy it. They knew Ruth was one in a million. "It's a good life being a ballplayer," Ruth said. "There's good money in it."

When the other Red Sox players arrived, they passed through the supply room on their way to the locker room. A few muttered hello, but most walked past. When a good portion of the peanuts had been bagged, Ruth got up to go, but not before tossing a few more bills, sometimes even a crumbled twenty—a fortune—onto the table. "Hey, Doc," he'd call to one of the bosses. "Split that up between my friends here. See you boys out on the field."

The boys hurried through the rest of their work, because once the peanuts were bagged, the boys were allowed on the field during batting and infield practice. Out on the grass, they approached the players, politely asking to borrow their gloves while they took their swings in the cage. But they only asked Red Sox players: the visiting teams were convinced the kids would run off with their gloves.

Tom Foley was fourteen years old and a familiar face at the park. His mother had died when he was three years old, and now living with his aunt in East Boston, he was expected to earn his keep. In addition to his job at Fenway, and sometimes at Braves Field when the Red Sox were on the road, Tom worked in a neighborhood grocery store. He had become friendly with Everett Scott, Boston's slender shortstop, and the two now had a private arrangement: Scott would wait for Tom to come out, then toss him his mitt. Only Tom got to wear Scott's glove, which was small, well-worn and stained with tobacco juice. With the leather mitt on his hand, Tom sprinted into the outfield, trying to look professional. He'd chase down the flies and line drives, rifling them back to the infield.

Afterwards, the boys went back under the stands and changed into their uniforms of starched white coats and white caps with black visors. If it was a very hot day, the boss might make the coats optional, but the identifying visor was always required.

Landing the job had been easy for Tom. At school one day, a friend asked, "Hey, you wanna get a job selling peanuts at the ballpark? They're looking for some boys." At Fenway, Tom was told he'd get a one-day trial: if he did well, he could come back; if not, goodbye. From school, Tom would either walk to Fenway or ride his bicycle; on weekends, he'd take the streetcar. One of Tom's classmates and fellow vendor was Maurice Tobin, who would later become mayor of Boston.

Most boys started out with a handful of scorecards, selling those to the early arrivals before moving on to food or drink. Right from the first day, selling peanuts was Tom's favorite job. He'd pack about fifty brown peanut bags into a burlap sack, sling the sack around his shoulder and make his way through the stands calling, "Peanuts! Get your red-hot peanuts here!"

Sometimes Tom sold soda, which was more lucrative, but was also much harder work. The vendors carried the sodas in a big bucket filled with water and cakes of ice, with 10 or 12 glass bottles wedged in. The supplies were located behind the plate, so quenching the thirst of fans in the sun-baked bleachers meant a lot of walking and heavy lifting. Selling hot dogs was another thankless job. They were also stored in heavy containers, only these were hot and held very few dogs, so the vendor had to race back and forth all afternoon. Peanuts were the easiest way for a boy to earn a few bucks. No matter what he was carrying, by the end of the game, Tom's shoes would be covered with spit from his cigar-smoking, tobacco-chewing customers.

Tom often passed the scores of gamblers congregated in the first base pavilion, either on his way out to the bleachers or when he worked the right field side of the park. There was a gap between the grandstand and pavilion known simply as "between the stands"—a wide path where trucks could drive from the street onto the field and where hot-headed fans often went to settle their differences.

The pavilion was conveniently located behind first base, and the area hummed with activity for all nine innings. Every afternoon, upwards of 200 men shouted out odds and wagers across the rows of seats, and other men accepted the bets with a wave of their arms. The gamblers, garishly dressed, always had an empty seat beside them and they sat sideways, facing home plate. Many of the bettors were professional gamblers who made a living off their knowledge of the players, the game and the odds, but a fair amount were doctors, lawyers or other professionals whose enjoyment of the afternoon was heightened by the risk of a few wagers.

Gambling was rampant in baseball throughout the 1910s. During the war years, the government closed the racetracks so horses could be used in the war effort. With nowhere else to ply their trade, the gamblers migrated to the ballparks.

"Three to one he doesn't hit this pitch," one man cried out.

Twelve rows back, a voice answered, "I'll take it."

Somewhere else: "I'll take eight to one he strikes out."

"Who'll give me two to one the next two pitches aren't balls?"

As far as Tom could tell, the men never wrote anything down and usually waited until after the game to settle up. If anyone asked, they were simply paying back a loan. Tom was intrigued by the gamblers and curious about the language he heard—"Red hot!"—as he passed by. If the person doing the shouting bought some peanuts, Tom would some-times ask him what the cry meant. The man's only answer was a quarter pressed into Tom's palm for a 10¢ bag: "It's nothing you need to know."

9

WORK-OR-FIGHT

Early in the morning of March 11, 1918, Albert Gitchell, an Army cook stationed at Fort Riley, Kansas, complained of a sore throat, fever and muscle pain. Two days earlier, soldiers had burned tons of manure nearby, causing a thick, yellow-black haze to roll out over the dusty plains. Gitchell figured he had become sick from the manure dust storm.

The camp's doctor told Gitchell he had pneumonia. A few minutes later, another solider walked in with similar symptoms. By noon, more than 100 soldiers were in the hospital; by week's end, the number had grown to 500. Then, just as mysteriously and quickly as it appeared, the sickness vanished. Forty-eight men at Fort Riley died of pneumonia that spring. Camp doctors had no idea why.

Over the next four months, the disease that had hit Fort Riley would circle the globe, infecting millions of people, before returning to the United States with an unexpected and unprecedented fury.* Misnamed the "Spanish flu," the 1918 influenza virus would become the deadliest epidemic in human history.

---

* Some accounts place the epidemic's origin at Camp Funston, Kansas, approximately one week earlier.

There were other outbreaks of the virus throughout the eastern part of the U.S. during that spring. The Cleveland Indians were hit hard by influenza, often called the "grippe," during the first two weeks of the season. Twelve players were out of action, including shortstop Ray Chapman, outfielder Jack Graney and pitchers Bob Groom and Johnny Enzmann. Most of the Detroit Tigers' pitching staff, including George "Hooks" Dauss, George Cunningham and Willie Mitchell, were also laid up.

When the Indians arrived in Boston in mid-May, they were tied with the Yankees for second place, 2½ games behind the Red Sox. But Cleveland was slumping, having won only 5 of 13 games thus far on their eastern trip. Eleven of those 13 games had been decided by one run, including seven of eight losses. With catchers Josh Billings sick and Steve O'Neill having left to care for his ailing wife, manager Lee Fohl put John Peters, a strong-armed recruit from New Orleans, behind the plate. In his second big league game, "Shotgun" Peters committed three throwing errors in the first inning and another in the fourth before he was benched. Peters had plenty of company—there were 14 errors in that game, 8 committed by the Indians—but he was released before the end of the month.

Babe and Helen Ruth picnicked at Revere Beach on Sunday, May 19, along with about 175,000 other people from the Boston area. Ruth's throat had been sore for about a week, but he was ignoring it. When Ruth arrived at Fenway Park on Monday morning, Ed Barrow took one look at the Big Fellow and immediately called the trainer.

Ruth's temperature was 104 degrees; he apparently had tonsillitis. The trainer dabbed the back of Ruth's throat with a cloth swab of silver nitrate, a commonly-used antiseptic. Suddenly, Babe began gagging and choking. The trainer had used too much of the irritating substance, and Ruth's throat was burning. Barrow put him in a cab and rushed to a nearby druggist, who neutralized the chemical. Ruth was then taken to the Massachusetts Eye and Ear Infirmary. (Another account says Ruth collapsed in a drugstore near the ballpark.) By nightfall, Babe was out of danger—he had suffered a swollen larynx and would be confined to bed for a week. His throat was swaddled in ice packs and he was under strict orders not to speak.

When Barrow returned to the park, he asked Carl Mays to take Ruth's place. Fans peered into the dugout during the early innings, looking for Ruth. Wild rumors about his absence spread all afternoon, including one report that he had died.

Cleveland and Boston were both scoreless when the Red Sox erupted for seven runs in the fifth inning. Mays tripled, Harry Hooper singled, and after Dave Shean grounded out, Amos Strunk walked. George Whiteman doubled, Stuffy McInnis bunted for a hit, then McInnis and Whiteman pulled a double steal. Fred Thomas tripled, Everett Scott tripled, and Scott came across on Tris Speaker's wild throw to the plate.

Boston led 9-1 when Mays walked Ray Chapman in the eighth, then threw a pitch that glanced off Speaker's cap and rolled toward the grandstand. Speaker was dazed, but remained on his feet. "You yellow bastard!" he shouted, glaring at the mound. "I played with you long enough. If you throw at anyone else on this club, you won't walk out of this park."

Several Red Sox came out of their dugout, poised for a fight. Mays kicked at the dirt on the mound, ignoring Speaker and acting annoyed with his errant pitch. The rest of the game passed without incident. Speaker and Mays had played together in 1915 and Mays led the American League with 14 hit batsmen in 1917. "They were always trying to intimidate me," he said after his career was over. "There wasn't a single batter who came up to the plate who didn't have but one purpose in mind—to knock me out of the box. So when the occasion called for it, I sat them down."*

---

* Mays will be forever remembered as the man who, while pitching for the New York Yankees on August 16, 1920, hit Cleveland's Ray Chapman in the head. Chapman had gotten to his feet and was walking towards the clubhouse when he collapsed. Shortly after midnight, doctors performed surgery, and he seemed fairly stable. But at 4:40 that morning, Chapman died, major league baseball's only fatality.

With Ruth unavailable until the end of the month, Barrow hoped Sam Jones could fill the gap in the rotation. The Red Sox were fortunate Jones was even with the team. In two years, he had pitched only 43 innings and when he announced he was enlisting after the 1917 season, Boston placed him on its "voluntary retired list." Over the winter, Jones changed his mind, but Harry Frazee never learned of the change and didn't mail him a contract. By chance, a man from Jones's Ohio hometown happened to be in Hot Springs during spring training and was surprised that Jones was absent. The man spoke to Barrow, who immediately telegrammed Jones, telling him to come to Arkansas as soon as possible.

So far this season, the 25-year-old right-hander had pitched in only two mop-up appearances and a late-April exhibition game. (After he was no longer with the Red Sox, Sam Jones would be nicknamed "Sad Sam" because of his downcast facial expression and the way he wore his cap pulled down low over his eyes.) On May 23, Jones looked like a seasoned ace against his former team. Unfortunately, Guy Morton was almost perfect. Amos Strunk's bouncing single through shortstop in the seventh inning was Boston's only hit. Joe Bush pitched the ninth as a tune-up for his next start and the Red Sox lost 1-0.

Before the final game of the Indians series, Frazee and Barrow visited Ruth in the hospital. Dick Hoblitzell, Harry Hooper and some of the other players had seen Ruth the previous day. Bill Carrigan, in Boston on business, also visited Ruth and attended the Cleveland games. By the end of the week, Babe was sitting up and talking, although he was still confined to bed. His room resembled a florist's shop, crowded with bouquets from fans and teammates.

"The time to get flowers is when you're alive!" Babe exclaimed in an uncharacteristically subdued voice. Nurses read him the Red Sox stories from the papers each day. He enjoyed hearing the team's good news— they won three of four games against both Chicago and Washington— and he appreciated the flowers, but he could not tolerate being trapped indoors. The convalescing Colossus was still leading the American League with a .426 batting average and he was looking forward to Sunday, May 26, when he would finally be discharged from the hospital.

Three days before Ruth's release, the first of several government rulings regarding military service was issued—proclamations that would toss professional baseball into disarray.

Every Man In Draft Must Work Or Fight

Crowder's Order, in Effect July 1, Hits Ball Players, Waiters, Bartenders and Clerks in Many Lines Classed as Non-Useful, as Well as Gamblers and Idlers

President Given Unlimited Draft Power in Army Bill Within Age Limits

House Committee Acts at Once On Baker's Request—Would Allow Army of 5,000,000

Boston Globe, May 24, 1918

On May 23, the House Committee on Military Affairs unanimously passed an amendment to the Selective Service Regulations requiring all men of draft age to either make themselves available for military service or find employment in a war-related industry. The country's military forces in Europe already totaled nearly one million men and more were heading overseas as quickly as ships could be provided. The new amendment extended President Woodrow Wilson's power to call an immediate army of nearly three million men. "Every man, in the draft age at least, must work or fight," announced Provost Marshal General Enoch Crowder. Among those affected by what became known as the

"work-or-fight order" were "people, including ushers and other atten-
dants, engaged and occupied in connection with games, sports and
amusements, except actual performers in legitimate concerts, operas or
theatrical performances."

In 1915, President Wilson had promised that the country would
remain neutral in the Great War: "Peace is the healing and elevating
influence of the world and strife is not." Yet while urging everyone to be
"impartial in thought, as well as action," Wilson's administration was
sending millions of dollars in essential munitions to England and
France. Iowa Congressman Henry Vollmer called the United States "the
arch-hypocrite among the nations of the earth, praying for peace...and
furnishing the instruments of murder to one side only of a contest in
which we pretend that all the contestants are our friends."

After German U-boats sunk several American and British passenger
ships in 1915, including the Lusitania (killing 1198), Wilson began a
nationwide "preparedness" campaign and a five-year expansion of the
Army. That program was accelerated after the detonation of more than
two million pounds of explosives in New York harbor on July 30, 1916.
The sabotage ripped holes in the Statute of Liberty, shattered windows
as far north as 42nd Street and woke people from sleep in Maryland and
Pennsylvania.

Germany increased its "sink on sight" submarine attacks in 1917, and
U.S. involvement was imminent. The newly re-elected Wilson made his
now-famous pronouncement to Congress: "The world must be made
safe for democracy." Nebraska Senator George Norris claimed that
American corporations benefitting from the war, such as DuPont and
U.S. Steel, were behind the push to fight. "We are about to put a dollar
sign on the American flag," he said. The Senate passed the War
Resolution by a vote of 82-6 and the House voted in favor 373-50. War
was declared on Germany on April 6, 1917.

Much of the country remained unconvinced of the need to fight and
many people were reluctant to support the war. American men did not

rush to enlist; only 73,000 volunteered in the first six weeks. Boston Braves catcher Hank Gowdy, the slugging star of the 1914 World Series, was a well-publicized exception, signing up with the Ohio National Guard in June and reporting for duty one month later.

Almost immediately after the declaration, Wilson began a monumental effort to mobilize the country's financial, physical and emotional resources. The largest and most effective part of this propaganda campaign was the Committee for Public Information (CPI), headed by veteran journalist George Creel, who called it "the world's greatest adventure in advertising."

The CPI sponsored 75,000 speakers, known as "Four-Minute Men," for the brief patriotic speeches they gave in thousands of public squares, theaters and movie houses across the country. Congress permitted the CPI to censor foreign cables, radio broadcasts, correspondence and military photographs, thereby controlling what war news reached the public. Creel also authorized the opening and examination of domestic mail. "German agents are everywhere," a CPI poster read. "Do not wait until you catch someone putting a bomb under a factory. Report the man who spreads pessimistic stories…or belittles our efforts to win the war." Creel sent guidelines for war-reporting to the nation's newspapers and magazines. Most editors cooperated, publishing thousands of Creel's press releases as news.

The government went to extreme lengths to control what citizens could and could not say in public. In July 1917 Kate Richards O'Hare was sentenced to prison for expressing anti-war views in a letter to her local newspaper. The Sedition Act, passed in May 1918 as an amendment to the Espionage Act of 1917, stated that:

> Whoever, when the United States is at war,…shall willfully utter, print, write, or publish any disloyal, profane, scurrilous, or abusive language about the form of government of the United States, or the Constitution of the United

States, or the military or naval forces of the United
States…or by word or act oppose the cause of the United
States…shall be punished by a fine of not more than
$10,000 or imprisonment for not more than twenty years,
or both…

At the time, the U.S. Army population stood at 108,000, the 17th
largest in the world and "poorly trained and equipped." Major General
Leonard Wood compared it to the strength of the combined police
forces of Boston, New York and Philadelphia. Considering the
Herculean task of recruiting, training and transporting overseas up to
one million men, plus the U.S.'s insistence on sending its own forces, as
opposed to joining the British or French ranks, it was optimistically
estimated that U.S. involvement in Europe would begin no earlier than
March 1918.

Conscription was the only way to raise a fighting force that quickly, but
the man in charge of the process, General Enoch Crowder, was himself
ambivalent about it. "A military draft is not in harmony with the spirit of
our people," he said. Recalling the Civil War draft riots of the 1860s, he
added, "All of our previous experience has been that it causes trouble and
that our people prefer the volunteering method." Nevertheless, Crowder
devised a plan under which 23 million men, ages 21 to 30, would register
at one of 4,500 polling stations across the country.

Of the three million men examined, one out of every four could not
read a paper or write a letter in English. Of the first 40,000 men called in
August, more than half were immediately dismissed. In the camps,
many men were unwilling or unable to cope with 10 hours of daily
training. There were no organized protests, but there was individual
resistance. An estimated 3.6 million men never registered and another
2.8 million were deemed fit but never reported. Some fled the country,
while others took drugs to appear unfit or feigned illiteracy.

Throughout the summer and autumn, 200,000 men worked continuously building roads, trains and ships, laying miles of railroad tracks and constructing barracks. The Army estimated it would need 17 million blankets, 125 million yards of tent canvas, 82,500 trucks, 2 million rifles, 100,000 machine guns, 20,000 planes and hundreds of miles of leather harnesses for mules and horses by November. In May 1918 the government commandeered all supplies of horsehide for the war effort, which meant that there would be no more new baseballs and gloves. "As for the fan who is wont to secret a ball knocked into the stands," *The Sporting News* advised, "let him know once and for all that such practice will hereafter be considered high treason against a national institution...."

The unprecedented manufacturing demands brought nearly one million rural workers, most from the South, to the nation's northern cities, all of them desperate for jobs. Working-class whites resented black laborers who were paid lower wages; race riots broke out in St. Louis in July 1917, killing 50 people, and in Houston seven weeks later, leaving 16 dead.

Families were urged to cut back on wheat, meat and sugar; wheatless Mondays and Wednesdays and meatless Tuesdays were introduced. "Now is the time to lay your double chin on the altar of liberty," said Herbert Hoover. But even with the conservation campaign of "heatless days," "lightless nights" and "gasless Sundays," the nation's coal production could not keep up with demand through the harsh winter of 1917–18. At Boston's Southampton Street wharf during the first week of 1918, men, women and children lined up at dawn in the sub-zero chill with wheelbarrows, baby carriages, wagons, boxes, baskets and pails. They purchased numbered tickets, then waited as Metropolitan Coal Company employees filled their containers. One morning nearly 1,000 people carted away much-needed fuel; after company employees came back from their lunch break, another 300 customers were waiting outside. All over Boston, it was much the same story, as police were stationed at each yard to keep order and prevent fights in the lines.

The number of women in the workforce quadrupled as women took jobs in munitions and metalworking factories, and became streetcar conductors. In the summer of 1918, young women began working as ushers at the Polo Grounds and at Cubs Park.* When waiters were included in the work-or-fight order, New York City hotels planned on hiring women, until an old law was found forbidding them from handling or serving liquor; the hotels began looking for older waiters.

Although women were aiding the war effort, they were not yet allowed to vote in national elections. (A few states, mostly in the West, had granted women suffrage.) In 1917, four women were sentenced to six months in jail for protesting on behalf of suffrage outside the White House. Labor activists saw the "work-or-fight" order as a means of stifling dissent and organized labor. There was some truth to this view. President Wilson himself threatened to ban striking machinists in Bridgeport, Connecticut, from any war-related industry for one year, which would immediately render them eligible for the draft.

The 1918 baseball season was about one month old when those shipyard and steelworking jobs began causing controversy. Stories were leaking out that ballplayers were being recruited and handsomely paid for their baseball skills. The public wanted to know if the men in these "bomb-proof" jobs were doing any war-related tasks or if they were merely collecting inflated paychecks as "ringers" for the company baseball teams.

Chicago White Sox outfielder Joe Jackson became a highly visible target in this debate; his case was a lightning rod for criticism of ballplayers' wartime decisions. Jackson, 28 years old and married, was initially placed in Class 4, the lowest classification, and not likely to be

---

* Built in 1914 for the Federal League Chicago Whales, the park was first called North Side Ball Park. After the Federal League folded, the Cubs began playing there in 1916 and it was known as Weeghman Field and Cubs Park. After William Wrigley took control of the club, he renamed the park Wrigley Field.

drafted. In mid-May, the White Sox were playing in Philadelphia when Jackson's draft board ordered him to report for a physical exam. He was redesignated as Class 1 and put on the list of draftees expecting a call-up by June 1. Jackson argued that, with three of his brothers already in the service, he was the sole supporter of his wife, mother, sister and brother. The draft board ruled that Jackson's wife, Katie, was an entertainer and not economically dependent on her husband, and denied his appeal. When the White Sox left for a series in Cleveland, Jackson wasn't with them. He had accepted a job with the Harlan and Hollingsworth Shipbuilding Company in Wilmington, Delaware.

Although Jackson's decision was one of the government's acceptable options for draft-age men, he was widely denounced as a "shipyard slacker" who was avoiding military service. Condemning him was an easy way to demonstrate one's patriotism. The *New York Herald* said Jackson had "conscientious objections to getting hurt in defense of his country and to associating with patriots." The *Chicago Tribune* promised that "good Americans will not be very enthusiastic over seeing him play baseball after the war is over." American League president Ban Johnson joined the chorus, suggesting that every Class 1 employee be "yanked from the shipyards and the steelworks by the coat collar and sent to the Western Front."[*]

When Jackson responded that his work was dangerous and three men on his gang of bolters had been killed in one day, *The Sporting News* sneered: "Come on, Joe. Show us the blisters and calluses on your hands; let us see your pay envelope to prove that it contains only the wages of an honest plate-fitter and not a fat bonus for playing ball for the amusements of slackers high and low."

---

[*] There was a near riot at Cubs Park on May 26, when a fan refused to stand or remove his hat while "The Star-Spangled Banner" was played. When several sailors and soldiers leapt on the man, a government agent came to his rescue and led him to safety.

Up until that time, the war's only significant impact on baseball had been on attendance. In 1917, crowds fell by 20%, then shrunk another 41% in 1918. In three years, total attendance in both leagues had declined from 6.5 million to 3 million. Charles Comiskey watched crowds for the White Sox drop by almost 75% in 1918—684,521 to 195,081. The Braves and Phillies experienced similarly sharp declines.

But now professional baseball seemed to be "non-essential," according to the government's definition, but no definitive ruling would be made until a specific case was appealed to General Crowder's office. The work-or-fight amendment would take effect on July 1; after that date, any player whose draft board had declared his job non-essential could file an appeal. Crowder would then base his final decision on one of those appeals. Allowing time for a player to be notified, for his draft board to rule and for the appeal process, a definitive decision could be 10 weeks away. Nevertheless, baseball officials flew into a panic.

"I don't care if they close all the ballparks," Ban Johnson said. "I don't believe the government has any intention of wiping out baseball, but I don't care if they do. The people must realize that we are in the most terrible war in the history of the world. We should eliminate everything that is unnecessary."

Johnson's speech was nothing more than pompous grandstanding. In 1916, prior to the declaration of war, Johnson had said there was no reason to suspend the game, and he cited the National League's continued operations during the Spanish-American War in the late 1890s. He also pointed to the $300,000 raised through the war tax on tickets, and the Liberty bonds purchased by owners, umpires and players as further proof of the game's importance. "I cannot understand the statement that the game is non-productive," he claimed. But that change of heart was weeks away.

National League president John Tener noted that for 13 months, both leagues had been "operating with the understanding that baseball was being encouraged by the government. I don't think baseball can be called non-essential simply because what it produces is intangible." But before any ballparks were closed, Tener said, "the clubs will try to find players not of draft age."

The Red Sox had only four players above draft age: Dave Shean (age 34), Frank Truesdale (34), George Whiteman (35) and Heinie Wagner (37). Other teams would be similarly decimated. Cleveland would be left with two players, a coach and a manager. In St. Louis, neither the Browns nor the Cardinals would be able to field half a team. The same was true in Chicago, where there would be a total of four players between the Cubs and the White Sox. And so on. A strict interpretation of the work-or-fight order would affect nearly 80% of baseball players.

"Just Think What He would Mean to the Yankees"

The first important series of the young season began on May 24. The Chicago White Sox, 1917 World Series champions, made their first appearance at Fenway Park, while the Cleveland Indians and New York Yankees tangled at the Polo Grounds.

American League Standings

	W	L	Pct.	GB
Boston	19	12	.613	-
New York	16	13	.552	2
Cleveland	17	14	.548	2
Chicago	14	12	.538	2½
St. Louis	15	13	.536	2½
Philadelphia	12	16	.429	5½
Washington	13	18	.419	6
Detroit	8	16	.333	7½

The White Sox were one of the few teams virtually unscathed by the demands of war, and were favored to repeat as pennant winners. Since spring training in March, however, bad luck had trailed them like a shadow. Eddie Collins had been spiked while stealing a base, ending his new record of 477 consecutive games played. Chick Gandil became ill with food poisoning, Fred McMullin had missed a week with a sore knee and Joe Jackson had taken a shipyard job. Oscar Felsch missed 10 games when his brother died after being thrown from a horse at a Texas Army camp. Buck Weaver tore cartilage in his right foot, but finished playing an 18-inning game anyway, and then could barely limp. After three days of rest, Weaver pronounced himself fit to battle the Red Sox.

Perhaps no player personified Chicago's terrible fortunes more than Eddie Cicotte. After putting down the bottle before the 1917 season, he blossomed into one of the top pitchers in the American League—28-12 with a 1.53 ERA. But in six decisions so far this year, Cicotte had not won a game, losing heartbreakers to Washington (1-0), Detroit (2-1 in 11 innings) and New York (1-0 in 14 innings). "In my last four games, the team scored only three runs and two of those I drove in myself," he lamented. "I held the Yankees without a run for 13 innings and still they couldn't win for me." Cicotte was getting the worst of it, but the White Sox were losing a lot of close games no matter who was on the mound. They were 2-7 in one-run games, four of the losses by a 1-0 score.

In the opening game, Joe Bush faced off against Red Faber. Center fielder Amos Strunk smacked a two-out triple to the flag pole in deep center in the fourth inning, but was out at home trying to stretch it into a home run. The Red Sox trailed 2-0 before they scored four times in the fifth. That frame was becoming a lucky inning for Boston; they had now scored 16 fifth-inning runs in their last four games. Bush drove in two of the runs against Chicago and in the ninth inning, he singled home the game-winner for a 5-4 win.

Wally Schang played a part in that ninth-inning rally, and the next day, he started another comeback with a one-out, tenth-inning double.

After Carl Mays lined out, Harry Hooper was intentionally walked. With 10,255 fans on their feet, Dave Shean got ahead in the count before lining the ball over left fielder Harry Leibold's head. The ball bounced to the scoreboard and Schang scored easily. The Red Sox won 3-2, and Mays's record improved to 7-2. It was the first extra-inning game of the year at Fenway and Chicago's sixth overtime contest in 12 games. Lefty Williams, who had recently lost an 18-inning complete game to Walter Johnson, took the tough loss.

Harry Frazee arranged a game on Sunday to benefit the Red Cross, but it turned out that Boston's blue laws would not be relaxed, even for charity. When Frazee argued that 42,000 people had been at Braves Field for an Army-Navy game three Sundays earlier, Police Commissioner Stephen O'Meara informed him that since no admission had been charged, the game hadn't violated city law. The game was moved to Monday, and morning showers and a threatening sky brought only 4,284 fans to the park. Dutch Leonard blew two two-run leads and the team lost 6-4. In the bottom of the ninth, Boston had the potential tying runs on base, but was down to its last out. The situation cried out for Babe Ruth, and in fact, the Big Fellow was at the park, having been released from the hospital the day before. But he was sitting in street clothes behind the Red Sox dugout, and all he could do was watch Dave Shean fly out to end the game.

Joe Bush had pitched the top of the ninth inning, again as a tune-up for his next start. On Tuesday, May 28, Bush pitched his finest game of the year, allowing only Oscar Felsch's first-inning single, and driving in the game's only run in the fifth inning. In order for the Red Sox to travel to Detroit at the end of the week, the Red Sox and Washington Senators rearranged their schedules and played back-to-back doubleheaders on Wednesday and Thursday. Ruth gingerly worked out under Ed Barrow's watchful eyes. "It will be a difficult task to keep Babe away from his uniform and his big bat," Barrow said, promising that Ruth would play on Saturday against the Tigers.

The Red Sox swept the first doubleheader. Carl Mays won the first game 4-2. Sam Jones allowed only five hits in the second game; his 3-0 shutout was his first victory in a Red Sox uniform. In Thursday's twin-bill, Dutch Leonard got an easy 9-1 win, as Boston put the game away with five third-inning runs. Dick McCabe, the team's main batting practice pitcher, made his major league debut in the nightcap, pitching well but losing 4-0. The highlight of the final game came in the eighth inning, when Ruth was announced as a pinch-hitter. Eleven thousand fans gave him a lengthy ovation, but Ruth failed to get a hit.

During the series, Harry Frazee addressed skepticism about the offer he had received for Ruth in late April: "Colonel Ruppert of the New York Yankees asked me if I would sell Babe for $150,000 and I told the Colonel I would not. I think the New York man showed good judgment in making such a big offer. Ruth already is mighty popular in New York, and just think what he would mean to the Yankees if he were playing for them every day and hitting those long ones at the left field bleachers and the right field grandstand."

Rumors circulated that Red Sox players Fred Thomas, Dick Hoblitzell and third-string catcher Wally Mayer would be drafted soon. Barrow was loathe to start the western road trip with only the 18 players currently on the roster. Frazee added right-handed pitcher Vince Molyneaux, who had been dumped by the St. Louis Browns. Molyneaux had kicked around the minors since 1914; in 22 innings the previous year, he had allowed a whopping 18 hits and 20 walks. Frazee figured the 29-year-old could throw batting practice and serve as insurance against injuries. Molyneaux appeared in one game before the road trip, throwing one perfect inning against the Senators.

At the same time, Frazee released John Wyckoff. His only appearance of the season had been two weeks earlier, when he pitched two innings in a loss to Washington. Soon after that, he was sick with influenza, and the Red Sox sold his contract to Minneapolis of the American Association. Wyckoff never truly fit in with the Red Sox. He exhibited tremendous accuracy in dropping bags of water from hotel windows, but was also the butt of many clubhouse pranks and was nicknamed "Mr. Gloom." The day after his release, he was denied entry to the Boston clubhouse. Wyckoff refused his demotion and returned home to Pennsylvania, where he owned a taxicab business.

Traveling from Boston to Detroit by train took about 20 hours. Team travel during the teens consisted of "cinder-polluted trains" running over "corrugated road beds" for hour after hour. There was no air conditioning and an open window often left passengers covered with soot and grime. Sleeping berths were small, airless compartments concealed by drapes; clothes and personal items were held in a net attached to the inside of the berth. The team's regular players, and often the next game's starting pitcher, were assigned the lower berths, which were slightly wider and featured a window. The upper berths were just big enough to hold an average-sized player.

The men played cards—hearts, blackjack, pinochle—their coats off and shirts open at the neck. The train porters, who were almost always African-American men, might stop and watch for a minute or two. The conductor often sat in on a few hands before continuing his ticket-collecting rounds. Players pored over the stories and the box score pages in *The Sporting News*, checking on their opponents and on possible prospects in the International, Eastern, Southern and Pacific Coast Leagues. Paul Shannon of the *Boston Post* always carried an armful of reading material; whenever Babe Ruth saw him, he'd ask, "Are you still going to school?"

The sportswriters were also on the train, often finishing their early edition stories in a separate car. Sports pages in those days rarely printed anything about the players' lives off the field. Game reports detailed every inning of play, but features on players were strictly biographical. The less savory side of players' lives—drinking, fighting, gambling, womanizing—was probably common knowledge but it never made the papers. Allusions to illicit behavior were written in a kind of code; for example, a player who contracted "malaria" probably had syphilis or gonorrhea. Although the press wore the same blinders for most public figures, the baseball writers enjoyed an especially cozy relationship with their subjects. Since they ate, drank and traveled at the teams' expense, they had a strong incentive to avoid anything that might sour their cushy deal. The game of baseball had to be presented in a favorable light, wholesome and free from taint.*

Some players passed the time reading books or doing word puzzles; others sang in impromptu quartets. Joe Bush entertained his teammates with his ventriloquism skills: he made superb animal sounds—a cow, a crow or the bray of a mule. "Those hours on the train together, and the hours in the hotels, are a sort of magic," Ruth once said. "We're all one big gang together. We know each other, trust each other, like each other. The boys get a few hours to themselves and have a chance to act natural."

During one train trip west, Harry Hooper accompanied Ruth to the dining car. The railroad line was known for its giant beefsteaks and Hooper could scarcely believe his eyes when Ruth "asked for a double order, cold, and cleaned it up."

Fred Thomas had a similar experience. A group of players had finished a huge dinner and were walking back through the train to their seats when Ruth suddenly blurted out, "You know, I could go back and eat another one of those steaks."

"Babe, you're going to die if you overeat like that," Thomas said.

"I have to die sometime," said Ruth, heading back in the opposite direction.

---

* Besides baseball, only boxing and horse racing commanded significant space in the nation's sports pages at that time. Golf and tennis received some coverage, but they were regarded as strictly upper-class recreation. Professional hockey was in its infancy; professional football and basketball leagues had yet to be formed.

George Ruth Jr., at age seven, wearing white cap at right. Shortly after his parents sent him to St. Mary's Industrial School in June 1902, he posed with friend John DeTullio. *(Transcendental Graphics)*

In 1912, Ruth was a star on St. Mary's championship baseball team, the Red Sox. The burly teenager, far left with glove and mask, was primarily a catcher, but he also pitched and played third base and shortstop. *(Babe Ruth Museum)*

An advertisement for George Ruth Sr.'s saloon at 36-38 South Eutaw Street, circa 1916-1918. (*Between the Covers Rare Books*)

During the off-season, Babe Ruth donned an apron and helped his father (right) behind the bar; the photograph probably was taken in December 1916. *(Babe Ruth Museum)*

Babe Ruth, 23 years old (at right), dressed for the drive from his home in Sudbury, Massachusetts, to Boston, before leaving for spring training in 1918. Ralph Sheridan, one of Babe's local pals, took this photo and the shot of Babe and his wife Helen (below right). The photo of Babe and Sheridan (below left) was taken by Helen Ruth. (*Babe Ruth Museum*)

A cartoon from the *Boston Post* in February highlights Harry Frazee's winter activities.

The *New York Times* accused Red Sox owner Harry Frazee (left) of trying to buy the 1918 American League pennant. Ed Barrow (right) was Boston's manager in 1918. (*Baseball Hall of Fame Library, Cooperstown, N.Y.*)

Babe Ruth, right, chats with evangelist (and former Cubs and Pirates outfielder) Billy Sunday in 1918 or 1919. The two are standing near a batting cage, probably at spring training. (*Transcendental Graphics*)

The Red Sox bench during a 1918 spring training game. From left:
Carl Mays, Harry Hooper, Sam Jones, Babe Ruth and the rest of the
team. (*Transcendental Graphics*)

Babe Ruth won all three World Series games in which he pitched, including a 14-inning battle in 1916. In 31 innings, he allowed only 19 hits and had a 0.87 ERA. (*Babe Ruth Museum*)

Ruth hit 11 home runs in 1918; five major league teams did not hit as many. Despite his limited playing time, Ruth finished second in the American League in doubles, third in RBI, fifth in triples—but first in strikeouts. (*Baseball Hall of Fame Library, Cooperstown, N.Y.*)

As early as Ruth's rookie season of 1915, Red Sox followers and sportswriters wondered how successful Ruth would be if he played every day. The Big Fellow's managers, however, were reluctant to take one of the game's best pitchers off the mound. (© *Bettmann/CORBIS*)

Babe Ruth is the only major league player to pitch in at least ten seasons and have a winning record in all of them. (*Baseball Hall of Fame Library, Cooperstown, N.Y.*)

Boston's Fenway Park, during a Red Sox game in 1917. (*The Brearley Collection*)

The Boston Red Sox won the 1918 American League pennant, their third flag in four years, with a 75-51 record. Nearly one-third of those victories were by one run, including eight wins by a 1-0 score. They had the best home record in the league: 40-21 at Fenway Park. (*Baseball Hall of Fame Library, Cooperstown, N.Y.*)

Harry Hooper: team captain, right fielder, leadoff hitter, and a shoulder to cry on. (*Transcendental Graphics*)

Dutch Leonard pitched a no-hitter against the Tigers on June 3, 1918. (*Transcendental Graphics*)

Boston's "Big Four"—pitchers Sam Jones, Carl Mays, Babe Ruth and Joe Bush—in front of the Red Sox dugout on September 10, 1918, the day of the Game Five delay. Jones lost to the Cubs 3-0 that afternoon. (© *Bettmann/CORBIS*)

I I

"I Quit!"

In 1914, Boston's Rube Foster threw a pitch that cracked Ty Cobb's ribs, sidelining the perennial American League batting champion for two weeks. Cobb was convinced the beaning was deliberate—and he was probably right. Bill Carrigan, Boston's manager-catcher, believed intimidation was as important to the game as bunting or hitting the cut-off man. For most pitchers, it was nearly automatic that if the count was 0-2, the next pitch would be high and inside.

There were hot heads and raw nerves in 1915 as the Red Sox and Tigers battled for the pennant. During an August series in Detroit, the Tigers' aggression angered the Red Sox, and a few Detroit players, including Cobb, accused Ernie Shore of doctoring the ball. Cobb got into a shouting match with Carrigan in front of the visitors' dugout, with Carrigan goading Cobb to fight him. And right there in the thick of it was 22-year-old rookie Carl Mays.

Even then, Mays ceded ground to no one. He was comfortable with the animosity he attracted and was fearless in brushing hitters off the plate. At night on the road, Mays would sit in bed and outline to his roommate his philosophy about knocking guys down: "Don't let them stand too close to the plate because they're taking the bread and butter out of your hand." One of Mays's catchers claimed the submarine pitcher had his own private signal for the beanball. Of course, Mays's attitude wasn't much different from that of his contemporaries. "If we saw a fellow get too close to the plate," Cleveland's Stan Coveleski said, "we'd fire under his chin."

In 1887 teams in the American Association began awarding first base to batters who were hit by pitches, as a way to cut down on headhunting by pitchers like Tony Mullane, known as "The Apollo of the Box." The National League adopted the same rule, but considered repealing it in the early 1900s because some owners were afraid of "sissifying" the game. Batting helmets didn't exist and no self-respecting player would have worn one anyway. It hadn't been that many years since catcher Roger Bresnahan was ridiculed and criticized for wearing shinguards.

The misanthropic Mays and Cobb, the most feared man in the game, exemplified the Red Sox-Tigers rivalry in all its pugnacious glory. In that August 1915 series, after Mays threw high and tight to Cobb, the Tiger batter pushed a bunt towards first base, knowing Mays had to cover the bag. When he did, Cobb spiked the pitcher's right leg, leaving a long, bloody gash.

When the two teams met in Boston a few weeks later, extra police were called in to control the crowds. The Red Sox were trailing in the first game when Mays threw at Cobb's head. The Detroit star hit the dirt and the crowd roared its approval. Cobb leapt up and flung his bat towards the mound. The umpires moved quickly to keep the two men apart. When play resumed, Mays drilled Cobb on the wrist and he jogged slowly to first base, snarling, as fans threw soda bottles onto the field. As soon as the game was over, dozens of fans ran onto the field, pelting Cobb with scorecards and other trash. He needed a police escort just to get to the dugout, where several teammates stood with bats in hand, just in case.

That year, the Tigers led the league in batting average, slugging average, runs scored and stolen bases, and finished with a 100-54 record—but Boston went 101-50 and won the pennant. It was the first time a team had won 100 games but failed to capture the flag.

Detroit finished third and fourth in the next two seasons and were not considered contenders for 1918. Like the Yankees, they had a good-hitting team, but were weak on the mound. Bobby Veach and Harry Heilmann were two of their stars, but Cobb was their best player by far. He won the 1917 batting title with a .383 average; he went more than two games without a hit only four times the entire season.

After losing four straight games to Boston in May, the Tigers—11-20, in last place, already 10 games behind—were desperate for revenge. The Red Sox arrived on Saturday, June 1 for the start of 17 games in the league's western cities, Detroit, Cleveland, Chicago and St. Louis.

As expected, the first game at Navin Field was full of rough words, hard slides and forceful tags. Detroit shortstop Donie Bush led the constant harassment of Joe Bush (no relation), which got an early boost when the Tigers scored three times in the first inning. The Red Sox clawed their way back; run-scoring singles by Dave Shean in the seventh and ninth innings tied the game 3-3.

When Ruth was sent up to bat for Bush in the ninth, he wanted to duplicate the unprecedented feat he had accomplished in batting practice—smashing the ball over the right field stands, onto Trumbull Avenue—but he was too eager against rookie Rudy Kallio and struck out on three pitches.

In the bottom of the ninth, Carl Mays walked slowly out to the mound, one of his two relief appearances in 1918. It was as though a large bull's eye had been pinned to his back. Many of the 10,000 fans—and then players on both benches—were spewing venom. Frank Walker doubled, Oscar Vitt singled and Cobb was intentionally walked. There was no one out and the winning run was 90 feet away. Mays got Lee Dressen to ground to first base, where Stuffy McInnis stepped on the bag and threw home to Wally Schang, who tagged Walker for a double play. Donie Bush struck out, but Schang dropped the third strike. He recovered and threw him out, but Bush collided with McInnis, nearly knocking him out of the game.

Everyone was calm in the extra innings. In the top of the 13th, Fred Thomas was robbed of a long hit by Walker in deep center. In the bottom half, Ralph Young singled, took second on a groundout and scored on Harry Heilmann's double over Amos Strunk's head in center. Detroit won the game 4-3. Meanwhile, the Yankees had beaten the White Sox 6-3 at Comiskey and moved within one game of Boston.

The reports of bitterness and rough play swelled Sunday's crowd, but if the 14,000 fans expected more fireworks, they were disappointed. The umpires arranged a pre-game handshake between Cobb and Mays in full view of the grandstand. Ruth begged Barrow to let him pitch. He had been out of the lineup for two weeks and the Red Sox were 7-5 without him. Barrow relented and although Ruth's spirit was willing, his left arm was weak. Donie Bush pasted his first pitch for a double. Two bases-loaded walks in the second put the Red Sox behind 4-0.

Leading off the sixth, Ruth, hitting ninth, which he did whenever he pitched, drove an 0-2 pitch into the right-center field bleachers, his fourth home run of the season. The *Boston Post* said, "it was the hardest hit ball of the year on the local park" and the *Herald and Journal* cried, "Cave Man Crashes Home Run." Boston came up short, 4-3, but overall Barrow was pleased with Ruth's outing. He allowed nine hits and walked three, but after the fourth inning, his control improved. Babe said he felt better than he had before his throat injury.

Dutch Leonard's struggles with his control had not abated. After ten starts, Leonard had a 5-5 record, 82 hits allowed in 82.1 innings, 43 walks, 28 strikeouts and a 4.60 ERA. Those dreary numbers were a pathetic performance from the pitcher who had dominated the American League in 1914 and 1915. Leonard was a warm weather pitcher and, despite having lost four of his last six starts, Barrow thought he would improve as the summer went on. The manager still preferred to take his chances with Leonard rather than one of the rookies. It was warm in Detroit, but no one was prepared for Leonard's start on June 3.

Amos Strunk had twisted his ankle the day before so Ruth played center field—his fourth position of the season. Babe gave his drinking buddy Dutch a 1-0 lead in the first with his fifth home run. It landed in the same remote area of the bleachers as his last four-bagger. The five home runs were a new season high for Ruth, tying him with Tilly Walker and George Burns for the league lead.

With one out, Leonard walked Bobby Veach and Barrow would have been forgiven if he thought trouble was on the way. But Leonard got the next two men without a problem, and put the Tigers away in the second and third. His confidence increased as he consistently painted the corners of the plate. After six innings, Boston led 5-0 and Detroit had not registered a hit. After Veach's walk, Leonard retired 17 batters in a row.

When he came out for the bottom of the seventh inning, the 3,500 fans became a one-throated mass, cheering louder for Leonard than they were for their own team. The Boston lefty worked through the seventh and eighth, cutting the Tigers down in order "as though he were at work on a bench or sitting at his meal." Up to that point, there had been four drives to the outfield, but they had been hit right at the fielders.

Twenty-three consecutive Tigers had been retired by the time Archie Yelle stepped into the box in the bottom of the ninth. Only now did Leonard betray his mask of calm. He blew into his clenched fist, mopped his brow and adjusted his cap. Yelle tapped a slow roller towards shortstop, the best hope for a hit all afternoon. Everett Scott ran in, grabbed the ball on the run and pegged it to McInnis for the out. Ty Cobb had been on the bench nursing an injured right shoulder, but he came up to hit for pitcher George Cunningham. Cobb worked the count to 2-2 before popping up an outside pitch. Fred Thomas raced over near the third base grandstand and squeezed it for the second out.

Leonard's first pitch to Donie Bush was a called strike, then Bush fouled one off. The 0-2 pitch came in at Bush's shoulders and he swung and missed. Leonard's masterpiece was complete.

It was the second no-hitter of his career. He had pitched the first one at Fenway Park against St. Louis on August 30, 1916. That no-hitter had been more special than usual, because the day before Leonard had faced only five Browns—allowing two hits and a walk, throwing a wild pitch and hitting a batter. Cy Young held the record with three no-hitters; now Leonard joined Addie Joss, Frank Smith and Christy Mathewson as the only men with two hitless games.

The next day, it looked as though it would be Bill James's turn for immortality. Through five innings, the Red Sox bats were dead silent against the Tigers pitcher and the game was scoreless. But in the sixth, Harry Hooper and Dave Shean singled, and Ruth pounded a three-run homer. That began a flood of runs that ended with a 7-6 Red Sox victory. Ruth had again tied the record for home runs in consecutive games.

Ed Barrow thought a 10-7 record on this trip would keep the Red Sox on top of the American League. Now after splitting four games with last-place Detroit, he wondered if an 8-5 mark the rest of the way was overly optimistic. As the Red Sox's steamer crossed Lake Erie to Cleveland that evening, Barrow knew the Yankees had lost three out of four games to the White Sox and were three games behind Boston.

Railroad construction magnate James C. Dunn purchased the Cleveland Indians in late 1915 and wanted a pennant-winning team within three years. It wouldn't be easy—the 1915 club had finished in seventh place, a distant 44½ games behind the Red Sox.

One of Dunn's first moves was getting Tris Speaker from the Red Sox to replace outfielder Joe Jackson, who had been traded to the White Sox by the previous owner. Lee Fohl was hired as manager in 1915, but once Speaker arrived at the start of the 1916 season, Fohl deferred to him on every decision, including pitching changes. The two men developed a series of hand signals so Speaker could relay orders from the outfield. Speaker led the league with a .386 batting average and the Indians improved by 20 games. The team rose to third in 1917, and Dunn's plan was right on schedule. The Indians were seen as contenders, although when Boston arrived at Cleveland's League Park, they were 22-22.

League Park's right field wall was similar to the left field wall at Fenway. It consisted of a 20-foot concrete fence topped with 20 feet of chicken-wire, and at only 290 feet from the plate, it was a more inviting target than either the left field line (385 feet), left center (415) or dead center (460). In order to cut costs, any ball hit out of the park could be returned at the gate for free admission. During batting practice, kids congregated on the street outside—a few lying on the ground near the exit gate, yelling under the door, begging an outfielder to please toss them a ball.

Cleveland starter Johnny Enzmann met with Fohl and Speaker to discuss how to pitch to Ruth. Whatever was said, the advice appeared solid. Enzmann retired Ruth his first two times up. But in the sixth inning, with the score tied 1-1 and Shean on second, Ruth yanked a 3-2 pitch over the right field fence and screen. "Babe Ruth Establishes World's Record Of Four Home Runs In Four Successive Days" shouted the *Boston Herald and Journal*'s banner headline. The *Globe* was more subdued: "Ruth's Fourth Homer In Four Days Goes To Waste," referring to the team's 5-4 loss. The *Post*'s only comment was that "Ruth kept up his home-run crusade by driving out the longest home run of the season."*

It was Babe's turn to pitch the following day, but with the press touting him as perhaps the hardest hitter the game had ever seen, going to the mound suddenly felt like a chore. Plus he had lost three of his last

---

* According to *Total Baseball*, Cleveland third baseman Bill Bradley was the first American League player to hit a home run in four straight games (May 1902).

four decisions. When Ruth saw Barrow, he told him that his arm was sore. Barrow wasn't completely convinced, but benching Ruth for refusing a pitching assignment would hurt the whole team. He had few choices. Barrow turned to Sam Jones, and once again, he came through. Pitching for the first time in a week, Jones threw his second straight shutout, a five-hitter that trumped the Indians in 10 innings, 1-0. Boston cobbled only three hits off Stan Coveleski—Harry Hooper's single in the first and two hits from Fred Thomas, in the second and the fourth. A walk, two errors by Coveleski and a force play gave the Red Sox their 10th inning run.

Despite the pitchers' duel, Ruth was still the center of attention. One of his batting practice drives had smashed two windows in a building beyond right field. Amos Strunk was back after missing three games, so Ruth played left field. He went 0-4, drawing a loud ovation when he struck out in the eighth inning, turning almost completely around with an all-or-nothing swing.

Cy Young drove up from his sheep farm in Paoli, Ohio, to watch the game. In 22 years, the legendary Young had pitched in 906 games, setting totals for wins (511) and losses (316) that are all but unbreakable. He spent most of his career in either Boston or Cleveland, wearing the uniforms of two teams in both cities: the Spiders (1890–98) and Indians (1909–11) in Cleveland; the Red Sox (1901–08) and Braves (1911) in Boston. Ruth's versatility, as well as that of Cleveland left fielder and former pitcher Joe Wood, impressed Young. "It reminds me of the old days," he said from his seat in the press box, "when we pitchers had to play the outfield when not working in the box."*

On June 7, Dutch Leonard made his first start since his no-hitter and lapsed back into his old habits. He was handed a 4-0 lead before throwing his first pitch and he crumbled in the third inning. A steady

---

* Young played first base five times early in his career, but he never played in the outfield.

succession of pitchers followed: Joe Bush, Ruth (summoned from left field to face three batters), Vince Molyneaux, Sam Jones and Dick McCabe. The Indians amassed 14 hits, 11 walks and 7 stolen bases, including both a double steal and a triple steal in the seventh inning. Boston led 4-0, trailed 6-4, regained the lead 7-6—and eventually lost 14-7.

Clarence "Brick" Owens had joined the American League's eight-man umpiring crew two years earlier and had been a big thorn in Boston's side. He got his nickname after someone had struck him with a brick during a game in Pittsburg, Kansas. Late in 1916, owner Joe Lannin accused an umpire, thought to be Owens, of conspiring against his team. Ruth had punched Owens in June 1917, and later that season, the umpire had ejected three Red Sox players for disputing his calls.

Facing Tris Speaker the next day, Carl Mays threw a two-strike pitch at the waist. Owens called it a ball—and Mays was furious. Speaker blooped a hit over the infield, and the usually sure-handed Mays mis-played a bunt, allowing a run to score. Later on, Mays thought he struck out Bob Roth, but Owens disagreed. Cleveland won 3-1 and according to the *Boston Post*, "All [Owens] needed was a uniform to get into the Indians' lineup."

Owens came under fire the next day, too, but this time, it was the Indians who did the kicking. Dutch Leonard cursed loudly on what he thought was a strikeout pitch and Wally Schang flung his mask down the line towards third base. Neither George Hildebrand nor Owens took any action. The Cleveland bench was dumbfounded.

In the eighth inning, Ray Chapman hit a hard grounder that Dave Shean fumbled before rushing a throw to first. Owens spread his arms, indicating Chapman was safe, then in the same motion, raised his right fist for the out. Chapman and pitcher Fritz Coumbe, coaching at first base, argued vehemently—and both were ejected. Owens refused to resume play until both men left the dugout. Coumbe took his time—getting one, then two large drinks of water—and the fans grew restless. Several soda bottles were tossed onto the field.

After the game, a sloppy 2-0 shutout for Boston, some fans stormed onto the field, gunning for Owens. As he made his way under the stands, Owens was punched a couple of times and a bottle was thrown at him, just missing his head. Several hundred agitated fans waited outside the park for nearly an hour until mounted police broke up the mob. James Dunn snuck Owens out a side exit and personally drove him back to his hotel.

It wasn't until 1911 that professional baseball employed more than one umpire for each game. Before that, it was virtually impossible for one official to watch everything happening on the field. The players took full advantage, doctoring balls, interfering with base runners, cutting second base in order to shorten the distance from first to third. Umpires in the early 1900s didn't suffer the vicious assaults, from players and fans alike, that were common in the 1880s and 1890s, but they still took a lot of abuse.

Pop bottles were a constant menace. Fans in St. Louis hurled bottles, cucumbers and other vegetables onto the field during a game in 1915; it took a dozen men five minutes to clean up the debris. In 1907, umpire Bill Evans's skull was fractured when he was hit by a bottle in St. Louis. That same year in Brooklyn, Cubs manager Frank Chance threw a bottle back into the stands, where it cut a boy's leg. Chance escaped the park in an armored car with a police escort.

Through the month of June, Ed Barrow and Babe Ruth argued over Ruth's role with the Red Sox—what Babe wanted for himself versus what was best for the team.

"Babe, how you doing?" Barrow would venture. "I could really use you to pitch today."

"I can't today, Eddie," Ruth would reply, perhaps mentioning his sore arm or that he was too tired from playing the outfield to also pitch.

"Tired? Of course you're tired! You're running around every night!"

Ruth would walk away and Barrow would call after him, "Maybe if you got to bed on time once in a while, you could play every day and not feel it."

Harry Frazee was concerned. "Simon, you'll ruin that big boy before you know it." Frazee wanted Babe back on the mound for good. Ruth's record stood at 4-5 and although he pitched well in his last start, his success on the mound was no longer guaranteed or even expected. Two months had passed since his last victory.

Ruth didn't help his case by slumping at the plate for the first time all year. After June 8, he hit safely in only 6 of his next 33 at-bats (.182). Yet even in a prolonged slump, Ruth was feared as much as, if not more than, any other hitter in the league. On June 13, Boston had a runner on third with two outs in the first inning and White Sox pitcher Eddie Cicotte walked Ruth intentionally.

On June 15 in St. Louis, Ruth tagged Allen Sothoron for an rbi-single and a two-run double before coming to bat with two men on in a 4-4 tie. Cries of "walk him" were heard throughout Sportsman's Park but neither pitcher Tom Rogers nor shortstop Jimmy Austin, in his third game as interim manager, listened. Ruth crushed Rogers's second pitch into the right field bleachers for a three-run home run and Boston won 8-4.

But Austin was a quick learner. After Babe whiffed in his first at-bat the following day, Austin had Ruth intentionally walked in the fourth, sixth and eighth innings, each time with men on base. The next game, Ruth was passed in the first and second innings, a string of five consecutive intentional walks. Barrow wondered how Ruth could contribute if he rarely got an opportunity to swing the bat.

The Red Sox won three of four games in Chicago and split four games with the Browns, finishing the road trip 9-8. Boston received superb pitching—seven of the nine wins were shutouts and opponents batted only .216. Four of the eight losses were by one run, evidence of the team's own anemic hitting. Harry Hooper and Dave Shean, the two men at the top of the order, did well on the trip (.343 and .315, respectively), but most of the regulars did not: Ruth (.239), McInnis (.224), Thomas (.222), Schang (.143), Strunk (.123) and Agnew (.111).

The Red Sox returned to Fenway Park on June 18 with a 1½-game lead over the Yankees and a three-game edge on Cleveland. The team was glad to be home where they were 22-7, a stark contrast to their 12-15 road record.

With the government's July 1 deadline for the work-or-fight order drawing closer, club owners were sending reports to Provost Marshall General Enoch Crowder in Washington, claiming that a strict interpretation of the order would affect the majority of major league players and cause huge financial losses.

It was difficult to predict how Crowder would rule on an appeal. As originally written, the work-or-fight order would likely include professional ballplayers. Baseball officials, of course, wanted the sport to be considered entertainment, like theater; actors and opera singers were exempt from the order. Although President Wilson had given baseball his full endorsement, officials feared Crowder might decide that the afternoon games drew men away from productive jobs. For about a year, the pool of Class 1 men had been adequate, but as the war intensified, men in the lower classifications were being called, and there was talk of expanding the draft to include men as young as 18 and as old as 45.

Meanwhile, attendance at ball games declined drastically in most cities. More and more men were working in war-related jobs and the papers stoked the public's dissatisfaction with the sport by insinuating that draft-age ballplayers were avoiding military service. Only the Washington Senators, boosted by the influx of servicemen in the nation's capital and the legalization of Sunday ball, were playing to larger crowds than usual. On June 12, the Red Sox-White Sox game attracted only 1,000 fans to Comiskey Park; that same afternoon, 300 people watched the Tigers host the Athletics.

The owners were willing to cancel the 1919 season and keep the game in storage until the war was over, but they wanted to finish the current season. Faced with the prospect of 300 players suddenly vanishing from major league rosters, alternative plans were discussed. One idea was to pool the remaining players into one eight-team league and schedule exhibition games throughout the summer. In cities with two teams— New York, Chicago, Philadelphia, St. Louis and Boston—the remaining players would form one club. Rosters could be filled out with minor lea- guers, retired players and any available amateurs.

National League secretary John Heydler asked for tolerance and a bit of "local pride" from the public during any transition period. "Every effort will be made to keep the game alive," he said. "Baseball is essential to the morale of the people," league president John Tener maintained. "A square deal is all that is wanted."

Detroit outfielder Ty Cobb, designated Class 2, said he was ready to answer Uncle Sam's call. "But I hate to see baseball pass out. It should not be stopped because of the war. There will be many left here, and they will want to go to the games to forget the horrors of the war, and also to get some fresh air."

As New York and Cleveland crowded Boston at the top of the stand- ings, there was continued uncertainty regarding the Red Sox roster. Dick Hoblitzell had left for the Army on June 9, though he hadn't played regularly in a month and his absence was barely noticed. Harry Hooper was named the new Red Sox captain the following day. Stuffy McInnis left the team a few days before the road trip ended, either because of an illness in his family or because he had been bothered by the 103 degree heat in St. Louis, and went home to rest.

Dutch Leonard also received permission to head east and meet with officials at the Fore River Shipyard in Quincy, Massachusetts. Sportswriter William Spargo hinted strongly that the pitcher was plan- ning to jump the Red Sox. Those rumors intensified four days later when Leonard's draft board moved him from Class 4 to Class 1.

Leonard met with Harry Frazee and reminded his boss that he had returned to the Red Sox instead of enlisting the previous winter. Now he wanted to do his part. Frazee hoped Leonard would reconsider, but when the team left for New York, Leonard was at his Brookline apartment waiting for word about his enlistment.*

Shortstop Everett Scott was moved to Class 1; since he was married and had a young son, Scott said he would appeal. If drafted, the Deacon would be very difficult to replace. He had gone 27 games without making an error and he hadn't missed a game since June 20, 1916.

Even recently married men, formerly exempt, now feared conscription. If newlyweds were being automatically reclassified to prevent men from avoiding service by getting married, Stuffy McInnis and Wally Mayer might then be called.

Carl Mays denied reports that he was considering shipyard work. "There is no danger of me quitting the Red Sox for a job in any shipbuilding plant," he replied. "If I'm drafted, I'll go, and if I decide to quit the team before that time, it will be because I want to enlist."

At age 35, Dave Shean wasn't eligible for the draft, but his health problems worried Barrow. In addition to neuralgia and ongoing foot troubles, Shean had contracted a stomach virus and missed a game (giving Frank Truesdale his first start of the season at second base). Coach Heinie Wagner invited Horace Ford, an infielder at Tufts College, to work out with the club. Meanwhile, Harry Frazee and team scout Billy Murray looked to the minor leagues for help.

Around the same time, former Red Sox pitcher Lore Bader was discharged from the Charlestown Navy Yard because of loose knee ligaments. Known as "Two Pairs" because he loved playing cards, Bader had pitched in 15 games in 1917, all but one in relief, and had a 2.35 ERA. When Bader joked a few days later that, instead of staying with the

---

* Despite his plans, Leonard did pitch for the Fore River company team at least three
  times, including a three-hitter with 18 strikeouts on July 4.

team, maybe he'd forget about baseball and return to his farm in Kansas, he got few laughs. The Red Sox, and every other team, needed any man who could play to don a uniform.

On June 25, Frazee announced he had purchased four players from the New Orleans Pelicans: first baseman Red Bluhm, shortstop Walter Barbare, third baseman Jack Stansbury and outfielder Ed Edmondson. They would meet up with their new team in Washington in a few days, once the Southern Association season ended. Only Stansbury was out of draft age.

The next day, Fred Thomas's finger was ripped open by a line drive. The injury coincided with his decision to enlist. Thomas didn't want a shipyard job, so when the New Orleans recruits joined the team, he left for his home in Mukwanago, Wisconsin. When the Army rejected him because of diabetes, Thomas visited a Navy recruiter. "They never asked me why I was 4-F," he said. "I never even took my clothes off for an examination. I was in before I knew it." Thomas was assigned to the Great Lakes Naval Training Station in Illinois.

"Barrow is making a mistake in not pitching Ruth in his turn," Joe Vila wrote in *The Sporting News* of July 4. "With Leonard gone, the Red Sox are trying to get by without left-handed strategy." But Ruth remained adamant about his new career as an outfielder, telling Barrow his arm remained sore. Babe's description—"It doesn't feel right"— seemed more than a little ambiguous. When Ruth started wearing a protective leather strap on his left wrist, Barrow didn't know what to believe. Furthering the confusion, Burt Whitman wrote in *The Sporting News* that Babe had a sprained *right* wrist.

"What else can I do?" Barrow asked Ruth. "Listen, I'm telling you right now. You're the only left-hander we've got and you're pitching against the Yankees on Monday."

Before that, though, the Red Sox would face the lowly Athletics at Fenway. Carl Mays was able to soothe Barrow's month-long headache over Ruth and the threadbare pitching staff with his second one-hitter of the year and third consecutive shutout. Philadelphia's only hit was a slow roller by rookie Jake Munch that died on the dirt path between the mound and home plate. Boston won the game 13-0.

The Athletics played an ugly game, committing seven errors. A shortage of players forced Connie Mack to move Claude Davidson from right field to third base. Munch played right field and nearly injured himself trying to catch a fly ball. Munch and first baseman George Burns traded positions, but Burns was no better. One observer said Burns "was lucky to escape with his life." He admitted he had no business masquerading as an outfielder: "You wouldn't call in a barber if you wanted an accountant."

The Yankees were hanging tough, only two games behind the Red Sox, and Miller Huggins was making sure he had quality players if the work-or-fight order depleted his roster. New York signed a quartet of minor league pitchers, including Little Rock's Hank Robinson, who had made a name for himself with the Pirates in 1912 and 1913. After being traded to the Cardinals, he had faltered and drifted into the minor leagues. First baseman Ham Hyatt, one of Robinson's teammates, was signed to replace Wally Pipp, who was scheduled to leave for M.I.T. to study aviation construction for the Navy.*

On the morning of the Red Sox's first game against New York, Barrow yielded to Ruth's complaints about his wrist and started Joe Bush. Bullet Joe usually had good success against the Yankees. Knowing most of their batters were permitted to swing only on hitters' counts, such as 2-0 or 3-1, Bush would often purposely throw two bad balls to fall behind. Then, when the hitter believed Bush was in a tight spot and more likely to come in with a fastball, Bush would throw a curve or an off-speed pitch and catch the hitter off-stride. "For the most part, the

---

* Another new Yankee was 27-year-old Dazzy Vance, who appeared in only two games, but would resurface with the 1922 Dodgers and begin a Hall of Fame career.

system worked to my advantage," he said. "Of course, sometimes the batter would lambaste the slow ball out of the park."

Bush failed to hold leads of 1-0 and 2-1, and with the game tied 2-2 in the ninth with a man on second, he gave up a long home run to right field by Wally Pipp. It was ruled a double, however, because only two bases were needed to score the winning run. Prior to 1920, a team batting in the bottom of the ninth or in the last half of an extra inning could not win by more than one run.

When Amos Strunk reinjured his ankle sliding into third base, Ruth replaced him in center field, off the hook again for pitching. Strunk was expected to miss two weeks, so Barrow moved Sam Jones into the regular rotation.

On Tuesday, June 25, in the top of the first inning, George Whiteman rapped a two-out single and the Big Fellow strode to the plate. A huge cheer rang out from the Polo Grounds fans. Allan Russell's first pitch was a high, hard one and Babe crushed it into the upper deck in right for his ninth home run of the year. Under the headline "Babe Ruth Menace Breaks Out Again," the *New York Times* reported, "If the right field grandstand hadn't been in the way, the ball would have gone down to 125th Street." Fred Thomas also hit a home run and Boston won the game 7-3.

Carl Mays carried a string of 31.1 scoreless innings into his start on Wednesday. In his last three outings—all shutouts—he had allowed a total of eight hits. It was a frustrating game for the ultra-competitive Mays. New York scored two runs in the first inning without hitting the ball out of the infield. Coach Heinie Wagner finished the game at third base, his first appearance in a big league game in four years.

In the sixth inning, Ruth hit a long foul ball that crashed into a seat near a napping fan. The man jolted awake, and kept his eyes open the rest of the afternoon. Ruth thought his injury might have been worsened when he slid into second base with a ninth-inning double. There were some anxious moments as he flexed his wrist. It was the second time during the series that Ruth had wrenched his left arm.

Babe struck out in his first two at-bats against George Mogridge in the series finale, which caused "more noise and commotion than there would be if any other player had poked the ball over the fence." Boston collected 15 hits off Mogridge and 2 more off Ray Caldwell, nearly double the number of hits allowed by Red Sox pitchers Joe Bush and Lore Bader. But hampered by slovenly base running, the Red Sox stranded 11 men on base and lost 7-5. When it was over, many of the 10,000 Yankee fans swarmed onto the field to celebrate—their team was now tied for first place.

Boston headed to Washington to face the Senators, who had just finished a five-game sweep of Philadelphia, and had quietly joined what now looked like a four-team race. After seeing Mogridge twice in four games, the injury-plagued Red Sox faced hot Washington left-hander Harry Harper, who had won five games in a row. Ruth said he couldn't pitch, so Bader got the ball. Barrow's tolerance for Ruth's excuses was wearing thin.

Harper was sharp. He allowed only one hit and four base runners, and Ruth was three of those runners. When the Washington infielders and outfielders played back a few steps when he led off the second inning, Ruth dropped a bunt in front of the plate. Catcher Val Picinich threw the ball past first for an error. Ruth got Boston's only hit when he walloped Harper's first pitch of the seventh inning over the right field fence. The blast tied the game 1-1, but the Griffith Stadium crowd cheered as Ruth rounded the bases—watching Ruth hit transcended home-team loyalty. A Ruth home run was an event, a sight to savor and recount to those not lucky enough to be present. It was Babe's 10th home run of the year, and the first time a home run had ever been the sole hit in a one-hitter. Bader gave up two eighth-inning runs and the Red Sox lost 3-1. He walked five Senators and hit two others, but Barrow believed a few more starts would fix Bader's rustiness.

In Philadelphia, the Yankees "slugged the ball so hard that it looked like one of Aunt Jemima's pancakes" and topped the Athletics 10-2. New York moved into first place, and Boston dropped into a second-place tie with Cleveland. On June 29, Everett Scott and new third baseman Wally Schang had four hits each as the Red Sox battered Doc Ayers for 13 safeties. Ruth drilled three balls over the right field stands during batting practice, but went 0-5 when it counted. Sam Jones gave another strong performance, but Boston again left too many men on base—14 in this game—and lost 3-1.

Pitcher Bob Shawkey rejoined the Yankees that afternoon on a weekend furlough from the Philadelphia Navy Yard, but New York lost 2-1. Cleveland scored 10 times in the eighth inning and hammered Detroit 13-4. The American League standings would get no tighter than they were on Sunday, June 30:

American League Standings

	W	L	Pct.	GB
New York	36	26	.581	-
Boston	38	28	.576	-
Cleveland	39	29	.574	-
Washington	36	32	.529	3
Chicago	30	31	.492	5½
St. Louis	30	35	.462	7½
Detroit	25	35	.417	10
Philadelphia	22	40	.355	14

Despite a steady drizzle, 15,000 fans watched Carl Mays pitch against Walter Johnson. Babe Ruth was back in the third spot in the order and Jack Stansbury, one of the Pelican recruits, was making his major league debut at third base.

Johnson ended the first inning by striking out Ruth, bringing the Senators fans to their feet, and then needed only four pitches to dispose of Boston in the second. In the third, Everett Scott singled, was bunted to second, and scored on Harry Hooper's single. Boston led 1-0.

Mays was perfect, retiring the first 16 Senators until Eddie Ainsmith singled with one out in the sixth. But no harm came from the hit and, even as the game was delayed three times by rain, Mays and Johnson battled on.

Washington tied the score in the bottom of the ninth and with two outs in the top of the 10th, Dave Shean rapped a clean single to right field. Then Babe Ruth sent Johnson's first pitch arching across the gray sky, over the scoreboard, the right field wall and out of the park, where it landed on U Street. The Senators got a man on in the 10th, but Mays struck out the side.

After the game, Johnson called Ruth "the most dangerous hitter I've ever seen. But he's not the best hitter. Babe can look worse in one game than Nap Lajoie would look in a whole season." The 1918 season was another banner year for Johnson; every one of his 29 starts was a complete game and 9 of them went into extra innings. He also pitched in relief 10 times, played four games in center field and batted .267.

Ruth's home run against Johnson was his third in his last six games and his 11th overall. In the previous 14 American League seasons, only three players had hit more than 11 home runs in one season: Harry Davis (1906), Frank Baker (1913) and Wally Pipp (1916) had each finished with 12. But astonishingly, Ruth had hit his 11 home runs in less than two months (May 4 to June 30), two weeks of which he spent in the hospital. It was an unprecedented explosion of long-ball hitting. Ruth started making headlines in other cities even when the Red Sox weren't in town. At this point, Ruth had played in only 43 of Boston's 67 games; with July, August and September still ahead, the American League home run record of 16, set by Socks Seybold in 1902, seemed well within his reach.

Sitting in Griffith Stadium's third base grandstand on that soggy Sunday afternoon was Ralph Sheridan, Babe Ruth's hockey and skiing buddy from the previous winter. After Ruth had left Sudbury for spring training in February, Sheridan took and passed the civil service exam, landing a job in the office of the Secretary of the Navy. Knowing his friend was in town, Sheridan and his roommate took in the Sunday game.

They arrived late. After Hank Shanks struck out to end the game, Ruth jogged in from center field with Harry Hooper. Sheridan and his friend walked down to the railing. "Babe! Over here! Hey, Babe!" Sheridan yelled, but Ruth disappeared into the dugout.

"Well, he sure was in a hurry," Sheridan said to his friend.

"Maybe he's got a big date tonight."

Monday was an off-day, but Sheridan made it a point to get to the park early on Tuesday. The Red Sox were taking batting practice, but he didn't see Ruth anywhere. Sheridan peered into the visitors' dugout, but the only person there was Ed Barrow, scribbling in a notebook. Maybe Babe is pitching today, Sheridan thought. He had never seen Ruth pitch; that would be an extra treat.

Everett Scott wandered over from the field to grab some chewing gum. Sheridan called out, "Hey Scotty, is Babe around today?"

"Yeah, he's over there." Scott jerked his thumb behind the plate.

Sheridan looked over and saw Ruth, sitting by himself on the ground against the backstop, looking glum and staring at the field.

"Hey, Babe," Scott shouted. "Come on up, somebody wants to see you."

Ruth trudged over and as soon as he saw Sheridan, his face brightened. "Wooo, what are you doing here?"

"Checkin' up on you," Sheridan said with a laugh. He could see something wasn't right—this wasn't the jovial fellow he remembered from Sudbury—and he suddenly felt awkward. "Say, Babe, isn't that Barrow there in the dugout?"

Ruth spat on the ground. "Yeah, that's the goddamned old shit-pot."

It was obvious that Ruth wasn't entirely joking. They chatted for a few minutes before Scott called from the infield, "Babe, it's your turn to hit. Get out there. It's the last time around."

"Don't bother with me," Ruth barked. "I'm not interested."

"Go on out there and hit a couple," Sheridan prodded. "I saw you whack that homer the other day, I'd love to see you hit a couple more."

Ruth relented, grabbing a bat and taking a few steps toward the plate. Then he stopped, turned around and flung his bat back to the dugout. It rolled in, coming to a stop at Barrow's feet. Then Ruth walked down the opposite foul line, towards right field.

The previous day, Ruth had visited his father and friends in Baltimore. Barrow had expected the slugger back early that Tuesday morning, but Ruth hadn't shown up until about an hour before the game, shortly before Scott pointed him out to Sheridan. Barrow was annoyed, but held his tongue.

Sheridan didn't get to see Ruth pitch that day. Babe was in center field and Joe Bush had the task of facing Harry Harper in his second start of the four-game series. Boston still had no luck against Harper. The Red Sox trailed 3-0 when Ruth led off the Boston sixth. It had been a tough afternoon for Babe; his first inning error had allowed one run to score and he struck out on three pitches in the third. Ruth took a vicious cut at Harper's first offering and missed. Although Boston's hitters had some autonomy at the plate, there was an unspoken rule not to swing at the first pitch.

Babe eventually struck out. Barrow didn't have even a sliver of patience left and by the time Ruth got back to the bench, the manager was seething.

"Can't you wait the pitcher out!" Barrow screamed. "What's the matter with you? Christ, we're down by three runs, show a little patience."

Ruth just glared at him and walked to the opposite end of the bench.

"A home run only counts as one!" Barrow yelled. "And that's if you hit the son of a bitch!"

Ruth turned around. "Why don't you go to hell, old man."

"You could use a good kick in the ass, that's what I think. You won't pitch, you show up late and now I have to watch this. That was a bum play."

"Don't you call me a bum," Babe said. "I'll give you a punch in the nose."

"That'll cost you $500!"

"The hell it will. I quit!"

Ruth stomped off to the locker room and Barrow turned back to the game. When the inning was over, a teammate went back to check on Ruth. He was sitting on a bench, his uniform shirt unbuttoned. "I've had it with that bastard and I've had it with this whole goddamn team."

"Where are you going?" the player asked.

"I don't know."

I 2

"HE'S NOT HERE. THAT'S ALL I KNOW."

Jack Stansbury grabbed his glove and ran out to center field. If he was a bit stunned, it was understandable. Only a few minutes ago, Ed Barrow and Babe Ruth had been shouting at each other so vehemently, it looked as if they might come to blows.

Stansbury had been with the Red Sox less than a week. In his heart, he might have known that at age 32, he was wearing a Boston uniform solely because of the wartime shortage of talent. Yet here he was, in Griffith Stadium, spitting into his glove, playing in his second major league game because Babe Ruth had thrown a tantrum and stomped out of the ballpark.

Exactly where Ruth went after changing into his street clothes is unclear. During the seventh inning, Ralph Sheridan heard a familiar voice behind him in the stands say, "Hello, hello." He turned around and there was Ruth, making his way down the aisle, chatting with fans.

"Hey Sherry, mind if I take a seat?" Ruth watched the last three innings with Sheridan, who was afraid to ask Babe why he wasn't on the field. After the game, Ruth said, "I'll see you in the woods next winter." It wasn't until Sheridan was on his way home that night that he learned what Ruth had done.* The *Boston Post*'s Paul Shannon wrote that Ruth left the game "suffering from stomach trouble."

Apparently, at 11:20 p.m., Ruth sent a telegram to Frank Miller, the manager of the Chester (Pennsylvania) Shipbuilding Company's baseball team, saying he'd like to discuss the possibility of playing ball for his team. Then Ruth boarded a train to Baltimore.

When William Spargo reported for work on Wednesday morning, July 3, the *Boston Traveler* sportswriter noticed a small story that had come over the wire: Babe Ruth had quit the Red Sox. As the news spread throughout the city, phone calls started flooding the *Traveler*'s offices.

The *Traveler* was an afternoon paper and its sportswriters specialized in interviews and background information, rather than reports of games, so it didn't have a writer assigned to travel with the team. Spargo put a call into Philadelphia's Hotel Adline, hoping to get confirmation from Ed Barrow on what remained an unconfirmed rumor. Spargo ended up talking to Heinie Wagner, and published the interview in that day's edition under the headline, "Ruth Not To Quit Red Sox":

> "Is there any trouble with Babe, Heinie?"
> "Well, he isn't feeling very well."
> "Has he had any trouble with Barrow?"
> "What, trouble with Barrow? No, where'd you get that stuff?"
> "There's a report here that he and Ed had a row and Babe has quit the team."

---

* Many details of Ralph Sheridan's account of the Senators-Red Sox series were astonishingly accurate when he described them in 1995. No newspaper reported that Ruth stayed at the park that day, so while Sheridan's account is entirely plausible, it is not verifiable.

"No, there's nothing to that. Babe hasn't been feeling well lately, so Barrow told him to stop off at Baltimore to see his old friends and get a little vacation to brace him up. Babe isn't sick or seriously ill, but he has been working mighty hard, so Ed thought he'd let him have a day off. He'll be back with us today or tomorrow."

Spargo described Wagner as "ever-reliable," but the Boston coach had been bluffing. Wagner and everyone else associated with the team had no idea when—or if—Ruth would return to the Red Sox.

George Ruth Sr. must have been surprised when his son walked into his Eutaw Street saloon late Tuesday night. After all, Babe had said goodbye and left Washington that very morning. Babe muttered something about wanting to spend the Fourth of July with his father, but later that night he told him the truth.

On Wednesday morning, while Wagner was assuring William Spargo that all was well, Ruth was meeting with a representative of the Chester Shipbuilding Company in his father's apartment. Shipyard employees were paid only for their company work, not the baseball games, so Babe would be taking a huge pay cut if he signed up. But that didn't seem to be an issue: the two men agreed that Ruth would play in Chester's July 4 exhibition game against Sun Shipbuilding. And although Ruth's walk-out was at least partially prompted by what he felt were unreasonable demands to pitch, Chester manager Frank Miller fully expected Ruth to take the mound. The company quickly printed up new advertisements for the game with Ruth's name featured prominently.

Baltimore Sun reporter C. Starr Matthews found Ruth that evening holding court at the bar. Ruth told Matthews that he hadn't made any long-term plans and was playing in the Independence Day game while "waiting for the Red Sox to show their hand." Ruth thought he would either pitch or catch. He also said that he would not be paying Barrow's $500 fine.

"I was too mad to control myself," Babe said of the dugout confrontation. Matthews told his readers, "Ruth is sore clear through—sore with Barrow—because he feels that he has not been properly treated."

Someone in the group asked if the impending work-or-fight order had affected Ruth's actions, but the slugger said no. "I'm in Class 4, being 24 years old and married, but we've all signed up to do our bit after the season."* Like several of his teammates, Ruth belonged to a reserve unit in Boston. "Anytime they want me, I'll go."

Matthews asked point blank, "Do you plan on returning to the Red Sox?"

"Just say I don't know what I'll do."

Matthews speculated that if Harry Frazee slipped Ruth "a little boost in salary," the Babe might ditch his fantasies of shipyard employment and get back to making a run at the single-season home run record.

In Philadelphia's Shibe Park, the Boston sportswriters already had the news of Ruth's shipyard exhibition when they spied Barrow and Frazee sitting in the back of the grandstand, watching the Red Sox take infield practice. "We've heard that Ruth has signed with the Chester shipyards. Either of you gentlemen want to comment?"

"I don't believe it," Barrow said, dismissing the statement with a wave of his hand—just as at the hotel that morning, he had denied that Babe had quit the team. "Ruth went home for a day, like he always does when we play in Washington. You know he lives in Baltimore. He'll be back tomorrow."

Frazee was more concerned. "Where is this shipyard? I'll put a stop to that move right away. I'll see if we can't get some protection from the courts. Ruth can't get away with it." Later that afternoon, Frazee issued a statement: "Ruth has signed a contract with the Boston club and must

---

* Ruth was 23 years old. At the time, he believed he had been born on February 7, 1894. He did not learn his correct birth date, February 6, 1895, until the mid-1930s.

play baseball with us until that contract expires. I shall notify both Ruth and manager Miller, and if they try to use him, I shall get an injunction. After that I will sue the Chester Shipbuilding Company for heavy damages, and I believe I will win. I wouldn't try to prevent Ruth from enlisting—or if he wants to build ships—but there's one thing he can't do for anybody else and that is play baseball."

Chester's Frank Miller responded, "The Chester team is supported by the employees, not the officials of the company. So if Mr. Frazee starts suit, he'll have to sue every employee that supports the team. As for getting out that injunction, well, I think he'll have a hard time getting one in Delaware County."

Miller was probably correct; it was doubtful that a judge would rule that Ruth's baseball contract superceded what could easily be interpreted as a war-related job. In any event, the courts were closed for the holiday. Frazee instructed his lawyers to prepare the necessary court papers and vowed he'd stop at nothing to set an example for the other owners and players. Barrow was now offering no comments beyond, "He's not here. That's all I know." There is some evidence that Barrow telegrammed Ruth, asking him to come to Philadelphia and talk things over.

As serious as it was, losing Ruth wasn't the team's only headache. When Dave Shean was sidelined with an infected foot, 37-year-old Heinie Wagner was pressed into service at second base. Jack Stansbury played center field and Wally Schang filled in at third. Weakened by their ragged lineup, or perhaps distracted by Ruth's defection, the Red Sox lost 6-0. Vean Gregg threw a four-hitter, two of which were infield scratches. All three of his shutouts this season had been against Boston.

After the game, "a Boston player, a friend" (most likely Wagner) received a telegram from Ruth. The two men had roomed together on the road and Wagner had been part of the group that lobbied Barrow to play Ruth every day. Babe was probably using Wagner as a go-between to respond to Frazee's public condemnations and Barrow's private invitation to talk. A few hours later, Barrow told Wagner to go to Baltimore.

"Maybe you can talk some sense into that thick skull of his. In any case, bring him back."

Wagner found Ruth in his father's bar. He bought a couple of beers from Babe's 18-year-old sister, Mary, who was tending bar, and Babe poured out his feelings.

"Sometimes I think that if it wasn't for baseball," he began, "I'd be in the penitentiary or the cemetery. I have the same violent temper as my father and his older brother. I don't want to be fighting and being fought with all the time."

"Nothing good is going to happen if you leave the Red Sox," Wagner told him.

"I just wanted to have a little fun tomorrow, so I took a chance on accepting a job to play with Chester. If I can't do that, I guess that's alright. I'm willing to get back to playing."

"I promise you we'll talk to Barrow and try to get this settled so everyone's happy. What do you say?"

Ruth telegrammed Frazee, saying he was on his way to Philadelphia with Wagner and would report on time for the next day's game. He also sent a short message to the *Boston Globe*: "I hear a lot of talk about [my] jumping the American League. It is not true. Babe Ruth."

But before his return could be made public, Red Sox fans awoke on July 4 to huge headlines: "Ruth Quits Red Sox After Row"; "Ruth Is Missing From The Red Sox"; "Ruth Deserts Red Sox To Join Chester Shipbuilding Team." One story said it all: "Fans in the Hub have worshiped at the shrine of the breaker of fences, and his desertion…was more than they could realize, believe or understand."

The coverage was less than kind. "His fellow players strongly resent his actions," said the *Globe*. "They think he should remain loyal to the Sox to the end and do his part in their efforts to win the pennant." The *Boston Post* reported, "Not a single player on the team is in sympathy with him, and the Red Sox first and last are disgusted with the actions of a man whom they say had his head inflated with too much advertising and his effectiveness impaired by altogether too much babying."

Ruth and Wagner arrived in Philadelphia at 2:00 a.m. on July 4. After a few hours of sleep, the two men were at Shibe Park for the morning game of a holiday doubleheader. Ruth might have expected a warm welcome, but Barrow ignored him. When the lineup was announced, Ruth's name was absent.

Amos Strunk's ankle had healed, but he remained mired in a five-week slump—8-for-73 (.110), dropping his average from .313 to .245—so Jack Stansbury was in center field. Wally Schang's three errors the previous day earned him a seat on the bench; Walter Barbare was the team's latest third baseman.

Sam Jones, Vince Molyneaux and Joe Bush were nothing short of abominable on the mound. The last-place Athletics whacked 15 hits, received seven walks, and took advantage of five errors, yet the Red Sox led by six runs. Bush nearly blew the 11-5 lead in the final two innings and George Burns's bid for a game-winning home run was caught by George Whiteman at the left field fence for the final out. The game lasted a lengthy 2 hours, 42 minutes, and Boston prevailed 11-9.*

Barrow avoided Ruth between games and, feeling snubbed, the slugger's conciliatory mood vanished. Ruth blew up again, yelling, "This time I'm quitting for good!" before Wagner, Harry Hooper, Everett Scott and a few others managed to calm him down.

"Ed, you've got to talk with him," Hooper said to Barrow. "I know you're still angry, but he came back and he understands what he did was wrong."

---

* In the deadball era, games usually lasted between 90 minutes and 2 hours. There were few pitching changes and less time between innings (and no television commercials). Also, pitchers didn't have to worry about the long ball, so they could ease up and work faster when there were no runners on base. In 2000, games routinely lasted more than 3 hours, with the average times around 2 hours, 50 minutes.

Over lunch, Barrow relented. "You're a great player, but you still have to follow the rules," he told Ruth. "There are a lot of players on this club and no man is above the rest of the team."

"I'm sorry, Eddie." The two men shook hands. "It won't happen again."

Ruth was in center field for the afternoon contest. In the bottom of the 11th, Merlin Kopp lofted a fly ball to shallow center with the bases loaded. Ruth caught it, but his throw home was poor, and Boston ended up on the short end of a 2-1 score. After the game, Barrow withdrew the fine and Ruth promised he would pitch the following afternoon. For the record, Sun Shipbuilding beat Chester 16-12.

Barrow had no idea what to expect when Ruth took the ball on July 5. Babe hadn't pitched in nearly a month and that had been only a three-batter relief stint; his last victory had been on May 15. But despite his long absence from the mound, Ruth pitched well. He allowed a first inning run, then settled down.

In the ninth, three outs away from a 3-1 victory, Ruth stumbled. Tilly Walker doubled and with one out, Cy Perkins walked. Joe Dugan singled home one run, and after a ground ball moved the runners to second and third, Charlie Jamieson was intentionally walked. The strategy failed when Ruth hit Kopp with his first pitch, allowing Perkins to score the game-tying run. Stuffy McInnis rescued the Red Sox in the 10th inning, when he tripled down the right field line after Ruth had walked.

"I like to pitch," Babe admitted after the 4-3 win, "but my main objection has always been that pitching keeps you out of so many games. I like to be in there every day. If I had my choice, I'd play first base. I don't think a man can pitch in his regular turn, and play every other game at some other position and keep up that pace year after year. I can do it this season all right. I'm young and strong and don't mind the work, but I wouldn't guarantee to do it for many seasons."

After the Fourth of July, the Chicago Cubs led the New York Giants in the National League by four games. The race had been a two-team contest all year; after the third day of the season, none of the other six teams held a piece of first place.

As the two teams began a series in Chicago, Jim Vaughn pitched a six-hitter, winning 1-0 in 12 innings. The next day, Phil Douglas threw a five-hitter for a 6-1 victory. The Cubs won the third game before the Giants salvaged the finale on July 10, Jim Thorpe's 10th-inning home run giving New York a 7-6 win. Chicago's lead stood firm at six games.

Cubs manager Fred Mitchell said the reason for his team's success was obvious. "We are up there because we are getting better pitching than any club in the league," he said. Just before the Giants series, Chicago swept a doubleheader from St. Louis, Lefty Tyler winning the first game 1-0 in 10 innings and Claude Hendrix taking the second also by a 1-0 score. "Will my pitchers stand up?" he asked. "I think so. Vaughn, Douglas, Tyler and Hendrix are big fellows, capable of with-standing a lot of work."

Sportswriters had wondered if the Cubs could contend after losing pitcher Grover Alexander, who pitched in only three games before being drafted. Bill Killefer, who had caught Alexander for six years, thought Jim Vaughn was Alexander's equal. "I don't think there's a lot of differ-ence," he said. "Alex is a sidearm thrower while Vaughn has an assort-ment of curves. As to their curves, there is little difference. Vaughn has a remarkably sharp curve that breaks as fast as Alexander's."

The Cubs' offense was led by rookie shortstop Charlie Hollocher, who, when he collected six hits in a mid-July doubleheader, became the first player to top 100 hits. He had also amazed everyone with his play in the field. "Never in all my connection with baseball have I seen a young-ster the equal of Hollocher," Mitchell said. "I reserved judgment on him early in the season, because frankly I didn't expect him to continue hit-ting, but when a player hits .300 for almost half the season during his first trial in the majors, the doubt must give way to certainty."

In mid-July, Hollocher received a notice from his draft board to report for a medical exam. He said he would serve if called, but it wasn't clear if or when that might happen. Killefer also thought he might be drafted, so the Cubs signed catcher Tom Clarke, who had played with the Reds from 1909 to 1917.

Mitchell also offered his thoughts on the American League race: "I believe New York is almost certain to see a World Series this fall. They have a great bunch of hitters and Miller Huggins is one of the smartest managers in the game. That's why I pick him to win."

13

SOCIALISM AND SALISBURY STEAK

The Red Sox limped back to Fenway Park after splitting their series with the Athletics. Despite owning the league's best home record (24-9) and beginning a 16-game stand on its own turf, Boston received a unfavorable and blunt assessment from the *Boston Post's* Paul Shannon: "The pitching staff is fairly shot to pieces, the infield is badly crippled and there is no help in sight."

With the league-leading Cleveland Indians coming to town, Harry Frazee considered luring two former pitchers back to the Hub. One was Ray Collins, a left-hander who had excelled for a few years before arm trouble led to his retirement in 1915. Collins, now 31, worked on his farm in Colchester, Vermont, and was a long shot to actually accept any offer. The more likely candidate was 27-year-old Ernie Shore, now studying at the ensign school at Harvard. Shore had joined the Red Sox with Babe Ruth in July 1914 and quickly established himself in the team's rotation, posting a four-year record of 58-32.

Other pitchers, such as Bob Shawkey of the Yankees and Red Faber of the White Sox, had pitched for their clubs on weekend furloughs and Frazee hoped Shore could do the same. When the lanky Southerner showed up with some Navy friends for the first game against Cleveland, William Spargo wrote, "Ernie Shore will pitch one game a week for the Red Sox beginning next Saturday afternoon and he will continue for an indefinite period."

Frazee also had his eye on former Yankees outfielder Hugh High. The Red Sox had discussed a trade involving High back in May, but nothing had come of it. High was employed at Sparrow's Point, a huge shipyard 14 miles outside Baltimore. Everyone thought he would join the team for the homestand, but he either had second thoughts or was unable to leave his job. Another possible addition was former Red Sox infielder Steve Yerkes, until he broke his leg in a shipyard game.

When the Indians arrived in Boston for five games, they held a half-game lead over the Red Sox and a 1½-game edge on the Yankees. The Senators had posted the league's best record in June (20-10) and were only 2½ games behind.

"We have our eyes on the pennant," Cleveland manager Lee Fohl said. "I think we have the best team in the league and we have a chance to retain almost everyone in our present lineup until the end of the season." Despite that confident prediction, on the eve of the Boston series, shortstop Bill Wambsganss was told to report for Army duty in three weeks. He filed for an exemption.

The Indians had won five of eight games against Boston thus far in the season and Frazee recognized them as a serious foe. "If we can beat these fellows," he said, "we'll win the pennant."

The start of Saturday's doubleheader was postponed 90 minutes because of menacing clouds. During the delay, former Red Sox Tris Speaker, Joe Wood and Chet Thomas hung around the Boston dugout, chatting with some of their former teammates. Ed Barrow was annoyed;

he hated his men talking with opposing players at any time.* The home team finally took the field at 3:00, meaning the 6,000 fans would see only one game. Joe Bush faced Indians lefthander Freddie Coumbe.

The Cleveland pitcher Fritz Coumbe now referred to himself as Freddie or Fred, his Germanic name a victim of the country's wartime fervor. He wasn't alone. Herman Schaefer changed his nickname from "Germany" to "Belgium," and Heinie Zimmerman of the Giants and Cincinnati's Heinie Groh both began calling themselves Henry.

When the war began in 1914, one-third of the U.S.'s population of 100 million was foreign-born or had at least one foreign-born parent. Nine million Americans spoke German and 15 million were of German heritage. But anti-German bigotry was pervading the entire culture. Fourteen states banned the speaking of German in public schools. The City University of New York reduced every course in German by one credit. In June 1918 former Boston mayor John Fitzgerald suggested burning every German book in the city's school system in a Fourth of July bonfire in Boston Common. In Pittsburgh, it was a crime to play Beethoven. A group of women tried to change the name of Bismark, North Dakota, and Baltimore's German Street was renamed Redwood Street. Sauerkraut became known as "liberty cabbage," frankfurters were called "liberty sausages" or "hot dogs" and hamburger became "Salisbury steak."

As false rumors spread of German spies putting ground glass in food and poisoning Red Cross bandages, suspicion and fear led to hateful actions. A mob of 200 people in Willard, Ohio, forced a German couple to salute and kiss the American flag. The husband was then ordered to fly the flag outside his cigar store. On April 4, 1918, Robert Praeger of Collinsville, Illinois, was lynched for allegedly making pro-German statements. The conductor of the Boston Symphony Orchestra, Dr. Carl

---

* Barrow had the rule book on his side. Even now, Rule 3.09 states, "Players of opposing teams shall not fraternize at any time while in uniform."

Muck, was accused of espionage, arrested and held in a Georgia internment camp for more than a year. Historians Merion Harries and Susie Harries call the summer and fall of 1918 "a period of mass paranoia to rival the later McCarthy era....[O]rdinary Americans volunteered to police the system, to spy on their neighbors, to condone violence and the abuse of civil rights, to participate in a shameful travesty of their former lives."

Labor leader and Socialist presidential candidate Eugene V. Debs was arrested in June 1918 for making an anti-war speech. Debs was sentenced to 10 years in prison, one of about 900 people imprisoned under the Espionage Act. In 1920, at age 64, he ran for president from his jail cell; "convict 9653" received almost one million votes. Debs was later pardoned by President Warren Harding and released on Christmas Day in 1921, after 32 months in prison.

Five thousand fans were at Fenway Park on Saturday, July 6, for the first game of the Red Sox's important series against first-place Cleveland. Early in the game, Steve O'Neill of the Indians was at the plate when he called time and pointed to a blinding glare coming from the right field pavilion. A police officer investigated and confiscated a hand mirror being manipulated by an overzealous Red Sox fan.

The Indians led 4-2 when Cleveland manager Lee Fohl replaced left-hander Fred Coumbe with Jim Bagby, a right-handed starter, in the sixth. "Fohl had a hunch Coumbe was due to explode," wrote Cleveland sportswriter Henry Edwards, but the manager forgot "that Bagby never did have any luck against Boston and that a left-hander is just the style of pitcher that annoys the Red Sox the most."

George Whiteman greeted Bagby with a double. Everett Scott followed with a single and with no one out, Whiteman stopped at third. The next hitter was Walter Barbare. The crowd had been calling for Babe Ruth all afternoon and now their cries grew desperate. With a righty on the mound, they got their wish. Ruth emerged from the dugout, swinging three black bats in an arc high over his head. The cheers were deafening.

Bagby's first pitch was outside. Ruth took ball two, then looked at a strike. He hit the 2-1 pitch on a line toward the right field corner. It dropped between Bob Roth and the foul line, bouncing up against the wall. Whiteman and Scott scored easily. Ruth went into third with a stand-up triple, and when Bill Wambsganss threw the relay into the visitors' dugout, Babe jogged home with the go-ahead run. The Red Sox led 5-4. Fenway Park was a madhouse. The Colossus had done it again.

Ruth strutted back to the bench where he was mobbed by the entire team, including Barrow. The late nights, the missed curfews, the petty complaints, the over-sized ego—Barrow would have to adjust. Ruth belonged in the lineup. Babe replaced Whiteman in left field in a double-switch, Joe Bush made the one-run lead stick and the victory allowed Boston to reclaim first place.

After the game, Barrow spoke about his opponents in the pennant race. "I told Frazee before the season began that it would be a close, hard struggle. However, I'm not afraid of New York. I've never seen a team of sluggers win a pennant. Have you? I'm much more fearful of a team with good pitchers and tight fielding, like Cleveland or Washington."

Saturday's unplayed second game meant a Monday doubleheader and 12,000 fans turned out, civilian Dutch Leonard among them. Stan Coveleski's control was shaky; he walked five Red Sox in the first three innings. Boston put at least one runner on base in each of the first six innings, but never struck the decisive blow. Sam Jones was stranded at third in the third inning; Everett Scott was thrown out at the plate in the fourth, then tagged out in a rundown between third and home in the sixth. By the end of the ninth inning, neither team had scored.

In the Boston 10th, Amos Strunk singled with one out. Ruth was next. He was 1-3; in the third inning, Coveleski intentionally walked him with runners at second and third and two outs. Passing Ruth now would move the winning run from first to second base. The Indians would take their chances.

Coveleski knew he had to keep the ball low and away. Babe stood slightly off the plate. The first pitch, a curveball, hung up in the strike zone and Ruth pulverized it. Right fielder Bob Roth watched the ball soar far over his head, but he didn't move. It landed about three-quarters of the way up the right field bleachers. The consensus in the press box was that a ball had never been hit so deep at Fenway Park. But Ruth's 12th home run of the season was ruled a triple since only three bases were needed to score Strunk from first with the winning run.

Melville Webb Jr. of the *Boston Globe* wondered whether Strunk could have deliberately run off the field or failed to touch a base and been called out, thus making Ruth's hit a home run. Strunk had been thinking the same thing. He jogged slowly around the bases and waited until Ruth trotted around third before stepping on the plate, hoping Ruth would thereby get credit for four bases. "There is no reason why the circumstance of having a man on base...should be turned to the disadvantage of the batter," Webb wrote. Ruth "was entitled to a home run in the records if any batter ever was." Home plate umpire Billy Evans agreed: "This has happened about three times already in the American League this year and I wouldn't be surprised to see some change made in the future."*

With the 1-0 victory, Sam Jones had now allowed the Indians only one run in 29 innings. It was his fourth straight win. Boston lost the

---

* Evans's count was correct: Irish Meusel of the Phillies lost a home run in April and the Yankees' Wally Pipp lost one against Boston in June. A little more than a week after Ruth's triple, another Yankee, Frank Baker, had a home run reduced to a single. That was the last of 40 "discredited" home runs; the rule was changed after the 1919 season. In November 1968 the Special Baseball Records Committee decided that these hits should officially count as home runs and that Ruth's career total should be increased to 715. The Committee reversed its decision the following year.

second game 4-3 when Harry Hooper lost Bill Wambsganss's ninth-inning fly ball in the afternoon sun. It was ruled a triple and Wamby scored on a wild pitch.

Stuffy McInnis played both games with boils on his neck and finally had them lanced that evening. This was good news for 24-year-old rookie Harvey "Red" Bluhm. "It looks like Stuffy isn't going to be in the lineup for awhile," Barrow told him. "I want you to work out with the regulars tomorrow. You'll be playing first base." Bob Gilks, a former Cleveland outfielder and Indians scout, called Bluhm "the best fielding first baseman I ever laid eyes on." He had begun the year in New Orleans; before leaving for the Red Sox, a "day" was held in his honor and fans pinned red flowers to their lapels.

While the Indians warmed up on Tuesday, Barrow addressed the team. "As you know, Stuffy'll be out of action for a few days, so we've got Bluhm at first base today. The lineup is Hooper in right, Shean at second, Strunk in center—"

"Hey Eddie, what's wrong with Stuffy?" It was Ruth.

Barrow explained about McInnis's boils. "Don't worry about a thing," Babe replied. "I can play first till he gets back."

"I'm hoping you'll pitch against the White Sox," Barrow said, referring to the game against Chicago in two days. "Besides, you told me your knee is acting up again."

"It's a little sore, but it's good enough for first base," Ruth insisted. "I'm starting to hit and we need these games. I can do the job."

Barrow sighed. "All right, Babe, you're at first. You'll hit fourth."

Bluhm never got another chance to play: he was sent back to the minors at the end of the month. His one at-bat as a pinch-hitter on July 3 would be his only major league appearance.

Ruth handled 11 chances that afternoon without incident, but took two jolts to his knee, once colliding with Ray Chapman and falling to the ground. Ruth's teammates rushed off the bench to his aid. He got up, shook his leg a bit, had a drink of water and pronounced himself fit.

Later, Jack Graney bumped into the Big Fellow while running out a ground ball.

For the second time in three games, the Indians and Red Sox played nine scoreless innings. Jim Bagby and Joe Bush were the pitchers this time and, unlike his relief appearance in the first game, Bagby was nearly untouchable, allowing only one runner to reach third base in 11 innings.

The star of the game, especially in the extra innings, was shortstop Everett Scott. In the 10th, Cleveland's Doc Johnston took a sizeable lead off second base as Joe Evans attempted to bunt. Scott snuck in behind Johnston as Evans took the pitch. Catcher Sam Agnew fired the ball to second, Scott spun around and tagged Johnston out. It was a potential game-saving play, because after Evans struck out, Steve O'Neill singled to right.

In the 11th, Jack Graney singled and was bunted to second. Tris Speaker hit the ball into the shortstop hole. Graney saw the ball get away from Scott and Jack Stansbury and sprinted to third. Manager Lee Fohl, coaching at third, yelled for Graney to stop, but Graney's head was down; he was intent on scoring. Scott grabbed the ball on the outfield grass and threw home to Wally Mayer, who had replaced Agnew at the start of the inning. Graney slammed on the brakes when he was halfway home and Mayer, playing in his first game at Fenway, tagged him in a rundown.

Then, in the Boston 12th, Scott reached second when Speaker dropped his fly ball. Frank Truesdale bounced back to the pitcher, and although Scott was caught off the bag, he evaded the Cleveland infielders long enough for Truesdale to advance to second. When Mayer singled to left, the Red Sox had a 1-0 win.

"The more I see of Everett Scott, the more I'm convinced we have the greatest shortstop in the game," Ed Barrow said. "There are other good ones—Donie Bush of Detroit, the White Sox's Buck Weaver, Art Fletcher of the Giants, and the Braves' Rabbit Maranville—but they aren't in the same class with Scotty. He can't hit like Babe Ruth or run the bases like Cobb, but efficiency is how much a player means to the ball club six days a week.

"That's where our boy shines. He makes play after play that ordinary shortstops wouldn't get close to. As a matter of fact, we expect him to make plays that we probably shouldn't count on. Scotty would attract more attention if he made his plays look as hard as they are, maybe tear around and flash a little pepper. After he makes a hard play, he acts as if nothing's happened. But when he gets back to the bench, he breaks out in a grin."

Scott's modesty wasn't at odds with his gritty intensity on the diamond. Scott was 21 years old and a wisp of an infielder—5 feet, 8 inches tall and 125 pounds—when he won the Red Sox shortstop job from Heinie Wagner in 1914. Two years later, after a vicious slide by Ty Cobb left him with a lacerated ankle, Scott took the unusual step of wearing padded shoes. "They help when you're tagging wild base runners with sharpened spikes," Scott said. His shoes got cut, sometimes to ribbons, but not his feet.

As the backbone of the Boston infield, Scott brought a base stealer's mentality to his position. Thinking his arm wasn't particularly strong, he studied the hitters, looking for any possible advantage, and tried to get a good jump on the ball. Scott modeled himself after the Senators' George McBride, who always seemed to make a strong, true throw to first base, even when he was off-balance or barely had time to look. Stuffy McInnis joked that Scott's "trolley line" throws to first base were boring and routine. "He wants us to quit pegging the ball over too accurately," Scott said of McInnis. "He's in his element when he's digging low ones out of the dirt or leaving the bag to pull in a wide heave."

Scott loved playing with the Red Sox because they "were an integral part of Boston. Every time you went downtown, or walked on Boylston Street or Massachusetts Avenue, you would be among friends and admirers."

It rained the next day, Wednesday, July 10, just after Boston took a 2-0 lead in the bottom of the fifth. The umpires waited the required 30 minutes before calling the game, but the field was already a mess. The game was official and Lore Bader had his first victory. He allowed five singles, three of which were immediately followed by a double play. The four Red Sox wins in the series pushed the Indians 2½ games out of first place.

Harry Frazee smiled as the rain poured down. "This series was a wonder. I doubt if any five games had more thrills in them than these did. There was great pitching on both sides. Jones and Bush did wonderful work for us, Hooper and Scott showed some great glove work, and old Babe Ruth, our man of all work, played the outfield and first base as if he had been there all his life. This series convinces me that we can beat all the others. I feel surer now than I ever did before that we'll win the pennant this year."

The entire Boston pitching staff had shone against the best hitting team in the league, putting up consecutive scoreless streaks of 19 and 17 innings, and holding Cleveland to only eight runs in 45 innings.

Triples by Ruth had led to three of Boston's four wins. "I want to give the club the best I've got, and that means playing every day," Babe said. "My hitting won three of four games. If I was pitching, I would have been in only one of those games, and who knows if it would have been a win?"

The Red Sox were at the halfway point in the season with a record of 45-32. Although New York and Cleveland were fielding stronger teams than they had in 1917, Burt Whitman of the *Boston Herald and Journal* felt that Barrow's deft juggling of his limited roster through enlistments, the draft, injuries and sickness was the primary reason the Red Sox were ahead of those clubs.

On July 11, before the start of the White Sox series, Barrow gave Ruth some advice on his batting stance. "That double to left yesterday before the rain was sweet," Barrow said. "You ought to try closing your stance, moving your left foot back, and poking the ball to left field more often. Everybody's pitching you away all the time. Take advantage of it." In batting practice, Ruth was soon sending screamers to the opposite field. In the game, Ruth smacked three doubles to left field off Chicago starter Eddie Cicotte, two of them on the first pitch.

Ruth's work at first base was the icing on the afternoon's cake. He stretched for a wide throw from Everett Scott in the second inning and hung tough on a bad-hop grounder in the third, beating the runner in a race to the bag. In the top of the ninth, Chicago loaded the bases with one out. When John Collins drilled a hot shot to the right side, Frank Wilson, the runner at first, froze between Ruth and the ball. Ruth scooped up the grounder, tagged the confused Wilson and dove towards the bag. When the dust settled, the game was over. Ruth had an unassisted double play—his 19th and 20th putouts of the day—and Boston had a 4-0 victory, a four-hitter by Carl Mays.

Boston's pitchers had not allowed a run in their last 26 innings. Three days later, Mays would beat the White Sox again, keeping all 27 outs in the infield.[*] A player described making contact with Mays's fastball as "hitting a chunk of lead. It would go clunk and you'd beat it into the ground."

But before Mays's second gem, the rumbling of thunder and sporadic flashes of lightning would offer a dramatic backdrop for Ruth's continued assault on the White Sox pitching staff. On July 12, Babe smacked a double and two triples, scored three times and knocked in four runs before rain ended the game after seven innings. A St. Louis writer called Ruth "without any question the greatest hitter of modern times" and said his work with the stick "was the most remarkable show in either league for years."

---

[*] Mays was also a superb fielder. In 1918, he set the Red Sox season record for assists by a pitcher (122); he also holds the second-best (118 in 1917) and third-best (117 in 1916) season totals.

Ruth maintained that he didn't have "what you'd call a regular system at the bat. They don't throw me very many good balls," he said. "Now and then, they'll slip the first one over, and if I get them in a hole, they have to pitch, but most of the time I have to make the best of what they give me. It's part of the game, I guess, but when I'm ready to give that ball a ride and that fellow out there passes me, I want to wring his goddamn neck. I'd rather take a punch in the nose than a base on balls."

Babe's goal was to smack a home run in all eight American League parks, something no one had ever done in one season. Ruth needed only three more parks: Comiskey, Shibe and Fenway. He thought Boston and Philadelphia wouldn't be too difficult, and even though the bleachers in Chicago were far away, he had seven more games in which to give it a shot.

Ruth's big cuts at the plate created an impression that he would "swing and pray," that he was all muscle and no control. "That's a lot of horse shit," Ruth told Ed Martin of the *Boston Globe*. "Until this season left-handers used to fool me some. They'd throw me curves and I'd chase a lot of them. I can pull those balls over to left or center, but the idea in hitting to right is to drive it out of the lot. Take a good cut and bang that old apple on the nose. They can't catch it then."

Martin ended his article by noting that Ruth, like his boss, enjoyed the theater. "He is not specially interested in W. Shakspere [*sic*] or G. Bernard Shaw, but give G. Babe Ruth a good vaudeville show, a smart musical or straight comedy…. Babe is somewhat of a thespian himself. Back in his school days he was in a sketch. 'This sketch was so funny that it used to give me a laugh,' said Babe. 'The other guy was a doctor and I was the comedian. It was immense. Wish I could remember that old sketch now.'"

Ruth's value to the Red Sox was also immense, not only because his versatility helped minimize the impact of the team's injuries, but because so many people came out to Fenway Park mainly to see him. "His name is on every lip these days," Martin wrote. "His appearance at the bat is a signal for a great outburst of applause. Men who have followed the game for years declare that they never knew of any player that drove the ball any harder than Ruth."

That sentiment was echoed in the *St. Louis Post-Dispatch*, which reported that the huge offer Frazee had received for Ruth earlier in the season "caused little astonishment in the inner circles" of the sport. "[I]t is extremely doubtful if there is a player in baseball so valuable. And this statement takes in Ty Cobb.... It is a gamble from now on how much longer Ty will last as a major leaguer, while Ruth is just getting into the best of his stride."

Babe also talked publicly for the first time about his sore arm. "My wing is a little off. If I had to go in now and pitch a game, I don't know how good a job I could do. Some fans probably think that the extra work I've been doing around the infield and outfield has ruined my arm. It hasn't. I realized before I started playing the other positions that my arm was sore." He insisted there was nothing "seriously wrong" with his arm, but was fortunate to "play somewhere where I won't have to put any strain on it." After Ruth's confession, all talk of the sore arm, and the "sprained wrist" mentioned in *The Sporting News*, stopped. Whether Ruth received treatment or the discomfort simply disappeared is not known.

Since he was spending more time in the outfield than on the mound, Ruth visited Harry Frazee's office to renegotiate the bonus portion of his 1918 contract. It was the right time to make the move. During the week of July 6–12, Ruth batted .478 (11-23) and slugged 1.087, with two singles, four doubles, five triples and six runs scored. On July 12, Ruth and Frazee signed the following agreement:

Mr. George H. Ruth, Boston, Mass.

Dear Sir:

This letter is to advise you that we agree to pay you the additional sum of $1,000 as a bonus for the season of 1918, over and above the amount stated in your contract for 1918. Also the additional sum of $1,000 if the Boston American League Club wins the pennant in the American League.

This letter cancels previous letter which you hold regarding bonuses you were to receive in the event of your pitching and winning a certain number of games.

> Yours truly, Boston American League
> Baseball Club, by Harry Frazee

Accepted by G. H. Ruth

Ruth's salary was now $8,000, and if the Red Sox won the pennant, he'd earn $9,000. There was no mention of a World Series bonus.

Facing St. Louis in the scorching heat, Sam Jones was plagued by an upset stomach; in the dugout, the trainer keep him alert with smelling salts. Joe Bush had the same trouble the following day, but his nausea passed by the third inning. The Red Sox managed to win both games.

Ruth continued his torrid hitting with a triple that banged off the wall below a Bull Durham tobacco sign in left-center field. The tobacco company had promised $50 to any player who hit the sign on the fly during a game; the advertisement had been brought over from the Red Sox's previous home, the Huntington Avenue Grounds.

On the morning of July 17, Carl Mays spied Ruth hurrying past the hotel where Mays and several other players lived during the season. Ruth was heading north on Huntington Avenue, carrying a suitcase.

"Where you going, Babe?"

"Baltimore," Ruth answered, without turning his head or breaking stride.

Mays panicked and phoned Ed Barrow. The manager thanked Mays, but assured him he didn't think Babe was really leaving town. Sure enough, Ruth appeared at Fenway right on time.

Stuffy McInnis was back in the lineup at first base, so Ruth moved to left field. Two new pitchers joined the club: Walt Kinney, a tall, 24-year-old left-hander who had been with Dallas in the Texas League, and Bobby Carruthers, who came from a Jersey City semi-pro team.

Late in the first game of the doubleheader, with Boston up by six runs, Barrow asked Ruth, "How are you feeling?"

"Fine. Want me to pitch the next game?"

"If your arm's all right, you can try it. I'll put Whitey in left field, so you can rest up."

"Oh no, I'm not going to lose a chance to get another whack at that ball," Ruth said. "Let me take my swings. I'll change my shirt and be ready for the next game." Ruth batted in the eighth inning, made an out, and George Whiteman took the field in the ninth.

A buzz went through the stands as Ruth began warming up for the second game, dark clouds looming overhead. Everyone knew Barrow was short on pitchers, but many in the crowd of 8,000 wondered if Babe had the stamina to pitch after playing eight innings in the heat. Ruth doubled home two runs in the first and his second double scored another run in the third. McInnis singled Ruth in and Boston had a 4-0 lead. After a short rain delay, the Browns began stalling, hoping for a cancellation before the game became official.

McInnis tried stealing second and was safe when Jimmy Austin intentionally dropped catcher Hank Severeid's throw. McInnis got up and dashed for third, but Austin didn't bother throwing. When McInnis figured he'd try to score, Austin made a half-hearted toss to the plate, and Severeid, allegedly "peeved because the play was made," pounded McInnis on the back with his glove for the out. McInnis lay on the ground for a few minutes, catching his breath.

After another delay, the game became a total farce. The Browns wasted time by throwing the ball around the infield. The Red Sox tried taking extra bases, hoping to be tagged out and thus move the game along. On another play at the plate, Severeid put a vicious tag on Wally Schang. In an instant, Schang leapt up and began choking Severeid. Both men laughed about the incident afterwards and even shook hands in front of the crowd, but the umpires reported it to Ban Johnson. Two days later, Johnson announced that neither player would be suspended.

St. Louis scored a run before heavy rains stopped play in the sixth. Since the top half of the inning was incomplete, the Browns' run was wiped out and the score reverted back to the last complete inning: Boston 4, St. Louis 0. But was the second game actually a shutout?

Browns first baseman George Sisler didn't think so. In a letter to Ed Martin, a *Boston Globe* writer and the game's official scorer, Sisler said he should have received credit for his double and run scored. Ernest Lanigan followed up the complaint in *The Sporting News*, quoting from the rule book:

> ...at any time after five innings have been completed, the score shall be that of the last equal innings played, except that if the side second at-bat shall have scored in an unequal number of innings, or before the completion of the unfinished inning, at least one run more than the side first at bat, the score of the game shall be the total number of runs each team has made.

That rule had remained unchanged since 1907; Lanigan sided with Sisler. Because Boston led the visiting team by more than one run, he argued, the final score should have been what it was at the moment the game was called—4-1. But no official action was taken. The shutout was the 17th of Ruth's career and his last regular-season whitewash. The sweep increased Boston's lead to 5½ games over the Indians and 6½ games over the Yankees.

St. Louis's stalling antics weren't the only absurdity that week. In Washington on July 18, Cleveland's Joe Wood singled and was safe at second when George McBride muffed the right fielder's throw. A Senators fan near the third base box seats suddenly hopped over the railing, placed his coat and straw hat on the outfield grass and walked over to the shortstop position. He spat in his bare hands, crouched down and shouted to the umpire, "Okay, start the game. Now they've got a shortstop who can play!"

No one knew what to do. McBride tried coaxing the man back to his seat. "I know you're better than I am," he said, "but it will delay the game while you get into a uniform."

"I don't need a uniform to play this position better than you," the man heckled. By that time, two policemen had arrived and the man was escorted off the field.

The on-field levity was quickly overshadowed by the long-awaited decision from Secretary of War Newton D. Baker regarding Eddie Ainsmith's appeal of his draft notice. Up to that point, there had been no national policy. Local draft boards considered each case individually, deciding whether or not a particular player was performing essential work, or if baseball employment was essential to his financial obligations. The first ruling against a ballplayer had come on July 8 when Sam Lewis, a pitcher for Dallas of the Texas League, was told to leave his team and find war-related work. But at least two major leaguers, Joe Finnerman of the Yankees and Hy Myers of the Dodgers, had won their appeals and were still playing ball. Baker's decision would trump all local and district rulings.

On July 19, the Secretary of War announced, "I have decided that the work-or-fight regulations include baseball." While acknowledging the social and entertainment value of the national game, he concluded that "the times are not normal. The demands of the Army and of the country are such that the non-productive employment of able-bodied persons cannot be justified."

Baker saw no evidence that the work-or-fight order would result in the death of professional ball and expressed hope that baseball would continue: "It would be an unfortunate thing to have so wholesome a recreation as baseball destroyed if it can be continued by the use of persons not available for essential war service."

Reaction throughout the baseball world to Baker's statement was divided. American League president Ban Johnson ordered the parks in his league to shut their gates in two days, after Sunday's games. National League president John Tener thought all 16 teams should "gladly sacrifice our business interest in the country's welfare." Jacob Ruppert of the Yankees simply said, "I guess that ends it."

"We accept the ruling without a protest," Johnson said. "I hope the great majority of our players will put on uniforms and shoulder a rifle." Johnson's blustery statements, like his outbursts when the work-or-fight order was first announced in May, only provided more fodder for some members of the press. St. Louis sportswriter John Wray wrote that Johnson was suffering under "the delusion that he is monarch of all he surveys...roaring madly and frightening supporters of the good pastime."

Cleveland owner James Dunn was one of Johnson's allies. "My men told me that they would not care to stand on the field and have leather-lunged fans shout at them to get useful jobs," Dunn said. "I agree heartily with them." Ruppert said he would also abide by any decision Johnson made.

National League secretary John Heydler was confident that "every effort" would be made to complete the schedule; National Commission chairman Garry Herrmann wanted a specific timetable from Washington before making any decisions. "This hasty closing down of ballparks seems wholly uncalled for," Herrmann said. "My plan is to send a delegation to Washington as soon as an audience with the President can be secured to discuss a reasonable time in which to arrange our affairs." Then, donning his other hat as president of the

Cincinnati Reds, Herrmann told manager Christy Mathewson to take the team to Chicago and "continue on the trip until further instructions are received." The Cubs, however, said that they had already decided to stop playing.

Once the initial shock had worn off, it became clear that a majority of owners wanted to finish the season that was already underway. Negotiations began with dozens of players from the American Association and the Pacific Coast League who were above or under draft age. For Brooklyn Dodgers president Charles Ebbets, it was purely a financial concern. "If we quit, we would have unfinished contracts with a number of high-priced stars. The difference between plunking down the balance due on salaries and continuing the game would not be very much. I know we won't play to empty parks."

Harry Frazee was also strongly opposed to Ban Johnson's order to close the ballparks. "It's not right and not necessary," Frazee said, adding that he would "prefer to refrain from further discussion until the final word comes from Washington." In the meantime, Frazee wired his own proposal to the National Commission:

> If, after an appeal to President Wilson, if such is possible, he affirms Secretary Baker's finding of today, I urgently suggest that the American and National leagues close season after playing 100 games, winner in each league to play nine games to decide world's championship.

The Red Sox's 100th game was scheduled for August 3, exactly two weeks away.

Frazee assured his players that the games at Fenway Park would go on as usual and that the team would leave for its western road trip the next week. But not being privileged to as much information as the owners, the Red Sox players were uncertain. The question that dominated Saturday's team meeting was when the players would be expected to find essential work. Of the 20 men on the roster, only 6 were exempt—Heinie Wagner, Dave Shean, George Whiteman, Frank Truesdale, Jack Stansbury and Horace Ford. Some players thought they should return home immediately; others were fearful of defying a government order and opposed the upcoming road trip. Wally Mayer, 28 years old, had received his draft notice that morning; he said that after visiting his mother and sister in Cincinnati, he'd be reporting to a South Carolina Army camp.

A few days after the Secretary of War's ruling, the Duluth-Mesaba Baseball League, a group of factory teams in Minnesota, sent out telegrams offering work to many of the game's stars, including Ty Cobb, George Sisler and Walter Johnson (who was offered $300 per game). Braves pitcher Hub Perdue signed with Duluth, and St. Louis shortstop Rogers Hornsby expected to do the same.

The Baltimore Drydock Shipbuilding Co. offered jobs to Babe Ruth, Cobb and Sisler. Ruth also received an offer and a pitching contract from the Hibbing, Minnesota, team of the Head of Lakes League; rumor had it that if the major leagues shut down, Ruth would head to Hibbing. The companies saw it as a buyer's market. One official stated flatly, "If they are not star players, it will be useless for them to apply as we are after the best."

News of players leaving their teams spread through both leagues. Many players quickly enlisted, others accepted factory jobs. When George Mogridge of the Yankees joined the Standard Shipyard Co. in Staten Island, New York, the *Globe* was thrilled: "Joyous News For Red Sox; Pitcher Mogridge Quits." The lefty had beaten Boston four times so far in 1918. In the confusion, no umpires showed up for a game between St. Louis and the Yankees on July 22. The game was officiated by Cozy Dolan, a former player who happened to be in attendance, and the Browns' trainer; the game was ruled a 4-4 tie, ending after 15 innings because of darkness.

While Frazee told his players they would keep playing baseball, Ed Barrow assured Boston's fans that the Red Sox would not be fielding a team of replacements. But it was questionable whether the national pas-time would last another week. On Saturday, 15,000 people came to Fenway Park, nearly three times the previous day's attendance. Ty Cobb had missed Friday's game and the crowd hoped it would get one more glimpse of the Detroit star. Cobb's batting average was nearly .390 and his 11th batting title in 12 years was almost assured. In 28 games from June 17 to July 13, Cobb had hit .469 (53-113) and scored 24 runs. He had showed no sign of slowing down on the field, but at age 31, Cobb was facing an uncertain future. He was considering quitting the game and enlisting in the chemical division of the armed services.

Cobb and Ruth received rowdy applause from the Fenway crowd, but neither man stood out. Babe couldn't hit George Dauss's curveballs out of the infield, although he did rob Cobb of a double with a leaping catch in the first inning. But the fans did see another superb pitching performance from Sam Jones, who was quickly becoming Boston's unsung hero. The 5-1 victory was his seventh straight win.

Cobb's one opportunity to excite the crowd came in the sixth inning, after he singled and took second on another hit. When he glanced towards third, he didn't recognize the Boston player covering the bag. "Hey Scotty," he said, turning to the Red Sox shortstop. "How good's that guy over there?"

"He's a marvel, best I ever saw at tagging base runners," Scott said. It was a blatant lie. Jack Stansbury was the club's sixth third baseman of the year and, Scott thought, the worst of them all. "If you're heading for third, you'd better watch yourself. He'll cut you if you come in too rough."

"Is that right?" Cobb mused, giving Stansbury a more careful look. "Well, I'm going on the next pitch, so we'll see."

It was a double steal. Catcher Wally Mayer got the ball to third in plenty of time—Stansbury was waiting, ball in glove—but Cobb some-how eluded his tag. When the inning was over, Stansbury was still mut-tering about the call on the Red Sox bench.

"What do you know about that play?" he moaned. "I had Ty by five feet."

Barrow shook his head in disgust. "Wally did, but you didn't. You haven't tagged Cobb yet."

Sunday's sports pages were packed with details of the upcoming league meetings, lists of which players would remain and column after column of speculation. Harry Frazee told his manager not to worry, that Baker's decision was not likely to be the final word.

Frazee's instincts proved correct. By evening, Ban Johnson had changed his mind, and was now telling all American League clubs to "play their scheduled games until ordered to the contrary by me." Johnson expressed confidence that the league would vote to end the season early at its meeting in Cleveland on Monday, July 22. The National League would convene two days later. Garry Herrmann said the option of "using men over the draft age was a question that must be settled. Personally I don't favor the idea—too much trouble in reforming your teams and not enough high class baseball to satisfy our patrons."

The *Boston Post* ridiculed the notion of continuing with "kids" and "old men." An editorial said the clubs "have a perfect right to play all the games they wish with men not of draft age in the lineups, but such aggregations would call out attendances of about 126 per game, after the first novelty had worn off." On July 22, an unmerciful sun drove near-record crowds to Revere Beach and City Point in South Boston. The *Globe*'s headline read, "It May Be Last Time To See Boys In Action" as Joe Bush and Carl Mays keyed a doubleheader sweep of the Tigers, 1-0 in 10 innings and 3-0. It was the second time in a week that Red Sox pitchers threw two shutouts in the same afternoon.

Boston finished its homestand with a sterling 14-3 record; 9 of the 14 wins were shutouts. Red Sox pitchers allowed an average of less than one run per game. Bush, Mays and Sam Jones each won four games.

Babe Ruth played first base in seven games and hit .522 (12-23), with 4 singles, 4 doubles and 4 triples. Boston had its largest lead of the season.

American League Standings

	W	L	Pct.	GB
Boston	55	34	.618	-
Cleveland	50	42	.543	6½
New York	46	40	.539	7½
Washington	47	41	.534	7½
St. Louis	40	46	.465	13½
Chicago	39	47	.453	14½
Philadelphia	36	49	.424	17
Detroit	36	50	.419	17½

The three members of the National Commission had assumed, naively, or perhaps arrogantly, that baseball would escape the work-or-fight order intact. The game's officials firmly believed that its business was essential to the war effort—if not directly, through the tax on tickets, then as diversionary entertainment—and saw no urgency to meet with War Department representatives. By contrast, representatives of the theater and film industries had met several times with Secretary Baker and thanks partly to their forethought, their industries had received exemptions. The order had been looming over the game since May 23, but league presidents Ban Johnson and John Tener had done nothing; no wonder Johnson claimed Secretary Baker's ruling "came out of the blue."

The National Commission itself was in disarray. An ongoing feud between the Boston Braves and the Philadelphia Athletics over the rights to pitcher Scott Perry had created a rift within the three-member body. Tener vowed he would not attend another meeting with Johnson and scoffed at Johnson's oft-stated intention to enlist, "He probably will wait until the American forces are occupying Berlin before he does."

An official clarification of the work-or-fight ruling was needed and Clark Griffith, manager and part-owner of the Washington Senators, decided to act. Griffith's Bat and Ball Fund had provided more than 3,000 baseball kits to American troops overseas. (Each kit contained a catcher's mask, mitt and chest protector, a first baseman's mitt, three bats, three bases, a dozen balls, a dozen scorecards and a rule book, "everything needed to play the game except pop bottles to throw at the umpire," quipped the *New York Times*.) Because of that effort and his geographical proximity to government offices, Griffith took the initiative and met with Provost Marshall Enoch Crowder on July 22.

"When a player is within draft age and found eligible," Griffith said, "he should join the colors just like any other young man without baseball ability. Baseball is full of men of draft age who are in deferred classes because they are married and have young children or other dependents. Few players are independently wealthy—not half a dozen. And not many of them could equal their present incomes in any other line of work. Few would be worth $15 a week in a shipyard if hired on their working skill."

At their meeting, Crowder told Griffith that his visit was the first contact he had received from any baseball official regarding the ruling. Griffith asked for an extension of time so that baseball could complete some semblance of a full season. Crowder said he would consider the request and agreed to meet with the National Commission. That same day, Harry Frazee arrived at the American League meeting at Cleveland's Hollenden Hotel with a chip on his shoulder. He argued that since rulings from local draft boards had been inconsistent, baseball stood a decent chance of being allowed to play out its schedule.

When news of the meeting between Crowder and the National Commission reached Cleveland, Ban Johnson initially declined to attend, but eventually relented under pressure. Annoyed at Johnson's timidity, Frazee decided to go to the Washington conference himself. Before the meeting adjourned, however, Frazee forced Johnson and

Garry Herrmann to admit that the National Commission—which the Boston owner usually referred to as the National Omission—had botched its responsibility by not approaching the government earlier. When asked why he hadn't sought a conference any sooner, Johnson claimed he had made "several trips to Washington on that errand," a statement contradicted by Crowder only hours earlier. The *Boston Herald and Journal* printed the news under the heading, "Commission Admits Sloth."

The July 23 heat wave reached 102 degrees in Boston Common and 103 in Harvard Square. Ice stations were set up throughout the city; four deaths were reported. Before the Red Sox left for Chicago that morning, Harry Hooper spoke to sportswriter William Spargo.

"I depend on baseball for my livelihood," said Hooper. "I have done that for years and with the money I have made out of baseball, I have bought a ranch in California. I now employ a dozen men on that ranch. The expenses now are greater than the income off the place and to meet these obligations, I need my salary as a ballplayer.

"If that salary is taken from me, my ranch will suffer. I'll have to get rid of the several families that derive their income from the place. I can't see where anyone—country, soldiers, war causes or myself—can benefit from that state of affairs. And there are dozens of other ballplayers in the same predicament."

Several Red Sox players met with Harry Frazee and demanded that their salaries be guaranteed until October 6, the last day of the season under the original schedule. The players—two of whom were likely Babe Ruth and Carl Mays—told Frazee they would not make the road trip unless their salaries were guaranteed. These "secret meetings" were becoming more common, not only for the Red Sox, but for the Cubs, Yankees and Cardinals—all players were concerned about receiving their full salaries should the owners decide to end the season early. During the winter, many owners, foreseeing a possible war-related work stoppage, had decided to pay salaries on a monthly basis, rather than an annual amount, as was customary. That way, if the season lasted only four or five months instead of the usual six, they would save thousands of dollars.

Before the road trip, Frazee cut the team's roster, sending Walter Barbare, Red Bluhm, Dick McCabe and Vince Molyneaux to Jersey City of the International League. On the way to Chicago, the Red Sox train stopped in Springfield, Massachusetts, and Eusebio Gonzalez got on board. Gonzalez had been one of the Eastern League's top infielders, and as a Cuban citizen he was not eligible for U.S. military service.

Boston signed right-hand pitcher Jean Dubuc from the Pacific Coast League's Salt Lake City club. Known for his slow ball, Dubuc had a 72-60 record with the Detroit Tigers from 1912 to 1916.* Dubuc, 29, had been rejected by his draft board three times because of knee damage. He had also received offers from the Indians and Phillies, but having been born in Vermont, he jumped at the Red Sox's offer. Frazee inked another PCL pitcher, Charles "Curley" Brown, a left-hander from Los Angeles. But while traveling to join his new team, Brown became ill and never played for Boston.

On Wednesday, July 24, Provost Marshall Enoch Crowder and Secretary of War Newton Baker met with National Commission members Garry Herrmann, Ban Johnson and John Tener. Commission secretary John Bruce, National League secretary John Heydler, Clark Griffith and Harry Frazee were there, along with representatives of the Senators, Giants, Cubs, Pirates, Phillies and Braves.

Johnson and Herrmann made short statements and submitted a four-page report claiming that Secretary Baker's ruling would leave fewer than 60 men in the major leagues and cause the immediate dissolution of the national game. Even if the clubs decided to recruit replacement players, the September 1 deadline did not allow enough time. The

---

* A slow ball is now referred to as a "change of pace" or a "change-up."

Commission asked for an extension to October 15, 1918, to comply with the regulations.

The Red Sox arrived in Chicago on Thursday and found Jean Dubuc and Wally Mayer waiting at the train station. Mayer's draft assignment had been delayed, so he returned to the team. At Comiskey Park a few hours later, Reb Russell took only 83 minutes to beat Boston 4-2. The lefty "didn't have enough speed to break a pane of glass," but his off-speed junk baffled the Red Sox. Chick Gandil went 3-4, driving in three runs and scoring the fourth one himself. Carl Mays, who had pitched Boston's last game, started on two days' rest and took the loss.

The next day, during the fifth inning, the Comiskey Park announcer informed the crowd of 2,500 that the War Department had granted baseball a new deadline—not October 15, but September 1—to comply with the work-or-fight order. Trailing 7-1 at that point, Barrow sent in the subs: George Whiteman replaced Harry Hooper in right field, Mayer went behind the plate, Eusebio Gonzalez took over at shortstop and Walt Kinney relieved Sam Jones. Gonzalez tripled to left-center field to begin the seventh inning and later scored; Kinney pitched the final four innings, allowing only one hit. It was both players' major league debut.

Even with the new deadline, questions remained. Would the leagues decide to play past the September deadline with draft-exempt players? What would the schedule look like if the season were cut short? When would the World Series be played? Baseball officials, naturally, were opposed to abandoning the autumn classic. Ban Johnson wanted the regular season to be played until August 20, with a World Series played and completed by September 1. But his plan gave the American League eastern teams and the National League western teams heavy home-field advantages. National League secretary John Heydler stated that a new schedule should be adopted, adding "a joke should not be made out of the pennant race."

Most of the National League and some of the American League owners wanted to take full advantage of Baker's edict and finish the season
on Labor Day. Teams would stop playing on Saturday, August 31, but
the players probably wouldn't be required to report to their new jobs
until Tuesday, September 3. Why couldn't the teams keep playing and
reap the extra revenue of the holiday weekend? The owners also calcu-
lated that if a player received his draft notice on September 2, the grace
period would leave him plenty of time to play in the World Series. The
two proposals only worked out to a difference of 10 or 11 days, but
many people believed that ending the season as early as August 20—
slashing five full weeks off the schedule—would tarnish the prestige of
the World Series.

Judging from the minuscule crowds at many of the games (often less
than 500 people), John Tener doubted whether the public would be suf-
ficiently interested in any post–Labor Day games. "I don't think any
World Series will be played this year."

I 4

"Burnt out by Gun Fire"

"The five Artillerymen who used their field piece like a rifle on the southern bank of the Marne in the opening hours of the fifth great offensive of 1918, scattering the Hun hordes that were crossing the river until every man of the five was killed, did not ask to be allowed to wait over a battle and come in on the next.... 'Work or fight' doesn't mean getting two base hits or catching fly balls between the hours of four and six."

This acerbic pronouncement from *Stars and Stripes*, the weekly newspaper of the American Expeditionary Forces, was part of its lengthy explanation of its decision to drop sports news from its pages. The editors confessed embarrassment at Senator Eddie Ainsmith's draft appeal to the Secretary of War; they condemned the "yellow-hearted cowardice" of professional athletes, saying they were "traitors to their country's good and worse than traitors to their own souls."

Hank Gowdy, the first big leaguer to enlist, was held up as a model of heroism for the paper's 145,000 readers. The former Boston Braves catcher "didn't scuttle into an easy job with a shipyard ball team.... He didn't suddenly remember that a whole flock of relatives were dependent upon him for support. He didn't say he'd wait until the season was over and then come in."

The editors concluded, "Back home the sight of a high fly drifting into the late sun might still have its thrill for a few. But over here the all absorbing factors are shrapnel, high explosives, machine gun bullets, trench digging.... the glorified, the commercialized, the spectatorial sport of the past has been burnt out by gun fire. The sole slogan left is 'Beat Germany.' Anything that pertains to that slogan counts. The rest doesn't."

At the National League's meeting on August 2, John Tener's suggestion to cancel the World Series found little support. "The National League will not stop its season on August 20," Pittsburgh Pirates president Barney Dreyfuss told the press. "We plan to play until Labor Day, regardless of what the American League does." Dreyfuss then left New York immediately to attend the American League's meeting in Cleveland.

Ban Johnson believed he had the votes to ratify his plan to complete the World Series by Labor Day. But there was dissension. Charles Comiskey didn't want to lose the revenue from the crowds his White Sox typically drew in the East. Clark Griffith wanted to play as many games as possible so his Senators might catch the Red Sox. Harry Frazee hated the idea of playing exhibition games before the World Series and protested any alterations to the schedule. Another reason the owners were not keen about closing on August 20 was because 14 of the 16 teams would have to pay their players for the remainder of the month with no games generating any revenue. One stockholder said, "Do you think I want to see my players all idle yet drawing pay and watching the World Series?"

No one wanted to call off the Series—the debate was simply a matter of when it would be played. There was some idle speculation that if a time for the Series could not be agreed upon, or was not sanctioned by the government, and if Boston and the New York Giants won their respective pennants, the two clubs might arrange a series on their own. In St. Louis, Branch Rickey proposed a 30-game "city challenge" series against the Browns.

Dreyfuss was prepared to accept an early season closing if the American League insisted, but as soon as he saw the acrimony and division, he took advantage. "My league has given me no alternative," he said. "If the American League quits sooner, that is its privilege, but I can tell you positively there will be no World Series." When a vote was finally taken, New York had joined Boston, Washington and Chicago in supporting the National League plan.

Cleveland president James Dunn was bitterly opposed to an early closing without a modification of the schedule. According to the current schedule, the Indians would have played only 58 of their 77 scheduled home games by Labor Day. The Red Sox would have played 71 of 77 home contests. Dunn counted on those September home games to cut into Boston's lead, and insisted that unless a more equitable schedule was drawn up, his team would refuse to begin its road trip on August 14. Johnson admitted "it may be impossible to deal fairly with every club." Several alternative plans were drawn up and voted down. The group eventually decided that the schedule would remain unchanged and the season would simply end on Labor Day.

After the meeting, still smarting from the defeat of his proposal, Johnson had more to say. Baker's ruling had been clear, he said, but if certain owners "wish to take a chance on acting contrary to the ruling of the War Department, that is their business." To Harry Frazee, Johnson's words were like waving a red flag in front of a bull. The Red Sox owner called several reporters into his hotel room, and speaking on behalf of Griffith, Comiskey and himself, condemned Johnson's "unwarranted misstatement of facts." Frazee defied "any person to show us where Secretary Baker has said he was opposed to baseball. To the contrary, in every statement he has made he has said he hoped that baseball would be able to continue regardless of the enforcement of the work-or-fight order.

"From now on the club owners are going to run the American League," Frazee declared. "We have nothing against Mr. Johnson personally, but he is in great measure responsible for the cloud under which baseball has lain all year. From now on, his 'rule-or-ruin' policy is shelved."

An official of the St. Louis Browns mentioned that he had seen several baseball men in the "wet goods section" of the hotel after the meeting. "Speeches made under 19th-hole conditions should not be given undue importance," he said, not mentioning any names.

Boston's western swing had been a mixed affair thus far. The Red Sox lost three of four games in Chicago and then swept four from St. Louis. Babe Ruth pitched two of the four wins against the Browns. George Cochran, the leadoff hitter for American Association pennant-winner Kansas City, joined the Red Sox and replaced Jack Stansbury—and became third baseman number seven. "Just when I get to know our third baseman well enough to call him by his first name," shortstop Everett Scott lamented, "Barrow gets another one."

Carl Mays rejoined the team in Cleveland on August 2, after spending four days at his home in Missouri. The last six weeks had been frustrating for Mays; his record during that stretch was 5-5—four of the losses were by scores of 3-1, 2-1, 4-3 and 4-2. Mays sputtered against Cleveland and left after five innings, trailing 6-2. Walt Kinney threw three perfect innings of relief, but it was too late. The next day, the Indians finally got their revenge on Sam Jones, smacking 11 hits, including five doubles, and winning 5-1. Alternating fadeaways and curves with an occasional fastball, Jim Bagby retired the final 12 Red Sox batters.

Now that the decision to end the season on Labor Day was official, exactly 30 days remained in the pennant race. Twenty thousand fans showed up at Cleveland's League Park for a Sunday doubleheader; 2,000 of the latecomers stood behind a rope stretched across the deepest part of the outfield.

In the first inning of game one, Guy Morton disregarded a sign to intentionally walk Ruth, and Babe rapped a run-scoring single. It was one of Morton's few mistakes. His curveball carried him through seven scoreless innings, but Ruth more than matched him. He gave his finest pitching performance of the summer, setting down the Indians in order in nine of the game's first 11 innings, allowing only four hits.

In the 12th, with the game tied 1-1, George Cochran reached on a two-out fielder's choice. He stole second and scored on Wally Mayer's single to left. Ruth took a 2-1 lead into the bottom of the 12th. Jack Graney led off with a grounder wide of first base. Stuffy McInnis grabbed it, but threw wildly past Ruth, who ran over to cover the bag. Graney sprinted to second. Mayer had backed up the play, and he fired the ball to Everett Scott. The throw was perfect. Graney slid in with spikes high, and Scott slammed the tag on him. The two men thrashed in the dirt and threw a few punches before umpire Tom Connolly separated them. Ruth got the next two hitters for his fifth straight victory. It was also Mayer's second 12th-inning, game-winning hit against Cleveland in less than a month.

If Carl Mays felt unlucky, he had nothing on Stan Coveleski. The Cleveland right-hander had led the American League with nine shutouts in 1917, but didn't pitch his first shutout this season until late July. Before that, he had pitched nine scoreless innings in four previous games, only to lose all four in extra innings. In the second game of the Boston doubleheader, Coveleski won a rain-shortened contest 2-0 and Cleveland moved 3½ games behind the Red Sox.

Babe Ruth, Red Sox, Is Year's Sensation
Pitches, Plays Infield And Outfield,
And Hits Ball Hard
Quit Team For Few Days But Trouble With Owners
Has Been Patched Up, And All's Well Now

Babe Ruth of the Boston Red Sox continues to be a regular Dick Merriwell. His exploits are becoming the talk of baseball back home. Ruth pitches, plays first and also the outfield, and besides that is among the leaders in the American League in batting. His feat of four home runs in four consecutive days is alone enough to make him famous. Ruth had some trouble with the owners of the club last week. He quit in a huff, but the trouble was soon patched up, and he is back clouting the ball again....

Babe always has been known among ballplayers as a slugger of parts, but it was generally said that if he had to play every day opposing pitchers would soon find his weak spot and make a fish out of him. This spring, when the Boston Red Sox found themselves short of batting strength, it was decided to use Ruth in the meadows or on first base when he was not pitching.... The longer he remained in the lineup, the better he got. Instead of the pitchers finding out his weakness, he found theirs.

Babe is a tremendously powerful man who handles a bat as though it weighed no more than a toothpick. He takes a full swing and hits the ball out in front of the plate, giving him tremendous drive. Home runs are his specialty.... He is credited with the longest hit ever made in the American League, driving one into the center field bleachers at Fenway Park, Boston, in a game against Detroit last year with Bill James pitching.

Any one that has ever seen Fenway Park will realize what a tremendous thump this was. The ball went into the 25-cent seats about four rows from the top. It was the first time in record that anyone ever had succeeded in putting one into this stand, though now and then someone hits a homer into the right field section....

In addition to being at present the boss hitter of the league, Ruth is also an accomplished first baseman and a fair out-fielder. His defensive play is improving all the time. And of course he is one of the best left-handed pitchers in the world. Aside from these few accomplishments and some speed on the bases, he is of practically no value to the Red Sox.

Stars and Stripes, July 19, 1918

Babe Ruth's transformation from the Red Sox's pitching rotation to their everyday lineup enabled him to excel at a level unprecedented in the game's history. Of his many nicknames—the Big Fellow, Tarzan, the Caveman, the Colossus—the last was particularly apt. As the Colossus of Rhodes was believed to have straddled the entrance to the harbor of ancient Greece, his New England namesake towered over the national sport in 1918, one huge foot planted on either side of baseball's pitching and hitting camps. What Ruth accomplished on the mound, at the plate and in the field from mid-July to early September was arguably the greatest nine-or ten-week stretch the game has ever seen.

The mere fact of Ruth's double duty was not unique. Guy Hecker had pitched, played the outfield and spent time at first base from 1882 to 1890. In 1884, he won 52 games for the Louisville Colonels of the American Association and had a 1.80 ERA. Although Hecker was rarely among the league's top hitters, his .341 average won the 1886 batting title. In the years after the establishment of the American League, pitchers who played the outfield or outfielders who pitched were either players with short careers (such as Washington's Dale Gear, Brooklyn's George Hunter and St. Louis' Jack Dunleavy) or their performances were unexceptional (Jock Menefee of the Cubs and Homer Hillebrand of the Pirates).

Washington Senators pitcher Al Orth pulled double duty in 1904, but two years later, when he led the American League in wins and complete games, he played only one game in the outfield. Similarly, Jack Coombs of the Athletics had both pitched and played the field in both 1909 and 1918, but during his best years on the hill, he never played another position.

The only players who had been even remotely comparable to Ruth were Doc White and Doc Crandall. White Sox pitcher White led the American League in 1907 with 27 wins and a 1.52 ERA, but appeared on the mound in all but three of his 49 games. In 1909, when he truly divided his time, he batted only .234 (although his on-base average was .347) and was 11-9 with a 1.72 ERA.

Doc Crandall played second base and pitched for the Federal League St. Louis Terriers in 1914, leading the club in both batting average (.309) and wins (13). The following year, as a pitcher and pinch-hitter, Crandall won 21 games and batted .284.

Babe Ruth was among both the elite pitchers and elite hitters for most of 1918. He began spring training by homering in his first two at-bats. (In his first plate appearance—that is, in the first inning of a meaningless game in March—Dodgers manager Wilbert Robinson had Ruth walked intentionally.) Every home run he launched during the season was described by the hometown press as "the longest hit ever seen on the local grounds" or some variation thereof. His slugging prowess commanded headlines all year long and every opposing team feared him. He was routinely walked intentionally in the first inning; the St. Louis Browns gave Ruth an intentional pass in five consecutive plate appearances over two days. When pitchers finally had to pitch to him, he made them pay. In one 10-game period during Boston's July homestand, Ruth hit .469 (15-32) and scored 10 runs; he hit four singles, six doubles and five triples for a .969 slugging average.

Off the mound, Ruth alternated between left field, center field and first base, depending on which other Red Sox players were available. His glove work in the outfield was solid and he was remarkably adept at first base, recording a near-record 20 putouts in one game against Chicago, including a game-ending unassisted double play.

And then, every fourth day Babe would take his turn on the mound and prove that he was one of the game's toughest pitchers. After returning from his Fourth of July defection and resolving most of his differences with Ed Barrow, Ruth made 11 starts and won 9 of them, including the pennant-clincher against Philadelphia. In his last 10 starts of the season, he allowed more than two runs only once.

When the season was complete, Ruth would lead both the National and American Leagues in slugging average by a wide margin and tie for the most home runs in both leagues. His 11 home runs were more than the home run totals of five other teams. Babe finished second in doubles, third in runs batted in and fifth in triples—all accomplished with 100 to 175 fewer plate appearances than his peers. His pitching record was 13-7, and his ERA of 2.22 was eighth best. He allowed an average of 9.52 hits and walks per nine innings, second only to Walter Johnson. Ruth had the third lowest opponents on-base average and fourth lowest opponents batting average.

Then, for an encore, he would give a historic performance in the World Series.

An oppressive heat wave blanketed the East and Midwest during Boston's road trip. In St. Louis, hundreds of people slept on their lawns and in public parks as the mercury hit 104 degrees. On August 6 and 7, Maryland hit a high of 115; Philadelphia reached 106 (the hottest day since record-keeping had begun in 1894) and Washington 106. A few days after the Red Sox left Cleveland, the city hit an all-time high of 107 degrees; in two days, the grueling heat claimed the lives of an adult and 30 infants.

On Detroit's Navin Field, one unofficial thermometer read 115 degrees. The players' thick, wool uniforms hung like dead weights from their shoulders. In the hotel rooms, players left the windows open and prayed for a breeze. Others would soak their bed sheets in cold water before lying down for the night. Babe Ruth's strategy for keeping cool in the dugout was to place a chilled lettuce leaf under his cap.

Carl Mays struggled for the second straight start. After the Red Sox rallied to win the game 7-5 in 10 innings, Mays was sent east to Boston for some extra rest. Before the next game in Detroit, the Red Sox players were filmed tossing baseballs and swinging bats for possible World Series newsreel footage. Once the game began, the Tigers pounded Joe Bush for six first-inning runs and won 11-8.

Hack Miller was the newest player plucked from the Pacific Coast League, where he had batted .316 in 102 games for Oakland. The son of a circus strongman, Miller was seldom modest about his own considerable strength. He swung a 47-ounce bat and claimed to occasionally use a 65-ounce stick "because it didn't sting my fingers." (An average bat weighed 32-38 ounces.) Miller sometimes entertained teammates by yanking small trees out of the ground, driving nails into planks with his hand and smashing stones with his fist.

In the final game against the Tigers, Miller played left field and had a double, a single and two rbis. Miller was in left because Ruth was pitching. When he gave up two singles in the second inning, Barrow told Sam Jones to get ready. But Ruth got out of the jam quickly. He surrendered only four hits the rest of the way, conserving his energy in the intense heat, baring down only when runners were on base. The Red Sox won 4-1, ending the road trip with a 7-7 record.

On the train to Boston, Barrow spoke for the first time about the Red Sox's chances in the World Series. "I figure the Cubs will be much easier to beat than the Giants," he said. "Jim Vaughn is a good pitcher, but I don't believe Chicago has any other curveballer who will or can bother us. And another thing, the Cubs will be without catcher Bill Killefer during the big games because of the draft."

Cincinnati Reds manager Christy Mathewson had suspected for weeks that his first baseman, Hal Chase, was taking bribes, gambling on the team and fixing games. Urged on by other members of the Reds, Mathewson suspended Chase for "indifferent play" on August 7.

For most players in both leagues, this was old news. Rumors and stories about Chase's crooked behavior had been around for nearly a decade. In the years to come, contemporaries would mention Chase, George Sisler and Lou Gehrig as the finest first basemen of all time, but "Prince Hal" would also become synonymous with the dishonest ballplayer. Chase not only threw games himself, he enlisted players to help him and tried bribing others, both on his own team and on opposing clubs. Though his reputation was well known, and despite 14 affidavits attesting to his dishonesty, all charges brought against Chase were dismissed.

The National Commission was loathe to acknowledge the extent to which gambling had infiltrated the game; it would have been too damaging to the sport's wholesome image. But Chase's acquittal was nothing short of an open invitation to unscrupulous players to fix games without consequences. The 1919 World Series fix—in which Chase was involved—is often described as an aberration. Actually, it was only the tip of a very corrupt iceberg.

The New York Yankees had held a slice of first place in late June, but since then, they had won only 11 of 37 games. They arrived in Boston in fifth place, mired in a seven-game losing streak and without many of their top players. In the final two weeks of July, Ping Bodie, Herb Thormahlen, Allan Russell and Zinn Beck left for various shipyards, Eddie Miller went to a munitions factory, Wally Pipp enlisted in the

Naval Aviation Corps and Armando Marsans went home to Cuba to care for his dying mother.

Against the slumping Red Sox, those absences would hardly matter, because New York manager Miller Huggins started the series with George Mogridge. Although Mogridge had bolted for a Staten Island shipyard, Huggins had managed to coax him back with $500. (Mogridge had quit the team twice before and both times returned for cash.) The lefty fanned Babe Ruth with the bases loaded in the fourth, escaped a one-out jam with runners at second and third in the seventh, and shut down an eighth inning rally. Joe Bush struck out 10 men, but he wilted in the 10th inning and the Red Sox lost 5-1.

In the second game, New York's Ham Hyatt was credited with a home run when his line drive disappeared into a hole under the right field fence. "I didn't know there was a hole in that fence," Barrow said. "The groundskeeper says he didn't know either. You can bet it's plugged up now. But why did that ball have to find that hole in a close series like this? And why couldn't a Red Sox player have been responsible for the fluke instead of a Yankee? It's uncanny. If I were superstitious, I would say the Yankees have a jinx on us."

His team's lackluster performance baffled Barrow. "I actually fear playing the weaker clubs more than the strong ones," he said. "The players don't deliberately lay down, yet it's evident they don't do their best. That's why I'm not worrying more about our lead right now. It's been cut down to a dangerous degree, but we're facing strong clubs on our home grounds. Under such circumstances, the Red Sox usually win. Nothing is certain in this game, but if we don't win the pennant now, after our good start, we ought to be run out of baseball on a fence rail."

Babe Ruth pitched a four-hitter on August 12, but his inattention early in the game allowed New York to beat him. He walked Del Pratt to start the second inning, then was late covering first on a bunt. A single to right field scored one run, then Ruth bobbled a suicide squeeze and a second run scored. When Ruth popped up for the final out of the game, he heaved his bat out past second base in frustration. Boston lost 2-1, their seventh loss in their last 10 games.

Winning pitcher Hank Robinson was dismissed by one Boston writer as "a National League discard" who was in the bigs only because of the draft. It was true that Robinson had gone a mediocre 39-33 with the Pirates and Cardinals years ago, but the denigration said as much about the Red Sox hitters as it did about the Yankees pitcher. Only one of Boston's three hits left the infield. The team's .247 batting average was seventh in the league; only last-place Philadelphia, at .239, was worse.

The Indians played their final home game of the season. Guy Morton pitched a two-hitter and Cleveland's 11-2 win moved them two games behind Boston. The Indians' final 18 games would be on the road.

The recurring rheumatism in Dave Shean's foot was so painful that no one knew if the second baseman would finish the season. Eusebio Gonzalez was on the bench as a substitute and Harry Frazee purchased infielder Jack Coffey as additional insurance. Back in 1909, Coffey had been the Braves' shortstop, batting .187 and committing 40 errors in 73 games. With Detroit in 1918, he had hit .209 in 22 games. The Tigers were ready to let Coffey go when the Red Sox were in town and a deal was made. Boston also signed catcher Norm McNeil and released Lore Bader, Jack Stansbury and Frank Truesdale.

More significantly, and more ominously, Babe Ruth, Amos Strunk and Sam Agnew all received draft notices, and Carl Mays was told to report for a pre-draft physical. This was serious. Ruth and Mays were irreplaceable. Losing Strunk, while not devastating, would be felt. Even if a diminished Red Sox squad could hold off the Indians and Senators, what would its World Series lineup look like?

And what about the World Series itself? It was nearly mid-August and there was still no word from the National Commission.

Then an unusual summer got a little stranger. On the same afternoon that the Red Sox draft notices arrived, Charles Comiskey and Clark Griffith both denied having anything to do with Harry Frazee's denunciation of Ban Johnson after the American League meeting. "I went to the ball game in Cleveland in the afternoon," Comiskey said, "and have no personal knowledge of a statement criticizing anyone. I did all my fighting in the meeting." Comiskey swore he never signed Frazee's statement and Griffith, in a separate interview, claimed he knew nothing about it at all.

Comiskey was technically correct, of course—since there actually *was* no written statement. "I never signed *my* name to any statement," Frazee said, nonplussed. "Some of the boys who haven't a lot of regard for me are using this to make it appear that I forged someone's name. As far as I'm concerned, my words are the same whether I've spoken or written them."

Paul Shannon of the *Boston Post* was stunned. He had been in the room when Frazee had made his comments, so he knew Griffith had been there, too, along with the Associated Press reporter, Henry Edwards of the *Cleveland Plain Dealer* and a writer from the *Washington Star.*

"Griffith was anxious to have the statement made in even more caustic language than Frazee used," wrote Shannon. "Besides this, Comiskey knew that this statement was to be given out, as he was in Frazee's presence at the hotel." Edwards agreed, "Frazee and Griffith together dictated the statement in question." When asked for his comments, Connie Mack identified Griffith and Frazee as "the chief complainants responsible for the criticism of Johnson."

Before boarding a train to New York the following evening to oversee some theater rehearsals, Frazee offered his version of the disputed event. "Clark Griffith and I were with three newspaper men and they asked our views on matters in general," he said. "I told them what I thought and Griff spoke as freely as I did. A little later, Charlie Comiskey came along and aired the same ideas as we did, and the newspapermen were at liberty to use our statements as they saw fit."

Shannon pointed out that both the White Sox and Senators had played games in Cleveland, "the city where Johnson holds forth," after the meeting took place. "It is evident that a movement is on foot to save Johnson's face and that Comiskey and Griffith are being whipped into line to try to make Frazee the goat."

The Chicago Cubs slumped in late July and their lead over the New York Giants in the National League shrunk to two games. The team was also on the verge of losing some key players. Shortstop Charlie Hollocher and catchers Bill Killefer and Bob O'Farrell planned on enlisting in the Navy. Third baseman Charlie Deal jumped the club for a shipyard job. With Deal gone, outfielder Dode Paskert was pressed into service at the hot corner until the team signed Charlie Pick from the San Francisco Seals of the Pacific Coast League.

But the Cubs won four of five games against the Giants at the beginning of the month, including a one-hitter from Jim Vaughn, and held a commanding 6½-game lead. Vaughn's win was also his 20th victory of the season. If the Cubs won only half of their remaining 26 games, John McGraw's Giants would have to win 19 of 24 to catch them. The defending league champs were not up to the challenge. On August 17, Chicago's lead had ballooned to eight games and Melville Webb wrote in the *Boston Globe* that unless the Cubs were "tipped out of the railroad cars somewhere," they were shoo-ins for the World Series.

But the actual plans for the Series were more guesswork than hard fact. The National Commission was keeping silent until the government granted permission for the Series. St. Louis sportswriter John Wray received an anonymous tip that "the World Series teams will not play at all unless they are guaranteed that the winners' share will be at least $3,000." That would pose a problem. In January, the National Commission had imposed a cap on the winning and losing shares; the maximum winning share was now only $2,000, less than half of what winning teams had received in recent years. "They may insist upon guarantees of amounts that cannot be paid," the insider said, "in view of the expected low attendance." In his opinion, the World Series would either be moved to the last week of August, before the work-or-fight deadline, when the players could make no bonus demands, or it would be abandoned completely.

15

"I NEVER SAW A CLUB HAVE THE LUCK BOSTON HAS HAD"

Cubs president Charles Weeghman was confident that the World Series would be played and that his club would be in it. Seeking to avoid the problems that plagued the crosstown White Sox in 1917, when loyal fans were denied the best tickets, Weeghman announced an innovative system of advance ticket registration. Anyone attending a Cubs game in July or August was advised to write his or her name and address on the rain check portion of the ticket stub, then drop the stub in a special box before leaving the park. The stubs would then be catalogued to measure fan loyalty and preference would be given to "the people who patronize the club during the regular season."

It was a brilliant idea, but by mid-August, there weren't many stubs in the box. Attendance figures dropped so low that visiting teams were borrowing money from their treasuries to pay the hotel bills. The Browns reportedly made little money in Boston, broke even in Washington and collected only $335 from a three-game series in

Philadelphia. During a weekday series at the Polo Grounds, the Browns cleared $141 on Monday, $215 from a Tuesday doubleheader and were hoping to net $75 from a meager Wednesday crowd. The four National League games played on August 22 were attended by a total of 2,525 people. At Cincinnati's Crosley Field, an average of 200 fans watched each game of a Reds-Cardinals series.

Ed Barrow wondered if he should toss his new gray hat into the nearest trash can. The White Sox had pounded Carl Mays for 10 hits and sent him to his fifth loss in six starts. Boston took two of three games against Chicago, but the team still had won only five of its last 13 games. Barrow thought his hat might be a jinx.

The Indians were only two games back in the standings when they arrived for a crucial three-game set beginning Saturday, August 17. Harry Frazee had returned from New York hoping for big crowds. In previous years, the warm weekend afternoon might have brought upwards of 30,000 to Fenway Park. The Saturday contest did draw the largest crowd of the year, which in the war-torn season was 15,129.

The starting pitchers were Guy Morton and Babe Ruth; whenever these two hurlers faced each other, a tense duel was virtually guaranteed. On June 1, 1917, Morton's bid for a no-hitter at Fenway Park had been dashed by Ruth's eighth-inning single, while Ruth had a one-hitter of his own that day until Cleveland broke through with three ninth-inning runs. Back on May 23, Morton had thrown a one-hitter against Boston. Two weeks earlier in Cleveland, the two pitchers had hooked up in a 12-inning duel. Would this game be another nail-biter?

Lee Fohl loaded his lineup with right-handed hitters against Ruth. A few days earlier, Fohl had benched Bob Roth for "laying down" and moved Joe Wood from second base to right field. Fohl now penciled Wood in at first base in place of Doc Johnston, who could not hit lefties.

Cleveland scored a run in the fourth when Jack Graney tripled and Tris Speaker doubled. The Red Sox fought back in their half of the

inning. Ruth grounded to second baseman Terry Turner, who was playing so deep that Babe beat out a single. Stuffy McInnis reached on an
infield error and Hack Miller cracked a single to left. Ruth streaked
around third and shouldn't have had a chance of scoring, but Graney's
throw bounced 10 feet up the line. Catcher Steve O'Neill chased the ball,
leaving the plate unguarded. McInnis tried scoring as Wood sprinted in
from first. Wood and Morton reached the plate at the same time as
McInnis and the baseball. Morton muffed the tag and Boston led 2-1.

Ruth escaped unscathed in the seventh, when Wood was doubled off
second after Harry Hooper caught a line drive in right. At that point,
Morton had surrendered only one solid hit, while his teammates had
slugged two doubles, a triple and a long single—but still trailed 2-1.

Jim Bagby replaced Morton in the eighth and just as they had back
on July 6, the Red Sox immediately pounded him. Hooper singled and
was forced by Dave Shean. Amos Strunk doubled to right, moving
Shean to third. Catcalls and boos filled the air as Bagby intentionally
walked Ruth. But McInnis got revenge, lining the first pitch to left,
boosting Boston's lead to 4-1.

Those two runs were a necessary cushion against Cleveland's ninth
inning rally. A single and a throwing error by McInnis put runners at
first and third with one out. With the infield back, Wood's grounder to
second scored a run. Ruth then got the final out and finished with a
five-hitter and his seventh win in his last eight decisions.

"I never saw a club have the luck Boston has had against us this year,"
said Cleveland's Ray Chapman. "We've got to score enough runs on
Monday and Tuesday to counter that. Guy had the best curveball of his
career this afternoon, but two fluke hits and Jack's throw beat us."

Ruth, Heinie Wagner, Wally Schang and a bunch of benchwarmers
spent Sunday in Connecticut playing an exhibition game against the
New Haven Colonials. The home team's lineup featured two ex-major
leaguers, Wally Pipp and Neal Ball. Ruth thrilled the crowd by belting
the ball over a bathing pavilion in right field. Naturally, it was the

longest home run anyone could remember at Lighthouse Point. Boston pitchers Bill Pertica and Walt Kinney lost the game 4-3.

Sam Jones took the hill on Monday for perhaps the most important game of his young career. Boston held a three-game on Cleveland and there were rumors that Carl Mays might be in the Army by the end of the week.

Indians manager Lee Fohl made sure that if his team was going to lose, it would not be because of Babe Ruth. In the first and third innings, with men on base, Stan Coveleski walked him intentionally. Ruth doubled in the seventh and when he batted in the eighth, with Boston ahead 6-0, Cleveland put on a shift with four men covering right field. Joe Wood, the right fielder, was back near the bleachers, Tris Speaker was in right center, second baseman Terry Turner stood in short right center and first baseman Doc Johnston played about 20 feet back on the outfield grass.

Ruth could have gone the opposite way or laid down a bunt, but, stubborn and confident, he tried to beat the shift. Taking a mammoth swing, he crushed the ball high and deep to right. Wood was already at the base of the fence, and he leapt and snared the long drive. Two minutes later, it was payback time. Leading off the ninth, Wood hit a line drive toward the left field corner. Ruth sprinted over, stuck out his mitt, banged into the wall—but held onto the ball.

Jones shrugged off the pressure like a veteran. He pitched a two-hitter; only three Indians reached second base. Tris Speaker had no doubt Jones was Boston's best pitcher. "That slow ball of his simply floats up there and you swing your head off," he said. "Then he's got a fast one that's on top of you before you realize it. Plus, he's got as good a curveball as anyone in the league."

Jones's 6-0 shutout boosted Boston's lead to four with 14 games remaining. That was enough for the *Boston Herald and Journal's* Burt Whitman to proclaim the pennant was in the bag. Edward Martin of the *Globe* agreed, writing that the Red Sox would soon "occupy a very fine looking residence on Championship Avenue."

In the series finale, Barrow brought Ruth back to pitch on two days' rest (although of course Babe had played nine innings on each of his days off). His fastball had plenty of zip—catcher Wally Mayer's hands became so sore, he was replaced by Schang in the fourth inning—but after a frustrating afternoon against Jones's breaking balls, the Indians welcomed some straight heat.

Barrow kept Ruth in for seven innings, ignoring plenty of free advice from the grandstand to give Babe the hook. That was enough time for Cleveland to rack up 13 hits and eight runs. The 8-4 loss was Ruth's worst outing of the season and the only one of his 19 starts he didn't finish. Cleveland sportswriter Henry Edwards thought any other hurler would have been yanked much earlier, but Ruth "is one pitcher whom Barrow dislikes to derrick, being much bigger than Barrow and extremely temperamental."

The game ended the season series between the two clubs. It was hard to imagine two more evenly-matched teams; each had won 10 games, and 14 of the 20 contests had been decided by either one or two runs.

Harry Frazee breathed a huge sigh of relief on Monday, August 19, when he learned that four Red Sox starters—Amos Strunk, Harry Hooper, Everett Scott and Stuffy McInnis—had been granted exemptions from their draft boards until September 15. The fate of Carl Mays was still up in the air.

Two days later, Mays got his 19th win by beating the Browns. It was Shriner's Day at Fenway and several hundred fez-wearing members of the Aleppo Temple were on hand with a fife-and-drum band to honor St. Louis catcher Les Nunamaker. When Nunamaker batted in the second, a delegation walked out onto the field and gave him a diamond emblem. Temple chairman J. C. Morse presented cigars to all the servicemen in the grandstand; any player who got a hit in the game was also given a box of cigars. After Barrow saw Heinie Wagner gaze longingly at his cigars, the manager broke down and gave the coach a box of his own. Barrow estimated they would last Wagner "until about 10 o'clock tomorrow night."

While the crowd puffed away, Jack Coffey slugged a fifth-inning home run. It was the only one of his career and just the second of the year for the Red Sox at Fenway Park. The Shriners held a party at Point Shirley that night; Red Sox attendees included Coffey, Sam Agnew, Sam Jones, Wally Mayer and George Cochran.

The rest of the schedule favored Boston: they would play 9 out of 11 games at home and face the league's weaker teams. And despite Barrow's belief that his club played poorly against second-division teams, Boston was a combined 33-12 against St. Louis, Detroit and Philadelphia.

On August 22, Secretary of War Newton Baker announced that the government had no objections to a World Series being played and he ordered local draft boards to give the participating players until September 15 to comply with the work-or-fight order. The Red Sox, as well as the Indians and the Cubs, could proceed with printing and distributing World Series tickets. Requests for tickets, mailed by fans prior to the ruling, were already piling up at Fenway Park.

Baseball officials expressed relief, but Baker's statement wasn't news. Indeed, for the past month, several people in government, including President Wilson, had expressed their support for baseball, saying they hoped it could continue. As far back as late July, Clark Griffith had told the Commission the government wanted baseball to continue. "All this talk about the government wanting baseball shut down is bunk. It just about tore their hearts out when they gave the order that baseball was non-essential. We will play right up to September 2 and then we'll play a World Series—bank all you have on that."

But the National Commission was paralyzed—it could not decide what to do with the 1918 season. The Commission and the owners didn't think it was proper to abruptly stop the season, but with attendance plummeting, they wanted to cut their losses. Their constant appeals for more time or clarification throughout the summer were a stalling tactic designed to give the impression that the government was making the final decision. Most sportswriters fell for the charade and parroted the Commission's line: the government was ordering baseball to shut down on September 1.

Before the game against the Red Sox, each player on the St. Louis Browns was told that in 10 days, his contract would be terminated and he would be released. The standard contract required a 10-day notice period, and August 22 was exactly 10 days before September 2, the final day of the shortened season. The Browns weren't the only players shocked by this news: only the two World Series teams did not cut their players loose.

After Labor Day, players were no longer being paid by any major league team, but that didn't mean they could offer their talents to other teams. The owners had made a "gentlemen's agreement" not to tamper with other teams' players. While the club owners saved approximately $200,000, the players lost their salaries, but remained yoked to the teams that had released them. "It was only natural that we should enter into an agreement to protect our interests," Philadelphia's Connie Mack said, overtly admitting the collusion. The *Boston Herald and Journal* assured fans, "Let there be no fear that these releases will be taken literally by any of the clubs."

In an overview of the 1918 season for the *Reach Official American League Guide*, editor Francis C. Richter explained that the players "would be 'free agents' all right if there were any clubs to bid for their services, but as no club will lift a finger to secure a player under reserve to another club the players' best, and indeed only, course is to make the best possible terms with the reserving clubs, or retire from the game. That's the immutable law of Organized Ball."

A few players went to court to recover their lost salaries. Jack Daubert's claim against the Dodgers for $2,150 (the balance of his $9,000 salary) was settled out of court, then Brooklyn owner Charles Ebbets traded him to Cincinnati. After Burt Shotton sued the Washington Senators for $1,400, he was released.

When news of the Browns' contract terminations filtered into the Red Sox locker room, the Boston players asked Babe Ruth to meet with Harry Frazee and find out exactly what was happening.

"Salaries will be paid until September 2," Frazee told Ruth. "That is the end of the regular season and that is the obligation I have as a club owner."

"What about the promise you made at the team meeting three weeks ago?" Ruth asked. "You told us we'd get paid until September 15."

"That was before Secretary Baker's decision," Frazee said, using the lie most of the owners were telling their players. "The Labor Day work-or-fight deadline automatically voids all contracts. It's a government order. All of baseball comes to an end at that point—except for the World Series, of course."

Ruth's response was clear: "Well, I've been told by the rest of the boys that if you don't stand by your promise, the Red Sox won't play in any World Series."

That afternoon, Joe Gedeon of the Browns tried to steal home with his team ahead 1-0 in the ninth inning. He barreled head first into Wally Schang and was tagged out, losing five teeth in the collision. St. Louis won the game 1-0, but Boston took the next two behind the pitching of Sam Jones and Ruth. On August 25, Ruth stole home as part of a double steal and wrenched his tightly-wrapped knee on the slide. Trainer Martin Lawler helped the Big Fellow back to the dugout. When Ruth came out to pitch the next inning, limping slightly and with a visible bruise on his left hand, he drew cheers from the 8,000 fans—and threw shutout ball for the rest of the game. Ruth won 3-1, and Boston now held a four-game lead with nine games remaining. The Red Sox needed only a 5-4 record against Detroit and Philadelphia to clinch their third pennant in four years.

As Ruth dispatched the Browns, the National Commission announced that the World Series would begin on Wednesday, September 4. Ten percent of the gate receipts would be donated to various war charities; ticket prices were reduced with the hopes of increasing attendance. Box seats that had sold for $5.00 in 1917 would now go for $3.00. All other prices were halved: grandstand seats were $1.50, pavilion seats were $1.00 and bleacher admission was only fifty cents.

"The first three games will be played in Chicago," Ban Johnson said, "and the others, if any, will be at the American League team's park." (The lopsided schedule was designed to cut down on travel expenses between Chicago and Boston.) Once again, Johnson had lit a match under Harry Frazee. Despite their periodic feuds, the two men were very much alike. Neither was a stranger to hyperbole; both could be pompous and full of bluster. This time, Frazee was angry over the words "if any"—it sounded as if it were possible that no games would be played at Fenway Park, that the 1918 World Series would be a best-of-five contest. Frazee called the schedule an insult to his city, his team and their fans, and he vowed that without significant changes, the Red Sox would not play.

And late that Saturday night, as Babe Ruth celebrated his victory over the Browns, his father lay dying in a Baltimore hospital.

16

"The First Time I Ever Saw George Cry"

Some time after midnight on Saturday, August 25, George Ruth Sr. had a fist fight with his brother-in-law outside his saloon. Ruth, standing near the edge of the curb when he was punched, lost his balance, stumbled back into the street and struck his head. Customers carried him into the bar. He was taken to University Hospital, but never regained consciousness, dying of a skull fracture early Sunday morning. Ruth was 45 years old.

Babe and Helen Ruth were looking forward to a relaxing Sunday afternoon at the beach when they heard the news. Ruth was unable to leave town until the following evening, and he telegrammed his stepmother to say Helen and he would arrive in Baltimore on Tuesday morning.

The circumstances and manner of George Ruth's death are clear, but the reasons behind the incident are not. The events leading up to his accidental death had been set in motion about a year earlier.

Some time after being widowed, George Ruth married Martha Sipes. Martha had a brother named Benjamin and a sister who was married to a man named Oliver Beefelt. In September 1917 Beefelt, then 33, met 15-year-old Emma Stopford at the home of one of her friends. They began a relationship that lasted for a couple of months until Emma's mother learned that Beefelt was married. Anna Stopford forbade her daughter from seeing Beefelt, but when Emma related this to her lover, Beefelt told the teenaged girl he'd kill her if she stopped seeing him. They continued to meet in secret.

Emma told her parents she had taken a job as a telephone operator; when she was supposedly working, she was actually at a room Beefelt had rented at 908 North Broadway. In the spring of 1918, Emma, then 16, moved in with Beefelt. Several weeks later, her parents discovered the truth and tried once again to end the relationship.

On Sunday, June 23, Emma left her parents' house to buy some ice cream. Some distance from the house, Beefelt drove up in his car and Emma got in. Beefelt took the girl to a dress shop and bought her a "dress fit to go away in." At Beefelt's request, Emma then wrote two letters, one to her father assuring him that she was in no danger, and the other attesting that she had left of her own volition. Then Beefelt drove to the train station and put Emma on a train to Cleveland, and said he would join her in six weeks.

As soon as Anna Stopford realized her daughter was missing, she contacted the police. On June 27, the truth about Emma's job was discovered, and Beefelt was arrested. At a hearing on July 1, Beefelt was accused of abducting Emma "for immoral purposes." In his defense, he produced the two letters Emma had written. The girl's father admitted the handwriting resembled Emma's but said Beefelt must have forced her to write them. Beefelt denied the accusation and was cleared of all charges.

In Cleveland, Emma took a room at a boarding house on East 55th Street. When she didn't have enough money for a week's rent, John

Fosland, the landlady's stepson, would pay her board. In July, Emma wrote to some friends in Baltimore; in one letter, she begged a friend not to reveal her whereabouts and asked what everyone was saying about her.

Meanwhile, searches for Emma were conducted in at least 20 cities. When information from one of Emma's letters leaked, the Baltimore police wired the Chief of Police in Cleveland. On Wednesday, July 31, Emma and John Fosland, who was with her at the time, were both arrested. Emma was detained for 10 days before being brought back to Baltimore.

Beefelt was again arrested, this time on charges of "criminal assault and enticing [Emma Stopford] from her home." On August 12, Emma testified about her relationship with Beefelt and the weeks she had spent in Cleveland. Beefelt made no statement and was later released on $500 bail.

During this time, Beefelt's wife, Martha Ruth's sister, had been living with George and Martha Ruth. Late during the night of August 25, Benjamin Sipes stopped by the Ruths' apartment to check on Mrs. Beefelt's health and to give her some money. When the wife of the philanderer saw her brother, she broke down in tears, telling him how horribly her husband had been treating her.

Downstairs, Sipes found Beefelt sitting in Ruth's saloon and began berating him. The two men argued loudly before Sipes left the bar and went to a cigar shop across the street. A few minutes later, George Ruth came out of the saloon's side door, walked up to Sipes and punched him in the face. Ruth landed another blow, and when Sipes dropped to the sidewalk, Ruth kicked him. When Sipes managed to get back on his feet, he punched Ruth, and the saloon owner fell into the street and struck his head.

Early Sunday morning, three policemen arrested Sipes at his home, charging him with "striking and causing the death of George H. Ruth" and took him to the Western Police Station. At a jury inquest that evening, Sipes admitted striking Ruth, but said that it was only after being knocked to the ground and then kicked. The jury decided that Sipes had acted in self-defense and he was released from custody later that night.

The *Boston Globe* and *Boston Post* printed short, nearly identical accounts of George Ruth's death, but they differed from the stories in the *Baltimore Sun*. The Boston papers reported that Sipes was angry at how his brother-in-law, George Ruth, had been treating his sister, Martha Ruth. Oliver Beefelt wasn't mentioned at all. The early Sunday morning story (with its inaccuracies) likely came off the wire and the Boston papers didn't have time to get more information or fact-check the report.

The three best-known biographies of Ruth—Robert W. Creamer's *Babe: The Legend Comes to Life*, Marshall Smelser's *The Life That Ruth Built* and Kal Wagenheim's *Babe Ruth: His Life and Legend*—all briefly mention the incident.

Creamer calls the charge against Beefelt "statutory rape." This seems plausible since Emma Stopford was 15 when the relationship began. After Beefelt was arrested for the second time, one of the charges against him was "criminal assault," a euphemism for rape. There is, however, little evidence that the relationship was actually illegal. Beefelt and Stopford had shared an apartment for several weeks, but Beefelt was arrested only after Emma was missing; the charges of "having spirited [her] away for immoral purposes [and] having abducted her" had been previously dismissed. There was the implication that Emma's parents wanted the affair stopped only because Beefelt was married.

Smelser tells a different story. He says Benjamin Sipes, a regular at Ruth's saloon, accused Ruth's bartender of taking money from the till; Ruth defended his employee and a fight broke out. Ruth may have tried ejecting Sipes, but "they went to fighting in the street outside" and Ruth fell to the sidewalk. Smelser makes no mention of Beefelt; his is the only account that includes the involvement of the bartender.

George Ruth Sr. was buried in Baltimore's Loudon Park Cemetery on Wednesday, August 28. One of Babe's relatives remarked, "It was the first time I ever saw George cry."

Back in Boston on the day of the funeral, one Red Sox player quipped, "The Ball Club did not get back today, but he'll be in there tomorrow."

17

"I MAY BE THE LUCKY FELLOW"

"It's an outrage to have a city like Boston turned down in this manner," said Harry Frazee, hot under the collar and always quick to speak his mind. Frazee may not have been, in the words of one sportswriter, "overburdened with popularity" in Boston, but Red Sox fans appreciated his strong reactions when he felt his team had been wronged.

Frazee said that if the World Series began with two games in Chicago, the next two games should be in Boston. "I'm absolutely opposed to playing three games in Chicago, and then, as President Johnson says, playing the remaining games, 'if any'—whatever that means—in Boston. The Series should be arranged so that each club has an equal chance to win. The expense of an additional trip between the two cities should not be a factor."

Ed Barrow thought Johnson must have been misquoted. "That 'if any' statement looks wrong to me," he said. "I don't think Johnson would ever intimate that the Series should be three games out of five."

The National Commission's schedule meant that Saturday and Sunday would be spent traveling from Chicago to Boston. Not taking advantage of the potentially lucrative weekend dates was puzzling, especially after a season of dwindling finances and lowered Series ticket prices.

The consensus in Boston was that Johnson was retaliating against Frazee. "Big Ban" was "putting the screws" to the Red Sox owner, said the *Boston Globe*. Frazee was a "young, independent and sometimes impetuous" owner who "had the temerity to question Ban's power in the American League and now, unquestionably, he is being asked to pay the penalty." The *Boston Traveler* said sarcastically, "Among the interviews we'd like to read is one from Byron Bancroft Johnson on 'How pleased I am to see the Red Sox win the pennant.'"

The National Commission had little reason to grant Chicago's Charles Weeghman any favors either. He bought the Cubs and joined the National League after the 1916 settlement with the Federal League and was viewed as an outsider. During the winter meetings, his ostentatious display of wealth—announcing he had a quarter-million dollars to spend—endeared him to no one.

Commission chairman Garry Herrmann answered Frazee's complaints: "Had Mr. Frazee waited until he had received his official bulletin with respect to the matter, possibly nothing would have been said by him. The schedule was made by the National Commission and not by Mr. Johnson. The schedule as arranged will be carried out, regardless of whether it suits Mr. Frazee or not."

The telegram smoothed Frazee's ruffled feathers. "I thought it was a baseball law that the Series should be played two games in each city," he said. "I guess we'll have a World Series even if we don't like some of the details. The fans will think more of us if we take the bad breaks and make a good fight. At first, it looked as if the Red Sox didn't have a chance, but the more I see how our players are not worrying, perhaps it isn't a bad arrangement. If we get a good start in Chicago, we should romp through the other games."

There was also uncertainty about where the Cubs would play their home games. Weeghman wanted to keep his North Side fans happy and not handicap his players with unfamiliar grounds for the most important games of the season. But he worried about Babe Ruth hitting in his small park. The right field line at Cubs Park was forty feet closer to home plate (321 feet) than at Comiskey Park (362 feet).

The Cubs playing a World Series at Comiskey would not be unprecedented. The Red Sox had used newly constructed Braves Field for the 1915 and 1916 Series because of its larger seating capacity. The Braves had played in Fenway Park during the 1914 Series. Boston's Royal Rooters were planning a trip to Chicago, even though Ban Johnson was discouraging fans from making the trip to another city in order to conserve fuel.

The day following his father's funeral, Babe Ruth was back in Boston, but he was not in the lineup. Hack Miller played left field as Carl Mays went for his 20th win. In the eighth inning, Ty Cobb slugged a ball to the opposite field. Miller played it poorly and the ball got past him; when he chased after it, he fell down. Amos Strunk was late backing up the play and Cobb easily circled the bases for a two-run, inside-the-park home run. Mays was furious. He was in line to receive an additional $1,500 if he won 20 games, and the rookie's blundering play might have cost him the bonus. Mays yelled at Miller from the mound, his voice audible throughout the grandstand. The Tigers won 6-3, their first victory of the year at Fenway in nine tries.

The next day, Joe Bush relied on nothing but fastballs. He struck out the side in the first inning, fanned two in the second and struck out the side in the third. With his eighth strikeout, Bush walked off the mound to a standing ovation. The Red Sox scored in the fourth on Stuffy McInnis's single. Bush added one strikeout in the fifth, two more in the seventh and one to start the eighth, but he had gone deep in the count on many batters and was tired. After he surrendered three eighth-inning singles and a line drive glanced off his glove, Detroit won again, this time 2-1. Bush finished the day with 13 strikeouts, three shy of the American League record set by Rube Waddell in 1908.

Cleveland began the day 3½ games behind Boston. The Indians trailed 3-2 in Philadelphia, but had the bases loaded with two outs in the fifth. Athletics first baseman George Burns knocked down Doc Johnston's line drive, but it rolled away. The tying run scored and Tris Speaker rounded third. Pitcher Roy Johnson got the ball, fired it home and Speaker was called out by umpire Tom Connolly.

Speaker ranted at Connolly for a full 15 minutes, at times being restrained by the other umpire and players from both teams. The more Speaker shouted, the angrier he became, eventually wriggling loose and punching Connolly in the head. He likely would have done more damage if Joe Wood and Rube Oldring hadn't finally dragged him away. The next day, Ban Johnson gave Speaker an "indefinite" suspension, which would undoubtedly cover the last six games of the season.

On August 28, with Joe Wood substituting in center, the Indians lost 1-0. But that was the only game Speaker missed. Both Cleveland and Boston were rained out the next day, and Speaker returned for Cleveland's final four games. The *Cleveland Plain Dealer* confused matters even further by reporting, "It is not expected that Tris Speaker will be suspended. Umpire Connolly did not have him chased from the field. Speaker did not strike the umpire."

Most accounts of the 1918 season call Speaker's suspension the "death knell" for the Indians' pennant chances. But the Indians were 2½ games out of first place when the suspension was announced, and they finished the season 2½ games behind. Speaker played in his team's last four games and they won them all. Cleveland simply ran out of season, as owner James Dunn had feared.*

---

* There were rumors that Ban Johnson was reluctant to suspend Speaker because of his own financial connection to the Indians. Johnson had always furiously denied any conflict of interest, but in August 1919, he finally admitted owning $58,000 in Indians stock.

If the schedule had been left to Ed Barrow, the Red Sox would not have played three doubleheaders in four days before the World Series. The Red Sox had twinbills against Philadelphia on both Friday and Saturday, then two games against the Yankees on Monday. The team would leave for Chicago on Tuesday.

Connie Mack arrived with a skeleton crew: three pitchers, two catchers, seven regulars and Rube Oldring as the all-purpose substitute. Carl Mays coasted through a 12-0 blowout in Friday's opener—the Red Sox led 8-0 after three innings—his 20th win and eighth shutout. His bonus secure, Mays asked Barrow if he could pitch the second game as well. Mays knew Scott Perry was getting $500 from Mack for every win over 20 and Perry had been razzing Mays during the first game. "I got mine," Mays told Barrow. "I'll be damned if I'll let him get his."

Babe Ruth didn't come out to warm up as expected for the second game. In those days, in an attempt to thwart gamblers, teams didn't formally announce their starting pitchers before games; doing so drew a $25 fine. So when the Red Sox took the field and Mays trotted out to the hill with a big grin on his face, the crowd was surprised.

Mays allowed four hits in what was arguably a better pitched game and ended the season with a 21-13 record. His two wins began a streak of 23 consecutive victories against Philadelphia; he would not lose to the Athletics for another five years, until July 24, 1923. At his draft examination the next day, physician Werner Rollins called Mays the most remarkable physical specimen he had ever seen.

Because Connie Mack had only three pitchers on his roster, John Watson pitched two complete games on Saturday, losing 6-1 to Babe Ruth and winning 1-0 with a one-hitter. Ruth's victory in the first game clinched the third pennant in four years for Boston. If Ruth was grieving, it didn't effect his performance. After returning from his father's funeral, Ruth went 5-15 with two doubles.

Once the Indians were officially out of the race, James Dunn told the Browns his team wouldn't be playing Monday's games in St. Louis since many players were beginning war-related jobs on Tuesday. But the games were not meaningless. St. Louis was in fifth place, only 1½ games behind New York. If the Red Sox swept New York and the Browns swept Cleveland, St. Louis would finish in fourth place, meaning that, under the National Commission's plan, they would collect a share of the World Series revenue. So on Labor Day, with pitcher Grover Lowdermilk acting as umpire, the Browns took the field and two pitchers threw the required five balls each, with a 10-minute break between "games." St. Louis claimed the two games as victories by forfeit. After Harry Frazee protested the Indians' action, Ban Johnson disallowed the forfeits, the clubs' records reverted to what they had been, and the Yankees finished in fourth place.

Boston's regular season ended before 15,000 fans at the Polo Grounds on September 2. Sam Jones won the first game; his 16-5 record was the top winning percentage in the American League. In the second game, Jean Dubuc battled George Mogridge and lost 4-3. In the final innings, Barrow pulled his starters; when it was over, pitcher Walt Kinney was in right field and catcher Wally Schang was at shortstop. That evening, the Red Sox boarded a train for Chicago. The World Series would begin on Wednesday.

American League Final Standings

	W	L	Pct.	GB
Boston	75	51	.595	-
Cleveland	73	54	.575	2½
Washington	72	56	.563	4
New York	60	63	.488	13½
St. Louis	58	64	.475	15
Chicago	57	67	.460	17
Detroit	55	71	.437	20
Philadelphia	52	76	.406	24

Earlier in the day, George Whiteman had taken a boat ride on the Hudson River with Burt Whitman of the *Boston Herald and Journal.* "I'm lucky against those left-handed pitchers," Whiteman said, referring to Chicago's Jim Vaughn and Lefty Tyler. "No one is figuring I'll do much in the Series and you know it's the unexpected fellow who usually does the heavy work."

Whiteman had honed his batting eye against Mogridge in the season finale, going 3-4, hitting a home run and scoring all three Boston runs. "I may be the lucky fellow," he told Whitman. "I feel lucky enough to win two World Series."

18

THE MATCH-UPS

The Chicago Cubs returned from Pittsburgh on September 3, picked up their home uniforms and headed to Comiskey Park on the city's South Side. Charles Weeghman had decided his club would play in the bigger ballpark. He had also hoped his men would wear newly-designed uniforms for the Series, something both the White Sox and Giants had done the previous fall. The players voted that down, however, fearing a jinx.

Only a few Cubs had ever played in Comiskey, so during infield practice the players watched the afternoon shadows cutting across the diamond and how the ball caromed off the outfield fence. They discussed how the white sign on the center field scoreboard made it difficult to see the ball while batting, especially for right-handed hitters against left-handed pitchers. Paul Carter and Dixie Walker, two pitchers unlikely to get any playing time in the Series, threw batting practice for about an hour.

"There'll be no change in our batting order after that practice," manager Fred Mitchell said while three groundskeepers worked on the lawn and others hung the traditional red, white and blue bunting. "My players are all set. Their work was snappy and accurate."

"Who are you starting in the opener tomorrow?" one reporter asked.

"A left-hander. But I'm not going to tip my hand to Ed Barrow. I had planned on Jim Vaughn, but I've changed my mind about that. Vaughn and [Lefty] Tyler will both warm up and I'll go with whoever's in better shape."

Once the worst of the summer heat had passed, Tyler's performance had improved. "He's never pitched with all his skill in the middle of the season," said Mitchell. "From being with him for many years with the Braves, I know his habits and as soon as the cooler weather of August comes along, he gets real good and at his best is one of the finest left-handers in the game."

Some writers believed the Red Sox held an edge because they played at Comiskey Park during the season, but Mitchell thought any advantage would be negligible. "The Cubs are a faster team and a better hitting team," he said. "Every man from Flack down to the pitcher can hit. We out-hit Boston by 20 points and we've stolen almost 50 more bases. The teams are about equal in defensive ability, but even assuming Boston's claim that the pitching staffs are equal, what chance do they have? From what I've heard, if you stop Babe Ruth and Harry Hooper, Boston has a tough time scoring runs."

Carl Mays, Joe Bush and Sam Agnew arrived from Pittsburgh that afternoon, where they had been scouting the Cubs on Labor Day. Unfortunately, they didn't see many key players. Catcher Bill Killefer had dislocated a finger on his throwing hand, so rookie Bob O'Farrell was behind the plate. Three pitchers, Vaughn, Tyler and Phil Douglas, as well as reserve infielder Bill Wortman and outfielder Max Flack weren't at the park that day, either.

The three Boston player-scouts watched a little of the Cubs' workout, then waited for their teammates at the Hotel Metropole, a short distance from Comiskey Park. A persistent and clandestine effort by Ed Barrow had secured a furlough for Fred Thomas, the most reliable of the 10 men he had used at third base during the season. Fresh from the

Great Lakes Naval Training School and dressed in his white sailor's uniform, Thomas joined the others at the Metropole.

Babe Ruth strolled through the door shortly after 4:00 p.m. with an equipment bag slung over his shoulder and the rest of the team right behind him. Mays jumped up. "Babe, am I glad to see you," he said. "Joe and I were starting to think we'd have to pitch the whole Series ourselves." The men hadn't seen Thomas since late June, and they mobbed him, pumping his hand and slapping him on the back.

"Come on, boys, we're going right out for practice," Barrow announced. "We don't have much daylight left."

Since leaving New York, the Red Sox hadn't talked much about the Cubs or the Series. They relaxed, played cards, thumbed through *The Sporting News*. Ruth lost money at the card table, but laughed it off, saying bad luck at cards meant success in his next game. Ed Barrow, Harry Hooper and Heinie Wagner met in the manager's compartment for a short skull session, talking over their pitching plans and general strategy.

Watching the Red Sox work out, George Robbins of the *Chicago Daily News* thought everyone "from Barrow to the mascot" exuded confidence. Lefty Walt Kinney was the busiest man on the field, pitching a ton of batting practice. "My team is the best defensive club in the major leagues," Barrow said. "Having Fred Thomas back in the infield plugs up our only weak spot. We have some long distance hitters on the Red Sox, but look out for a surprise or two."

They didn't have to wait long. The Red Sox hadn't been on the field more than 10 minutes when Dave Shean dove after a line drive. The ball struck his throwing hand, ripping the nail and skin off the tip of the middle finger. Trainer Martin Lawler wrapped the injured finger in a splint. It seemed unlikely Shean would be able to play in the opening game; one report claimed that "the bone protruded from the hanging flesh." If Shean was out, Jack Coffey would start. (Coincidentally, Boston's second baseman in the 1916 World Series, Jack Barry, had been knocked out of commission when he was hit on the hand by a pitch.)

Besides Shean's injury, Stuffy McInnis's leg remained sore after he had twisted it chasing a foul ball in New York, and Harry Hooper was battling hayfever.

In the 15 years since the National and American Leagues had begun playing a post-season series, a team from either Boston or Chicago had been involved 11 times, but never during the same year. The Cubs won their pennant by 10½ games, so they were slightly favored. During the season, Chicago finished with a better record than Boston (84-45 to 75-51) and a higher batting average (.265 to .249), higher on-base percentage (.325 to .322) and higher slugging percentage (.342 to .327). The Cubs scored more runs (538 to 474) and had a higher average margin of victory (1.1 to 0.8). Their team ERA was lower (2.18 to 2.31) and was lower relative to the league average (-0.58 to -0.46). Both clubs relied heavily on pitching and it was clear that the men on the mound would dictate the course of the Series.

Starting Pitchers and 1918 Season Statistics
(league-leaders in bold)

	AGE	W/L	ERA	IP	H	BB	K	SH	OBA	OOB
Chicago Cubs										
Jim Vaughn	30	**22-10**	**1.74**	**290.1**	216	76	**148**	8	.208	.266
George Tyler	28	19- 8	2.00	269.1	218	67	102	6	.226	.279
Claude Hendrix	29	20- 7	2.78	233.0	229	54	86	3	.259	.305
Phil Douglas	28	10- 9	2.13	156.2	145	31	51	2	.246	.285
Boston Red Sox										
Carl Mays	26	21-13	2.21	293.1	230	81	114	8	.221	.284
Joe Bush	25	15-15	2.11	272.2	241	91	125	7	.242	.307
Babe Ruth	23	13- 7	2.22	166.1	125	49	40	1	.214	.277
Sam Jones	26	16- 5	2.25	184.0	151	70	44	5	.230	.312

SH=shutouts; OBA–opponents' batting average; OOB=opponents' on-base average.

The Cubs' 2.18 ERA was the best in baseball; Boston's 2.31 ERA was second only to Washington in the American League. Chicago had pitched 23 shutouts and Boston led the majors with 26. Both teams had the lowest opponents batting average in their respective leagues, Boston at .231 and Chicago at .239. Almost one-third of the Red Sox's 75 victories had been decided by one run.

It was no secret that Fred Mitchell would use his two left-handed aces as often as possible to stymie the entire Boston lineup and try to minimize Ruth's slugging. Jim "Hippo" Vaughn had completed the best season of his 10-year career. The six foot, four inch, 215-pound pitcher led the National League in wins, shutouts, ERA, strikeouts, most strikeouts per nine innings, fewest hits allowed per nine innings and lowest opponents batting average.

On May 2, 1917, Vaughn was involved in perhaps the most remarkable baseball game of all time. He faced the Cincinnati Reds in Cubs Park and after nine innings, both he and Fred Toney had no-hitters. Vaughn finally allowed a hit in the top of the 10th, and lost the game 1-0 when his throw home on Jim Thorpe's swinging bunt bounced off his stunned catcher's chest protector. Toney finished with a ten-inning no-hitter. Toney set a record two months later by winning both ends of a doubleheader and allowing only three hits in each game.

Vaughn had a hard fastball and good control, but carried a reputation of buckling in important games. Burt Whitman of the *Boston Herald and Journal* wrote that "Vaughn's record for 'gameness' has been none too solid and substantial in big games" and claimed that Mitchell was skeptical of Vaughn's "mental balance" as a Game One pitcher.

George "Lefty" Tyler had pitched for the Boston Braves for eight years before being traded the previous winter. He had faced some older members of the Red Sox during spring training in 1915, including Ruth, then a rookie. Tyler, a dairy farmer in New Hampshire during the off-season, was smaller than Vaughn, but what he lacked in size he made up for in stamina. On July 17, Tyler had pitched 21 innings against the Phillies—the longest complete game in Cubs history.

William Spargo of the *Boston Traveler* believed Tyler would have better luck against Boston than Vaughn. "Tyler hasn't the speed of
Vaughn," he wrote. "He throws a sweeping outcurve ball, delivered with
a cross-fire motion, a good slow ball and a better change of pace than
Vaughn." Boston won only 11 of 29 games against left-handed pitchers
in 1918; junkballers such as Reb Russell, George Mogridge and George
Tyler could frustrate the Red Sox hitters. Harry Hooper believed that
left-handed hitters like himself, Amos Strunk and Ruth would do just
fine against Tyler, but Barrow disagreed. The manager decided that
Ruth wouldn't start against Tyler; George Whiteman would be the left
fielder.

Why would Barrow purposely leave his best hitter on the bench? Did
he question Ruth's concentration so soon after his father's death? It
made no sense. Followers of the game believed that Ruth didn't hit as
well against left-handers, but Babe didn't buy it and it was not borne
out by his statistics. "I've been just as sure against left-handers after the
first few months of the season as I have been against right-handers," he
said. "I can see one just as well as the other now."

Ruth's time at first base and in the outfield had limited him to only
19 starts as a pitcher, a significant drop from his 41 and 38 starts the
previous two seasons. Yet on the eve of the World Series, Ruth was the
hottest man on the staff, having won 9 of his last 11 starts; he had batted
.354 as a pitcher.

Carl Mays had slumped in the last five weeks of the season. In 10
starts from July 25, his record was 4-6, and he allowed four or more
runs in seven of those games. Barrow considered using Mays when Bill
Klem was the plate umpire, since Klem generally called a lower strike
zone and Mays kept the ball down. Klem would be behind the plate for
Game Three.

After Dutch Leonard had left the team and when Ruth would refuse
to pitch, Sam Jones had been the answer to Barrow's prayers. After a few
erratic performances when he was used sporadically, Jones went 13-2

and had won his last five games, including two by shutout. He had a superb slow ball and his deceptive delivery made his fastball appear even quicker; the common complaint was "it's on top of you in a second."

Joe Bush had the lowest ERA of any Boston pitcher, but bad luck and poor run support left him with a 15-15 record. In the last month, Bush had gone 1-6; four of those losses were by scores of 2-0, 1-0, 2-1, and 1-0. Bush tied a league record by winning five 1-0 games—that record still stands. His opposite number on the Cubs was Phil Douglas, who had a 10-9 record despite a similarly low ERA.

Thirty-year-old Bill Killefer was one of the National League's top catchers, having been sold to the Cubs after seven years with the Phillies. He was a weak hitter (.233 in 1918) with little power, but he had a strong, accurate arm and a talent for working with pitchers. "If anything should happen to Bill Killefer," Hugh Fullerton wrote in the *New York Evening World,* "the Cubs would lose this Series almost beyond doubt." Killefer's injured finger was not expected to keep him out of any games.

Either Sam Agnew or Wally Schang would catch for Boston. Schang was the better hitter (.244 to .166), especially against left-handers, but the rifle-armed Agnew had a better glove.

Both teams showcased World Series veterans at first base: Stuffy McInnis had played in three World Series with the Athletics (1911, 1913 and 1914) and Fred Merkle was making his fifth World Series appearance after seasons with the New York Giants (1911, 1912, and 1913) and Brooklyn Dodgers (1916). McInnis was a speedy runner and a good bunter, although his batting average had been the worst of his career (.272). Merkle had a fantastic season, hitting .297, one of the highest marks of his 12-year career; he was fourth in the league with 65 rbis, fourth in doubles and fifth in total bases.

In 1917, Dave Shean looked like a weak hitter past his prime, but he had found a home in Boston, hitting a career-high .261 and working well with shortstop Everett Scott. His recent injury cast doubts on his effectiveness, despite his claims that his taped finger would not hinder his fielding or batting grip.

Rollie Zeider, known as "Bunions" because of his chronic foot trouble, had played for three Chicago teams in his career, the White Sox, Whales and Cubs. In 79 games in 1918, he batted .223. Charlie Pick spent time at both second and third, batting .326, much higher than his .241 mark as the Athletics third baseman in 1916.

Charlie Hollocher was the only Chicago batter to hit over .300. The 22-year-old rookie had been a highly touted prospect with Portland in the Pacific Coast League, but he exceeded all expectations in 1918. He led the National League in hits (161) and total bases (202), was second in on-base percentage (.379), third in stolen bases (26), and fourth in runs scored (72) and batting average (.316). He struck out only 30 times in 509 at-bats and had good range in the field.

Everett Scott (.221) was not in Hollocher's class as a hitter, but the Deacon had what one writer called "gambler's nerve"—an ability to remain clear-headed and composed under pressure—and his glove work was unrivaled. In 1918, Scott committed only 17 errors; other shortstops, by comparison, had 32 (Buck Weaver), 37 (Joe Dugan), 48 (Donie Bush), 49 (Ray Chapman) and 57 (Doc Lavan). Jimmy Austin of the Browns had 18 errors, but he had fielded only 293 chances compared to 706 for Scott. With 53 errors, Hollocher's fielding percentage was .929, fifth best in the National League.

The return of third baseman Fred Thomas boosted the entire team's confidence even though he hadn't played major league ball since late June. As a rookie, Thomas batted .257 in 44 games. A few weeks before the end of the season, Ed Barrow had contacted the commanding officer at the Great Lakes Naval Training Station and asked if Thomas could get a furlough in order to play in the World Series. Fortunately for Boston, Thomas's work at the facility was expendable and because he worked in the athletic department, he had been playing ball nearly every day.

Charlie Deal had been the Cubs' third baseman until he jumped the club for work in a munitions plant. When he heard the World Series would be played, Deal called Fred Mitchell about getting his job back. Deal played for Mitchell on the 1914 Braves and was a solid infielder who guarded the foul line well. He batted .239 for Chicago, his fifth team in seven years.

Deal happened to have an odd connection to Babe Ruth. In the summer of 1917, about the time Ruth was suspended for punching umpire Brick Owens, the National Commission investigated a claim filed by Deal against Ruth for $100, the balance due on a car Babe had bought from him in 1916. Ruth hadn't contested the claim, which the Commission took as an admission of guilt, ruling that Ruth could not return to the Red Sox until he paid the $100. Once the Commission discovered that the debt had already been settled, Ruth was given an apology and put back in good standing.

Les Mann, Chicago's 24-year-old left fielder and one of their on-field leaders, hit .288, the second highest mark of his six-year career. In 1918, Mann also reached personal bests in doubles, stolen bases and walks. He covered more ground, had a stronger arm and was superior in the outfield to both George Whiteman (.266) and Hack Miller (.276 in only 12 games).

But no one thought too much about those men. Everyone assumed that when he wasn't pitching, Babe Ruth would play left, even if the Red Sox had been giving out information to the contrary. Ruth had played in 95 games, batted .300 and with approximately 80 fewer plate appearances, tied Tilly Walker with 11 home runs. At .555, Ruth's slugging percentage topped both leagues. His talents as both a hitter and a pitcher made him unquestionably the sport's most valuable player.

After seven years with the Philadelphia Phillies, Dode Paskert was traded to the Cubs in 1918. The 37-year-old center fielder had his best season since 1912, batting .286 and finishing with 125 runs produced, second behind George Burns of the Giants (127).* Les Mann was third with 122.

Red Sox center fielder Amos Strunk hadn't been happy leaving his hometown of Philadelphia, where he had played since 1908, and it showed. Strunk had a horrible year, batting only .257, driving in a meager 35 runs and walking only 36 times in 114 games.

Harry Hooper and Max Flack were both terrific right fielders with strong arms, but Hooper held an edge as the better leadoff hitter. The Red Sox captain tied for second in the American League in both doubles and triples, was third in runs scored and walks, and fifth in runs produced and on-base percentage. Hooper had also helped Ed Barrow steer the team through the stormy summer.

Flack had broken in with the Federal League and joined the Cubs in 1916. He batted .257 and his on-base percentage of .343 was 50 points lower than Hooper's. Flack finished second in the National League with 56 walks; Hooper had 75.

Hugh Fullerton, one of the country's top sportswriters, looked at the Cubs–Red Sox match-up in a 10-part preview in the *New York Evening World*, "Doping The World's Series." Fullerton used a personal statistical formula to measure "Position Strength" which included "hitting, waiting out pitchers, long-distance hitting, getting hit by pitched ball, speed" and defense. He would calculate "each man's value and then figure how his values, both in attack and defense, will be affected by the opposing team." Fullerton concluded that the margin was "too small to indicate any marked superiority for either team," but in his final analysis, he believed the Cubs would prevail in six games.

Most of the other scribes agreed with Fullerton's dope, including Henry Edwards of the *Cleveland Plain Dealer*, Thomas Rice of the *Brooklyn Eagle*, Bill Phelson of *Baseball Magazine* and George S. Robbins of the *Chicago Daily News*. New York syndicated writer Joe Vila

* Runs produced is equal to runs batted in plus runs scored minus home runs.

thought Chicago would win because of its left-handed pitchers and the "yowling, heartless rooters" at Comiskey Park.

Connie Mack of the Philadelphia Athletics thought the schedule gave Boston an edge. Eddie Hurley of the *Boston Evening Record* said the Red Sox "are the better defensive club of the two" but questioned whether the team could score enough runs to win. Burt Whitman of the *Herald and Journal* said Boston would win in six games: "On paper, the Cubs figure 'to beat' the Red Sox…[but] this series will not be played on a typewriter."

As soon as the Red Sox left the Polo Grounds on September 2, rumors flew about who would start Game One on Wednesday. Mays was the early candidate during the Yankees series. On Monday, Ruth became the favorite, but by evening, as the team traveled west, it was Jones. Bush looked like Barrow's choice on Tuesday, and on Wednesday, the speculation had come full circle, back to Mays. Hugh Fullerton speculated that Mays might not pitch in Chicago at all because his unusual delivery was ill-suited to Comiskey's higher mound.

Harry Frazee had been in Pittsburgh for the premier of one of his theatrical productions and arrived in Chicago on Tuesday. Frazee made it clear that Ruth's bat was more important than his arm; he didn't want Ruth on the mound at all. Barrow said next to nothing: Mays, Ruth and Bush were ready, although he conceded Bush would be his choice on an overcast day, since his fastball would be hard to see.

Boston sportswriters Burt Whitman, Edward Martin and Paul Shannon chatted with Ruth in the lobby of the Hotel Metropole. "Babe, I hear Barrow's going with you tomorrow."

"I hope he'll start me," Ruth said. "I can win and start the team off right. Hell, I'd pitch the whole Series, every game, if they'd let me."

The men chuckled. "I could do it," Ruth insisted, sounding a little wounded. "I used to pitch three games in one day when I was at school. I pitched a 13-inning game one Saturday when I was with Baltimore and then pitched a doubleheader the next day—and the second game went 13 innings, too! Damn, what are all those guys that have been boosting me going to think if I'm not in there?"

And Ruth had plenty of boosters.

"The mighty shadow of Babe Ruth falls athwart Chicago tonight like a menace," Whitman wrote. "Never did one man count so heavily in the before-the-game pressure of a World Series…. [T]here he is, a huge, human, horrifying prospect for Mitchell and his men, absolutely unruffled and calm. He is the difference between defeat and victory…. If the Sox win the Series…H. H. Frazee should erect a statue to the Colossus of Clouters."

Another *Herald and Journal* writer opined, "If Babe Ruth can get the proper focus of the Chicago stockyards, he might cause a stampede among the cattle by walloping a home run out in that direction."

American League umpire Billy Evans, covering the Series for the *Chicago Daily News*, wrote that Ruth "is one of the most remarkable players in the history of the game" and called his swing "a thing of beauty. He doesn't hold back, regardless of who is doing the pitching…. It is curtains when he meets the ball squarely. On a warm day he keeps the catcher and umpire cool because of the air disturbance due to his giant swings." The *Daily News* described Ruth eating "enough for three ordinary persons" and "prepared to strike terror in the [Cubs]."

The papers made it sound as though a rampaging conqueror had arrived, the likes of which Chicago had never seen. Fred Mitchell bristled at all the attention paid to Boston's slugger. "The Sox are a one-man team," he said, "and his name is Ruth. But we have studied his ways and his mental processes and we will spike his guns. We will out-hit the Sox and out-fight them. Vaughn and Tyler will be able to stop Ruth's batting."

Harry Frazee, top row far left, in the only photograph of him with the 1918 Red Sox. Walt Kinney and Babe Ruth—Boston's hat-smashing duo—stand side-by-side with arms crossed, top row, third and fourth from left. (*Transcendental Graphics*)

The 1918 Chicago Cubs. Back row: Bill Killefer (second from left), Otto Knabe (fourth from left), Rollie Zeider (second from right). Middle row: Max Flack (far left), George Tyler (second from left), Jim Vaughn (second from right), Dode Paskert (far right). Front row: Charlie Deal (far left), Charlie Hollocher (third from left), Manager Fred Mitchell (fourth from left), Les Mann (third from right). (© *Bettmann/CORBIS*)

Above, iron-man shortstop Everett Scott. (*Baseball Hall of Fame Library, Cooperstown, N.Y.*) Top right, ticket stub from Boston's 4-3, 10th-inning victory at Philadelphia on July 5, 1918. (*Author's Collection*) Submarine pitcher Carl Mays, bottom right, won 21 games in 1918. (© *Bettmann/CORBIS*)

Carl Mays, top left, was Boston's other ace and in many ways the antithesis of Babe Ruth. (© *Bettmann/CORBIS*). Stuffy McInnis, top right, played first and third base for Boston in 1918. (*Baseball Hall of Fame Library, Cooperstown, N.Y.*)

Babe Ruth signs bats for U.S. military camps. (© *Bettmann/CORBIS*)

Left, Sam Jones on September 4, 1918, before Game One of the World Series in Chicago.

Right, center fielder Amos Strunk came to Boston from Philadelphia in a trade.

(Baseball Hall of Fame Library, Cooperstown, N.Y.)

At age 35, after 13 years in the minor leagues, outfielder George Whiteman became a World Series hero. (*Baseball Hall of Fame Library, Cooperstown, N.Y.*)

Shean scoring; fourth inning, first game, Killefer, Vaughn and Umpire O'Day watching the play; Scott stepping out of batter's box while play is in progress.
Photo by Burke, Chicago.

WORLD SERIES SCENE, CHICAGO, 1918.

Top, a page from the *1919 Reach Official American League Guide.*
Above, Chicago's Comiskey Park, site of the first three World Series
games. (*Transcendental Graphics*).

An evening paper tells the tale of Babe Ruth's Game Four heroics.

The Cubs warming up at Fenway Park, with the left field wall, "Duffy's Cliff" and the flag pole in the background. (*Transcendental Graphics*)

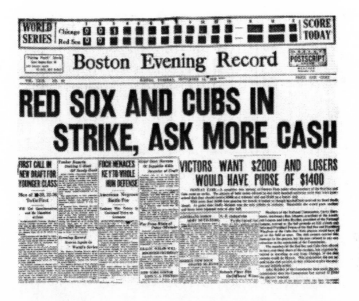

News of the players' delay before Game Five hits the streets. Below, several Red Sox players on the first base side of Fenway Park, with the sparsely populated center field bleachers behind them. *(Transcendental Graphics)*

Previous page and above: lineups for the Cubs and Red Sox as printed in the score cards sold at Fenway Park for ten cents. The numbers beside the players' names were not worn on their uniforms, but were used only to identify them on the scoreboard.

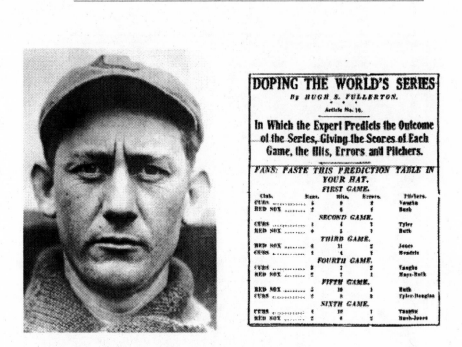

Left, Gene Packard: Did he fix the 1918 World Series? (*Baseball Hall of Fame Library, Cooperstown, N.Y.*)

Right, Hugh Fullerton, *New York Evening World* sportswriter, previewed the Series and offered his predictions.

Umpire Bill Klem calls Chicago's Fred Merkle out at third base in the ninth inning of Game Four. Boston's Fred Thomas took the throw from Stuffy McInnis on Bill Wortman's bunt. In the center of the photo is Red Sox pitcher Joe Bush, who relieved Babe Ruth. Boston turned a double play on Bush's next pitch, which ended the game, a 3-2 victory for the Red Sox. (*Baseball Hall of Fame Library, Cooperstown, N.Y.*)

Front page news, *Boston Post*, September 10 and 12, 1918.

Boston's Last Champions. Top row: Secretary Larry Graver, Walt Kinney, Carl Mays, manager Ed Barrow, Wally Mayer, Sam Agnew, John Coffey, trainer Martin Lawler. Middle row: George Whiteman, Heinie Wagner, Harry Hooper, George Cochran, Joe Bush, Babe Ruth, Dave Shean, Amos Strunk. Bottom row: Everett Scott, Jean Dubuc, Bill Pertica, Stuffy McInnis, bat boy, Sam Jones, Wally Schang, Hack Miller. (*Author's Collection*)

19

GAME ONE:
"THANKS FOR CONVINCING
ME I WASN'T A CATCHER"

Shortly before sunrise, it began to rain. The dreary weather, with strong winds off Lake Michigan and a hint of sleet, was expected to last all day and possibly into the night. The night before the White Sox hosted the New York Giants in the 1917 World Series, more than 2,000 fans had camped outside Comiskey Park. They huddled under blankets, built bonfires and drank coffee as they speculated on the Series. Chicago hotel managers were forced to put cots in hallways to accommodate the crowds. When a group of policemen arrived at Comiskey Park on Wednesday morning, ready to maintain order, they found only 50 people bunched near the grandstand entrance. A few salesmen were at their carts preparing sandwiches. Inside the park, 15 sheep grazed on the outfield grass.

Herman Schultz had taken the train from Goodland, Indiana, to attend the Series with his friend Isabelle Huncker. They waited near the front of the ticket line until 9:00 a.m. before leaving to dry off, confident they would have no problem getting good seats. Even though the Cubs were selling tickets to individual games rather than the usual three-game packages, it was unlikely that the game would sell out. It was the first time newspaper advertisements had been needed to announce World Series tickets and thousands still remained available.

Local gamblers were surprised at the lack of interest. On the city's South Side, fans stayed true to the American League and bet on the Red Sox. One person willing to wager on the Cubs was Phillies manager Pat Moran, who bet $500.* Chicago sportswriter Matt Foley was shocked— Moran was such a skinflint, Foley said, he was "one of those fellows who would ask odds before betting a nickel that there is a war."

For fans unable to go to the ballpark, the only way to hear about the games was to grab an afternoon or evening paper, which would have the linescore above the headlines and the raw details inside, or to hang out in front of the various bars and newspaper offices where special score-boards had been erected. The boards varied in size and in the amount of information displayed. A telegraph operator would receive an update from the park, and the news—balls, strikes, men on base, runs scored— would be posted, recreating the game pitch-by-pitch.

A Boston promoter promised that at Tremont Temple, each game would be "completely reproduced" courtesy of "Howell's Baseball Machine." Helen Ruth decided to follow the action at the Boston Arena on St. Botolph Street, where the advertisement read:

> Real Life! Real Action! Watch The Ball!
> Doors Open at 1:30. Game starts at 3 P.M.
> A Comfortable Seat for 25¢ and 50¢.
> Bring the Ladies. Direct Wire to the Game.

---

* Moran managed the Cincinnati Reds the following year in the crooked World Series against the Chicago White Sox.

National Commission chairman Garry Herrmann phoned Charles Comiskey from the Congress Hotel Wednesday morning, checking conditions at the ballpark. "The umpires tell me the outfield is soaked," Comiskey reported. "Even if the rain stops by noon, the field won't be ready this afternoon." Herrmann met with interim National League president John Heydler (John Tener had resigned in early August) and at 10:20, they postponed the game. Notices were tacked up throughout downtown Chicago announcing that the three games would now be played on Thursday, Friday and Saturday. The games in Boston would not be affected.

With the schedule change, ticket sales for Saturday's third game picked up, further proof that not planning weekend dates had been a huge mistake. Harry Frazee and Charles Weeghman probably hoped the rain would continue and force a game on Sunday as well.

The postponement was fine with Ed Barrow, who thought the Red Sox could use another day of rest. Jack Coffey took indoor fielding practice, just in case Dave Shean couldn't play. "It's nothing," Shean told anyone who asked about his finger. "I'll be in there every game." Babe Ruth didn't mind the time off, saying, "It only postpones the killing one more day."

A soggy infield would hinder the speedier Cubs and the extra day of rest might work against their pitchers; Vaughn and Tyler were both "notoriously in line for wildness after a layoff."

After hearing of the postponement, some players went back to bed, a few hung out in the hotel lobby and read the papers, while others went to the movies. Several Red Sox visited the War Exposition in Grant Park, which included mock soldiers digging trenches and fighting ground and air battles.

Herrmann held court in his hotel suite, where he presided over a huge feast that included roast chickens, boiled hams, blood pudding, baked beans, cole slaw and plenty of drink. "Garry was a walking delicatessen," one observer wrote, "a connoisseur of sausage. He carried his own wherever he went."

Boston vaudeville musician Joe Daly treated the Red Sox to an hour of music at the hotel that night. Joe Bush sang along with Daly on several songs, including "The Land of Wedding Bells." Sam Jones won $44 at poker and remarked, "I hope it rains tomorrow."

Harry Frazee wanted a change in the umpiring system. In previous World Series, the plate umpire had always been from the home team's league. Because of this year's unorthodox schedule, Frazee wanted the umpires rotated for each game; his request was granted.

Early Thursday morning, a police wagon pulled up alongside Comiskey Park, and a half-dozen men were arrested. Rumors spread that it was a "slacker raid"—a round-up of men who were violating the work-or-fight order—but it turned out to be only a crackdown on the crap games being played in the ticket line.

Raids had been conducted in many cities all summer, but after the Labor Day work-or-fight deadline, they became more frequent. Men were pulled off the streets by soldiers and sailors, even by volunteer vigilantes. In hotels, saloons, dance halls and pool rooms throughout Chicago, men were stopped and asked for their draft card; anyone without a card was detained at a makeshift internment camp on a city pier. On Tuesday morning, September 3, in New York, early risers found all the subway entrances blocked; thousands were taken, some forcibly, to detention centers, where they waited all day and night to be questioned. In New Jersey, nearly 30,000 men were rounded up: 800 were inducted immediately and 12,500 more were reclassified. Congress ignored protests against the raids; the country needed fighting men.

Back at Comiskey, more than 300 people waited in the cloudy, damp chill for the remaining tickets that went on sale at 9:00 a.m. Fans wore overcoats and carried blankets to shield themselves against the wind. Vendors along the street sold food, gum and balloons. A few "speculators" tried to sell tickets for double or even triple face value with no success—cigar stores and hotels were offering excellent seats at regular prices.

The Red Sox were on the field two hours before game time, warming up, before the Cubs appeared. The grounds crew worked quickly to repair the ceremonial bunting damaged by the rain. A 12-piece brass band entertained the crowd and Babe Ruth hammered Walt Kinney's first batting practice pitch deep into the right field bleachers. Many early arrivals, seeing the Big Fellow for the first time, cheered.

A group of Royal Rooters, led by Johnny Keenan, had arrived from Boston the previous day and were in good spirits. The Red Sox players also had friends and family in town for support. Everett Scott's father was there with a rooting party from Buffington and Auburn, Indiana. Wally Schang's wife had traveled with the team from New York, and Schang's father and one of his brothers came up from Cincinnati. Joe Bush and Wally Mayer both had siblings in the crowd. Fred Thomas's father drove down from Milwaukee for the first game. He was a dead ringer for his son; upon seeing the elder Thomas, Red Sox scout Billy Murray said, "If Tommy wasn't playing, Barrow could put Thomas Sr. on the hot corner and get away with it."

The morning edition of the *Chicago Evening Post* listed Boston's lineup with Ruth in left field and Joe Bush on the mound, so it was no surprise when Bush started warming up in front of the Red Sox dugout. Five minutes later, Ruth was throwing beside him, and the fans were abuzz. When Barrow handed his lineup card to umpire Hank O'Day, it read, "Whiteman, lf" and "Ruth, p."

"Everyone expects me to start with Carl," Barrow had told Ruth that morning. "Jim Vaughn is almost sure to start for the Cubs, and if he does, I want to cross them up and pitch you. Don't say anything. I want this to be a surprise."

Chicago sportswriter Ring Lardner, the author of the recently published collection of baseball short stories, "You Know Me, Al," thought the truth was more complex. He claimed that Fred Mitchell chose

Vaughn as his pitcher only after Barrow had tapped Ruth; Mitchell actually preferred Lefty Tyler because, unlike Vaughn, Tyler could pitch the third game on one day's rest. Vaughn would have pitched Game Two, the travel day giving him an extra day off before Game Four in Boston. But now that Ruth had been announced, Mitchell was forced to play Vaughn, since he was a better hitter against left-handers. If Lardner's theory was correct, Barrow had accomplished his goal of disrupting Mitchell's pitching plans.

Harry Hooper stepped into the batter's box in the top of the first inning. Many White Sox fans were rooting for the American Leaguers and Hooper was warmly cheered. He looked at strike one, then tapped a swinging bunt to first base. Fred Merkle grabbed the ball with his bare hand and tossed it to Vaughn, who had hustled quickly off the mound. Dave Shean, in his normal spot in the order, punched an 0-2 pitch the other way, singling down the right field line. Amos Strunk forced Shean at second and Vaughn's first pitch to George Whiteman rolled away from Bill Killefer. Strunk took off for second, then inexplicably slowed down halfway to the bag, and was thrown out.

Babe Ruth's last World Series appearance, and his only Series pitching performance, had been against Brooklyn in 1916. In what remains the longest World Series game by innings, Ruth outlasted Sherry Smith 2-1 in 14 innings. Against the Cubs, Ruth got two quick outs before Les Mann's grounder hit a rock and bounced over Shean's head for a single. Mann had the green light to steal and even with Ruth's pitchout, Sam Agnew's throw was late.

Dode Paskert whacked a low liner to left. The ball dropped 10 feet in front of Whiteman and he misplayed it off his shin. His awkward, off-balance throw to third sailed over Fred Thomas's head and Ruth's alert backup behind the bag kept Mann from scoring. Paskert jogged into second.

Ruth started off Fred Merkle with a strike, but then kept the ball away, nearly throwing a wild pitch on ball three. The fourth ball was intentional and it loaded the bases for Charlie Pick.

Mitchell's choice of the left-hand hitting Pick was questioned as the game went on. More than a few writers thought Rollie Zeider's experience and right-handed bat made him a more logical choice against Ruth. Pick took ball one. Knowing Babe couldn't afford to fall behind 2-0 with the bases loaded, he should have been ready for the next pitch—but he wasn't. It was a called strike. Ruth moved Pick off the plate with ball two, then retired him on a fly ball. Whiteman was shallow and he drifted over into left-center field where he made the catch knee-high.

A fan sitting behind the Red Sox bench called Agnew over. "Sam, tell Babe to keep the ball inside on these fellows," he said, adding that he had $300 riding on Boston. "I've seen 'em all summer. Brush 'em back and he'll have no more trouble." When the Red Sox retook the field, Agnew and Ruth walked out of the dugout together. "Everything's okay, old boy," the catcher called over. "Babe says he'll do that."

There had been talk of more rain in the morning, but by 2:00 p.m. the sky was clear. The sun was shining, but it was still cool enough for overcoats. Attendance was disappointing. The upper tier of the grandstand was nearly deserted, and a number of box seats remained empty. It looked as though only the hard-core fanatics had shown up.

Ruth, batting ninth in the order, the pitcher's spot, had his first at-bat with one out in the third inning. A huge roar went up, as prolonged as any cheer made for the Cubs. Right fielder Max Flack backed up to the bleachers. Ruth lined Vaughn's 1-1 pitch to right-center field. Paskert slipped on the damp grass, but recovered quickly for the catch.

Vaughn had problems with his control early on, going to full counts on several Boston batters and allowing a hit in each of the first three innings. He began the fourth with four inside pitches to Shean. Strunk tried moving the runner to second, but that had been one of his weaknesses all season. This attempt was no different. On the first pitch, Strunk popped to Vaughn and Shean darted back to first.

Whenever the Red Sox had a man on first in the early innings, they would try hitting behind the runner. Max Flack was very shallow in right field and his strong arm made it unlikely that any Boston runner would advance to third. With Whiteman up, Flack again crept in behind the Chicago infield. But Whiteman pulled the pitch and drove a single to Hollocher's right and into left field. Shean stopped at second.

To Hugh Fullerton, sitting in the press box, Hollocher seemed horribly out of position. He was playing way over near second base against the right-handed hitting Whiteman, the same spot he had been in for Whiteman's previous single in the second, and Hooper's hit in the third. What's wrong with Mitchell? he wondered. Hadn't these guys scouted the Red Sox?

Stuffy McInnis took a fastball high. Mann was a little shallow in left field, hoping to prevent Shean from scoring on a single. But McInnis was a pull hitter—Joe Bush said he "couldn't toss the ball up by himself and hit it to right field"—and Mann was standing nearly 50 feet off the line. McInnis gave Shean the hit-and-run sign. Shean took his lead off the bag, leaning back as Hollocher bluffed a play. With Vaughn's pitch, Shean took off. McInnis guessed curveball and whacked the ball over Deal's head into left field, where it rolled slowly on the soggy grass. Mann made a hurried throw home, but Shean, who *The Sporting News* said "runs like a turtle on an iceberg," scored without a play. Boston led 1-0.

Whether Pick and Hollocher allowed Shean too large of a lead was questionable, but clearly Mann had been out of position. In the dugout, Shean gave Barrow and Lawler an update on his finger: he would remain in the game.

Ruth settled into a rhythm, retiring the Cubs in order in the fourth and getting two quick outs in the fifth before hitting Max Flack in the head with a pitch. The Cubs' leadoff man sat on the ground for a minute, then got up and jogged to first. Hollocher popped up and the inning was over. Ruth took a seat in the dugout next to Barrow. "Well, Eddie, I guess I took care of that Mann guy for you."

Barrow was confused. Before the game, when he and Ruth discussed the Chicago hitters, Barrow had mentioned Les Mann. "Don't let up on that guy," he had warned Ruth. "He's tough against lefties, so don't let him dig in. Dust him off a little if you want." But he hadn't said much about Flack.

Once Barrow remembered that Ruth never could recall names or faces, it made a bit of sense. Mann and Flack were about the same height, although Flack was thinner; more to the point, thought Barrow, Mann hits right-handed and Flack bats left-handed.

In the bottom of the sixth, the Cubs Claws, a bunch of Chicago rooters sitting behind their team's dugout, starting cheering for a rally against Ruth. Paskert and Merkle both singled and with runners at first and second and one out, Barrow, methodically pacing in the afternoon chill, told Sam Jones and Joe Bush to loosen up their arms.

In the other dugout, Fred Mitchell had some decisions to make. In the first inning, Charlie Pick had a poor at-bat with the bases loaded and was overmatched when Ruth struck him out in the fourth. Should Mitchell let him bat again or send Zeider in as a pinch-hitter? He decided to have Pick bunt and take his chances with the next batter, Charlie Deal.

Pick did his job, half-bunting, half-swinging a roller to McInnis, who took the play himself. With men at second and third, Ruth came inside to Deal and fell behind 2-0. The crowd started to make a little more noise.

Ruth battled back and Deal hung in, fouling off three straight pitches, the last one a rope down the left field line. Then Deal swung at a pitch that was probably ball four, and hit it to left center. Whiteman raced over and although the wind was strong and the ball almost popped out of his glove, he caught it to end the rally.

During the seventh-inning stretch, the brass band began playing an impromptu version of "The Star Spangled Banner." All the players faced the flagpole in right field; at third base, Fred Thomas stood at attention in a military salute. Only a few fans sang along initially, but by the end, most of the crowd had joined in—and then burst into the loudest cheers of the afternoon.

In the middle of the ninth, with their Cubs still trailing 1-0, some fans gave up and left. With two outs, Deal reached on an infield single and Chicago native Bill McCabe went in to pinch-run. Killefer swatted the longest fly ball of the afternoon to right field. Harry Hooper caught it on the run and in 1 hour, 50 minutes, Boston had upset the dope and won the opening game. It was the first shutout in a World Series opener since 1905, only the second 1-0 World Series game in 12 years.

Ruth's sixth-inning stumble had been his only lapse in concentration. From the sixth to the ninth, using his fastball and mixing in his curve to keep the hitters off stride, Ruth retired 10 straight batters. Coupled with his victory in 1916, Ruth had now pitched 22 consecutive scoreless World Series innings. Christy Mathewson's record of 28 innings was within reach in his next start. Sitting in the locker room, Ruth considered sending a telegram to Brother Matthias: "Thanks again for convincing me that I wasn't a catcher." But it was only a momentary thought, quickly forgotten amid his teammates' celebration.

"We got the jump on them today," Ed Barrow said. "First blood counts for a lot in a short series. We knew Ruth was the man to beat the Cubs, and Babe came through as expected. I'll certainly give him another start back in Boston."

The other star of the game was George Whiteman, whose father had come north from Texas to see his son in a big league game for the first time. At 35, Whiteman was the second oldest player on either roster (Dode Paskert was 16 months older) and had been completely ignored in the pre-Series hoopla. One of his two singles sparked Boston's rally and he made five catches in left field, three of which were tough chances on a windy afternoon that gave fits even to sure-handed stars like Hooper and Paskert.

The crowd was announced at 19,274, roughly 13,000 fewer fans than had attended the first game of the 1917 Series. Home plate umpire Hank O'Day thought it was also one of the quietest World Series games he had ever seen. There hadn't been a lot of cheering, not even from the Cubs Claws, and nothing approaching the usual umpire baiting. Gate receipts totaled $30,348, the lowest for a Series opener in more than a decade. Charles Comiskey put on a brave face and said, "When you stop to think that most of our boys between 21 and 31 are gone, and most of those at home too busy to get away, I think the attendance was large. Also, there are fewer out-of-town fans because of the high railroad prices."

White Sox catcher Ray Schalk watched the game with teammates Buck Weaver and Oscar Felsch. "Everything was done right," Schalk said. "No bad plays were pulled and the club that got the break won." It had been an afternoon of sizing up the other side: both teams testing the opposing catcher's arm and Boston trying a few hit-and-run plays but neither side had taken many risks.

"The whole thing in a nutshell is they hit one at the right time and we didn't," Fred Mitchell said. "That's all there is to it. But we aren't discouraged. We don't think the Red Sox showed they had anything on us." Mitchell said he and his coaches had "found the weak spots of the Red Sox and the score will tell a different story tomorrow." Clarence "Pants" Rowland, the White Sox manager, was covering the Series for the *Chicago Daily News*, and in his opinion, Babe Ruth was the American League's most consistent left-handed pitcher. "I wouldn't say the Red Sox are the strongest team that ever represented their league," Rowland wrote, but "the Cubs will have to play exceptionally high grade ball to win."

While everyone assumed Lefty Tyler would pitch Game Two, Barrow wouldn't commit to either Carl Mays or Joe Bush. But perhaps the bigger question for the Red Sox manager was who would play left field.

Ruth had struck out twice against Vaughn, the *Boston Globe* calling him "about as useful as a broken umbrella in a rainstorm." When it came to swinging the lumber, the *Boston Evening Record* noted, "Ruth looked like a thin dime...while Whiteman looked like ready money."

At 3:10 that afternoon, after perhaps three innings of the Ruth-Vaughn duel, a bomb concealed in a suitcase exploded inside the Adams Street entrance to Chicago's Federal Building. It was one of the busiest times of day: nearly 100 people were in the corridor when the bell in the building's dome signaled the clerks' change of shifts. Four people were killed and 75 were injured.

The suitcase had been hidden behind a radiator. The force of the blast tore the radiator out of the floor, hurling it 20 feet into the street, where it struck and killed a horse. Desks were destroyed, marble was torn out of the walls, and the street was filled with plaster, stone and broken glass. Every window on the first three floors of two buildings across the street were blown in; some windows as high as the 10th floor were shattered and many pedestrians suffered serious wounds from huge shards of falling glass.

The surrounding streets were quickly roped off and bayonet-wielding soldiers kept the crowds at a distance. A man suspected of planting the bomb was chased down Dearborn Street by a mob and caught after a wild chase. He was quickly surrounded and only the arrival of the police prevented a lynching.

Ninety-five members of the International Workers of the World, a socialist organization, had been recently convicted of obstructing the government's war program. The trial had begun in April 1918 and continued for five months, at that time the longest trial in U.S. history. The Department of Justice believed the Chicago blast was an act of revenge by the I.W.W.

William "Big Bill" Haywood, general secretary-treasurer of the I.W.W. (often called the Wobblies), was on the building's eighth floor when the explosion occurred; the courtroom of Federal Judge Kenesaw M. Landis, who had presided over the Wobblies' trial, was on the sixth floor. Within 15 minutes of the blast, police raided two I.W.W. headquarters, arresting nine men. By late afternoon, 20 suspects were in custody and a general roundup of Chicago's I.W.W. members had begun.

20

Game Two:
"An Inglorious Hunk of Poor Judgment"

On his way to Comiskey Park on Friday morning, Everett Scott spied two young boys peeking through a knothole in the outfield fence. A pile of school books lay on the sidewalk nearby.

"Hey, you kids," he called out.

They whirled around, startled.

"You boys trying to see the game?"

The kids exchanged glances and nodded warily. Scott introduced himself—and their worried looks changed to smiles. "It should be a good game today," the Boston shortstop said. "Let's see if we can find you boys a couple of tickets." They grabbed their books, Scott put a hand around each of their shoulders and they all walked in the direction of the box office.

A little while later, Ed Barrow informed Joe Bush he had the Game Two assignment. "We're sure to get Tyler," Barrow told the entire team. "He's a good left-hander. We won't make many hits off him, but he's not as fast as Vaughn. If we wait for our chance, we can beat him."

Barrow was saving Carl Mays for the third game. Mays's unique "bowling" style of delivery was bad news even for hitters who faced him regularly, so he was a strong bet to pitch well against the Cubs. He'd either put Boston up by three games or break a Series tie.

The weather was perfect—clear skies, 70 degrees—but the turnout was only slightly larger than the day before—a crowd of 20,040. There were plenty of sailors, dressed in their stark white uniforms, rooting for fellow "Jackie" Fred Thomas. Someone counted less than 100 women in attendance, which was low for a World Series game.

The brass band had set up in foul territory while the Cubs took batting practice. But after a few hard-hit balls whistled past and one musician was struck in the leg, the band moved further away. The Red Sox were in good spirits, laughing, even dancing a bit when the band played ragtime. Babe Ruth joked with some early arrivals during batting practice. When he missed two consecutive pitches, the crowd razzed him. "Watch this one," he laughed. He hit the next pitch into the bleachers and yelled, "I told you so!" Later, he and George Whiteman tossed a few beat-up balls to the fans in left field.

Groups of fans had also brought musical instruments and were playing and singing so loudly that they drowned out the reading of the lineups. Fans who did hear the announcements learned that both lineups remained identical, except for the pitchers.

Bush and Tyler had faced each other in Game Three of the 1914 World Series at Fenway Park, Tyler for the Boston Braves and Bush for the Philadelphia Athletics. In that game, both clubs had scored twice in the 10th inning before Bush's 12th-inning error allowed the Braves' Les Mann to score the winning run. The Braves finished their miraculous four-game sweep the next day. Seven players from that Series were in uniform today, including Charlie Deal, Stuffy McInnis, Wally Schang and Amos Strunk. Cubs manager Fred Mitchell had been the Braves' manager that season.

Before the game, the National Commission made two decisions that had players on both sides grumbling. For the first time, the Commission would mail World Series checks to individual players rather than leaving the distribution to the two teams. And every player on the winning and losing rosters would receive an equal share. That meant Boston pitcher Bill Pertica would receive as much as Babe Ruth; Charlie Pick, who had joined the Cubs in the season's final month, would take home the same amount as Charlie Hollocher, who had played in every one of Chicago's 131 games. Veterans on both sides were angry. The *Boston Herald and Journal* said it was a miserable mistake, but conceded the arrangement was "part and parcel with every move the Commission has made in its asinine plans for the Series."

Meanwhile, George Whiteman was in left field again. Ruth sulked for a while at one end of the dugout, but as soon as Harry Hooper walked to start the game, Babe was on his feet, shouting encouragement and razzing the Cubs. There had been some heckling in the opener, but now the volume and intensity of the bench-jockeying was intense. The fans picked up on the players' enthusiasm and became more animated, too.

The ugly feelings between the teams got a jump-start from Tyler's eighth pitch of the game. After Hooper walked, Dave Shean swung and missed an 0-2 pitch, and Hooper broke for second base. As Bill Killefer threw to second, Shean stepped across the plate, bumping Killefer's right arm with his bat. The ball landed in the middle of the diamond. Killefer protested and plate umpire George Hildebrand called Shean out on strikes and Hooper out on the batter's interference.

In the bottom of the first, Les Mann lofted a fly ball to short center. Amos Strunk jogged in, caught and then dropped the ball. He recovered right away, and threw to Shean for a force on Charlie Hollocher at second base. More than a few Cubs suspected Strunk had dropped the ball intentionally to erase the lead runner.

Whiteman walked on four pitches to start the second. The Chicago fielders, having learned their lesson the day before, shifted over to the left side for McInnis. But he crossed them up and bunted the other way, to the first base side. Tyler and Killefer chased after it, but they ran into each other and no play was made. Killefer called time. First baseman Fred Merkle, third baseman Charlie Deal, Tyler and on-deck batter Everett Scott gathered around. Merkle borrowed a handkerchief from umpire Hildebrand, wet one end of it and removed some dirt from Killefer's eye.

When play resumed, Scott bunted and Tyler narrowly missed colliding with Killefer again. The catcher threw the ball to Charlie Pick, who was covering first. With one out and runners at second and third, Fred Thomas grounded to second. Pick's sidearm throw home was awkward, but it was in time to get Whiteman. Sam Agnew popped the first pitch to Flack in right field foul territory and Tyler escaped unscathed.

Joe Bush had trouble controlling his fastball right away, so he relied on his curve, not his best pitch. He walked Merkle, then Pick bunted a high, inside pitch that dribbled towards Fred Thomas. He tried barehanding it on the run, but it rolled between his legs and the kindhearted official scorer ruled it was a single.

Deal popped up, then Killefer drilled a first-pitch double down the right field line, and Merkle scored. Hooper hustled and cut it off, eliminating any chance of a triple. Mitchell told Pick to stop at third, a decision which brought a chorus of boos when Hooper's throw went to second base instead of through to the plate.

The Red Sox infield came in on the grass. Tyler poked a fastball on the ground towards center. Scott dove to his left, but it scooted past him. Pick scored and Killefer rounded third. Amos Strunk's throw home was too late to get Killefer, so Sam Agnew came forward towards the mound, got the ball on one hop and fired to second. Scott slammed a hard tag on Tyler as he slid in, shaking up the pitcher.

Max Flack was safe on a close play on his grounder to McInnis, but he overslid second on a steal attempt and was tagged out.

Otto Knabe, the Cubs' first base coach, had been yelling at Bush throughout the three-run rally. "Look out, Joe!" he called as Tyler's single got through the infield. "You're not ducking fast enough! You'll be killed if you stay out there much longer."

The Boston players despised Knabe. In the spring of 1910, when he was the Phillies' second baseman, Knabe had an altercation with Heinie Wagner and Bill Carrigan. No punches were thrown, but resentment had lingered. Knabe had baited Ruth during Game One, but Ruth didn't react, later saying he hadn't heard them. When Wagner told Ruth about it, Babe went looking for Knabe, but the coach had left the park.

As the Red Sox left the field trailing 3-0, Wagner walked across the infield to take his spot in the third base coaching box; he met Knabe going in the same direction, towards the Cubs dugout. It is not clear exactly what was said—maybe a remark about Scott's hard tag on Tyler, the call at first on Flack's grounder, or Knabe's wish to fight some of the Red Sox—but both men started cursing.

"I'll knock your goddamn head off," Knabe yelled.

"If you wanna fight, you dirty bastard, let's go right now." Wagner pointed to the alleyway leading to the Cubs' clubhouse—the same place where Chick Gandil of the White Sox and Boston pitcher Lore Bader had squared off a year ago.

Wagner grabbed Knabe's arm and tried dragging him along the dugout floor. The chunky Knabe outweighed Wagner by at least 20 pounds—"A guy might as well try to wrestle a depth bomb," wrote one observer—with the Boston coach further handicapped by a splinted broken finger. Knabe quickly subdued Wagner, and Jim Vaughn apparently knocked him down before he, Knabe, Claude Hendrix and a few others started punching. Wagner claimed Knabe had also kicked him while he was on his back. "I wouldn't mind it if I was hit with a fist," he later said.

The crowd learned of the fracas when Carl Mays, Sam Agnew, George Whiteman and Hack Miller leapt off the bench and ran across the infield. Agnew, still wearing his shinguards, tossed his chest protector aside as he ran. A second wave of players, including Walt Kinney, Wally Schang and Babe Ruth, followed.

The brawl ended quickly, although Wagner remained on the floor. Several Cubs separated the two coaches, and Hendrix and infielder Bill McCabe met the Red Sox brigade near the on-deck circle. The umpires did not get involved; afterwards, third base umpire Hank O'Day, who had been closest to the Cubs dugout, said he hadn't seen or heard any fighting.

When Wagner finally emerged from the dugout, it was clear he had received the worst of it. His hair was a mess, his face pale and bruised, the back of his uniform torn and muddy. Agnew and Ruth hung over the rail of the Cubs' dugout, complying with the umpires' request to return to their bench only after they were sure Wagner wasn't seriously injured. Barrow told Ruth, "I need you to pitch in this Series, Babe, not fight."

When Knabe took his spot near first base in the bottom of the third, a steady stream of profanity poured out of the Boston dugout. Several Cub supporters moved down to the front of the grandstand, taunting the visitors and jeering anyone in a gray uniform. A policeman was stationed near each dugout for the rest of the game.

At that point, Bush began pitching almost exclusively inside—way inside. After Hollocher grounded out, Bush buzzed a fastball near Mann's head. Mann cursed Bush, but got no response. On the next pitch, Mann pushed a bunt up the first base line. Stuffy McInnis made the play unassisted, but when Bush dashed off the mound to cover the bag, he tried tripping Mann on his way to first. Then Bush made the next batter, Dode Paskert, duck away from a beanball before retiring him on an infield pop-up.

Tyler walked the Red Sox's leadoff batter in each of the first three innings, but the Red Sox were unable to exploit his lack of control. They didn't force him to throw strikes, swinging early in the count and chasing poor pitches.

Chicago had an opportunity to widen its 3-0 lead in the sixth. Hollocher tripled into the right field corner. With the infield in, Hollocher had to stay put on a ground ball. On a pickoff attempt, Sam Agnew's throw got under Fred Thomas's glove, but Thomas deliberately tangled himself up with Hollocher, so the runner couldn't advance. Already in a foul mood, the crowd howled for Thomas's blood.

Hollocher broke for home when Paskert chopped a grounder to short. It was a foolish play, perhaps borne of frustration, and Scott's throw was in plenty of time for the out. Paskert raced to third on Merkle's hit-and-run single to right, but Merkle was tagged out in a rundown on a double steal attempt.

Where Jim Vaughn used a hopping fastball and a sharp curve, Tyler relied on a floater and a rising pitch that crossed the plate at the neck and shoulders. Through five innings, Tyler had been just wild enough to be good, using the entire strike zone and keeping the Red Sox off balance.

Boston kept trying to chip away at Tyler. Leading off the sixth, Dave Shean smacked a line drive to left-center field. Paskert ran over and kept the ball in front of him, bare-handing it and holding Shean to a single. Paskert appeared to have strained a leg muscle on the play and limped for the rest of the game. Any hope of a Red Sox rally disappeared quickly, as Strunk grounded into a force and Whiteman hit into a double play.

In the seventh, McInnis grounded to Hollocher, whose wide throw pulled Merkle off the bag. The first baseman smacked McInnis in the neck with his glove as he ran past for the out. Was this retaliation for McInnis's hard tag on Hollocher the day before?

Wally Schang pinch-hit for Agnew in the eighth. His hot shot took an odd bounce and hit Hollocher in the stomach. One out later, Hooper singled to right, but Flack made a perfect one-hop throw to Charlie Deal at third and Schang was dead. It was a crucial out—instead of runners at first and second and one out, Boston had a man at first and two outs. Shean bounced to first and the threat vanished.

With the Red Sox down to their last three outs, Amos Strunk led off the ninth with a triple over the right fielder's head that hit the concrete wall on one bounce. Whiteman took a strike and then drove the ball over Paskert's head to center field. Outfielders usually played fairly shallow and were more concerned with snagging line drives punched over the infield than long balls flying over their heads. They also wanted to cut off hits between outfielders; in the more spacious parks, a ball in the gap could roll a long time. Whiteman's hit came to a rest near the word "Buy" on a war bond billboard. A faster runner would have circled the bases, but Whiteman had only a triple. Chicago's lead was now 3-1 and the potential tying run was at the plate. The many fans making their way towards the exits stopped.

Tyler had allowed two hits through seven innings, but he was tiring. In the eighth and ninth, Boston had struck for four hits, including two triples. Phil Douglas and Claude Hendrix were warming up, the third time in as many innings that Mitchell's bullpen was active. Killefer jogged out to the mound for a word with Tyler, as McInnis took a few practice swings outside the batter's box.

Instead of squeezing the runner home, McInnis swung away. He tapped a weak grounder right back to Tyler, who checked Whiteman back to the bag and threw McInnis out. Everett Scott was up next, then Fred Thomas. Fred Mitchell thought about intentionally walking Scott, but he knew Barrow would then pull Thomas, who was 0-6 in the Series and had hit only one ball out of the infield. Should Mitchell bring in Hendrix or Douglas—and risk one of his right-handers dealing with Babe Ruth as the game-tying run?

"When Tyler slipped a bit, I was thinking of changing," Mitchell said afterwards, "but I couldn't. I had to stay with my left-hander." Tyler didn't give Scott anything too good, and actually got ahead in the count 1-2, but ended up walking him.

Barrow had strongman Hack Miller on the bench and he also considered sending Ruth up against the lefty anyway. But knowing Babe had struck out twice against Vaughn, Barrow played the percentages. He sent up pitcher Jean Dubuc, a right-hand hitter. It was an odd choice. Dubuc, whose name was mispronounced "Dee-buck" by the Comiskey Park announcer, had batted .269 and .267 while with Detroit, but he had only six at-bats with Boston. If Barrow was intent on having a pitcher at the plate, Carl Mays, whose .357 on-base percentage was fourth best on the team, would have been a better option.

Tyler's first pitch was low and inside and Dubuc fouled it off. He took ball one, then looked at strike two. Dubuc kept battling, fouling off four consecutive pitches, the count holding at 1-2. Tyler came back with a slow curve that started high and outside, then broke sharply down. It was about a foot off the plate, but Dubuc reached out and swung anyway: strike three. There were two outs.

Schang was next, and Ruth waited on the dugout steps, black bat in hand, ready to hit for Joe Bush if Schang could keep the inning alive. Considering how hard Tyler had worked to get Dubuc, Schang should have looked at a few pitches. But he swung at the first one he saw, popping it up. Hollocher moved a few steps to his right, made the catch and ran quickly off the field, disappearing into the dugout with the baseball still in his glove. The Series was tied at one game apiece.

For the Red Sox, it was a game of missed opportunities. The leadoff batter had reached base in five of the first eight innings. Tyler toughened in the pinches, working slowly with his baffling curves and deceptive change-ups. His performance may not have appeared as commanding or as scintillating as Vaughn's, but most Red Sox hitters admitted that Tyler had given them more fits.

Bullet Joe Bush had good speed, but intermittent control. The Cubs were a good fastball-hitting team and they hit Bush harder than the 3-1 score indicated. (One writer suggested an amended nickname: Shrapnel Joe Bush.) He compensated by pitching inside, intimidating Chicago's 3-4-5 hitters; Mann, Paskert and Merkle were a combined 1-10, after batting 4-11 in the opener.

The Boston press was dumbfounded by Barrow's ninth-inning strategy. More than one writer demanded to know, "Where was Ruth?" Eddie Hurley of the *Boston Evening Record* thought Barrow showed "an inglorious hunk of poor judgment"; letting Ruth sit on the bench in the ninth inning was "nothing but criminal."

The Series was even, but Boston held an advantage: the Cubs had already used their two aces, while the Red Sox still had Carl Mays and Sam Jones. When asked which pitcher he would choose, Barrow said he hadn't committed himself to anything except a porterhouse steak for dinner. Rumors circulated that Jim Vaughn might return for the Cubs on one day's rest.

Back east, the Red Sox office announced that all 4,000 box seats for the games at Fenway were sold out. All remaining grandstand seats would go on sale Saturday morning, and there would be 19,000 "rush" (day-of) tickets for each game, alleviating the need for fans to sleep overnight outside the park.

Matt Foley of the *Chicago Herald and Examiner* thought the Cubs would get a rude reception at Fenway Park if the squabbling between the two teams continued. "Boston fans are notorious for their skill at 'riding' visiting teams," he wrote. "White Sox players can vouch for the deadliness of the Boston species of fanatic, and with a World Series at stake, the Hub customers can be expected to outdo their worst exhibitions."

George E. Phair, another *Herald and Examiner* writer, offered a lengthy poem after the second game:

The Unharmonious Series

I.

War, with its rampant spirit, rough and rude,
Came busting in and queered the quietude.
There was a rough house, underneath the stand,
A noble scrap which none but athletes viewed.

II.

Ofttimes the athletes mingle blow for blow
Beneath the stand, nor let the public know.
Why don't they fight upon the open field?
And give the fan some action for his dough?…

VI.

No more the athletes care for ball or strike.
Their minds are on the knuckle and the spike.
Come on, you Cubs! Come on, you Hose of Red!
For that's the kind of baseball game I like….

IX.

No more the athletes play in harmony.
They battle now in wild and ghoulish glee,
So why not change the baseball rules to-day
And can the umps and hire a referee?

21

GAME THREE:
PICK'S MAD DASH

More than one thousand high school students were among the fans lined up outside Comiskey Park on Saturday morning for tickets to the last major league baseball game to be played in Chicago until the end of the Great War. All the reserved seats were gone by noon; the Cubs anticipated a near-capacity crowd. Latecomers had to choose between the bleachers or haggling with sidewalk "speculators," some of whom were asking—and getting—as much as $5.00 for a $1.10 ticket.

Susan Constance Sawyer, the girlfriend of Red Sox third baseman Fred Thomas, and her older brother Wilfred had driven down from East Troy, Wisconsin, for the game. Connie, who used her middle name, had been writing to Fred at the Navy camp over the summer and now she finally had a chance to see him at the team's hotel. Fred arranged for Connie and her brother to sit behind the Boston dugout in the first base grandstand.

Red Sox starter Carl Mays hadn't pitched since his back-to-back wins against Philadelphia a week earlier. Ed Barrow and Harry Hooper were convinced that spitballer Claude Hendrix would pitch for Chicago, so they had Bill Pertica throw batting practice. Pertica had appeared in only one game for Boston and was nearly left off the Series roster, but his spitter had baffled Pacific Coast League hitters earlier in the summer, so Barrow brought him along to Chicago.

Hendrix warmed up before the game with a bit of slippery elm bark that his parents had brought from Kansas. He hoped the sticky bark would give his pitches some extra dart and dive and further bedevil the Red Sox. But when the Cubs took the field, Hendrix remained on the bench. It was Jim Vaughn who strode out to the mound.

The Red Sox were shocked. The crowd, equally surprised, gave Vaughn a standing ovation. Ruth sat on the dugout steps, disappointed, his black bat by his side; Vaughn's return on one day's rest meant Babe would spend the day on the bench. For the third day in a row, the Chicago crowd was treated to a pitching duel that kept them hanging on every pitch.

George Whiteman started the second inning with a single and the light rain that had begun a few minutes earlier began falling a little harder. People in the pavilion seats moved back under the grandstand roof, while fans in the bleachers used newspapers and scorecards as improvised umbrellas. Bill Klem, the plate umpire, saw no reason to pause the game, and it drizzled off and on all afternoon.

With Whiteman on first, Stuffy McInnis fouled off three bunt attempts and struck out. Wally Schang whiffed on a pitch up around his eyes. Vaughn was pitching as strongly as he had on Thursday. In fact, his fastball seemed to have even more zip. On the third strike to Schang, Whiteman stole second, then moved to third when Cubs shortstop Charlie Hollocher bobbled Everett Scott's slow grounder. Vaughn cut off the threat by getting Fred Thomas to fly to right.

Boston rallied again in the fourth. After freezing Amos Strunk with strike three, Vaughn worked Whiteman inside and ended up hitting him in the back. McInnis tried to hit-and-run on the first pitch, but fouled it off. When he swung and missed the next pitch, Whiteman was trapped off the bag. Bill Killefer hesitated for an eyeblink before throwing to first baseman Fred Merkle, and that slight pause allowed Whiteman to dive back safely.

Vaughn's 0-2 pitch was high and inside and McInnis punched it into left field. Schang followed with a single to center; Whiteman scored. McInnis slowed as he reached third, hoping to draw a throw so Schang could take second. But Dode Paskert didn't take the bait and tossed the ball to second base. Boston led 1-0 with runners at the corners. "Take him out," several frustrated fans shouted from behind the Cubs' dugout.

Ed Barrow was not a fan of the suicide squeeze, but he may have also suspected that the Cubs knew that. So with Scott, a good bunter, at the plate, the play was on. Scott dropped the first pitch right in front of the plate—a beautiful bunt—too far out towards the mound for Killefer to field it. As Vaughn reached down, he glanced at McInnis sprinting past, and the ball ran up his arm like a spooked mouse. Vaughn still had time to throw to first, but there was no one at the bag; Merkle had run in on the bunt and second baseman Charlie Pick didn't cover first. Vaughn was left holding the ball, visibly shaken. Boston led 2-0.

Thomas followed with a single to right field, his first hit of the Series. Heinie Wagner wanted Schang to stop at third, which would have loaded the bases and kept Vaughn on the ropes, but Schang ran through the stop sign. Flack's throw was perfect and Schang was easily tagged out. Mays lined out to center field and Vaughn, who had been on the verge of being sent to the showers, escaped with minimal damage.

For the Red Sox, Mays was nearly perfect. He walked the first hitter he faced, then set down 10 in a row, breezing through the third inning on only five pitches. Facing Mays for the second time, the Cubs had a clue about his repertoire and a better read on his delivery—and they hit him hard. Les Mann doubled with one out and the crowd chanted for a rally. Paskert whacked a fly ball to left center that looked like it might carry into the bleachers. Back, back, back, Whiteman sprinted, until he was literally against the wall—and grabbed the ball with a leap at the fence.

Paskert's long fly probably would have carried out of Cubs Park for a home run. But in Comiskey, Whiteman's catch silenced the crowd. The fans in left field, not known for acknowledging opposing teams' talent, stood slowly and applauded. Had playing their home games in another park hurt the Cubs? Chicago had 10 flyouts in Game One—gusts of wind and deep fences were keeping the balls in play.

If Carl Mays was worried about anything before the Series, it was whether National League umpires, unaccustomed to his unusual pitching style, would call his low pitches for strikes. The high-ball-hitting Cubs were laying off the low ones, but plate umpire Bill Klem was calling them strikes as long as they were even with the batter's knees. Mays worked calmly and deliberately; when there were men on base, he slowed his rhythm even more and threw repeatedly to first. Mitchell and Knabe asked Klem to check a few of the balls, but no illegalities were found.

After his near-disastrous fourth inning, Vaughn was untouchable. He kept the ball in the infield in both the fifth and sixth innings, and at one point retired 13 Red Sox in a row. Meanwhile, his teammates threatened to tie the game again and again.

Charlie Pick's fifth-inning grounder slipped under Everett Scott's glove and slowly rolled into center field. By the time Amos Strunk could grab it, Pick was on second. (Scott was initially given a two-base error, but the call was changed to a double.) After Deal flew out, Killefer banged a single off Scott's bare hand into left. Whiteman charged in, but there was no play to make. Pick scored, cutting Boston's lead to 2-1. Killefer, perhaps thinking the Red Sox defense was unnerved, broke for second on Mays's 2-0 pitch to Flack. Schang's throw was low, but Everett

Scott dug it out of the dirt and put the tag on Killefer's spikes as he slid into the bag.

Mann and Paskert both singled with two outs in the sixth, but were stranded when Merkle struck out swinging. With one out in the seventh, Deal was safe on an infield hit to third. All of Chicago's six hits had come within the last 14 batters—nearly every other Cub was reaching base. Mays threw over to first several times as his rhythm slowed from deliberate to tedious. Tired of waiting in the batter's box, Killefer complained to the umpire and Klem ordered Mays to pitch. When Killefer bounced back to the mound, Mays threw him out. Deal took second but died there when Whiteman made a splendid catch of Vaughn's long fly to left.

In the eighth, Mays retired the top of the Cubs' order 1-2-3. Facing the daunting prospect of winning three games at Fenway Park, where opponents had won only one out of every four contests all season, Chicago scraped together one more rally in the ninth. Paskert took two strikes, then two balls, before grounding out to Scott. Merkle tapped a pitch in front of the plate. Mays and Schang went after the ball "like a starving man going after a frankfurter." Mays grabbed it and tossed to McInnis for the second out.

Charlie Pick was the Cubs' last hope. If George Whiteman was the Red Sox's most surprising player in the Series, his Chicago counterpart was Pick. Mitchell had taken a lot of heat for playing Pick, but the second baseman was 2-8; both hits had led to runs, including Chicago's only run against Mays. When Pick fell behind 0-2, the Cubs' batboy began gathering up equipment. Pick tapped a skittering ground ball towards right field. Dave Shean made a one-handed stop on the edge of the outfield grass, but couldn't make a good throw and held the ball. Pick was safe on first.

Fred Mitchell sent Charlie Deal back to the dugout and brought in Turner Barber, a left-handed singles hitter. Barber had batted .236 in 55 games and was 4-20 (.200) as a pinch-hitter. Mays's first offering was ball one. On the next pitch, Pick sprinted to second. Wally Schang tended to throw the ball in the dirt, as he had done in the fifth. This time his throw was right on the money—but Shean bobbled it. Pick made a great fall-away slide and the Cubs were still alive.

Barber waved his stick frantically, awaiting the 1-1 pitch. He reached out and smacked a line drive that landed about six inches foul down the third base line. Schang again set up outside, but Mays threw too far outside. The ball glanced off Schang's mitt and rolled a few yards to his left behind the plate. As Pick ran to third, Schang fired a throw to Fred Thomas. Pick and the baseball arrived at almost the same time. Umpire George Hildebrand began calling Pick out, then saw Thomas hadn't held onto the ball. He spread his arms: "Safe!"

Thomas and Pick were tangled in the dirt. Pick had overslid the bag and was on his stomach, trying to crawl back and touch the base with his hand. Thomas was yelling at Hildebrand, arguing that Pick had kicked the ball out of his glove. Fred Mitchell, coaching at third base, shouted at Pick: "Get up! Get up! Go, go, go!"

The ball had stopped rolling about 20 feet away in foul territory. Pick took off. Thomas finally ran over and grabbed the ball. He had no time to set himself, but his throw was straight and true. Pick slid in, spikes high, and Schang tagged him in the ribs a foot or two from the plate. The crowd exhaled a huge, collective groan. The Cubs had come so close, but Boston's razor-thin victory gave them a 2-1 lead in the Series, with every remaining game at Fenway Park.

Boston players ran out and swarmed Schang, Thomas and Mays. During the celebration, Joe Bush tripped on the top step of the dugout and was helped to the locker room by a couple of teammates. Barrow feared Bush had sprained his ankle.

During Pick's slide and his collision with Schang, he had spiked umpire Klem's thigh. Klem limped off the field, convincing evidence he had been in perfect position to make the call.

"What the hell do I have to do to win one of these things?" Vaughn shouted in the locker room. With the exception of the fourth inning, he had out-pitched Mays. After Vaughn cooled down and had some time to think, he said, "It was my fault. They gave me one run and that should have been enough to win for us.

"Do you remember that one McInnis hit? That was supposed to be a bean ball. It was bad enough to let that curve get away and hit Whiteman, but that probably wouldn't have beaten me. After I got the first two past McInnis for strikes, I wanted to drive him back from the plate. But my control was bad and I got it almost over the plate, just where he likes them. Schang's hit followed, but it might not have done any damage if I had got McInnis out of the way. I think that one pitch beat me."

Mitchell's strategy was on everyone's mind as they packed for the evening train to Boston. Should Mitchell have sent Pick? Why had he kept Vaughn in the game when Boston threatened in the fourth? Should Vaughn have pitched the third game at all? How would that effect the team's rotation for the rest of the Series?

Mitchell explained that because of Pick's speed and the need for a quick and accurate throw from Thomas, it was a gamble worth taking. "We took a desperate chance and lost," he said. "I have no kick to make on that play. It's now up to Tyler to put us back on even terms on Monday."

Mitchell admitted second thoughts about only one decision: letting Vaughn bat with two outs in the seventh inning and a runner on second. A single might have tied the game, but Vaughn was pitching so well at that point, Mitchell hadn't wanted to pull him in a one-run game. Now he regretted not using a pinch-hitter. "I thought Vaughn would beat them," he said, "but it seems we can't get runs for him."

That was an understatement. The Cubs had scored only one run for Vaughn in 18 innings. In Game Three, Chicago batted nine times with a runner on second or third and only once scored a run.

The slim Series budget meant there was no special train for the 27-hour trip to Boston. Instead, five extra cars were attached to an already-scheduled Michigan Central that would arrive in Boston late Sunday night: one car each for the Red Sox, the Cubs, Harry Frazee and his guests, the newspaper men and the National Commission and its entourage. Charlie Weeghman would leave with a group of 50 friends on Sunday morning. Newspapers from west of the Mississippi called their writers home after Saturday's game and relied on the reports of the syndicated writers.

Walking through Illinois Central Station, the Red Sox felt confident. The Cleveland Indians, who had led the American League with 504 runs and a .260 team batting average, had won only 4 of 11 regular-season games at Fenway Park. How could a team like Chicago beat them on their home turf? Ed Barrow was grinning like a Cheshire cat.

"I held Mays back two days because I felt I had a secure winner in him," Barrow said. "His delivery baffled the Cubs just as we thought it would. Do you remember before the Series I said that if we left Chicago a game in front, we'd win easily? Well, that's what we're doing tonight, and we'll carry out the other part of that prediction in a few days."

22

THE TRAIN RIDE

Harry Hooper grabbed an evening paper before boarding the train to Boston on Saturday evening. Looking over the gate receipts and the corresponding players' shares for the first three games, Hooper saw a dismal picture. He wasn't sure if anything could be done about the paltry figures, but he wanted to discuss it with both his teammates and the Cubs.

While Hooper mulled over his options, the Red Sox's other leader—Babe Ruth—was occupied with less serious matters. The train hadn't even left Chicago when Ruth, fellow pitcher Walt Kinney and a few others began racing through the cars, grabbing every straw hat they could find and ramming their fists right through them. They capped off their mischief with a dining-car feast of sandwiches and pickles.

Since the National Commission had assumed control of the World Series in 1905, the two pennant-winning teams had split a portion of the receipts from only the first four games. The idea was to prevent the teams from dragging out the Series in order to boost their earnings. An exception was made only once: in 1910, when poor weather caused a paltry Game Four crowd, the Commission added the Game Five receipts, too.

For much of the decade, each member of the World Series champion team had received between $3,000 and $4,000, often as much or more than his annual salary. The National Commission decided this was too much money, and during the winter of 1917–18, they sought ways to reduce the players' profits. One proposal called for letting all but the last place teams share the World Series money. The Commission ended up adopting Ban Johnson's suggestion of awarding a share to each of the top four teams in both leagues.

Supporters of this plan thought it was unfair that a pennant race could go down to the wire, only to have the first place team reap all the rewards while the second place team got nothing. They also hoped the new system would hold the interest of players and fans whose teams had no chance of winning the pennant. *The Sporting News* reported that the players didn't need to be involved in the decision, because they "always have been hungry for money."

So in 1918, the two World Series teams would split 55½% of the players' share, not all of it as in previous years. This 55½% amount would then be split 60–40 between the winners and losers. The remaining balance would be divided proportionately among the second, third and fourth place teams, with the higher placed teams receiving larger shares.

The players' total share in 1917 had been approximately $150,000; based on that amount, the 1918 winning and losing shares would be $1,835 and $1,215, respectively. In January, the Commission had announced a per-player cap of $2,000 and $1,400 for the World Series participants, anticipating 1918 revenues would be higher than the previous year's. But they had changed the distribution plan without considering either the war's effect on game attendance or the reduced ticket prices.

Meanwhile, most players, writers and fans had the impression that the $2,000–$1,400 figures were guaranteed, and that the other six teams would get a cut only if the receipts exceeded $150,000. In reality, the plan called for the two Series teams to split 55½% of the players' share—whatever the amount.

How and when the players learned the truth about the revenue plan is not clear. Harry Hooper first heard about it on the way to Boston, after Game Three. One newspaper reported that each player had been given a hefty legal document loaded with fine print before the Series began. However the information was received, here were the figures Hooper saw:

	Game One	Game Two	Game Three	Totals
Attendance	19,274	20,040	27,054	66,368
Gate Receipts	$30,348	$29,997	$40,188	$100,553
Players' Share of Receipts	$16,387	$16,198	$21,663	$54,249

If Game Four added approximately $20,000 to the players' share, the total would be roughly $75,000, half of what the White Sox and Giants had split the previous fall. Hooper figured a best-case scenario would be $1,200 for the winners and $800 for the losers, but the final numbers could fall as low as $900 and $600. Either way, it would be the smallest amounts ever awarded to World Series players.

Hooper broke the grim news to his teammates, then sought out Chicago's Les Mann. Though only 24, Mann was a six-year veteran and one of the most trustworthy men in the game. Hooper found Mann chatting with George Whiteman about signing up players for YMCA work in Whiteman's home state of Texas after the Series.

There were a few reports that animosity from the diamond had carried over to the train, but the majority of sportswriters claimed just the opposite. In fact, the *Philadelphia Inquirer* said "never before has there been so much fraternization." It's entirely possible that some writers purposely didn't report on the players' meetings.

Players on both sides had spoken about the low attendance as early as Game One, but the meeting on the train was the first formal discussion. Both teams were furious that they had been pressured into donating 10% of their earnings to war charities before even knowing how meager those earnings would be. Some of the veterans privately fumed about every player receiving an equal share. And everyone was angry that the original schedule hadn't included any weekend games (which would have brought in more fans), since there would have been time to begin the Series on Friday and still have finished by the work-or-fight deadline.

The players wanted the Commission to honor what they believed to be a promise, apparently broken because of the poor turnout in Chicago. Some suggested that they refuse to finish the Series. But knowing they held little bargaining power, the players came up with two alternatives: postpone the revenue-sharing plan until after the War, or guarantee reduced shares of $1,500 and $1,000. Hooper, Mann, Dave Shean and Bill Killefer were chosen to arrange a meeting with Garry Herrmann as soon as possible.

The players' committee tried meeting with Herrmann on Sunday afternoon, but he refused to see them, saying that he couldn't make any official decisions without Ban Johnson, who wasn't on the train. Hooper and Herrmann agreed to a meeting with all three Commission members in Boston on Monday morning.

Ballplayers had attempted to organize a union a few times in the past—the Brotherhood of Professional Base Ball Players (1885) and the Protective Association of Professional Baseball Players (1900) were two such efforts—but with little success. In 1912, the Base Ball Players Fraternity was formed, headed by David Fultz, a former player. Most of the Fraternity's victories concerned procedural matters: how suspensions, demotions and trades would be handled, and how much advance notice a player should receive. In 1916, the Fraternity was able to amend the injury clause, which obligated a team to pay an injured player for only 15 days. Most teams already had been paying injured players for the duration of their absence, but this made it official.

The Fraternity was mocked and derided in the sports pages, but for all the abuse it took, it was fairly conservative. After the demise of the Federal League in 1915, when players faced pay cuts of up to 50%, the Fraternity didn't get involved. Fultz didn't think salary disputes were a Fraternity issue, and believed the reserve clause was an evil necessary to insure the success of the sport.

In early 1917, when Fultz announced that more than 600 players would refuse to sign their contracts and would go on strike to protest poor minor league conditions, the National Commission severed all relations with the Fraternity, saying any striking players would "suspend themselves" and lose their jobs. As players capitulated, Fultz realized he had been too optimistic, thinking major leaguers would risk their jobs for "bushers." The Fraternity was dead.*

Bob O'Farrell's uncle had attended the three games at Comiskey Park and happened to be on the same train as the ballplayers, on his way home to Buffalo, New York. When O'Farrell, the Cubs' backup catcher, stopped by the passenger car to chat with his uncle, Arolene Edwards and her mother were sitting nearby. The women lived in Churchville, New York, a small town between Rochester and Buffalo; Arolene's father was working in Chicago and they were returning from a visit.

O'Farrell always claimed that Arolene started flirting with him. They introduced themselves and got acquainted, and when Arolene and her mother moved to Chicago a year or two later, she and O'Farrell renewed their friendship. The couple was married in 1928, 10 years after their chance meeting on the World Series train.

---

* It would be 48 years until the Major League Baseball Players Association was formed (1966) and another 10 years before the reserve clause was struck down (late 1975), allowing players to be free agents and giving them a greater measure of control over their careers.

Walt Kinney wasn't with the Red Sox very long before he struck up a friendship with Babe Ruth. At 6 feet, 2 inches, they were the tallest men on the team, but that wasn't all the pitchers had in common. Ruth and Kinney shared a love of pranks, crude jokes and generally adolescent behavior. They would box, wrestle on the floor and carry on like two hyperactive kids.

Kinney and Ruth had already destroyed most of the straw hats they could find on the train. On Sunday evening, they were at it again. Kinney's 25th birthday was the next day and it seems that he and Babe started the party a little early.

> Babe Ruth…narrowly escaped serious injury on the baseball special outside of Springfield last night. He was standing in the aisle of the Sox car, talking to Carl Mays, when the train lurched, sending the Colossus aspinning and crashing against a window. The heavy glass was shattered and fell clattering, inside and outside. Babe did not know how seriously he had been injured, but he had the presence of mind not to put out his hands, and was fortunate enough to escape with only a small cut in his trousers.
>
> *Boston Herald and Journal*

> A slight accident made its appearance in the Sox camp on the way home from the middle West. Saturday night Babe Ruth was walking out of the smoker when the train gave a lurch and he was thrown against the side of the car. He put out his left to save himself from a fall and bent the third finger of his left hand so far that the middle joint was slightly strained. It swelled a little, but Doc Lawler was on the job with iodine and it isn't in any serious condition this morning.
>
> *Boston Traveler*

Battering Babe Ruth did bump one of his pitching fingers "fooling" on the train, but the digit was not affected badly enough to harm his hurling ability.

Boston American

[L]ast night Ruth put his pitching hand on the bum. Babe made a playful swing at a brother athlete in the smoking room of the Pullman. The brother athlete dodged and Babe bent the third finger on his left hand. The steel coach stayed on the track and finished the trip to Boston.

Chicago Herald and Examiner

When Ed Barrow found out, he hit the roof. "You damn fool!" he bellowed. "You know I've picked you to pitch tomorrow and you go and bust up your hand that way. What the hell's the matter with you?"

"Don't worry, Ed," Ruth said. "It's okay. I'll be in there pitching for you, if you still want me to."

When the Red Sox arrived in Boston, Ruth began searching for a hat, but couldn't find one that was still intact. He asked a few teammates if they had an extra one that he could borrow.

"Why don't you ask in the dining car for a dish pan?" Joe Bush suggested.

"No, I think a barrel would be a better fit for his swelled head," said Heinie Wagner.

Babe eventually put his own smashed boater on his head and insisted it would bring him good luck in Game Four.

23

GAME FOUR:
"BALL STARS IN CLASH OVER COIN"

The *Boston American* assured its Monday morning readers that the rumors of a players' strike were unfounded and the Red Sox and Cubs were unlikely to revolt. The players' committee tried meeting with the National Commission at the Hotel Touraine, but Garry Herrmann, Ban Johnson and John Heydler refused to speak to them, claiming they first needed the complete revenue figures. The three men suggested getting together after that afternoon's game, when the actual receipt totals would be known. The players huddled, discussing the possibility of refusing to play, but Harry Hooper reluctantly agreed to a meeting that evening. When Hooper and Les Mann reported back to their respective teams, both groups were angry. The general feeling was that if the players weren't satisfied, they wouldn't finish the Series.

Cubs players and their fans staying at the Hotel Brunswick got their first earful of "Tessie" that morning, courtesy of the Royal Rooters. Taken from the musical comedy "Silver Slipper," the song had made its ballpark debut during the 1903 World Series against Pittsburgh:

> Tessie, you make me feel so badly;
> Why don't you turn around?
> Tessie, you know I love you madly;
> Babe, my heart weighs about a pound.
> Don't blame me if I ever doubt you.
> You know I couldn't live without you.
> Tessie, you are my only, only, only.

Hearing 300 Rooters sing the song during every Boston at-bat had driven the Pirates crazy. "We laughed at first," third baseman Tommy Leach said, "but after a while it got on our nerves. They kept singing it over and over, and so damned loud." Outfielder Fred Clarke said, "I kept hearing those damned words in my sleep all winter."

During the games in Chicago, fans in Boston followed the Series re-creations in the theaters and on the various scoreboards around town, but the crowds were small and the cheers half-hearted. With the country at war, food and fuel being rationed, and influenza making its devastating and deadly return, the World Series was perhaps a distant afterthought.

The Red Sox's Game Three victory, however, lit a spark in their fans, and excitement about the upcoming contests grew. It rained intermittently on Sunday, but Fenway Park was busy as fans bought tickets or picked up those they had reserved by mail. At the end of the day, only 1,500 grandstand seats were available for the remaining games.

With his team ahead in the Series, Ed Barrow said Babe Ruth would pitch if Chicago started a right-hander; if George Tyler started, Joe Bush or Sam Jones would pitch and George Whiteman would play left field (the injury to Bush's ankle after Game Three had not been serious). Paul Shannon of the *Boston Post* thought Jones deserved a start. He had no World Series experience, but he pitched well in the pennant race and had a 10-2 record at Fenway. Cubs manager Fred Mitchell was reasonably certain Jones would be the one, and he was considering Tyler, Phil Douglas or Claude Hendrix. There was also speculation that Jim Vaughn might return—again on one day of rest—for Game Four.

Whether Ruth pitched in Game Four or Five, his next start would give him a chance to break Christy Mathewson's World Series record of 28 consecutive scoreless innings. Ruth's current string was 22.1, which included 13.1 innings from 1916. A few Red Sox players were so confident that Saturday's 2-1 loss had demoralized the Cubs that they made plans to leave town on Tuesday, immediately after the fifth game.

Game Four would be Boston's first Series game in Fenway Park since 1912. One hundred fans spent a wet night outside the gates and once the sun broke through the morning clouds, people began arriving in droves. The park opened at 11:00, and within an hour, every reserved seat had been snapped up. Ten minutes before the first pitch, fans who had left home at the last minute were howling and shoving their way inside. The outfield was soaked from the overnight rainstorm, but the infield was dry—the grounds crew poured oil on the infield dirt and ignited it to burn off the excess water.

Massachusetts Governor Samuel McCall closed his offices at the state house, excused his staff for the day and headed to the park. Former Red Sox manager Jack Barry and his wife were also present, as was the club's previous owner Joe Lannin. Dutch Leonard—sporting a "mean-looking coat with a nifty belt"—visited his former teammates.

The fans with the highest profile were undoubtedly the 54 soldiers who had returned from France only three days earlier. While recuperating at City Hospital, they had talked about the World Series, lamenting that they couldn't get out for the remaining games. The *Boston Globe* heard about the situation and asked if some of the men could attend the games as guests of the newspaper. The hospital happily obliged and the soldiers were driven to the park in automobiles supplied by the Red Cross. Some hobbled in on crutches, others cradled stumps that recently had been limbs, many held blankets, but they were all dressed in crisp blue and khaki uniforms. The doughboys were a bigger attraction than the men on the diamond: they received a thunderous ovation when they took their seats, fans stopped by to greet them during the game, and hundreds more waited outside to hail them as they exited.

Most of the soldiers rooted for Boston, although a few, including Harry Hansen, a private from Percy, Illinois, cheered for the Cubs. Hansen had lost an arm at Chateau-Thierry; his uniform was decorated with the Croix de Guerre and a bronze palm leaf, representing three citations for unusual bravery. Another solider admitted that the game was not foremost in his thoughts; he glanced repeatedly up at the sky, as though he feared enemy planes overhead.

As Boston fans had done the previous week, Cubs fans gathered and followed the games by telegraph. An ad in the *Chicago Daily Tribune* read:

> See World's Series in Comfort at the Coliseum:
> Exactly as played on the field.
> Most wonderful invention in the world.
> You see live news made by telegraph.
> Doors open 12M. Game starts at 1:30 P.M.
> 50c, 75c and $1.00. Bring the ladies.

Babe Ruth walked to the mound promptly at 2:30 p.m. Fans in the box seats could see yellow iodine stains on his left hand and a "rubber cot" on his middle finger. It was obvious from his first pitch that the injury was bothering him. Even though Ruth gripped the ball loosely when throwing his fastball, he had difficulty getting the proper spin on his curve. Chicago put men on base in each of the first three innings, but were turned back by Ruth's gutsy pitching and Boston's airtight infield.

Cubs leadoff hitter Max Flack was an early goat. He was caught off first base by Sam Agnew in the opening inning, and Ruth ended the third by picking him off second base.* Agnew appeared to have also nabbed Charlie Deal off first base, but umpire Hank O'Day ruled otherwise.

Ed Barrow altered his lineup slightly, putting left fielder George Whiteman in the cleanup spot and batting Ruth sixth. Babe had been in the sixth spot only once before—back on May 6, the day he debuted at first base. Barrow gave no explanation for the switch. The Chicago outfielders played deep when Ruth came up in second inning. He swung viciously at Tyler's first pitch, missing it by about a foot. Then he ripped a foul ball by first that nearly wiped out O'Day. On the 0-2 pitch, Ruth grounded to Pick at second, who fielded the ball back on the right field grass.

Tyler, a Braves pitcher for eight years and a vital part of the 1914 championship team, was cheered when he took the mound and before each of his at-bats. The game was scoreless in the fourth when Tyler walked Dave Shean. With right-hand hitters George Whiteman and Stuffy McInnis coming up, Amos Strunk tried to bunt. After two failed attempts, he lined out to center field. Shean took advantage of Tyler's leisurely windup to Whiteman and stole second without a throw. The crowd stomped its feet in unison, clamoring for a run. Tyler couldn't find the strike zone and walked Whiteman. The roar increased as Claude Hendrix came out of the third-base dugout and began warming up in foul territory.

McInnis hit the ball right back at Tyler. The pitcher grabbed it, then paused for a split second before throwing to Deal and forcing Shean at third. His slight delay meant Deal's relay to first was late. Boston now had runners at first and second with two outs—and Babe Ruth was up.

---

* Flack is the only man picked off base two times in one World Series game.

Tyler stepped off the hill, rubbed the ball and looked over at his dugout, waiting for a sign from Fred Mitchell. Should he pitch to Ruth? Was Hendrix coming in? Should he walk Ruth intentionally, loading the bases for Everett Scott? Barrow called the Big Fellow over from the on-deck circle. "I don't know whether they'll let you hit or not," the manager said, "but if they pitch to you, you can win your own game. I know you can do it."

Ruth hadn't faced Tyler in Game Two; Scott went 0-2 against him and was 1-11 in the Series. All summer long, Ruth had been walked in situations like this, often as early as the first inning. Mitchell probably knew Ruth had yet to hit safely in a World Series game, wearing an 0-10 collar dating back to 1915. But that may not have mattered, since the man taking his practice swings had become a much better and more dangerous hitter during the last four years.

After conferring with Otto Knabe, Mitchell decided Tyler should pitch carefully to Ruth, and hope he'd chase a bad ball. Max Flack was at normal depth in right; he had been much deeper on Ruth in the second inning, but Babe had grounded out, and now he stayed where he was. Tyler turned and waved him back. Flack didn't move.

Tyler's first three pitches were low and outside, well off the plate. Ruth was patient and everyone in the park could see this was an "unintentional intentional walk." Then Tyler slipped a slow curve on the inside corner. Ruth took a big swing and missed, spinning nearly all the way around. The crowd gasped. Three balls and one strike.

Ruth thought Tyler's next pitch was too high and a bit outside. He tossed his bat aside and started jogging to first.

"Strike two!" Brick Owens yelled above the din.

Ruth glared at Owens and kicked the dirt. The fans howled. Babe retrieved his bat.

Up in the press box, Eddie Hurley of the *Boston Evening Record* was shaking his head. "The pitch was a foot off the plate and that bum Owens calls it a strike."

"He's not going to have a chance to call a third one," White Sox manager Pants Rowland said. "You know Babe, he'll swing at anything close now."

Tyler again checked his outfielders. Mann was fine and so was Paskert, but Flack still seemed too shallow. Tyler motioned him "to pitch his camp nearer the fence," but the outfielder backed up only a small step or two. Killefer called for a curveball—Tyler's strongest pitch and Ruth's weakest—but the lefty came back with another fastball, and this time it was belt high.

Ruth pulverized it, sending it screaming into right field. Flack took a half-step forward, not seeing the ball until it rose out of the shade of the grandstand. By that time, it was too late. He turned, ran wildly back towards the bleachers and leapt, but the ball sailed two feet over his glove and bounced once before banging against the fence.

The crowd was on their feet as Flack and Paskert chased the ball. Whiteman and McInnis scored easily. Charlie Pick threw the outfield relay over Charlie Deal's head at third base as Ruth slid in with a triple. Tyler had backed up the play and prevented Ruth from scoring.

Boston 2, Chicago 0.

Everett Scott tried twice to squeeze Ruth home before flying to center for the third out. The crowd never stopped roaring as Ruth ran back to the dugout, grabbed his mitt and returned to the mound. Tyler's failed attempts to reposition Flack were similar to an incident in the famous 1908 playoff game between the Cubs and the New York Giants. New York pitcher Christy Mathewson told Cy Seymour three or four times to play deeper in center field on Joe Tinker, but Seymour refused. Tinker tripled over Seymour's head, helping the Cubs go on to the World Series.

Ruth began losing his control in the sixth inning—apparently, the iodine on his finger was rubbing off on the ball, causing it to sail—and it was only Boston's strong infield that saved his hide. Tyler walked on five pitches to start the inning. Flack grounded straight back to Ruth.

He turned and fired to second base, but it was a poor throw—shortstop Scott hadn't quite reached the bag and it looked like both runners would be safe. Dave Shean normally would have been about 10 or 12 feet behind the bag, but playing a hunch, he backed up the play only a few feet from the base. Shean was on his knees when he gloved Ruth's errant toss. He dove toward the base, crawled on his stomach in the dirt, and tagged the bag with his mitt just ahead of Tyler's foot.

It was a stunning play, all the more spectacular because of Shean's injury. The next two Cubs grounded out and as Ruth took McInnis's throw to retire Mann at first and end the inning, it was official: Babe had set a new World Series record of 28.1 consecutive scoreless innings. But with the record securely in his pocket, Ruth's control only got worse. Fred Merkle walked with one out in the seventh. Rollie Zeider pinch-hit for Pick and walked on five pitches. Joe Bush began warming up.

Bob O'Farrell, another pinch-hitter, replaced Deal and hit the ball hard. It looked like it would bounce through the infield, but Scott raced over, scooped it up and flipped to Shean. The second baseman pivoted quickly and McInnis scooped his throw out of the dirt for an inning-ending double play.

After Ruth's triple, Tyler retired the next seven Boston hitters and prayed his teammates would rally. Killefer walked to open the eighth, Ruth's third walk to the last four batters, his fourth in two innings. Bush was joined on the first base line by Carl Mays.

Claude Hendrix, a right-hand hitter, batted for Tyler. For a pitcher, Hendrix was a good hitter, with a .264 average, three triples and three home runs. Mitchell's move paid off when Hendrix singled to left. Flack bunted the first pitch foul, then Ruth threw one in the dirt. It skipped past Agnew's glove for a wild pitch, and the Cubs had men at second and third.

The Cubs bench was heckling Ruth from the dugout. Anxious Red Sox fans were poised on the edge of their seats. An irate Stuffy McInnis went to the mound and yelled at Ruth to bear down. Flack bounced the next pitch to first and McInnis gloved it along the line and tagged the batter for the first out. Hendrix must have thought Killefer broke from third on the play because he was halfway to third before he realized his mistake. Everett Scott yelled for the ball, but Hendrix was able to get back.

McInnis may not have seen or heard Scott, but Fred Mitchell, coaching at third base, did. With a chance to tie the game and possibly even the Series at two games apiece, the Cubs manager wasn't taking any chances. He had wanted Hendrix to pitch the eighth inning, but Mitchell pulled him and sent Bill McCabe as a pinch-runner at second.

Charlie Hollocher, slumping at 1-13 in the Series, hit a sharp ground ball to Shean. The second baseman might have had a shot at Killefer at home, but he opted for the sure out at first. Killefer scored and Boston's lead was 2-1. Les Mann singled to left and McCabe's run tied the game. Ruth avoided further trouble when Paskert grounded out to third and the Big Fellow's scoreless innings record ended at 29.2.*

When the Red Sox batted in their half of the eighth, they faced a right-handed pitcher for the first time in the Series. Walking in from the bullpen with the dragging gait that gave him his nickname was Shufflin' Phil Douglas. He had been in the majors since 1912, but his excessive drinking—days-long binges he referred to as "vacations"—had sapped his talent and tarnished his reliability. Douglas, now 28, joined the Cubs near the end of 1915, missed the 1916 season completely and returned the following year to appear in a league-high 51 games. This year, his record in 25 games was only 10-9, but he had a very respectable 2.13 ERA. He threw a strong fastball and a nasty spitter. For the Series, he was wearing two sets of socks for good luck.

Wally Schang, a switch-hitter, batted for Agnew. Unlike his ninth-inning appearance in Game Two, this time Schang was patient. He

---

* Ruth's scoreless streak—the record of which he was most proud—stood for 44 years, until Whitey Ford of the Yankees pitched 33.2 scoreless innings in 1960-62.

worked Douglas to a full count before singling into center field. It was
no secret that Douglas was "easy meat for bunters" and Barrow vowed
that if Douglas pitched at all, the Red Sox would bunt on him. But
before Harry Hooper could lay one down, Killefer allowed his second
passed ball of the game and Schang took second. Would Barrow now
take the bunt off? Zeider, now playing third base, conferred with
Douglas on a possible play at third.

Even though Schang was on second, Hooper still bunted. Douglas
gloved it on the third base side, but when he turned to throw to third, he
found Zeider standing right beside him. The pitcher whirled the other
way and made a hurried throw to first. The ball sailed over Merkle's
head and down the right field line.

Bill Wortman, a replacement at second base, didn't back up Merkle
and the ball rolled and rolled into foul territory. Schang scored and
although Hooper missed first base and had to run back, he was still safe
at second before Max Flack threw the ball back in. Boston had regained
the lead, 3-2. Douglas took a minute to regain his composure, then
retired the next three hitters: Shean flew out to left, Strunk flew out to
center and Whiteman grounded to third.

Ruth now stood three outs away from his second victory in the
Series, but he was clearly out of gas. Merkle singled through the shortstop hole and when Zeider walked, Barrow decided he had seen enough.
Ruth knew he was done and was walking off the mound even before
Barrow gave Joe Bush the sign. If the Cubs tied the game or took the
lead, Ruth would bat second in the bottom of the ninth, so Barrow dou-
ble-switched, sending the visibly exhausted Babe out to left field to
replace Whiteman.

McInnis came in from first base and talked with Bush while Carl
Mays continued throwing on the side—just in case. Wortman, with a
puny .186 lifetime average, would probably be bunting.

When he was on, Bullet Joe Bush could throw as hard as Walter
Johnson. And here, in the ninth inning, Bush was throwing smoke. His

first pitch was a fastball for a called strike. Then he went outside for ball one. Wortman squared around on the 1-1 pitch and laid off a ball that was just outside.

"Christ! What the hell's the matter with that?" McInnis screamed at umpire Brick Owens, after racing in to field a possible bunt. Wortman got his bat on the next pitch, and McInnis was on it in a flash. The ball hadn't rolled 10 feet before Stuffy stepped in front of Bush and fired the ball to third. Merkle was forced by about 30 feet.

Next, Turner Barber came up to hit for Killefer. Barber had been at the plate when Pick tried to score on the final play of Game Three. Now he once again found himself in a last-inning nailbiter. Barber lined the ball on the ground towards Scott, and the sure-handed shortstop flipped the ball to Dave Shean to start a double play. The game was over. Bush had saved the win for Ruth, and the Red Sox were one victory away from their fifth World Series title.

"That was a fastball Tyler fed me," Ruth said after the game. "I was a little sore because the ball just before that was a ball in my opinion, but the umpire called it a strike. So I figured that if I was having strikes called on me, I might as well swing at them. I put plenty of beef behind that swing and gave it a good healthy wallop."

Jim Vaughn thought Tyler had been too confident and tried fooling Ruth with a heater. "Babe was swinging his bat with fire in his eyes," Vaughn said. "Ruth's always dangerous, but a left-hander can usually tie his hands behind his back. I fed him nothing but curves and slowballs. As I remember, I gave him only two fastballs."

Ruth confessed he had been in pain the entire game. "I still don't know how I did as well as I did," he said. "I was lucky to get that far." Now that Ruth had survived and Boston had won the game, Edward Martin could tell the *Boston Globe*'s readers that Babe's hand "was bruised during some sugarhouse fun with W. W. Kinney."

Tyler pitched a much better game than Ruth, allowing only three hits in seven innings, but the Nashua milkman had no luck or support. Babe gave up seven hits and six walks, and threw one wild pitch, but the game had been a litany of missed opportunities by the Cubs. In both the eighth and ninth innings, Chicago had two men on base with only one out. In fact, the Cubs had men on base in all but one inning. A total of 13 men reached base, but only two scored; by contrast, three of Boston's seven runners crossed the plate.

Much of Chicago's inability to bring those runners home could be chalked up to the phenomenal play of Everett Scott. The Deacon handled 11 chances flawlessly, several of which robbed the Cubs of hits up the middle. Scott also started two double plays in the final three innings. "I've made only one hit but I've spoiled several for the Cubs," Scott said. "That is the fielder's way of hitting and it's just as important as batting, if not more so."

Mitchell's decision to use a left-hander for the fourth consecutive game was questioned. Now his team was in a must-win situation and both of his aces were probably unable to pitch the fifth game. It appeared as if Mitchell had no faith in his right-handers, and Phil Douglas's performance hadn't given him any reason to think otherwise. Mitchell was also second-guessed on his use and choice of pinch-hitters. The outlook for the Cubs was grim, but back in the 1903 World Series, Boston had trailed Pittsburgh 3-1 before winning four games in a row. Of course, that had been a best-of-nine series—no team had come back from a 3-1 deficit in a seven-game series. Could Chicago pull it off?

Jim Vaughn cursed the "evil luck" of the Cubs. "Let one of our pitchers make any kind of slip and before we knew it, it would materialize into a run for the Red Sox," he said. "Tyler pitched a better game than Ruth. He was in hot water almost every inning." New York sportswriter Hugh Fullerton agreed, saying that the Cubs were playing better baseball, but Boston had a ton of luck on its side. The Cubs, he wrote, "had Ruth seemingly at their mercy at several stages and could not follow up." The Red Sox enjoyed their edge despite batting only .180 as a team, while the Cubs were hitting .227.

Unlike Mitchell, Ed Barrow seemed to possess a magic touch. In the tradition of Connie "The Tall Tactician" Mack, Frank "Peerless Leader" Chance and John "Little Napoleon" McGraw, the *Baltimore Sun* dubbed Barrow "The Man Who Dared." He had out-guessed and out-managed Mitchell at every turn. Almost all of Barrow's decisions had paid off: starting Ruth in Game One and putting Whiteman in the cleanup spot, batting Wally Schang sixth in Game Three and Ruth sixth in Game Four, and bringing in Bush as a relief pitcher, albeit a bit late.

The Fenway crowd had been 22,183 and now the players knew exactly where they stood financially, and it was on even lower ground than they expected. The players' pool was slightly more than $69,000, a distant cry from the $150,000 that had been shared in 1917. Making no attempt to hide their anger, the players spoke freely to each other and to the press about the possibility of leaving town without finishing the Series. Many Chicago players wanted a guarantee of at least $1,000 each before suiting up for Game Five.

The Red Sox and Cubs were honored guests at the Shubert-Majestic Theater that evening for a play called "Experience." Harry Hooper, Everett Scott, Les Mann and Bill Killefer declined the invitation and went to the Copley Plaza Hotel for their much-anticipated meeting with the National Commission. The hotel's switchboard operator told the group that Garry Herrmann, Ban Johnson and John Heydler were not in. The Commission "had ducked, in its customary backstairs policy" and was at the theater. The four players hung around the lobby until 1:00 in the morning, but they knew they had been stood up.

No one knew what would happen the next day—except perhaps Madame Lora. Elsewhere that night in Boston's theater district, after a demonstration of mental telepathy at the Bowdoin Square Theater, Madame Lora told her audience that she had correctly predicted the winning team in each of the first four World Series games. Her forecast for Game Five?

Sam Jones would pitch and the Red Sox would win.

24

GAME FIVE: "HARRY, OLD BOY, WHYN'T YOU STOP ALL THIS AND PLAY BALL?"

On Tuesday morning, the players' discontent became public. Wedged into the lengthy reporting and analysis of Boston's victory were brief notices about the simmering dissension. Many sportswriters had avoided or downplayed the issue, but that was no longer possible. The scribes maintained that, despite the chorus of complaints, the World Series would continue to its proper finish. The *Boston Globe* was confident—"There is nothing approaching a strike or walkout"—and the *Chicago Daily Tribune* reported, "Threats of a strike and refusal to complete the Series are mere rumors."

The players' representatives finally met with the National Commission that morning. Unbeknownst to the players, Ban Johnson had invited several sportswriters to the meeting in his suite.

"We do not think we have been treated fairly," Hooper said nervously. "We believe we were promised $2,000 and $1,400. We are asking that the other first division clubs not receive any Series money this year."

Garry Herrmann explained that the $2,000 and $1,400 figures were based on past gate receipts and he handed Hooper a copy of the Commission's report regarding the 1918 Series. The Chairman read from the report:

> If for any reason the players' fund for 1918 shall be less than $152,894.48, the respective shares of the players participating shall be scaled in the proportion and to the extent of the decrease in the aggregate players' revenue of 1918 as compared with 1917.

He emphasized the single word—"if"—that gave the Commission the right to limit the players' income. "The Commission's hands are tied," Herrmann said. "The financial breakdown is a matter for the American and National Leagues. The two leagues are responsible for these terms."

What Herrmann meant, of course, was that the players' hands were tied. The two leagues had decided by fiat nine months earlier to limit the players' prize money. But Hooper couldn't figure out why, amidst the turmoil and uncertainty of the previous winter, the owners hadn't anticipated 1918's receipts being significantly lower.

"The players have made baseball the national game," argued Hooper, "and it is the players that have made the World Series the sporting attraction it is. The crowds come out to see us—and we're getting a lousy return for our efforts."

"I understand your concern, Harry, but to change these rules, it would be necessary to get the consent of both leagues. Unfortunately, the game receipts were much less than anticipated. The Commission is sorry, gentlemen, but what can it do?"

Hooper pressed his case. "We didn't have a voice in making the rule that took away the big portion of our money, which was all wrong. We earn it, and the earner should be considered. We aren't a bunch of burglars. Baseball is our business and a man can't be blamed for looking after his business." He also asked why the winning players should accept $900 or less when at least one of the umpires, Bill Klem, was being paid $1,000 to work the games.* He received no answer.

Hooper then proposed a compromise of $1,500 and $1,000. John Heydler, the acting National League president, said he'd be willing to discuss the matter with the National League owners some time in the future—he couldn't make any promises, of course, but he would bring the issue up. It was a worthless suggestion. Heydler was merely filling in as league president after John Tener's resignation and there was no guarantee he would remain in the job.

The two sides were at an impasse. Herrmann said he would review the matter and make his final decision before that afternoon's game. Then, after a quick word with Commission secretary John Bruce, Herrmann corrected himself: his decision would come *after* the game, around 5:30 p.m. He told the players not to worry and promised them the right thing would be done.

"Well then," Hooper cracked, "I suppose we shall have to throw ourselves upon your tender mercies." With that, the players left. Hooper's sarcasm went right over the Commission's collective head. As one reporter noted, speaking of Herrmann and Johnson, "the thick-headed Czar of the triumvirate and his man Friday interpreted the speech as a backdown" and spread the news that the players had surrendered.

---

* The other three umpires were each paid $650.

At noon, both teams gathered in the Red Sox clubhouse. Most of the men were still in street clothes, although Stuffy McInnis, Fred Merkle and Bill Killefer had changed into their uniforms.

"They want to put us off until the Series is over," Hooper told them. "We've tried to meet with them since Sunday, and every time we do, they have a new excuse. If the Red Sox win the fifth game, the Series will be over. And what power will we have then? The Commission would simply say 'tough luck.' They told us they would give us an answer today—I think we should sit here until we get it."

Word of the meeting got out. Cubs business manager Walter Craighead telephoned Herrmann at the Copley Plaza and told him the players were refusing to take the field. Herrmann said that if one of the players called him, he would render his decision over the phone.

Shortly after 1:00, Les Mann took him up on it. "The players have decided they will not wait until 5:30 for the Commission's decision," he said over the phone. "We want a decision now."

"The Commission cannot change the rules. As I told you this morning, it was proposed and agreed to by both leagues months ago and it's up to them."

"We weren't even told about that decision until the Series had already begun," Mann countered. "And we're the only ones who will suffer."

"I'm sorry, Les. The club owners couldn't have anticipated the ill effects of the war."

"So that's it?" Mann asked, his voice rising in anger. "Is that the Commission's final word? You'd better decide right now if that's it, because I've got forty players here who aren't putting on their uniforms until we get a satisfactory agreement."

"If the players intend to strike," Herrmann yelled back, "you'd better go out in front of the park and tell them to stop selling tickets and letting fans through the gates."

"We're waiting for you and your decision," Mann said. "As far as the fans go, they'll wait just like us until the Commission shows up and tells us its decision face to face. If that takes until 5:30, so be it." Mann slammed the phone down.

The chance to see the Red Sox clinch another World Series title had brought more than 20,000 people to Fenway Park. One of them was Bobby McGarigle, who had spent some of his hard-earned income as a newsboy for a seat in the first base pavilion. Bobby hated missing batting or infield practice—he especially loved the pepper games the players put on along the sidelines—so he always tried to get to the park early. But as he came up the runway, no players were on the field. At 2:00, just a half-hour before game time, Fenway's green pasture was empty. So were the dugouts. Bobby found his seat and thought about lunch as vendors hawked their wares. Hot dogs and soda pop sold for a nickel apiece, but Bobby usually bought chewing taffy. It was a good bargain—sometimes he could make it last five or six innings.

A group of wounded veterans and soldiers arrived and took seats in the grandstand. The crowd stood, removed their hats and cheered as the 12-piece band struck up "Over There." Some fans gave the soldiers cigars or bought them peanuts and soda. During the delay, the band also played a song pointedly titled "Don't Bite The Hand That Feeds You."

With no explanation for the delay, some fans grew restless.

"Where are the players?" one shouted.

"Let's play ball!" yelled another.

When word that the players weren't taking the field reached the nearest police precinct, Sergeant Tom Goode immediately thought of a possible riot. Through the years, baseball had certainly seen its share of destructive and dissatisfied fans, so Goode dispatched extra officers to the park. Several mounted policemen rode onto the outfield, fanning out and facing the center field and right field bleachers. The crowd was neither hostile nor rowdy and gave the policemen a round of applause. It wasn't much of a line—only five horses in the vast expanse of the

Fenway outfield—but as the delay wore on, some foot patrolmen joined them.

Between 2:00 and 2:15, five Cubs—Claude Hendrix, Charlie Deal, Charlie Pick, Dode Paskert and Phil Douglas—walked through the grandstand in street clothes. "Everything's off," Hendrix called up to the press box. "There's not going to be a game today."

Word of a strike spread through the crowd, and impatient voices turned angry.

"Bolsheviki!"

"Shameless hold-ups!"

Fans had little sympathy for the players, evidenced by an anonymous telegram the National Commission had received that morning: "As a patriotic duty to slackers, kindly donate the players' shares to Red Cross and put them in front line trenches as targets to locate the Huns." Many people thought the athletes should have been off fighting in Europe, not playing baseball, and they agreed with their favorite sportswriters, who indignantly insisted that the players should be content with their lot. After all, the small Series shares were still more than the $30 monthly pay drawn by American soldiers.

"The government gives them a chance to make a little more money and they show their appreciation by going on strike!"

"If I had my way," said one Army officer in the stands, "every one of them would be wearing khaki tomorrow."

Ban Johnson was enjoying his lunch at the Copley Plaza, drinking and celebrating the Commission's triumph over the players, along with Taylor Spink, the publisher of *The Sporting News*, and Charley Riley, a fishing-tackle manufacturer from Bristol, Connecticut. Johnson and Riley were trying to outdo each other with boasts of their fishing exploits.

At Fenway, numerous visitors to the clubhouse were urging the players to reconsider their delay: former Red Sox managers Bill Carrigan and Jack Barry, umpire Tom Connolly (who attended, but did not work the Series), White Sox manager Pants Rowland, even former Mayor John Fitzgerald. Harry Frazee and Charles Weeghman also made their case, but when the two club presidents refused to guarantee any additional money, the players ignored them.

Johnson and Garry Herrmann didn't arrive at Fenway until five minutes before the game was scheduled to start (they had also almost missed the start of Game Four). "If Frazee or Weeghman have conceded anything to those bastards," Johnson said, "I'm through with baseball. I'm through, I'm through, I'm through."

"If anything's going to happen, it'll happen mighty quick," said Herrmann.

Under the stands, the two men spoke with Frazee. "Harry, the players have to take the field immediately."

"Let's try to get an amicable solution to this," said Frazee. "I don't want a scandal."

At first, Johnson and Herrmann refused to meet with the players at all, and as much as 30 minutes passed before the two Commission members made their way to the umpires' dressing room, off the Red Sox's locker room. Hooper, Mann, a few other players, some reporters and "not a few fans" were packed inside the "tiny, little, super-heated coop."

"What the hell is all this?" Johnson bellowed, squeezing his way in. "Why aren't these players on the field?"

Hooper took one look at Johnson and instantly knew that the meeting would not go smoothly. The American League president was holding on tightly to Herrmann's and Heydler's shoulders, undoubtedly to keep from falling over. Johnson was "pretty well oiled" and Herrmann appeared more than a little tipsy as well.

The American League president's penchant for getting intoxicated at the World Series was no secret. Sportswriter Fred Lieb had been covering baseball since 1911 and he couldn't recall a single game at which

Johnson was sober. Stories of Johnson's tippling were legion. He once urinated in an elevator after a league banquet, much to the dismay of the lift's operator. On another night, Johnson staggered back to the hotel and up to his room. When he turned on the light, he found a man sleeping in his bed. Johnson had the right room number—but the wrong hotel. Lieb said that Johnson showed up at Fenway that September afternoon "about three sheets to the wind."

In the umpires' room, Herrmann began loudly recounting the glorious history of the National Commission and all the wonderful work it had done on behalf of the great game of baseball. After about a minute, Johnson shoved him out of the way.

"I went to Washington," he slurred in a high-pitched voice, "and had the stamp of approval put on this World Series. I made it possible. I did." He thumped his chest with his fist. "No one else could have got it but me, Harry. If I hadn't gone…"

"But Mr. Johnson, please—" Hooper interrupted. In a moment, Johnson was in tears. He flung his arm around Hooper's shoulder and leaned heavily on him. "Harry, old boy, old boy. Whyn't you stop all this and play ball?" he blubbered. "Huh? Harry, you know I love you. I want you to go out to the field because there's 25,000 people waiting. Harry, go out and play the game. You'll win easier than yesterday. The crowd is waiting for you."

"But what are we going to do about—"

Suddenly Herrmann blurted out, "Let's arbitrary this matter."

Johnson took no notice and continued crying on Hooper's shoulder.

"Harry, do you realize you're a member of one of the greatest organizations in the world, the American League? Do you realize what you will do to its good name if you don't play? I love you, Harry. Go out there. For the honor and glory of the American League, go out and play."

"If the players refuse to finish the Series," Herrmann threatened, "then their entire shares will be given to the Red Cross."

"That's fine with us," Hooper countered. "We're willing to give the receipts to charity. All we ask is that the club owners and the Commission do the same. Let nobody get any money out of it."

"No," Herrmann said. "If there is a strike, we'll end the Series right now and we'll divide the players' money among the club owners. The Commission has the final say of how to dispose of the receipts, not the players."

Until that point, John Heydler hadn't spoken a word. Hooper thought he looked worried and couldn't tell if he was drunk or sober. Finally, Heydler suggested, as he had that morning, that the players play the fifth game and the two leagues would try to adjust the finances afterwards.

"Hold on there now, let me arbitrate," Herrmann again interjected.

Hooper repeated his offer of playing for charity. "We'd rather play for no money than disgrace the game as the Commission has done," he said. "The public has paid to see the ballplayers, not the National Commission." In a corner of the small room, Boston writer Arthur Duffey thought to himself, I'll bet there are plenty of fans who'd pay to see the Commission right now.

Hooper pushed Johnson aside. "This is a waste of time," he said to Les Mann. "I want to get back to the other players." Before he left, Hooper told the reporters, "You can see our predicament, gentlemen. These men are not in any condition to hear our arguments. We have nobody we can talk to—nobody who can talk."

Both teams were waiting in the Red Sox locker room. "Johnson's drunk and crying and Herrmann's no better," Hooper said. "Nothing's going to be settled today. We have to decide ourselves whether we're going out there."

In a "stormy session," the players discussed their options:

"Part of the reason for not jumping to the shipyards was the shot at the money they promised us."

"We're making just about as much as the second place clubs."

"The Commission cut our share almost in half, but they're taking their 100%."

"What chance do we have? If we play, the Series could be over, and then the Commission will never hear us."

The players could hear the crowd cheering as more soldiers arrived, and some impatient fans grumbling. The brass band had taken a break and was sitting on the grass in front of the Boston dugout. The Red Sox batboy perched on the top rail of the dugout was the only person in a baseball uniform the crowd had seen so far. Hooper thought that walking out on the Series would punish the fans who had supported them all season.

The players took a vote. A majority wanted to call off the Series, but it was eventually decided they would play. Hooper and Mann went back to the umpires' room." The players feel it's in everyone's best interest to stop all this silly talk," Hooper said. "We will go on with the Series today—but we do it only for the good of baseball and not because we think we're being treated fairly. We had no voice in making these rules, and we have no voice now. I'd ask that we be allowed to address the crowd and tell them the reasons for the delay. Also, we want some assurance that no action will be taken against the players. I suppose we'll just have to let it go at that."

Johnson threw his arms around Hooper's neck. "That's right, Harry, do that for me. Go out and play," he blubbered. "Everything will be all right. No action will be taken. For the honor and glory of the American League, go out and play."

Herrmann tried grasping Hooper's hand and began speaking, but Ed Barrow pushed him away. "We've wasted enough time already," said the Boston manager. "To the field, everybody!"

Johnson watched them go. "By golly, I did it. I *did* it."

It would be several weeks before Hooper realized he had made a crucial mistake. "I should have had them sign an agreement that no action would be taken," he said later. "But with the room full of sportswriters, I never imagined they would go back on their word."

John Fitzgerald walked out of the first base dugout and onto the field at 3:15. Shouting into a megaphone, he read the short statement Hooper had hastily scribbled, recapping the ballplayers' reasons for playing and announcing that the game would begin in 15 minutes.

When the Cubs took the field, most fans cheered, though there were some boos. Most of the jeers seemed aimed at Otto Knabe, but any hatred between Knabe and Heinie Wagner was in the past—the two men walked onto the field together, engrossed in conversation. While the teams briefly warmed up, the sportswriters in the press box typed their accounts of the delay and its resolution.

"It's a mighty good thing that professional baseball is dead," Arthur Duffey of the *Boston Post* began his "Sports Comment" column. "The game has been dying for two years, killed by the greed of players and owners. Professional baseball in the past four years has only been a mad scramble for money. The wrangling of the players and magnates yesterday over the spoils furnishes a disgusting spectacle.... All decent sporting spirit has long ago fled and the game just reeks with scandal after scandal."

"Americans like to think of baseball as a sport," wrote J. V. Fitz Gerald in the *Washington Post*. "They don't want the dollar mark stamped on it in letters so all can read." The *Chicago Daily Tribune* said the fifth game was played "under the sinister shadow of the dollar" as the players fought "over the pennies on the corpse's eyes." The *Brooklyn Eagle* called the delay "the most pitiful exhibition of demoralizing selfishness in all the annals of sports.... Their lofty manifesto about playing the game merely from a high sense of duty [was] one of the saddest and dreariest jokes of a depressing season."

Hugh Fullerton wrote that baseball "is buried deep in the slime of selfishness [and] the muck of commercialism.... The conference was...a fitting finish for the game, which has been disgraced so long by its officials."

A few Boston writers sympathized with the players. Harry Casey wrote, "No one blames the players for trying to get all they can." Eddie Hurley reported, "There is no doubt but what the players have been given the worst of it." And Burt Whitman wrote that the players "were absolutely disgusted and rightly so with the miserly money prizes allotted them by what is left of the unsteady National Commission."

As was the custom of the time, Johnson's intoxication was only alluded to indirectly. Whitman called the Commission "unsteady." Others said Johnson gave a "ridiculous exhibition" and "was a bit groggy." Another paper wrote,"[N]ation-wide prohibition will put the National Commission out of business." The *New York Tribune* stated that Johnson and Herrmann "stood together because they would fall alone."

Sam Jones hadn't pitched in eight days and had trouble finding his rhythm. He seemed nervous as he began Game Five by walking Max Flack on four pitches. When Charlie Hollocher followed with a hard-hit single up the middle, Carl Mays began warming up.

Les Mann bunted the runners over and the Red Sox infield played back, willing to concede an early run. Dode Paskert's sinking liner to left was caught on the run by George Whiteman. There was no play on Flack, who tagged up and ran home. Without stopping to set himself, Whiteman fired the ball to Dave Shean at second base, where Hollocher, perhaps thinking the ball would drop, had taken a reckless lead. He was doubled up for the third out with Flack still 20 feet from the plate.

After pitching complete game losses in the first and third games, Jim Vaughn took the hill, convinced "the time had come for something to break." After a leadoff single by Harry Hooper, Vaughn retired seven batters in a row.

But Chicago's sour luck reemerged in the third when Flack slapped a grounder to the right of Everett Scott. The ball took a crazy hop, bounding high and back to Scott's left. The shortstop shot out his gloved hand, snared the ball and threw out the runner. "We gotta get the breaks soon, boys," Fred Mitchell shouted from the coach's box. "This tough luck ain't gonna last. Let's go from here."

Both Mitchell and Hollocher had noticed that on pickoff throws from the catcher, Stuffy McInnis always swung around to his right when applying the tag. It was the fastest way to make the play, but it left McInnis's back to second base. When Hollocher walked on four pitches in the fourth, the Cubs knew they had to take a risk.

Hollocher took a long lead off first, daring Sam Agnew to throw. It worked—the Boston catcher called for a pitchout, McInnis took the throw and turned towards the bag—but he swiped at nothing but air. Stuffy's teammates yelled from the bench, but he didn't hear them. When he whirled and raised his arm to throw to second, he could only curse as Hollocher slid into second with a stolen base.

Mann followed with a double into the left field corner, scoring Hollocher and giving Chicago a 1-0 lead. For the first time in the Series, after pitching for 21 innings, Jim Vaughn was working with a lead.

It had been a dull three innings for the home fans: Hooper's first-inning single and Jones's walk in the third was the extent of the Red Sox's offense. The Fenway crowd cheered as Amos Strunk led off the fourth inning. He kept the faith by driving Vaughn's first pitch to deep right. The ball nearly went over the fence and Strunk stopped at second with a double. But Whiteman popped up a bunt attempt and McInnis lined into a double play, Merkle to Hollocher.

In the fifth, Vaughn was probably getting tired: he was pitching his 23rd inning in only six days. The Red Sox began hitting him hard and Claude Hendrix starting warming up. But for all their line drives, Boston came up empty. Mann made a nice running catch on Scott's liner and after Fred Thomas singled, Agnew hit into a double play.

Jones pitched well through five innings, having allowed only two hits and one run. In the sixth, though, Hollocher singled and Paskert walked. Merkle singled to left, but George Whiteman made a great throw to the plate and Agnew tagged out Hollocher to keep the game at 1-0.

Babe Ruth came out to coach first base in the bottom of the seventh, and the crowd roared, hoping his presence on the field might spark a rally. With one out, Whiteman singled, but another double play, the third by the Cubs in the last four innings, killed any hope of a rally.

Flack walked for the second time in the eighth and Hollocher dropped a perfect bunt. Jones and Thomas watched the ball move slowly along the third base chalk line, but instead of rolling foul, it struck a small rock, veered in about three inches and stopped. It was Hollocher's third hit of the game, and with minimal effort Chicago had runners at first and second with nobody out.

Carl Mays and Jean Dubuc were busy in the bullpen as Jones erased Mann on a pop-up. Paskert whacked a double off the wall in left-center and two runs scored. After Merkle struck out, Charlie Pick got his sixth hit of the Series when his ground ball got away from Shean. He recovered in time and Paskert was tagged out in a rundown near the plate—Shean to Agnew to Thomas to McInnis.

Scott, Thomas and pinch-hitter Wally Schang went down in order in the eighth. With one inning left for the Red Sox, still trailing 3-0, Hack Miller batted for Jones. He smashed the ball to deep left. Mann ran up the embankment, then slipped and fell. But from a sitting position on the slope, he caught the ball in his lap. It was a tough break for their team, but the Red Sox fans applauded the unlikely play.

Hooper popped to short left field. It looked like it would drop for a hit—there was no chance Mann could run in fast enough—but Hollocher, his hands outstretched, raced back and grabbed it. Instead of a double and a single, Boston was instead down to its last out. Shean hit safely to the right of shortstop, but Vaughn zipped three pitches past Strunk for his fourth strikeout and the final out of the game.

Vaughn finished with a 3-0 shutout, a five-hitter, but admitted it wasn't his best effort of the Series. "I didn't have so much stuff today as I had in my first appearance," he said. "And I didn't pitch so good a game. But I won. The games have been so close that a single badly pitched ball has decided every one of them."

"We played smarter ball today," Fred Mitchell said. "The men were more like themselves than in any game of the series."

No Red Sox player reached third base; in fact, Boston never had more than one base runner in any inning. Barrow had few words for the press, saying curtly, "I don't care to talk about it. The Cubs' win today merely prolongs the Series. We expected to end it today, but things broke too well for Chicago. So we'll win tomorrow with Mays or Bush."

Players on both teams insisted on another meeting with the National Commission before Fenway's gates opened for the sixth game. "When we saw that there were over 20,000 fans waiting," said Les Mann, "including dozens of wounded soldiers, we simply could not quit. If our demands are not granted tomorrow morning, we will announce our decision in time to protect the fans."

Harry Hooper seemed to contradict Mann when he said, "I'm certain the Series will be finished without trouble." Harry Frazee wasn't so sure. After the Cubs' victory, Frazee told his employees to stop selling tickets to Game Six.

25

GAME SIX:
ALL THE GLORY TO BOSTON

The Cubs refused to leave the Brunswick Hotel. "What's the point?" one Chicago player asked. "If we lose the Series, we'll get little more than the teams that finished second or third." They vowed not to throw a baseball or swing a bat until the National Commission guaranteed them a greater share of World Series revenue.

The Red Sox backed them up. "We'll stick with Chicago," said one Boston player, speaking for the team. "If they play, we'll also play, but if they refuse to go to the park, we will also hold out."

The players' committee—Harry Hooper, Dave Shean, Les Mann and Bill Killefer—met with Harry Frazee, Charles Weeghman and several shareholders of both clubs at the Copley Plaza shortly before 11:00 on Wednesday morning. At the players' request, no one from the National Commission was present. By all accounts, the hour-long meeting was cordial and professional.

"We've decided to go through," Hooper told a group of reporters in the lobby afterwards. "Our case appears hopeless, but the club owners have promised to use their influence with the National Commission and do their best to secure the money we are entitled to. Tell the fans that we'll be out there today."

Both locker rooms were much calmer than the day before, so quiet that several writers had the feeling that some behind-the-scenes settlement had been reached. Hugh Fullerton overheard whispers that another strike had been averted because Weeghman and Frazee guaranteed the players approximately one-third more than the announced shares, perhaps a bonus from that afternoon's receipts. Cutting the players an extra slice of the World Series pie was certainly preferable to the nightmare of turning away thousands of ticket-holders, but both Frazee and Weeghman officially denied making promises of any kind. It was reported that neither owner would make any money, after paying salaries, overhead and travel expenses, if the Series did not go more than five games.

Charles Dryden of the *Chicago Herald and Examiner* reported that Frazee and Weeghman had plenty of replacement players waiting to take the field in case the Red Sox and Cubs abandoned the Series. Under the headline, "Strikebreakers On Job," he wrote, "The strikers were not aware that on a railroad siding near the ballpark were two box carloads of strike breakers from adjacent shipyards and the paint and putty league, ready to jump in and finish the game." Dryden was the only writer to mention this and he provided no other information.

With their fans bundled up in heavy coats, furs and blankets on a day that was "cold enough for football," the Red Sox took the field at the scheduled time. One of the players' many superstitions held that accepting flowers before a game was bad luck. Fred Mitchell had been presented with a large floral horseshoe before Game One and his team had lost 1-0. Another taboo was laying claim to an award before it had been won. The Red Sox broke with convention and posed for a World Champions team photo 30 minutes before the game.

Joe Bush was promised the starting assignment, but at the last minute, Ed Barrow gave the ball to Carl Mays. Bush was told he'd pitch the seventh game, if it was necessary. Fred Mitchell sent Lefty Tyler back to the Fenway mound. Barrow's strategy remained conservative: George Whiteman was in left field. Barrow could have played Ruth in center, but he stayed with left-hand hitting Amos Strunk despite his dismal showing at the plate. His only change was putting Wally Schang, Mays's preferred catcher, in the eighth spot.

The band played "The Gang's All Here" but a casual glance through the Fenway stands made it obvious that much of the gang had not arrived. The park was half full, with large empty sections, including the best box seats. Rumors that there would not be a sixth game had begun almost as soon as Game Five had ended. The city's newspaper offices had fielded calls all morning from readers asking if the game was on. Word of Hooper's confirmation traveled slowly and the afternoon papers wouldn't be out for a few hours, so several thousand fans were arriving in the third and fourth innings. But nothing could keep the diehards from watching what they hoped would be another title-clinching contest, neither hints of a strike nor a morning temperature of 48 degrees. After the lineups were given, it was announced that if the Cubs won, tickets for Thursday's seventh game would be sold after the final out.

Mays was in peak form again and retired the first four Cubs on ground balls. Charlie Pick singled, but Mays picked him off first base. Eight of the first nine outs were made by the Boston infield. Barrow's switch from Bush to Mays looked like another successful hunch.

Tyler faltered in the bottom of the third when he walked Mays on four pitches. Harry Hooper poked a bunt towards the mound and Tyler's only play was to first as Mays took second. When Dave Shean walked on a 3-2 pitch, Mitchell motioned for Claude Hendrix to get up in the bullpen.

Amos Strunk hit four vicious foul balls before grounding to second. Pick bobbled the ball slightly, saw he had no chance for a force on Shean, and threw Strunk out at first. The Red Sox now had runners at second and third with two outs. The next batter, George Whiteman, had been involved in all but one of Boston's seven runs so far in the Series. Tyler talked to his infielders. If he walked Whiteman, the bases would be loaded for Stuffy McInnis.

The Cubs took their chances with Whiteman, and Tyler kept the ball outside. But as he had done with Ruth two days earlier, Tyler left a fastball a little too close to the plate. Whiteman reached for it and lined the ball to right field. Max Flack, playing deep, was slow to react. He took a half-step backwards, then sprinted towards the infield. The ball was dropping and Flack tried catching it on the run at his waist, but it hit the side of his glove and fell on the ground. Mays and Shean scored easily. It should have been the final out of the inning, but the two-base error gave the Red Sox a 2-0 lead.

Everyone was surprised by the misplay. Flack had a reputation as "one of the very surest catchers in the game" and it looked like an easy catch; he didn't even have to dive for it. One writer wondered if Flack thought there was only one out and was thinking about throwing home. Fred Mitchell said it was simply "an out and out muff."

Stuffy McInnis legged out a grounder to Hollocher's right, but Whiteman got greedy and tried to advance. Fred Merkle fired back across the diamond to Charlie Deal, who tagged Whiteman out as he slid head first into third.

Three Army officers in the press box made a note of the time—3:05 p.m.—and released a carrier pigeon to bring news of the just-completed inning to Camp Devens, 40 miles away in Ayer, Massachusetts. One bird was sent after each inning; the birds usually circled the park once or twice before leaving, reaching their destination about a half-hour later. It was the first time World Series news had been transmitted by pigeon.

Flack tried to atone for his error by singling up the middle to start the fourth inning, then taking second on Hollocher's groundout. Mays hit Les Mann in the leg with an inside pitch and Mann fell to the ground, writhing in the dirt and rubbing his leg. Mays thought he might have deliberately stayed in the ball's path, but in any event, Mann was now on first base.

Dode Paskert was at the plate and the hit-and-run was on. Mays made a few pickoff attempts to keep Flack close at second. Catcher Wally Schang saw Mann take a few halting steps off first and when Paskert laid off an outside pitch, he fired the ball to McInnis. Before Mann could get back, Stuffy fell against him, effectively blocking the bag and tagging him out.

Mann protested bitterly, but to no avail. Mays ended up walking Paskert and Flack stole third on ball four. The Cubs might have had the bases loaded and one out; now they had first and third with two outs. Fred Merkle lined a first pitch single to left, scoring Flack and cutting Boston's lead to 2-1. Pick followed with a hard drive to short right field, very similar to Whiteman's liner to Flack. Harry Hooper raced in and grabbed it for the final out of the inning.

From that point on, the Cubs and Red Sox battled through what Hugh Fullerton called "one of the most desperately contested games I have ever seen."

Right away, the Red Sox tried putting the game out of reach. Everett Scott hit an infield single and was sacrificed to second. Schang walked. Mays caught Deal flat-footed at third with another bunt and Boston had the bases loaded with one out. Scott was forced at the plate on Hooper's ground ball, then Dave Shean, again with the bases loaded, drilled a grounder to third. Deal knocked it down a few feet behind the bag. At first, he couldn't find the base, but was finally able to put his foot on the bag, lunge flat-out in the dirt and grab the ball for the force on Mays to end the threat.

It was a decent rally, but the Red Sox bats, already anemic, became comatose. Boston had hit only two balls out of the infield through four innings, both by Whiteman. The vanishing offense hardly mattered, however, because Mays returned to the mound determined to hold off the Cubs. After his stumble in the fourth, he regained control and kept the ball low, around the knees, and Chicago hit ground ball after ground ball after ground ball.

In the fifth, both Deal and Killefer grounded back to the mound. In the sixth, Mays, a superb fielder, speared a hot shot headed up the middle and threw to Shean for a force out. The other Red Sox were just as sure-handed. McInnis robbed Hollocher of a hit in the fifth and Schang threw Mann out at second to end the sixth. Fred Thomas knocked down Merkle's smash in the seventh with his bare hand, recovered the ball in foul territory and fired a strike across the infield to McInnis.

Mitchell went to his bench in the eighth, trying to shake up his team. Turner Barber lined the ball over shortstop. From the third base dugout, the Cubs could see that the sinking liner would drop for a hit and they started cheering. The crowd grit its teeth as Whiteman chugged forward on his aging legs.

His hustle seemed pointless. If the ball got past him, it would roll and roll and roll—three bases at least—since Amos Strunk wouldn't have time to back up the play. But just as the ball was about to hit the ground, Whiteman dove forward, stuck out his glove in front of him and snagged the ball a few inches off the grass. He landed head first, but rather than break his fall with his hands and risk losing the ball, he tucked his head in and turned a full somersault, bouncing back to his feet with the ball securely in both hands. Whiteman came up staggering a bit, but he was grinning. He tossed the ball in to Everett Scott, who whipped it around the infield. The Fenway crowd leapt to its feet and hollered for a full three minutes for their unlikely hero. Scott, Thomas and Strunk yelled out over the ovation, asking Whiteman if he was hurt, but he waved them off, still smiling.

The next batter, pinch-hitter Bob O'Farrell, popped up to short left field. There was no way Whiteman could reach this one—he wasn't even running hard. But Scott glided out and made a difficult catch look almost routine. At that point, with two outs, Whiteman jogged in from his position, rubbing his neck. As he crossed the infield, the crowd rose to its feet and applauded again.

Whiteman had made the last out in the previous inning. Barrow now wanted Ruth in the lineup in case the Cubs tied the game, so he told Babe to grab his mitt and go out to left field. Mitchell's third pinch-hitter of the inning, Bill McCabe, lifted a foul ball near the third base stands. Scott caught that one, too, and the inning was over.

The first three hitters in Chicago's lineup were due up in the ninth, and right to the end, luck was with the Red Sox. Flack was ahead in the count and Mays's 3-1 pitch was way inside. It was clearly ball four, but as Flack ducked away, the pitch glanced off his bat for strike two. Flack popped up the next pitch and Thomas caught it near the third base grandstand.

Charlie Hollocher managed only a lazy fly ball to left. When Ruth squeezed it for the second out, the fans roared and the Babe took a graceful bow. Les Mann, the Cubs' last hope, knocked a routine grounder to Shean, who scooped it up and threw to McInnis for the final out.

Boston 2, Chicago 1.

The Red Sox were World Series champions for the third time in four years, the first franchise to win five World Series titles.

The band broke into "Tessie" and the crowd sang along as several enthusiastic fans jumped the railings and ran onto the field. McInnis held the ball aloft in his right hand and led the scramble to the clubhouse. The Rooters mobbed the players in front of the dugout, shaking their hands and then hounding Barrow for souvenirs. He tossed them a few old baseballs.

But most of the 15,238 fans merely buttoned up their coats and departed for the warmth of their homes and hotel rooms. It was a strangely silent and unenthusiastic exit. Perhaps the public's taste for baseball had reached its limit. Perhaps, as Burt Whitman mused in the *Herald and Journal*, Boston fans simply had become too accustomed to World Series games, and the championship no longer had much meaning.

There was no official voting, but it was widely felt that George Whiteman was the Series' most valuable player. In the final month of the season, Whiteman hadn't been playing regularly and when he did, he was unreliable in the outfield. "I had about given up hope when this chance came," he said, referring to his spring signing with Boston.

Whiteman now stood near the grandstand, thanking well-wishers and cradling the bat with which he had hit his now-famous line drive. He and Babe Ruth had shared the bat for most of the summer, but Whiteman was taking it home to Houston. "I've been waiting 12 years to get a crack at the World Series," he said, "and I made good. I'm satisfied if I never play ball again."

Barrow praised his men for playing "machine-like baseball. The Cubs gave us a great battle. We presented a defense the Cubs could not break down. I felt our pitching staff and defensive play would offset our offensive weaknesses. We made only one error in the six games. When you consider that all of our victories were by one run, you realize what that near-perfect fielding meant. There were probably a half-dozen times in each of those games where a boot would have changed victory into defeat. But my boys never faltered."

In the final game, Carl Mays faced only three batters over the 27-man minimum. Chicago hit the ball out of the infield only twice in the last five innings and no Cub reached second base. Mays confessed making one mistake in Game Six—his first pitch to Fred Merkle in the fourth inning, which Merkle hit for a run-scoring single. It was either "a mistake of judgment or I was careless," he said, "which amounts to the same thing." After that inning was over, Mays set down the Cubs in order in the fifth, seventh, eighth and ninth innings, the last three crucial frames in which Chicago desperately needed a man on base. Mays thought he was sharper in Game Three. "The records say I pitched better ball today," he said, "but I don't believe I did."

"Boston has never lost a World Series," Harry Frazee boasted, referring to the Red Sox's five titles in 1903, 1912, 1915, 1916 and 1918, and the Braves' sweep in 1914. "The championship deserves to remain here until the war is won." McInnis hung on to the last ball of the game. In the clubhouse, it was signed by every Red Sox player and presented to Governor Samuel McCall, who said it would be placed among the state's cherished trophies.

Max Flack was immediately compared to Fred Snodgrass, who, in 1912, dropped a routine fly ball that helped Boston beat the New York Giants in the 10th inning of the final game of the World Series. Although he made a sensational catch on the next batter—and a mix-up by Fred Merkle and Christy Mathewson on a pop-up later in the inning was probably more damaging—Snodgrass would be remembered for that error the rest of his life. The New York Herald dubbed Flack's error the "$8,000 Muff"—the difference between the winning and losing team's shares and a reference to Snodgrass's error, known as the "$30,000 Muff."

"Honestly, I can't explain it," Flack said when asked about Whiteman's line drive. "I never felt surer of a fly ball in my life. Not that it was such an easy play, but it was a play I should have made and expected to make. I don't know now why I didn't do it. It wasn't overconfidence, I'm sure of that. I butterfingered the play and am unanimously elected as the goat. Ten years from now the scribes will write of how Flack's muff cost the series of 1918. It's the way of the old game."

Bill Killefer planned on enlisting once he was back in Chicago. "I'll never forget this Series, even if I am in no-man's land," said the Cubs catcher. "I never saw or heard of one that was lost by so many tough breaks. No doubt we should be sportsmen enough to give the winners credit, but I can't say that the better team won. I'll give the Red Sox credit for playing tight baseball, but I must say they were lucky." The *Washington Post* agreed: "The Red Sox have often been called the luckiest ball club in the world. They lived up to their reputation again today."

"This Series between teams of supposedly low ability," Hugh Fullerton wrote, "will go down in the records as the best played of all World Series." He also believed "the best team did not win" and that if the Series were played over again, "the majority of the experts who have watched all of the games would wager on Chicago."

Fred Mitchell was more magnanimous. "All the glory that goes with winning the world championship belongs to Boston," he said. "The pitching on both sides was the best in years. It was a tough series to lose. The scores of the games prove that. The Red Sox played clean, hard baseball. Luck went against the Cubs, and in a hard-fought series, luck is invariably the deciding factor. I won't say all the breaks were in favor of the Red Sox, but I'd say three-fourths were. Look at that fourth game. Ruth throws the ball to second base so wide that even Scott can't get it but Shean does, then crawls on his belly and tags the bag. If that isn't bull luck, what is it?

"I'm not trying to detract anything from the Red Sox. They are a great team and proved it. But I'd like to play the series over again if such a thing were possible.... I shall always contend that with an even break, we would have won. That's all I have to say on the subject."

The Red Sox would return to Fenway the following day to collect their Series shares. "They have not much to collect," Eddie Hurley wrote, "but that is no fault of theirs. They did their best and fought for what was rightly theirs. They must be given credit. They went through the season intact in the face of more upsets and more unpleasantness than was ever the lot of a championship team before. They've got the stuff that makes heroes. Is it any wonder they won?"

2 6

DISGRACEFUL CONDUCT

The winning share turned out to be $1,108.45 per player, the lowest amount ever awarded to the World Series champions. Ed Barrow, Heinie Wagner and 13 regulars—Babe Ruth, Joe Bush, Carl Mays, Sam Jones, Wally Schang, Sam Agnew, Wally Mayer, Stuffy McInnis, Dave Shean, Everett Scott, Harry Hooper, Amos Strunk and George Whiteman—were each awarded a full share. The Cubs' losing share was $671 per player.

The regulars spent the better part of an hour arguing whether the team's part-timers should receive a half-share or less. In the end, Fred Thomas received $750; Walt Kinney, Bill Pertica, Hack Miller, Jean Dubuc, George Cochran, Jack Coffey, Dick Hoblitzell and Dutch Leonard were each awarded $300. Comparable amounts went to team secretary Larry Graver, trainer Martin Lawler and groundskeeper Jerome Kelley; the team mascot and clubhouse boy were each given $25.

The Red Sox also distributed 10% of the team's share to various war charities. "After getting a peek at the members of the National Commission before the fifth game," McInnis explained, "we decided that we'd better dispose of that 10% ourselves. We'd be sure of it reaching the proper channels." The $2,300 check was split among Barrow and the regulars; each man chose his own charities (Hooper divided his among the Knights of Columbus, the Red Cross, the YMCA and the Salvation Army).

With baseball going into hibernation until the war's end, the sports pages were filled with fond farewells to the many stars unlikely to return, among them Ty Cobb, Frank Baker, Tris Speaker and Walter Johnson. After the Red Sox team meeting, Harry Hooper added his name to the list.

"I've been with the Red Sox for ten years," said the 31-year-old Hooper, "and yesterday I felt that I was playing in my last big game. I'm getting old for big league ball. And the outlook for the sport seems so dark—I don't anticipate there'll be any baseball next year. Then, when the game is resumed, salaries will be low and I may not be able to afford to come across the continent.

"I'll be sorry to leave Boston. I've made many friends here, I've had lots of good times. I wouldn't have remained in the game for so many years if I'd been playing in any other city."

The players signed baseballs for each other and bid each other good luck and goodbye. Many left the city by train that afternoon. Some were off to war-related jobs—Whiteman was working in "ground aviation work"; Miller had a job in the quartermaster's department on the West Coast; Jones, Coffey and Cochran planned on working in the oil fields out West; and Scott was considering a job with an Ohio electrical company.

September 12 was also another National Registration Day, as the draft age was expanded to include men age 18 to 45. Pertica enlisted in the Navy the day of Game Six, Thomas returned to his Navy base and Mays was awaiting a call from the Army. Other players pondered shipyard offers. After Harry Frazee had signed the remaining salary and bonus checks (paying the players through September 15), he and Ed Barrow left Boston for New York City.

After Babe Ruth pocketed his World Series share, he spent that evening acting as the official "starter" for bike and motorcycle races at the Revere Beach track. The following week, he refereed a local boxing tournament and attended the George Chaney–Lew Tendler fight on September 18 in Philadelphia. Babe mulled over at least seven shipyard offers, and a motion-picture producer contacted him about a possible film featuring the game's newest slugger offering baseball tips.

Ruth turned down an offer to play ball in California's War Service League, but did grab his bat and glove for a few games in New England. Four days after the World Series ended, Ruth pitched a 1-0 shutout for the Polis club before a huge crowd in Hartford, Connecticut. Reports of how much Ruth was paid for the exhibition varied from $350 to $1,300; the latter figure, if true, was nearly $200 more than his World Series share. A week later, Ruth relieved Walter Johnson in an exhibition game against the New Haven Colonials.

Ruth wasn't the only Red Sox playing in exhibition games. Joe Bush, Wally Schang, Wally Mayer and Amos Strunk formed a barnstorming club with several other major leaguers (four other Boston players, Sam Jones, Everett Scott, Sam Agnew and Hack Miller, may also have been part of the team). The team was advertised as the "Red Sox." After a loss to the Baltimore Dry Docks and Shipbuilding Company, Harry Frazee caught wind of the operation. "It's not the Red Sox team," he complained. "They have no right to use the club's name or call these players the world's champions."

On September 25, Ruth accepted a job with the Bethlehem Steel Company; he and Helen relocated to Lebanon, Pennsylvania. "It looks as though it's hard work all winter for me," Ruth wrote in a letter to Boston sportswriter Eddie Hurley. "All the boys have gone to work at some essential occupation and of course I'm big enough to do my bit. Before it's all over, I may be 'over there' yet."

A week after the Dry Dock loss, the ersatz Red Sox, now billing themselves as the "All-Stars," faced Ruth and his Lebanon mates. Babe played first base, batted fourth and struck out twice against Joe Bush, who three-hit Lebanon and won 4-2. Lebanon played four more games before its season ended on October 12, but Ruth didn't appear in any of them.

The sudden influx of players into the shipyard industry wasn't exactly a boon. Many were hired as "ringers" for the company teams and assigned nominal duties such as carrying blueprints or paint cans from one spot to another; some supposedly arrived wearing fancy clothes, bragging about their big league careers. More than 2,000 workers at the Cramps shipyard near Philadelphia went on strike, protesting that ballplayers, actors and other inexperienced men had been given supervisory jobs. One striker complained that a ballplayer-foreman kept calling the hold of the ship the "cellar" and the deck "upstairs."

After his three-hitter clinched Game Six, Carl Mays hung up his glove and spikes. He stayed in Boston and on September 19, married Marjorie Fredericka Madden, a student at the New England Conservatory of Music. Madden was a baseball fan and had met Mays shortly after he joined the Red Sox in 1915 (the Conservatory was very close to Putnam's, the residential hotel used by many of the players). Mays carried a photograph of her sitting on the roof of the Red Sox dugout. The pitcher's only guest at the wedding was Ralph McDonald, a former ballplayer at Tufts College. The bride and groom left that afternoon for a short honeymoon in Missouri before Mays reported for military service.

Mays was appointed leader of a group of 18 men traveling by train from Mansfield, Missouri, to St. Louis; Mays called it "the saddest and most ill-fated trip" of his life. "We were sworn in on November 6, only five days before the Armistice was signed, but ten of those men never made it back alive. Some never even got to put on a uniform." They had arrived in St. Louis just as the influenza epidemic was hitting its peak.

Some men were quarantined immediately, and Mays never saw them again.

Influenza had appeared in the spring, but in September it returned to the East Coast with a vengeance. Boston was a busy port for returning servicemen, and American soldiers had apparently brought back with them an even stronger strain of the disease. From Boston, the virus spread to New York and Philadelphia, then across the country. More than 195,000 Americans died from influenza in October 1918 alone.

Boston Globe sportswriter Edward Martin was one of them, passing away the day after his wife had succumbed. Two months later, Harry Casey of the *Boston Evening Record* also died, as did American League umpire Francis "Silk" O'Loughlin. For 24 years, O'Loughlin had been one of the game's more colorful umpires, often cutting short a player's argument with a wave of his arm and the words, "Get out of here. I never missed one in my life, too late to start now. The Pope for religion, O'Loughlin for baseball: both infallible."

Babe Ruth apparently contracted influenza twice. In mid-September, a Baltimore newspaper said that Ruth had fallen victim to the "Spanish flu" while visiting his relatives in Baltimore. Roughly a month later, a story from Lebanon, Pennsylvania, stated Ruth was recuperating from "Spanish influenza" in Baltimore. Neither instance was deemed serious, and apparently no other Red Sox players were affected.

The death toll from the 1918–19 epidemic reached 675,000 in the United States and between 20 and 40 million worldwide. It is still considered the deadliest infectious disease in human history.

In October, Ban Johnson returned from his annual hunting trip with Charles Comiskey and renewed his attacks on the Red Sox. Johnson demanded receipts proving that the Boston players had donated the proper portion of their World Series earnings to charity. He also announced that Joe Bush, Wally Schang, Amos Strunk and Wally Mayer were under investigation for post-season barnstorming violations.

Players on World Series teams were prohibited from playing exhibition games after the season; ostensibly a way to maintain the "purity" of the World Series, the rule was also a way to limit players' earnings, especially baseball income outside the control of the National Commission.

Johnson also announced that as punishment for the players' one-hour delay before Game Five, the Commission was withholding the traditional championship emblems, which were similar to lapel pins and the equivalent of modern-day World Series rings. In 1916, the Commission had also tried to withhold the Red Sox's emblems because of a barnstorming tour. After intense criticism, they reversed the decision, but fined each player $100, the approximate value of the emblems. This time, however, the Commission wasn't backing down.

Stuffy McInnis was furious and disgusted. "This is just another link in the chain of antagonism he has been forging against our team for some time," he said. Shortly before Christmas, each Red Sox player received a letter from John Heydler informing him that he would not receive an emblem "owing to the disgraceful conduct of the players in the strike during the Series."

At the American League meeting in December, Ban Johnson was asked about his promise to Harry Hooper that the Red Sox players would not be punished for their Game Five delay. Johnson denied having said it.* As a show of thanks that winter, Harry Frazee presented several of his players with pocket watches engraved with their names and the words "RED SOX 1918 CHAMPIONS."

---

* Eighteen years after Harry Hooper's death, in September 1993, the Red Sox held a ceremony at Fenway Park celebrating the 75th anniversary of the 1918 championship team. There were no surviving players, but replica emblems were awarded to a dozen of their descendants.

27

"I Have Never been a Disturbing Element on the Red Sox"

Babe Ruth's New Year's resolution was simple—make more money. In January 1919 he announced that he was underpaid and wanted $15,000 for the upcoming season—nearly twice his 1918 pay—or a three-year contract totaling $30,000, threatening to retire if he was denied.

Frazee called Ruth's demand "absurd" and offered a smaller increase to $8,500. A compromise seemed unlikely. One Boston paper suggested that the Big Fellow's boost in salary could be raised through public contributions. As spring training neared, Frazee hinted that Babe's time in Boston might be running out. "If Ruth doesn't want to work for the Red Sox at the handsome salary offered him," he said on March 16, "maybe we can make an advantageous trade for him."

Five days later, however, the two men agreed on a three-year deal—$10,000 per season for 1919, 1920 and 1921. Ruth headed south for camp in Tampa, Florida. In his first exhibition game, he belted a home run that a group of sportswriters measured at 579 feet.

On April 18 and 19, Ruth played two exhibition games in Baltimore. "I was afraid some of my old neighbors didn't believe all that they've read in the papers about me," he said. "This was my chance to show them what I could do." In six at-bats, he hit six home runs.

During the season, Ruth squabbled with Ed Barrow about his nocturnal ramblings and what position he would play. Ruth was suspended for one game in late April and two months later, he gave his bosses an ultimatum: he would either pitch or play the outfield, but not both. At the end of the year, Babe had spent 111 games in the outfield, 4 at first base and 17 on the mound, where he finished with a 9-5 record and a 2.97 ERA.

Ruth astounded the baseball world that summer by hitting 29 home runs, nearly double the former American League record of 16. Frank Baker, Tilly Walker and George Sisler hit 10 apiece as runners-up. Gavvy Cravath hit 12 to top the National League for the third consecutive year. At the time, the accepted home run record was Buck Freeman's 25 in 1899. But sometime during the 1919 season, someone had unearthed Ned Williamson's mark of 27 for the Chicago White Stockings in 1884.[*]

Ruth's 29 home runs accounted for 12% of the American League's total. Eleven major league teams hadn't hit that many home runs in 1919. Ruth topped the major leagues in slugging percentage (.657), on-base percentage (.456) , runs scored (103), runs batted in (114), and

---

[*] In 1884, the White Stockings ruled that any ball hit over the short right field fence at Lake Park (215 feet away) would be a home run instead of a double. That season, the team hit 142 home runs, 131 of those at home. The second highest team total was Buffalo with 39. Williamson hit 25 of his 27 home runs at home. The rule was abolished the following year and Williamson hit only three home runs.

total bases (284) and drew the second most walks (101). He either drove in or scored one-third of Boston's runs and more than half of his 139 hits were long hits: 34 doubles, 12 triples and 29 home runs. His .322 batting average was by far the highest on the team.

Yet after May 22, Boston spent only one day above fifth place, finishing 66-71, 20½ games behind the White Sox. What went wrong? The pitching staff had crumbled. Ernie Shore and Dutch Leonard were traded to the Yankees before the season began, Joe Bush injured his arm in spring training and made only two starts, and Sam Jones and Herb Pennock were hurt for weeks at a time. In mid-July Carl Mays walked out on the team and was traded to the Yankees. Boston's staff ERA ballooned to 3.31.

After another stupendous season in which he had exceeded all expectations, Ruth was now the undisputed star of the game. He announced that the three-year deal he fought Harry Frazee for less than 12 months earlier was now inadequate—a salary of $20,000 was more appropriate. Ruth hired an agent, which was highly unusual, and once again vowed he'd go into boxing (an annual threat) or begin a movie career if he wasn't properly compensated.

Ty Cobb, who was fanatical about being the highest paid player in the game, called Ruth a "contract violator." Babe responded, "A player is worth just as much as he can get, and Cobb has been paid all that he is worth, believe me, for quite a few years. I wouldn't say anything against Cobb if he held out for $100,000, why should he say anything about me?"*

The New York Yankees finished the 1919 season in third place. When owner Jacob Ruppert asked his manager how the club could improve, Miller Huggins replied, "Get Ruth from Boston." Huggins knew that Joe

---

* Ruth's belief in players' rights never changed. At spring training in 1948, he said, "Ballplayers should get all they can in the way of salary from their bosses and there should be no ceiling on salaries."

Lannin had been pressuring Harry Frazee for payment on some of the notes Frazee used to buy the team. "Ruth hit 29 home runs," Huggins told Ruppert. "Bring him to the Polo Grounds and he'll make it 35, at least."

On December 21, 1919, Paul Shannon of the *Boston Post* called Ruth a "disturbing element" on the Red Sox, a "Second Frankenstein" whose oversized ego and demands for more money put "a big dent in his popularity" and irritated management. Shannon concluded that "Red Sox fans need not be greatly astonished if the burly batter is allowed to pass on through some deal."

Ruppert and Frazee worked out their deal in secret and signed it the day after Christmas. Two days later, when asked about his winter plans, Frazee said cryptically, "I'll trade anyone but Harry Hooper." Ruth's sale to the Yankees was announced on January 5, 1920. It hit Boston like a bomb.

> Boston's greatest baseball player has been cast adrift. George H. Ruth, the middle initial apparently standing for "Hercules," maker of home runs and the most colorful star in the game today, became the property of the New York Yankees yesterday afternoon.
>
> *Boston Globe,* January 6, 1920

"It was an amount the club could not afford to refuse," Frazee said. "With this money, the Boston club can now go into the market and buy other players and have a stronger and better team in all respects than we would have had if Ruth had remained with us.

"I do not wish to detract one iota from Ruth's ability as a ballplayer nor from his value as an attraction, but there is no getting away from the fact that despite his 29 home runs, the Red Sox finished sixth last year. What the Boston fans want, I take it, and what I want because they want it is a winning team, rather than a one-man team that finishes in sixth place."

Frazee called Ruth's home runs "more spectacular than useful" and his insistence on doing whatever he pleased both on and off the field created resentment among his teammates who were naturally expected to follow the rules.

The cash deal was reported as both $100,000 and $125,000—either way the most money that had ever been paid for one ballplayer. Another part of the agreement, a $350,000 loan from Ruppert to Frazee, with the Yankees holding the mortgage on Fenway Park, was kept secret. (The Yankees held the mortgage until 1933.)

Public opinion of the sale was mixed. Two former members of the Boston Braves supported Frazee. Fred Tenney, a first baseman, said, "Frazee knows his business best. Ruth is a great attraction, but no player is indispensable to a team." Hugh Duffy hinted at Ruth's selfishness: "Star players do not make a winning team, and men of ordinary ability working for the interest of the club are greater factors in a winning machine than one individual."

Johnny Keenan, the leader of the Royal Rooters, disagreed. "It will be impossible to replace the strength Ruth gave the club," he said. "Management will have an awful time filling the gap caused by his going."

Another fan, Orville Dennison of Cambridge, wrote to the *Globe*: "It is not strange that the first reaction to the Babe Ruth story was negative to most Hub fans, but to me it was a positive one. I admire Frazee's willingness to incur the enmity of the fans, at least temporarily, in his efforts to produce a happy, winning team. Many sane followers of baseball claim that there is no player in the game who is worth paying $100,000 for, and that if the Boston club obtained such a sum, it is the gainer."

Ruth was in California when the deal was announced. "My heart is in Boston," he said. "I have a farm in Sudbury and I like New England. I'm not stuck on the idea."

A few days later, he sent a telegram from Los Angeles to the *Boston Herald and Journal*:

Wish you would print the following message to the Boston fans for me:

"All of the interviews credited to Frazee which have been printed in the Los Angeles papers, and I suppose they were the same as printed in Boston, are untrue and can be meant only to put me in bad with the Boston fans. I was as much surprised on hearing of the deal that transferred me to New York as were the Boston public.

"I never have been a disturbing element on the Red Sox. This can be proven readily by asking any of the boys who are on the club. I am friendly with all of the fellows and I firmly believe that they all would go to the limit for me and regret my leaving the club as much I do going.

"If there is any doubt about my being on friendly terms with the fellows, I will pay willingly any expense that the fans and press might incur to take the trouble to find out. This propaganda has been sent out to try to pacify Boston people over the sale. It is a rank injustice to both them and me, for there is not any of it true.

"I am thinking very seriously of taking the matter to court to prove these statements untrue and show Boston fans that they are being tricked by the so-called sportsman Frazee.

"The Boston club is my favorite, and naturally I wanted to remain there, but as the deal is completed, I suppose I will have to go to New York. I hadn't the slightest idea that this deal was on and I think that Frazee surely showed himself up in his true colors when he tries to belittle me to cover up his blunder.

"I appreciate the stand taken by the Boston people and very shortly hope to be in Boston to thank them in person for their support.

"Thanking you for past favors and wishing you success, I remain, your friend,

                         Babe Ruth"

28

THE FIX?

Fred Krehbiel had often done odd jobs around Comiskey Park when his uncle, Bill Veeck, owned the White Sox, and even after Veeck had sold his interest in the team, Krehbiel stayed on. One summer afternoon in 1963, Krehbiel was working in one of the park's many storage rooms when he discovered a hole in the wall. The hole, hidden behind the thick leg of a wooden table, was stuffed with papers—"two old note-books, one a hard-cover ledger book and the other a long, old-fash-ioned legal pad."

Krehbiel showed his find to Veeck. The ledger gave the White Sox's financial data for 1920; tucked into the ledger was a list of the players' salaries for 1918 and 1920. Veeck knew the team's records were intact up to and including 1919—and then again after 1921. The missing year was the season in which it was discovered that eight White Sox players had conspired to lose the previous year's World Series to the Cincinnati Reds.

The legal pad contained approximately two dozen pages of hand-written notes by Harry Grabiner, Charles Comiskey's secretary and right-hand man during the 1910s and 1920s. Veeck had become friends with Grabiner when the two men were partners in the Cleveland Indians front office. Grabiner had mentioned his baseball "diary" on several occasions, but Veeck never pressed him about it at the time, although every once in a while he and his nephew would search for it in the club's old files.

In *The Hustler's Handbook*, Veeck explained why Grabiner's notes (which Veeck also called a diary) and the financial data had been hidden:

> [T]he very first paragraph shows, beyond any doubt, that the White Sox front office had more than some inkling what was going on from the very first game of the 1919 World Series.... [I]t is perfectly evident that Harry sat down after the World Series was over to get the first part of the story down on paper.... Harry is doing his best at all times to put the blame elsewhere, particularly upon Comiskey's enemies.

Grabiner's notes almost exclusively concern the activities of the White Sox front office in the months following the 1919 World Series. But they also mention several apparently fixed games played late in the 1920 season (Cleveland–St. Louis and Cleveland–Detroit) that helped the Indians win the pennant. Near the end of his notes, in an entry possibly dating from January 1921, Grabiner wrote, "Saw Landis.... He asked regarding players that I knew that were even mentioned in any wrongdoing so told him complete list on page 27."

The list that Grabiner referred to Commissioner Kenesaw Mountain Landis named 27 players, including pitcher Grover Alexander and infielders Joe Gedeon and Rabbit Maranville. Another name on the list was one that few baseball fans would recognize. He had been teammates with Max Flack, Claude Hendrix, Les Mann, Rollie Zeider and Otto Knabe. Later in his career, he played with Heinie Zimmerman and Eugene Paulette, both of whom were banished by Landis amid allegations of game-fixing. This player was an above-average pitcher in the National and Federal leagues from 1912 to 1919, and the circumstances surrounding his departure from the game are murky.

Next to the name Gene Packard, Grabiner wrote: "1918 Series fixer."

Grabiner wasn't the only person who believed the Series was corrupt. According to a biography of Ban Johnson, the American League president "had information that a professional gambler planned to fix the 1918 World Series between the Cubs and Red Sox but dropped the idea of an investigation when he was unable to raise sufficient funds to carry it out."

Much of the other information in Grabiner's diary was verified decades later. But his assertion that the 1918 World Series was fixed—and who fixed it—has never been examined.

Eugene Packard was born on July 13, 1887, in Colorado Springs, Colorado. His father, Douglas Packard, had been a ballplayer and hoped his three sons would learn the finer points of the game. In their yard, he ran a rope through the center of three baseballs and hung them vertically from a tree limb. The line was anchored to the ground so that the three balls were at shoulder-, waist-and knee-height. The elder Packard would call out "high," "low" or "waist," as well as "inside" or "outside," and his sons would pitch, trying to hit the corresponding ball. All three Packard boys would eventually play professional baseball: two became pitchers and the other an infielder.

Gene attended high school in Helena, Oklahoma, and began his career in 1907, earning $100 a month with the Independence team in the Oklahoma-Kansas-Missouri League. In 1911, while he was with the Columbus Senators (American Association), Packard married Lutye Jackson, the daughter of a Helena minister. The couple honeymooned in Phoenix so that Packard could pitch twice a week in a winter league.

Packard made his major league debut with the Cincinnati Reds on September 27, 1912, pitching a complete game victory. The following season, the left-hander was 7-11 with a 2.97 ERA for a team that finished near the National League basement. Packard was earning $2,500 with the Reds and when he received a more substantial offer from the Federal League, he signed with the Kansas City Packers. Packard was the only pitcher to win 20 or more games in both years of the Federal League's existence, although he never finished among the leaders in any statistical category. In June 1915 Packard's younger brother, Milo, a minor league pitcher, was killed by lightning while working in a wheat field. Packard adopted "Milo" as his own middle name.

When the Federal League dissolved, Packard, then 29 years old, took a substantial cut in salary and joined the 1916 Chicago Cubs. After posting a 10-6 record with the Cubs, he was traded to the Cardinals early the following season. Packard also pitched for St. Louis in 1918, and in September, he was reportedly hoping for a job in Dayton, Ohio, but failing that, he'd try his luck on the West Coast. After the season, the St. Louis papers don't mention him again. If Packard attended any of the World Series games, he did so without attracting attention.

In July 1919 Packard, now pitching for the Phillies, led a drunken protest against the club's management in the center field bleachers. Packard was fined $200 and pitched in only two more games before announcing his retirement in August, saying he was joining a semi-pro club in Massillion, Ohio.

Eugene Paulette joined the Phillies on the day of Packard's protest. When he held out for a higher salary in 1921, Paulette was charged with throwing games and accepting bribes for games dating back to 1918. Two of his supposed St. Louis gambling connections, Carl Zork and Elmer Farrar, were well-known: Zork's name surfaced during the trial of the 1919 White Sox players. Commissioner Landis banned Paulette from baseball. About three weeks later, Paulette signed with the same semi-pro team in Massillion, Ohio, that Packard had joined less than two years earlier.

In the late 1800s and early 1900s, gambling and baseball were as inseparable as peanuts and Cracker Jacks. Admission to a game was first charged around 1860; reports of suspected corruption surfaced about two years later. The National League was plagued by a game-throwing scandal in its second year of existence, when four Louisville players conspired to lose the 1877 pennant. An umpire was banished in 1882 for advising gamblers how to bet in games he worked.

During the deadball era, suspicions about the integrity of the pennant races and the World Series were practically an annual occurrence. In 1903, Boston's Cy Young refused a bribe of about nine times his annual salary to throw a crucial World Series game. Two years later, gamblers got to Philadelphia pitcher Rube Waddell, who missed the entire Series because he had supposedly tripped over a suitcase. Gamblers tried fixing the National League pennant race in 1908. There were serious doubts about the honesty of the 1914 World Series, in which the Boston Braves swept the heavily-favored Athletics, as well as the 1915 and 1916 National League races. In 1917, the Chicago White Sox gave money and gifts to players on both Detroit and St. Louis for tanking in games against them in September.

Whenever a new allegation or rumor came to light, it was either hushed up or flatly denied, depending on who was making the accusation. When umpire Bill Klem, known for his upstanding reputation, revealed that he had been offered $3,000 to make sure the New York Giants won their 1908 playoff game against the Chicago Cubs, the National League appointed a committee to investigate. The inquiry was supervised by John T. Brush—the owner of the Giants. Unsurprisingly, Brush recommended that no further action be taken. (It was later discovered that the Giants' trainer, who had political connections in New York, had bribed Klem.)

In 1918, when the government closed the nation's racetracks, gamblers swarmed to the ballparks to set up shop. Many of them were intimate with both players and club owners; some gamblers even kept a few players on weekly salaries.

That year, there were ample motives for a fix. The World Series shares would be the smallest ever. No one knew if or when baseball would be played again and players were worried about money and their families' security. On top of that, the Red Sox and Cubs felt cheated by the National Commission, which had unilaterally decided to share their World Series revenue with six other teams. Combined with the players' well-justified antagonism towards their employers and the legions of gamblers working in nearly every ballpark, the situation was ripe for exploitation and dishonesty. All of this was happening at the end of a decade soaked with greed, betrayal and anger, one of the most wretchedly disorganized eras in baseball history. Given the circumstances, it is easy to understand how some players could have been willing to entertain the idea of a fix.

But as the Red Sox and Cubs prepared for their showdown, betting— like the public's interest in the Series—was on the wane. *The Sporting News*, the half-dozen dailies in both Boston and Chicago, and papers from Washington, Philadelphia, New York, Cleveland, San Francisco and New Orleans, all reported that gambling was minimal. On Chicago's South Side—White Sox, and thus, American League territory—what little betting there was on the opening game favored the Red Sox, who were slim 6-to-5 favorites.

During the 1918 World Series, no suspicions of foul play were reported in any of the Boston or Chicago newspapers. In 1919, by contrast, Chicago's hotel lobbies were buzzing with gamblers and sportswriters Fred Lieb and Hugh Fullerton both heard rumors of a fix. When Bill Burns, a former pitcher and inveterate gambler, advised Fullerton to "get wise" and bet on the underdog Reds, Fullerton was convinced the rumors were true. He confided his suspicions to Christy Mathewson, who, as manager of the Reds in 1918, had dealt with the crooked Hal Chase. Mathewson told Fullerton that the difference between an effective pitch and a disastrous one, or a fielding gem and a near-miss, was almost undetectable, even to the other players on the field. And how could one tell if a hitter wasn't trying his hardest? Fullerton and Mathewson agreed to independently circle on their scorecards any plays they found suspicious, then compare notes after the game.

What if we could have sat in that same Comiskey Park press box in early September 1918—what would our scorecards look like? What plays would we have circled?

The best, and perhaps the only available, way to analyze the 1918 World Series is to look closely at each game through the accounts of the men who were there. The sportswriters watched the games, talked with the players, and wrote their impressions and opinions for publication either later that evening or the following morning. Their collective day-by-day reports are as close as one can get to a running narrative of the Series.

In the 1919 opener, White Sox pitcher Eddie Cicotte hit Cincinnati's Morrie Rath in the back with his second pitch, a pre-arranged signal to everyone involved that the fix was on. There was nothing as obvious as that in Boston's 1-0 Game One victory in 1918. Surprise starter Babe Ruth did falter in the early innings, but he pitched a masterful game. After the Red Sox scored their run, he was untouchable.

The Cubs threatened to score in three separate innings, but "lacked the punch that [had] carried them" to the pennant. Two aspects of this game are worth examining. One is Chicago manager Fred Mitchell's choice of Charlie Pick at second base. Pick joined the Cubs late in the season after the Pacific Coast League shut down. He was a left-handed batter and hit .326 in 89 at-bats; that hot streak should be balanced against his .241 mark as the full-time third baseman of the 1916 Athletics. Many writers thought Rollie Zeider, a veteran right-handed batter, was the logical choice against the southpaw Ruth. Hugh

Fullerton blamed the Cubs' 1-0 loss partly on Mitchell's decision to start "an inexperienced player" like Pick over the "brainy, gritty and clever" Zeider.

In the first inning, Pick, batting with the bases loaded, appeared unprepared and flew out to left field. Ruth struck him out in his next at-bat. At that point, Mitchell should have been "tipped off" to Pick's weaknesses, but acted "deaf, dumb and blind"—allowing him to hit in the sixth with men at first and second. His soft grounder to first advanced the runners, but the Cubs failed to score. Pick was pulled for a pinch-hitter in the ninth, but Mitchell often went to his bench for fresh blood in the final frame. And the Cubs had no one on base at the time. Fullerton called Pick "an easy mark for Ruth. There is no telling what Zeider would have done, but he could not have done worse."

The second noteworthy aspect was the fielding of Pick's infield partner, Charlie Hollocher. The rookie shortstop had impressed everyone with his glove work during the season, but however flashy he may have been, he handled only 5.7 chances per game, among the lowest for National League shortstops, and committed 53 errors. In the first four innings, Fullerton wrote that Hollocher "was in the wrong position for almost every batter.... He was out of position on Whiteman in the second inning.... The kid was also in the wrong position for Hooper in the third...and in the fourth, when the lone run of the game was registered, he was sadly misplaced on Whiteman again."

Hollocher and Pick also drew criticism for not holding Dave Shean closer to second base in the fourth; Shean's long lead allowed him to score on Stuffy McInnis's single. "Shean and Whiteman started for third and second respectively as Vaughn wound up," wrote Paul Shannon in the *Boston Post*. "As McInnis' bat met the ball, Shean was well-nigh two-thirds of the way to third.... Mann made a nice throw home and Shean was just able to beat the ball to the rubber."

Cleveland writers Henry Edwards and James Lanyon thought left fielder Les Mann was also out of position, standing "fully fifty feet from the spot to which McInnis generally hits," where Stuffy promptly deposited "one of his famous left field hits." Nine of the Cubs had played in the American League and McInnis had starred on World Series teams in 1913 and 1914—shouldn't at least one of them have known McInnis was strictly a pull hitter?

Mitchell's lineup was the same for Game Two. Overnight, Pick had apparently "shook off his nervousness": he singled, walked and scored a run against Joe Bush, his former Athletics teammate, and handled eight chances at second base without incident. Fullerton thought one of them, an on-the-run grab of Everett Scott's fourth-inning bouncer behind first base, was the play of the day. Fullerton also noted that the Cubs battled the Red Sox for the entire game, an attitude distinctly absent in the opener. The Red Sox had few scoring opportunities against Lefty Tyler, and Bush had been undone by another dose of the rotten luck and poor run support that had plagued him throughout the season.

If there had been a fix, and if the outcome of the Series was pre-destined while the teams were in Chicago, would a Red Sox victory in Game Three have been necessary? With a win, Boston would take a 2-1 advantage, and the rest of the Series would be at Fenway Park. But a Cubs win in Game Three probably would have heightened the drama for the following games, since the Red Sox would have needed to battle back in their own yard.

Jim Vaughn returned for Game Three, and like his performance in Game One, was marred only by a brief lapse in the fourth inning, when Boston turned a hit batsman and four consecutive singles into two runs. The Cubs put men on base in seven of the nine innings, but they "could not hit when they had to have hits."

Mitchell later insisted that sending Pick home had been a necessary gamble. Though the *Chicago Daily Tribune* claimed "there is not a dissenting voice" against that decision, it was actually just the opposite. Nearly every writer in the press box thought the decision was desperate and foolish, "a frantic effort" and "reckless base-running." Pick had still been on the ground when Mitchell yelled at him to run; the manager's failure to consider how long it would take Pick to scramble to his feet before racing home turned the play into "baseball suicide."

Paul Shannon wrote that the ball rolled "toward the Chicago dugout. Pick started home, stopped for a fraction of an instant till he saw that Thomas had lost track of the situation and then resumed his hurried journey to the plate." Shannon noted that Pick's hitting was "one of the big surprises of the series"—he was 3-9—but "like Lot's wife, he looked around at a critical moment only to invite disaster." One possible explanation for Pick's hesitation was that he couldn't hear Mitchell's shouts over the crowd, which was cheering loudly after Schang's passed ball and errant throw to third. But Shannon claimed Pick had already started toward the plate when he momentarily stopped running and "the instant lost was fatal."

Chicago writer Charles Dryden reported that "awful complications would have followed a tied score," but did not elaborate. Did he mean Mitchell's pinch-hitting strategy would have weakened the Cubs lineup? It's doubtful. Pinch-hitter Turner Barber was batting when the game ended; had Pick been safe and the game gone into extra innings, Mitchell simply would have put Barber at third, replacing Charlie Deal (the man he hit for).

The Cubs had a reputation as a smart club, but so far, Henry Edwards of the *Cleveland Plain Dealer* wrote, "they have not used their heads." Earlier in the third game, Les Mann might have cost his team a run by not tagging up on Dode Paskert's deep fly to left. If the ball had fallen safely, Mann could have walked home. But he had taken a twenty-or thirty-foot lead while watching the play and was forced to retreat to the bag. There were also several times when first baseman Merkle and the Chicago pitcher were confused about who would field bunts.

Keeping in mind Hugh Fullerton's comments about Charlie Hollocher playing out of position in Game One, we should note that the Cubs shortstop committed a two-out error on Everett Scott's grounder in the second inning of Game Three. The error allowed George Whiteman to advance to third base, but Fred Thomas made the third out and Boston didn't score.

In the three games at Fenway Park, nothing changed between the foul lines. Boston took advantage of Chicago's mistakes and the Cubs sabotaged themselves several times with base-running gaffes. After Boston won the Series in six games, Chicago's right fielder Max Flack was the goat with the biggest horns.

Flack began Game Four with a single and was picked off first by Sam Agnew. In the third inning, Flack was on second when pitcher Babe Ruth and shortstop Everett Scott worked "a very pretty play" and picked him off again. Several minutes later, Flack misplayed Ruth's line drive into a triple. And of course, his error on Whiteman's hit in Game Six had been crucial to Boston's Series-clinching victory.

In Game Four, Chicago nearly doubled Boston's hit total (seven to four); Ruth walked six Cubs in eight innings and had just one 1-2-3 inning. But the Red Sox won because of their "quick thinking," the "analytical eye" of their infielders, and a late-inning throwing error by Cubs reliever Phil Douglas. In addition to Flack's mental lapses on the bases, Agnew almost picked Charlie Deal off first in the second inning and Fred Merkle was nearly nabbed in the seventh. The Cubs hit into three inning-ending double plays.

When Tyler faced Ruth with men on first and second, "the last thing which anybody expected was that Tyler would make the mistake of putting the next one over the plate, waist high, but that is exactly what he did." Ruth smacked the ball over Flack's head.

Tyler was pulled in the eighth for pinch-hitter Claude Hendrix, who would then stay in the game and pitch. But after Hendrix wandered off second base, Mitchell replaced him with Bill McCabe, thereby making him send a different pitcher, Phil Douglas, to the mound in the 2-2 game. Douglas gave up a single and threw a wild pitch before his error on Harry Hooper's bunt—a play on which Douglas had "plenty of time"—allowed the go-ahead (and game-winning) run to score.

Hugh Fullerton's recaps sounded eerily similar: "[F]or the third time [Chicago] threw away a game which seemed to be won…. It looks as if the Cubs are whipped, and whipped not by superior play, but by their own shortcomings."

Douglas was a good pitcher—when he was sober. But that wasn't often, and he was traded to the New York Giants in 1919. In the 1922 pennant race, after being chewed out by manager John McGraw, Douglas got drunk and wrote a letter to Les Mann, his former teammate and now a Cardinals outfielder.

> I want to leave here. I don't want to see this guy [McGraw] win the pennant. You know I can pitch, and I am afraid if I stay I will win the pennant for him.
> Talk this over with the boys, and if it is all right send the goods to my house at night and I will go to fishing camp. Let me know if you all will do this, and I will go home on the next train.

When he sobered up, Douglas probably remembered that the straight-laced Mann was the last person he should try to enlist in a dishonest endeavor. Douglas telegrammed Mann, begging him to destroy the letter, but Mann turned it over to his manager, Branch Rickey, who then passed it along to Commissioner Landis. When Douglas admitted writing the letter, Landis banned him from baseball for life.

On August 31, 1920, Douglas's former teammate, Cubs pitcher Claude Hendrix, was scratched from a scheduled start against Philadelphia. Cubs president Bill Veeck had received two anonymous phone calls that morning claiming the game had been fixed for the Cubs to lose. Hendrix had allegedly sent a telegram to gambler Frog Thompson that said he was betting $5,000 against his own team. Thompson denied everything, as did Hendrix. There were also allegations that Hal Chase and Fred Merkle were involved. Chase had already been banned from baseball for gambling-related infractions and while Merkle was neither suspended nor banned, he did retire at the end of the season. When Chicago released Hendrix after the season, no other team signed him and his career was over.*

Is it a coincidence that Douglas and Hendrix, both of whom would be exiled from baseball within three years, played essential roles in the game that put the Red Sox one victory away from the championship? Fred Van Ness of the *New York Herald* thought the Red Sox "were crowned with horseshoes" in the fourth game, but other writers were more blunt: "Chicago presented the fourth game to Boston." The Cubs "made costly misplays at critical stages and displayed minor league judgment in teamwork…. They had chances galore to win and tossed them away…."

In Game Five, Jim Vaughn returned and threw a five-hitter—his third complete game in six days. "For the first time in the series, [the Cubs] made absolutely no blunders, mentally or physically" and Chicago won 3-0. Charlie Hollocher reached base four times and scored two runs, and Les Mann and Dode Paskert both contributed run-scoring doubles. Chicago turned three double plays, which ended Boston's fourth, fifth and seventh innings.

The game had begun an hour late, after the players' protest of the division of the World Series gate receipts. For the next two days, there were rumors that Harry Frazee and Charles Weeghman had promised the players a cut of the ticket revenue of any additional games, in an attempt to persuade them to finish the Series. If that were true, it's possible the players might have conspired to prolong the Series.

---

* The Cubs-Phillies scandal led to a general investigation of gambling and baseball. This revived long-held suspicions about the 1919 World Series—which is how the White Sox scandal came to light. During questioning, Charles Weeghman, who by then had sold his interest in the Cubs, testified that Chicago gambler Monte Tennes told him in August 1919 that the upcoming World Series would be fixed. This was *before* either of the pennant races had been decided.

Before Max Flack's third-inning error in Game Six, bases on balls again caused trouble for the Cubs. Lefty Tyler "suffered the fate of the pitcher sent too often to the well…. [He] paid the penalty for his brief lack of control…[and] shattered the hopes" of the Cubs.

"Flack's muff was just one of the many evidences of Boston luck," J. V. Fitz Gerald of the *Washington Post* wrote. "The Cubs could not rise to an emergency in the fashion of their rivals. When they did get on base they didn't seem to know what to do."

Flack was known as one of the better right fielders in the National League. Should he have been playing as deep as he was? Whiteman didn't possess Ruthian power, but he had belted a triple to right-center off Tyler in Game Two and flown out to Flack three times in the Series. It wasn't uncommon for Whiteman to hit to the opposite field, so perhaps Flack's outfield position was justified. It's impossible to know if Flack intentionally dropped the ball, but when this error is considered alongside his misjudgment of Ruth's triple and the three times he was picked off base, Flack's play becomes a little more suspicious.

But Flack wasn't the only friend the Red Sox had in Game Six. Carl Mays picked off Charlie Pick to end the second inning, then caught Les Mann in the fourth. A total of five Cubs were nabbed: four on the bases and one for oversliding the bag. Another oversliding gaffe had given Pick a slow start home in Game Three.

When compiling *The Reach Official American League Guide* for 1919 (a collection of recaps and statistics from the previous year), the editors thought it was peculiar "that in all of the defeats suffered by the [Cubs] southpaws, they started their own downfall either with a base on balls or hit-by-pitcher, and in no case was the winning rally started with a [Boston] hit."

In the coming years, three members of the 1918 Red Sox would be suspected of involvement with gambling and game-fixing.

When Boston released Jean Dubuc, the pitcher signed with the New York Giants. After a good season in 1919, he was inexplicably dumped. The reason would become clear a year later, when news of the White Sox World Series fix became public. Dubuc admitted before a grand jury that he had been in the Ansonia Hotel room in New York when the details of the fix were finalized. (Giants manager John McGraw believed Dubuc, Hal Chase and several other Giants helped throw the 1919 pennant race to Cincinnati.) By the time the White Sox trial began in 1921, Dubuc had fled to Canada, where he played semi-pro and minor league ball. Two years later, he was back in the U.S., playing minor league ball in upstate New York. He was never punished for his advance knowledge of the 1919 fix.

Both Carl Mays and Joe Bush were traded to the New York Yankees, Mays in July 1919 and Bush during the winter of 1921. New York sportswriter Fred Lieb claimed that Yankees owner Jacob Ruppert and manager Miller Huggins were convinced that both pitchers intentionally lost World Series games. In Game Four of the 1921 Series, Mays, after supposedly receiving a signal from his wife in the Polo Grounds stands, allowed three eighth-inning runs and lost the game to the New York Giants 4-2. Mays also lost Game Seven 2-1, and the Giants won the best-of-nine series five games to three. Oddly enough, Mays's pitching opponent in both of his losses was Shufflin' Phil Douglas.

In 1922, the Yankees again met the Giants in the World Series. In Game One, Joe Bush blew a 2-0 lead by allowing three eighth-inning runs, and lost 3-2. Mays self-destructed in Game Four, giving away a 2-0 lead by surrendering four runs in the fifth inning and losing 4-3. Then, in the deciding game, Bush *again* lost a lead by giving up three runs in the eighth inning. The Giants beat New York 5-3 to complete a sweep of the Series.

According to Lieb, Ruppert voiced his suspicions one night when the two men had been drinking, but Lieb never followed up on the story. Most historians believe that Carl Mays is not a member of the Baseball

Hall of Fame because of the 1920 beaning that killed Ray Chapman. But Lieb always insisted the real reason for Mays's exclusion was his questionable World Series performances.

From the available evidence, it cannot be determined whether or not the 1918 World Series between the Red Sox and Cubs was fixed. There is enough information from newspaper reports to place question marks beside much of the Cubs' on-field performance. White Sox secretary Harry Grabiner, writing in what he believed would remain a private journal, linked Gene Packard to a 1918 World Series fix. Not much is known about Packard's career and the circumstances surrounding his retirement. He was an eight-year veteran who won a total of 85 games, yet when he died in 1959, *The Sporting News* did not publish an obituary. Packard associated with several dishonest players, including members of the 1918 Cubs, some of whom were later banished from the game. Eugene Milo Packard remains a mystery man. The possibility of a World Series fix in 1918 also remains a mystery.

2 9

EPILOGUE

Before the Red Sox began spring training for the 1919 season, **Sam Agnew** was sold to the Washington Senators, where, in 42 games, he batted a career-high .235. Agnew then headed west, playing eight seasons with the San Francisco Seals of the Pacific Coast League. He also managed three minor league teams and in 1939 he purchased the Meridian (Mississippi) club of the Southeastern League. Agnew died in 1951 at age 64.

Lore Bader's five games with the Red Sox were the last of his big league career. After serving in the Army in 1919, Bader returned to baseball in 1920, winning 19 games for Toronto of the International League and later working as a coach for both the Red Sox and Braves. He also managed several minor league teams in New England. During the Depression, Bader was a WPA director in Coffey County, Kansas. Bader died in 1973 at age 85.

Walter Barbare spent two years as a utility infielder for the Pittsburgh Pirates before returning to Boston in 1921 as the Braves' regular shortstop. He also played, managed and umpired in the minor leagues. Barbare died at age 74 in 1965.

Red Bluhm's one at-bat on July 3, 1918, was his only major league appearance. Because the official box score sent to the American League office mistakenly did not include his name, Bluhm's debut was not verified until 1962, 10 years after his death at age 57.

In the spring of 1919, **Joe Bush** injured his arm and pitched only nine innings. While warming up one day in 1920, he gripped the ball between his index and middle fingers and developed a forkball. After a 16-9 season in 1921, Bush was traded to the New York Yankees, along with Sam Jones and Everett Scott. Bullet Joe won 26 games for New York in 1922, leading the league in winning percentage. Bush also played for the St. Louis Browns, Senators, Pirates and New York Giants before finishing his career where it had begun, in Philadelphia, with the 1928 Athletics. Later in his life, Bush worked as a clerk at racetracks in New Jersey and Florida. He died in Fort Lauderdale, Florida, on November 1, 1974, at the age of 81.

George Cochran's 24 games with the Red Sox were his only major league experience. His biographical folder at the Baseball Hall of Fame Library in Cooperstown, New York, contains no information about his baseball career. According to his obituary, Cochran's last job was as a retail clerk at the Jim Dandy Market in Hawthorne, California. He and his wife Wilma had four children. Cochran passed away in 1960 at age 71.

Jack Coffey's major league career ended in 1918. He returned to Fordham University, where he had coached in 1909, and served as athletic director there for 37 years. In 1955, the school renamed its baseball field in his honor. Coffey was fluent in French, Spanish, Italian and German and spoke a little Latin and Greek; at various times, he lived in France, Germany, Spain, Mexico, South America and Australia. Coffey said his biggest baseball thrills were hitting one home run in each league and being teammates with both Ty Cobb and Babe Ruth in 1918. Coffey died in the Bronx, New York, in 1966 at age 79.

The Red Sox invited **Jean Dubuc** to spring training in 1919, but returned him to the minors before the season began. Picked up by the

New York Giants, Dubuc appeared in a league-leading 31 relief appearances. He was sent to Toledo in 1920 and in October of that year admitted his complicity in the 1919 World Series fix. Dubuc returned to the major leagues as a scout for the Detroit Tigers in 1928. His biggest contribution was signing slugger Hank Greenberg from under the nose of the New York Yankees. Dubuc died at age 69 in 1958.

Eusebio Gonzalez was sent back to Springfield, Massachusetts, in the Eastern League in 1919. He never made it back to the major leagues. Gonzalez died on Valentine's Day in 1976 in Havana, Cuba, at age 83.

Dick Hoblitzell's last at-bat for the Red Sox, a pinch-hit single on June 7, 1918, was also the 29-year-old's last big league appearance. In 1919, Hoblitzell served in the military, stationed at Nitrate Plant No.1 in Sheffield, Alabama. He played in the minors until 1931 and then umpired for two seasons in the International League. Hoblitzell was 74 when he died in 1962.

Harry Hooper did not retire after 1918. He returned to Boston and played two more seasons before a salary dispute with Harry Frazee led to a trade to the Chicago White Sox. Hooper spent five years in Chicago, and was the baseball coach for Princeton University in 1931 and 1932. Between 1937 and 1951, he received only 22 votes for the Hall of Fame, but due to the tireless efforts of his son John, Hooper was elected by the Veterans Committee in 1971. Hooper leads all Red Sox players in career triples (130) and stolen bases (300), and is fifth in walks (826). Hooper petitioned each baseball commissioner from Kenesaw Landis to Bowie Kuhn to award the World Series emblems to the 1918 Red Sox. They all refused.

In 1919, **Sam Jones** lost 20 games. After rebounding in 1921 with 23 victories, he was traded to the Yankees and helped them win their first World Series title. Jones played for the Browns, Senators and White Sox before retiring in 1935. While managing Toronto of the International League in 1940, Jones, then 48 years old, boasted a 2.25 ERA in eight games. After retiring from baseball, Jones returned to his native Ohio and was president of the Woodsfield Savings and Loan Association for many years until his death in 1966 at age 73.

Walt Kinney led the 1919 Philadelphia Athletics' pitching staff with 43 appearances; his nine wins were exactly one-quarter of the team's season total. Kinney also batted .284, collected two of the staff's three saves and had the fourth-best ratio of strikeouts per nine innings in the American League. He left the Athletics in May 1920 when an independent team in Franklin, Pennsylvania, offered him more money. Kinney was denied reinstatement by Commissioner Landis the following spring, but did return to pitch five games in 1923. He is one of only 35 players to hit a home run in his final major league at-bat (May 9, 1923). Kinney was living with his daughter in Escondido, California, when he died in July 1971 at age 77.

Dutch Leonard was traded to the Yankees in December 1918, along with Ernie Shore and Duffy Lewis. Leonard was sent on to Detroit before the 1919 season began and finished his career with the Tigers. Among Red Sox pitchers, Leonard has the fourth-lowest career ERA (2.13) and is fifth in shutouts (25). In 1926, Leonard was involved in a major scandal when he produced two letters apparently revealing that he, Ty Cobb, Tris Speaker and Joe Wood had agreed to fix and bet on a late-season game in 1919. Speaker denied all accusations; Cobb admitted only that bets had been made. Leonard refused to travel from the West Coast to testify. No formal charges were brought against anyone and Cobb and Speaker were "permitted to resign" by Commissioner Landis. Leonard died at age 60 in 1952.

In February 1919, **Wally Mayer** was sold to the St. Louis Browns for $5,000. Playing part-time, he batted .226 in what was his seventh and final major league season. One of his post-baseball jobs was working as a cigar clerk. Mayer died in November 1951 at age 61.

In 1919, **Carl Mays**'s mother's house burned to the ground while he was at spring training and he suspected arson. During that season, Mays refused to pitch if Jack Barry played second base and openly criticized his teammates for poor run support. On Memorial Day in Philadelphia, fans pounded on the roof of the Red Sox dugout until Mays threw a ball into the stands, hitting a man in the head. Mays was already reviled in Philadelphia for the 1917 beaning of prospect Buck Thrasher and was able to avoid arrest only after Athletics manager Connie Mack convinced the man not to file charges.

In mid-July, Mays walked out on the team. Harry Frazee sold him to the Yankees, where he won 26 games in 1920 and 27 more in 1921. Mays also won 20 games with Cincinnati in 1924. Although his career was worthy of the Hall of Fame (208-126, 2.92 ERA), Mays will always be best remembered for throwing the pitch that led to Ray Chapman's death in 1920. Mays passed away at age 79 in 1971.

In addition to his three appearances with Boston, **Dick McCabe** pitched in three games for the 1922 White Sox. He played in the minors until 1933 and was a fixture in Buffalo, New York's amateur and semi-pro baseball communities. McCabe later served as vice president of the William Simon Brewery. He died in April 1950 at age 54.

Stuffy McInnis was Boston's first baseman until he was sent to Cleveland in December 1921. At the time, he was in the middle of what became a major league record of 1,700 consecutive chances—163 games—without an error. McInnis holds the American League record for fewest errors at first base in a season: one, in 1921. In his 19-year career, McInnis also played for the Boston Braves and Pittsburgh Pirates, and was a member of five World Series championship teams. He managed the Philadelphia Phillies to a last-place finish in 1927 and later worked as a baseball coach at both Harvard and Norwich Universities. McInnis was 69 years old when he passed away in February 1960.

The Red Sox sent **Hack Miller** back to Oakland of the Pacific Coast League for 1919. After batting .347 for two straight seasons, Miller was signed by the Chicago Cubs. When Miller hit 12 home runs in 1922, Cubs president Bill Veeck installed bleachers in left field, shortening the distance to the fence by 18 feet. It worked: Miller drilled 20 homers the following year. In 1924, Miller split his time between playing for the Cubs and teaching high school in Alameda, California. He also worked as a longshoreman on the San Francisco-Oakland waterfront for 25 years. He died in Oakland in 1971 at age 77.

In 1919, **Vince Molyneaux** pitched for Reading in the International League and did not return to the major leagues. He died in 1950 at age 61.

Bill Pertica pitched two more seasons with Los Angeles in the Pacific Coast League before returning to the big leagues with the St. Louis Cardinals. From 1921 to 1923, his record was 22-18. Pertica's last job was as a bartender; he died at his home in Los Angeles in 1967 at age 69.

Babe Ruth has the fourth-best winning percentage (.659) and the fifth-lowest career ERA (2.19) of all Red Sox pitchers. His nine shutouts in 1916 is second in club history to the 10 each posted by Cy Young in 1904 and Joe Wood in 1912. In addition to his many batting achievements, Ruth is the only player to have pitched more than 10 seasons and have a winning record in each of them. He played on 10 World Series champions—three in Boston and seven in New York.

Ruth's first two seasons with the New York Yankees—1920 and 1921—were arguably the two greatest batting performances of all time. His name quickly became synonymous around the world with baseball. In his 22-year career, he led the American League in home runs 12 times, runs batted in 6 times, runs scored 8 times, walks 11 times, on-base average 10 times, and slugging percentage 13 times. He won the 1924 batting title (.378); the previous season, he hit .393, giving some credence to his claim that if he had tried to hit singles instead of home runs, he would have batted .600.

Ruth was without question the greatest player to ever wear a baseball uniform. He died on August 16, 1948, in New York City.

Wally Schang was traded to the Yankees in the winter of 1920 and, as he had done in Philadelphia and Boston, helped his new team win a pennant right away. Over an 11-year period, Schang played in six World

Series with three different clubs. In 1936, as a coach with Cleveland, Schang roomed and worked with a 17-year-old fireballer named Bob Feller. In the 1940s, Schang retired to his farm in Dixon, Missouri. He died in 1965 at age 75.

Everett Scott regained his batting stroke in 1919, hitting a career-high .278. He led the American League in fielding percentage for eight consecutive seasons (1916 to 1923), a major league record since tied by Luis Aparicio. Scott was named captain of the Red Sox in 1921, and then traded to the Yankees that winter. His consecutive game streak stood at 386 after the 1918 season, and it ended at 1,307 games, when he was benched for Pee Wee Wanninger on May 5, 1925. Less than one month later, rookie Lou Gehrig would pinch-hit for Wanninger and begin a streak of his own. Scott also bowled competitively and owned two alleys with his sons in Fort Wayne, Indiana. He passed away at age 67 in 1960.

Dave Shean finished his career with the 1919 Red Sox, hitting .140 in 29 games. Working with Nathan Robbins & Co., he remained a familiar figure in Boston's market district. He died in Boston in May 1963 from injuries suffered in a car accident. He was 79 years old.

In 1919, **Jack Stansbury** was back in the minor leagues. After his playing days, he settled in Beaumont, Texas, living there for 40 years and working for the Magnolia Refinery Company. Stansbury died at age 85 in 1970.

Amos Strunk began 1919 as Boston's center fielder and was batting .272 when he was traded back to Philadelphia in late June. He also played 3½ seasons with the White Sox. Strunk worked as an insurance broker for 50 years, living in Llanerch, Pennsylvania, with the former Ethel Kennedy, his high school sweetheart, who he had married in 1915. Strunk was 89 years old when he died in 1979.

In March 1919 **Fred Thomas** was sold to the Philadelphia Athletics, and in 1920 he played for the Washington Senators. Thomas bounced around the minors until he retired in 1924. With his wife Connie, Thomas opened a resort on Lake Chetac in Birchwood, Wisconsin.

Thomas remained good friends with former teammate Everett Scott; the men often fished together at the resort. Thomas was the longest surviving member of the 1918 Red Sox; he died in December 1986 at age 93.

The 1918 Red Sox were **Frank Truesdale**'s last major league stop. Truesdale lived with his wife, Bonnie, in Gamerco, New Mexico and worked as a watchman. He was 59 years old when he passed away in 1943.

In 1927, when Bill Carrigan was rehired as Red Sox manager, **Heinie Wagner** returned to the team as a coach. The two men couldn't restore any lasting glory to the Red Sox. For three seasons, Boston improved slightly, but never escaped the cellar. Wagner managed the team in 1930 and finished last with a 52-102 record. He was 62 when he died in 1943.

George Whiteman's jog off the field at Fenway Park after his remarkable somersault catch in Game Six of the 1918 World Series was his final appearance in the major leagues. The Red Sox kept him under contract through the spring of 1919 until Harry Hooper and Babe Ruth were signed. Whiteman was then sent to Toronto. He beat the bushes for another 11 years before hanging up his spikes in 1929 at age 47. His minor league totals include 3,282 games, 3,388 hits and a .283 batting average.

In the early 1920s, Whiteman wrote several letters to Ban Johnson and Garry Herrmann asking for his World Series emblem. Both men agreed that Whiteman deserved his emblem, but neither man did anything about it. Whiteman eventually gave up. He later served as a deputy constable in Houston, Texas, where he lived for 40 years. Whiteman died on February 10, 1947 at age 64.

John Wyckoff's last major league season was 1918. He was working in his yard on May 8, 1961, when he suddenly collapsed and died. He was 69 years old.

Edward Barrow managed the Red Sox in 1919 (6th place) and 1920 (5th place). In October 1920 he accepted the job of general manager of the New York Yankees. Within weeks, Barrow acquired Wally Schang and Waite Hoyt from Harry Frazee. In July 1922, when Barrow grabbed

Joe Dugan from Boston, the St. Louis Browns accused the Red Sox of helping the Yankees win the pennant—and thus arose the mid-summer trading deadline that exists today. Barrow was rumored as a successor to Ban Johnson as American League president in 1927, but he stayed with the Yankees. Barrow was named club president in 1939 and along with his assistant, George Weiss, he developed the most consistently successful organization in baseball history. Barrow was elected to the Hall of Fame in September 1953. He died six months later at age 85.

Harry Frazee has been vilified through the decades as the man who destroyed the Red Sox, but the truth is never so simple. In his first two years, Frazee spent lavishly to maintain Boston's winning tradition and then struggled to keep the franchise financially afloat in the early 1920s. He allegedly clipped and saved dozens of negative articles written about him in the Boston newspapers, filling two large scrapbooks. When Frazee sold the Red Sox in 1923, no member of the 1918 team remained. Shortly after the sale, Jacob Ruppert denied a report that Frazee had purchased an interest in the Yankees. Frazee, who suffered from Bright's disease, died after a sudden relapse in June 1929, at age 48. Ed Barrow attended his funeral, as did former team secretary Larry Graver and former Chicago Cubs owner Charles Weeghman.

The **Boston Red Sox** finished the 1919 season with a 66-71 record. It was the team's worst showing since 1907 and the first of 16 consecutive losing seasons. Boston would not finish over .500 again until 1935. The Red Sox won the American League pennant in 1946, 1967, 1975 and 1986. In each World Series, they lost in the seventh and deciding game.

Appendix A

Boston Red Sox

1918 Season Day-by-Day

Date	Town	Home Team	Score
March 17	Hot Springs, Arkansas	Brooklyn	Boston 11, Brooklyn 1
March 24	Hot Springs, Arkansas	Boston	Boston (ss) 7, Brooklyn (ss) 1
	Little Rock, Arkansas	Brooklyn	Boston (ss) 18, Brooklyn (ss) 1
March 27	Little Rock, Arkansas	Brooklyn	Brooklyn 3, Boston 2
March 30	Little Rock, Arkansas	Boston	Boston 4, Brooklyn 3
March 31	Little Rock, Arkansas	Brooklyn	Boston 7, Brooklyn 4
April 1	Little Rock, Arkansas	Boston	Boston 3, Brooklyn 2
April 2	Dallas, Texas	Brooklyn	Boston 7, Brooklyn 6 (16 innings)
April 3	Waco, Texas	Boston	Brooklyn 2, Boston 1
April 4	Austin, Texas	Brooklyn	Boston 10, Brooklyn 4
April 5	Houston, Texas	Boston	Brooklyn 5, Boston 3
April 7	New Orleans, Louisiana	Brooklyn	Brooklyn 4, Boston 3 (13 innings)
April 8	Mobile, Alabama	Boston	Boston 6, Brooklyn 6 (13 innings)
April 9	Birmingham, Alabama	Brooklyn	Brooklyn 3, Boston 1

Date	Score	Winning Pitcher	Losing Pitcher	Record & Standing
Home				
April 15	Boston 7, Philadelphia 1	Ruth	Myers	1-0; —
April 16	Boston 1, Philadelphia 0	Mays	Perry	2-0; +½
April 17	Boston 5, Philadelphia 4	Leonard	Adams	3-0; +1
April 18	Rained out (vs. Philadelphia)			3-0; +1
April 19	Boston 2, New York 1	Bush	Russell	
	Boston 9, New York 5	Ruth	Thormahlen	5-0; +2
April 20	Boston 4, New York 3	Mays	Love	6-0; +2
April 21	Off			6-0; +2½
April 22	New York 11, Boston 4	Mogridge	Leonard	6-1; +1½
April 23	Boston 1, New York 0	Bush	Thormahlen	7-1; +1½
Away				
April 24	Philadelphia 3, Boston 0	Gregg	Ruth	7-2; +1½
April 25	Boston 6, Philadelphia 1	Mays	Adams	8-2; +1½
April 26	Boston 2, Philadelphia 1	Leonard	Perry	9-2; +2
April 27	Boston 4, Philadelphia 1	Bush	Myers	10-2; +2
April 28	Exhibition			
	Boston 7, Bridgeport (Conn.) All-Stars 0			10-2; +2
Home				
April 29	Rained out (vs. Washington)			10-2; +2½
April 30	Boston 8, Washington 1	Ruth	Harper	11-2; +3
May 1	Washington 5, Boston 0	Johnson	Mays	11-3; +2½
May 2	Boston 8, Washington 1	Leonard	Shaw	12-3; +2½

Date	Score	Winning Pitcher	Losing Pitcher	Record & Standing
Away				
May 3	New York 3, Boston 2 (11 innings)	Love	Bush	12-4; +1½
May 4	New York 5, Boston 4	Russell	Ruth	12-5; +1½
May 5	Exhibition			
	Boston 3, Doherty Silk Sox 1			12-5; +2
May 6	New York 10, Boston 3	Mogridge	Mays	12-6; +2
May 7	Washington 7, Boston 2	Johnson	Leonard	12-7; +2
May 8	Washington 14, Boston 4	Harper	Bush	12-8; +1
May 9	Washington 4, Boston 3 (10 innings)	Johnson	Ruth	12-9; —
Home				
May 10	Boston 4, St. Louis 1	Mays	Davenport	13-9; —
May 11	St. Louis 4, Boston 2	Gallia	Leonard	13-10; —
May 12	Off			13-10; +½
May 13	Boston 7, St. Louis 5	Bush	Sothoron	14-10; +½
May 14	Rained out (vs. St. Louis)			14-10; +½
May 15	Boston 5, Detroit 4	Ruth	Dauss	15-10; +1½
May 16	Boston 7, Detroit 2	Mays	James	16-10; +1½
May 17	Boston 11, Detroit 8	Leonard	Finnerman	17-10; +1½
May 18	Boston 3, Detroit 1	Bush	Erickson	18-10; +2½
May 19	Off			18-10; +2½
May 20	Boston 11, Cleveland 1	Mays	Bagby	19-10; +3
May 21	Cleveland 6, Boston 5	Coumbe	Leonard	19-11; +2½
May 22	Rained out (vs. Cleveland)			19-11; +2½
May 23	Cleveland 1, Boston 0	Morton	Jones	19-12; +2
May 24	Boston 5, Cleveland 4	Bush	Danforth	20-12; +2
May 25	Boston 3, Chicago 2 (10 innings)	Mays	Williams	21-12; +3

Date	Score	Winning Pitcher	Losing Pitcher	Record & Standing
May 26	Off			21-12; +2½
May 27	Chicago 6, Boston 4	Shellenback	Leonard	21-13; +1½
May 28	Boston 1, Chicago 0	Bush	Cicotte	22-13; +2½
May 29	Boston 4, Washington 2	Mays	Harper	
	Boston 3, Washington 0	Jones	Johnson	24-13; +2½
May 30	Boston 9, Washington 1	Leonard	Shaw	
	Washington 4, Boston 0	Ayers	McCabe	25-14; +2
May 31	Off			25-14; +2

Away

Date	Score	Winning Pitcher	Losing Pitcher	Record & Standing
June 1	Detroit 4, Boston 3 (13 innings)	Cunningham	Mays	25-15; +1
June 2	Detroit 4, Boston 3	Erickson	Ruth	25-16; +1
June 3	Boston 5, Detroit 0	Leonard	Dauss	26-16; +2
June 4	Boston 7, Detroit 6	Mays	Boland	27-16; +3
June 5	Cleveland 5, Boston 4 (10 innings)	Bagby	Bush	27-17; +2
June 6	Boston 1, Cleveland 0 (10 innings)	Jones	Coveleski	28-17; +2
June 7	Cleveland 14, Boston 7	Coumbe	Ruth	28-18; +1
June 8	Cleveland 3, Boston 1	Morton	Mays	28-19; —
June 9	Boston 2, Cleveland 0	Leonard	Coveleski	29-19; +1
June 10	Boston 1, Chicago 0	Bush	Shellenback	30-19; +1½
June 11	Chicago 4, Boston 1	Faber	Jones	30-20; +1½
June 12	Boston 7, Chicago 0	Mays	Danforth	31-20; +2½
June 13	Boston 6, Chicago 0	Leonard	Cicotte	32-20; +2½
June 14	St. Louis 5, Boston 4	Sothoron	Bush	32-21; +1½
June 15	Boston 8, St. Louis 4	Jones	Davenport	33-21; +2½
June 16	St. Louis 2, Boston 1	Shocker	Leonard	33-22; +1½
June 17	Boston 8, St. Louis 0	Mays	Gallia	34-22; +1½
June 18	Off			34-22; +1½

Date	Score	Winning Pitcher	Losing Pitcher	Record & Standing
Home				
June 19	Philadelphia 5, Boston 0	Geary	Bush	34-23; +½
June 20	Philadelphia 2, Boston 0	Gregg	Jones	
	Boston 3, Philadelphia 0	Molyneaux	Perry	35-24; +1½
June 21	Boston 13, Philadelphia 0	Mays	Adams	36-24; +2½
June 22	Rained out (vs. Philadelphia)			36-24; +2
June 23	Off			36-24; +2
Away				
June 24	New York 3, Boston 2	Mogridge	Bush	36-25; +1
June 25	Boston 7, New York 3	Jones	Russell	37-25; +2
June 26	New York 3, Boston 1	Love	Mays	37-26; +1
June 27	New York 7, Boston 5	Mogridge	Bush	37-27; —
June 28	Washington 3, Boston 1	Harper	Bader	37-28; 1 GB
June 29	Boston 3, Washington 1	Jones	Ayers	38-28; —
June 30	Boston 3, Washington 1 (10 innings)	Mays	Johnson	39-28; +½
July 1	Off			39-28; —
July 2	Washington 3, Boston 0	Harper	Bush	39-29; —
July 3	Philadelphia 6, Boston 0	Gregg	Bader	39-30; —
July 4	Boston 11, Philadelphia 9	Jones	Watson	
	Philadelphia 2, Boston 1 (11 innings)	Perry	Mays	40-31; 1 GB
July 5	Boston 4, Philadelphia 3 (10 innings)	Ruth	Geary	41-31; ½ GB

Date	Score	Winning Pitcher	Losing Pitcher	Record & Standing
Home				
July 6	Boston 5, Cleveland 4	Bush	Bagby	42-31; +½
July 7	Off			42-31; +½
July 8	Boston 1, Cleveland 0 (10 innings)	Jones	Coveleski	
	Cleveland 4, Boston 3	Morton	Mays	43-32; +½
July 9	Boston 1, Cleveland 0 (12 innings)	Bush	Bagby	44-32; +1½
July 10	Boston 2, Cleveland 0 (5 innings, rain)	Bader	Coumbe	45-32; +2½
July 11	Boston 4, Chicago 0	Mays	Cicotte	46-32; +2½
July 12	Boston 6, Chicago 3	Jones	Benz	47-32; +3½
July 13	Chicago 5, Boston 0	Russell	Bush	47-33; +2½
July 14	Exhibition			
	Boston 5, Queen Quality of Jamaica Plain (R.I.) 2			47-33; +3
July 15	Boston 3, Chicago 1	Mays	Danforth	48-33; +3
July 16	Boston 2, St. Louis 1	Jones	Leifield	49-33; +4
July 17	Boston 7, St. Louis 0	Bush	Wright	
	Boston 4, St. Louis 0 (4 innings, rain)	Ruth	Rogers	51-33; +5½
July 18	St. Louis 6, Boston 3	Davenport	Bader	51-34; +4½
July 19	Boston 5, Detroit 0	Mays	Bailey	52-34; +5½
July 20	Boston 5, Detroit 1	Jones	Dauss	53-34; +6
July 21	Off			53-34; +5½
July 22	Boston 1, Detroit 0 (10 innings)	Bush	James	
	Boston 3, Detroit 0	Mays	Kallio	55-34; +6½
July 23	Off			55-34; +6½
July 24	Off			55-34; +6½

Date	Score	Winning Pitcher	Losing Pitcher	Record & Standing

Away

Date	Score	Winning Pitcher	Losing Pitcher	Record & Standing
July 25	Chicago 4, Boston 2	Russell	Mays	55-35; +6
July 26	Chicago 7, Boston 2	Cicotte	Jones	55-36; +5
July 27	Boston 6, Chicago 4	Bush	Shellenback	56-36; +5
July 28	Chicago 8, Boston 0	Russell	Mays	56-37; +4½
July 29	Boston 3, St. Louis 2	Ruth	Sothoron	57-37; +5
July 30	Boston 11, St. Louis 4	Jones	Bennett	58-37; +4½
July 31	Boston 8, St. Louis 4	Bush	Gallia	59-37; +4½
August 1	Boston 2, St. Louis 1	Ruth	Leifield	60-37; +5½
August 2	Cleveland 6, Boston 3	Coveleski	Mays	60-38; +4½
August 3	Cleveland 5, Boston 1	Bagby	Jones	60-39; +3½
August 4	Boston 2, Cleveland 1 (12 innings)	Ruth	Enzmann	
	Cleveland 2, Boston 0 (6 innings, rain)	Coveleski	Bush	61-40; +3½
August 5	Off			61-40; +3½
August 6	Boston 7, Detroit 5 (10 innings)	Mays	Kallio	62-40; +3½
August 7	Detroit 11, Boston 8	Jones	Bush	62-41; +3½
August 8	Boston 4, Detroit 1	Ruth	Boland	63-41; +3½
August 9	Off			63-41; +3½

Home

Date	Score	Winning Pitcher	Losing Pitcher	Record & Standing
August 10	New York 5, Boston 1 (10 innings)	Mogridge	Bush	
	New York 4, Boston 1	Caldwell	Mays	63-43; +3
August 11	Off			63-43; +3
August 12	New York 2, Boston 1	Robinson	Ruth	63-44; +2
August 13	Off			63-44; +2
August 14	Boston 5, Chicago 3	Jones	Russell	64-44; +2

Date	Score	Winning Pitcher	Losing Pitcher	Record & Standing
August 15	Chicago 6, Boston 2	Quinn	Mays	64-45; +2
August 16	Boston 2, Chicago 0	Bush	Cicotte	65-45; +2
August 17	Boston 4, Cleveland 2	Ruth	Morton	66-45; +3
August 18	Exhibition			
	New Haven (Conn.) Colonials 4, Boston 3			66-45; +3
August 19	Boston 6, Cleveland 0	Jones	Coveleski	67-45; +4
August 20	Cleveland 8, Boston 4	Bagby	Ruth	67-46; +3
August 21	Boston 4, St. Louis 1	Mays	Sothoron	68-46; +3
August 22	St. Louis 1, Boston 0	Davenport	Bush	68-47; +3
August 23	Boston 6, St. Louis 5	Jones	Houck	69-47; +3
August 24	Boston 3, St. Louis 1	Ruth	Leifield	70-47; +4
August 25	Off			70-47; +4
August 26	Detroit 6, Boston 3	Cunningham	Mays	70-48; +3½
August 27	Detroit 2, Boston 1	Kallio	Bush	70-49; +2½
August 28	Boston 3, Detroit 0	Jones	Dauss	71-49; +3½
August 29	Rain vs. Philadelphia			71-49; +3½
August 30	Boston 12, Philadelphia 0	Mays	Johnson	
	Boston 4, Philadelphia 1	Mays	Perry	73-49; +3½
August 31	Boston 6, Philadelphia 1	Ruth	Watson	
	Philadelphia 1, Boston 0	Watson	Bush	74-50; +3
September 1	Off			74-50; +2½

Away

Date	Score	Winning Pitcher	Losing Pitcher	Record & Standing
September 2	Boston 3, New York 2	Jones	Love	
	New York 4, Boston 3	Mogridge	Dubuc	75-51; +2½
September 3	Off			

World Series
Comiskey Park, Chicago

		Winning Pitcher	Losing Pitcher	Series Standing
September 4	Rained out			
September 5	Boston 1, Chicago 0	Ruth	Vaughn	Red Sox lead 1-0
September 6	Chicago 3, Boston 1	Tyler	Bush	Series tied 1-1
September 7	Boston 2, Chicago 1	Mays	Vaughn	Red Sox lead 2-1
September 8	Off			

World Series
Fenway Park, Boston

September 9	Boston 3, Chicago 2	Ruth	Tyler	Red Sox lead 3-1
September 10	Chicago 3, Boston 0	Vaughn	Jones	Red Sox lead 3-2
September 11	Boston 2, Chicago 1	Mays	Tyler	Red Sox win 4-2

APPENDIX B

1918 Boston Red Sox
Batting and Pitching Statistics

Batting

	G	AB	R	H	2B	3B	HR	RBI	SB	BB	K	BA	OBA	SLG	POS	PO	A	E	PCT.
Sam Agnew	72	199	11	33	8	0	0	6	0	11	26	.166	.221	.206	C-72	254	104	13	.965
Walter Barbare	13	29	2	5	3	0	0	2	1	0	1	.172	.172	.276	3B-11	6	13	4	.826
															SS-1	0	1	0	1.000
Red Bluhm	1	1	0	0	0	0	0	0	0	0	0	.000	.000	.000	PH-1				—
George Cochran	24	60	7	7	0	0	0	3	3	10	6	.117	.264	.117	3B-22	12	39	3	.944
															SS-1	1	0	1	.500
Jack Coffey (Bos.)	15	44	5	7	1	0	1	2	2	3	2	.159	.213	.250	3B-14	11	31	2	.955
(Season)	37	111	12	21	1	2	1	6	4	11	8	.189	.268	.261	2B-23	1	6	0	1.000
Eusebio Gonzalez	3	5	2	2	0	1	0	0	0	1	1	.400	.571	.800	SS-3	1	2	0	1.000
Dick Hoblitzell	25	69	4	11	1	0	0	4	3	8	3	.159	.266	.174	1B-19	209	15	1	.996
Harry Hooper	126	474	81	137	26	13	1	44	24	75	25	.289	.391	.405	OF-126	221	16	9	.963
Wally Mayer	26	49	7	11	4	0	0	5	0	7	7	.224	.321	.306	C-23	63	18	3	.964
Stuffy McInnis	117	423	40	115	11	5	0	56	10	19	10	.272	.306	.322	1B-94	1066	71	9	.992
															3B-23	34	42	1	.987
Hack Miller	12	29	2	8	2	0	0	4	0	0	4	.276	.276	.345	OF-10	10	0	0	1.000
Babe Ruth	95	317	50	95	26	11	11	66	6	57	58	.300	.410	.555	OF-59	121	8	7	.949
															P-20	19	58	6	.928
															1B-13	130	6	5	.965
Wally Schang	88	225	36	55	7	1	0	20	4	46	35	.244	.377	.284	C-57	202	52	10	.962
															OF-16	31	1	3	.914
															3B-5	2	8	3	.769
															SS-1	1	1	1	.667

	G	AB	R	H	2B	3B	HR	RBI	SB	BB	K	BA	OBA	SLG	POS	PO	A	E	PCT.
Everett Scott	126	443	40	98	11	5	0	43	11	12	16	.221	.242	.269	SS-126	270	419	17	.976
Dave Shean	115	425	58	112	16	3	0	34	11	40	25	.264	.331	.315	2B-115	241	341	20	.967
Jack Stansbury	20	47	3	6	1	0	0	2	0	6	3	.128	.241	.149	3B-18	12	37	1	.980
															OF-2	4	0	0	1.000
Amos Strunk	114	413	50	106	18	9	0	35	20	36	13	.257	.316	.344	OF-113	230	13	3	.988
Fred Thomas	44	144	19	37	2	1	1	11	4	15	20	.257	.331	.306	3B-41	54	97	5	.968
															SS-1	0	0	0	—
Frank Truesdale	15	36	6	10	1	0	0	2	1	4	5	.278	.350	.306	2B-10	14	28	4	.913
Heinie Wagner	3	8	0	1	0	0	0	0	0	1	0	.125	.222	.125	2B-2	2	7	1	.900
															3B-1	0	0	0	—
George Whiteman	71	214	24	57	14	0	1	28	9	20	9	.266	.335	.346	OF-69	95	5	7	.935
Lore Bader	5	9	0	1	0	0	0	0	0	0	3	.111	.111	.111	P	1	2	1	.750
Joe Bush	36	98	8	27	3	2	0	14	0	6	11	.276	.317	.347	P	16	81	2	.980
Jean Dubuc	5	6	0	1	0	0	0	0	0	1	2	.167	.286	.167	P	2	2	0	1.000
Sam Jones	24	57	6	10	1	0	0	1	0	13	14	.175	.329	.193	P	11	41	2	.963
Walt Kinney	6	5	6	0	0	0	0	0	0	0	1	.000	.000	.000	P	2	3	0	1.000
Dutch Leonard	16	43	2	8	0	0	0	3	0	6	6	.186	.286	.186	P	4	25	2	.935
Carl Mays	38	104	10	30	3	3	0	5	1	9	15	.288	.357	.375	P/PH	16	122	8	.945
Dick McCabe	3	2	0	0	0	0	0	0	0	0	0	.000	.000	.000	P	1	3	0	1.000
Vince Molyneaux	6	2	0	0	0	0	0	0	0	0	2	.000	.000	.000	P	1	3	0	1.000
Bill Pertica	1	1	0	0	0	0	0	0	0	0	0	.000	.000	.000	P	0	1	0	1.000
John Wyckoff	1	1	0	0	0	0	0	0	0	0	1	.000	.000	.000	P	0	0	0	—
TOTALS	126	3982	474	990	159	54	15	—	110	406	324	.249	.322	.327		3356	1721	154	.971

League leaders in bold.

Pitching

	W	L	ERA	G	GS	CG	IP	H	ER	BB	K	SHO	SV	OBA	OOP	WHIP
Lore Bader	1	3	3.33	5	4	2	27.0	26	10	12	10	1	0	.271	.369	13.7
Joe Bush	15	15	2.11	36	31	26	272.2	241	64	91	125	7	2	.242	.307	11.1
Jean Dubuc	0	1	4.22	2	1	1	10.2	11	5	5	1	0	0	.268	.348	13.5
Sam Jones	16	5	2.25	24	21	16	184.0	151	46	70	44	5	0	.230	.312	11.2
Walt Kinney	0	0	1.80	5	0	0	15.0	5	3	8	4	0	0	.106	.263	9.0
Dutch Leonard	8	6	2.72	16	16	12	125.2	119	38	53	47	3	0	.254	.332	12.5
Carl Mays	21	13	2.21	35	33	**30**	293.1	230	72	81	114	**8**	0	.221	.284	9.9
Dick McCabe	0	1	2.79	3	1	0	9.2	13	3	2	3	0	0	.351	.385	14.0
Vince Molyneaux	1	0	3.38	6	0	0	10.2	3	4	8	1	0	0	.086	.256	9.3
Bill Pertica	0	0	3.00	1	0	0	3.0	3	1	0	1	0	0	.273	.273	9.0
Babe Ruth	13	7	2.22	20	19	18	166.1	125	41	49	40	1	0	.214	.277	9.5
John Wyckoff	0	0	0.00	1	0	0	2.0	4	0	1	2	0	0	.400	.455	22.5
TOTALS	75	51	2.31	126	126	**105**	1120.0	**931**	287	380	392	**26**	2	**.231**	.302	10.8

OBA   Opponents batting average
OOP   Opponents on-base percentage
WHIP   Hits and walks allowed per nine innings
League leaders in bold.

APPENDIX C

1918 World Series

Box Scores

FIRST GAME—At Chicago, Thursday, September 5.

Boston.	AB.	R.	H.	TB.	P.	A.	E.
Hooper, rf.........	4	0	1	1	4	0	0
Shean, 2b..........	2	1	1	1	0	3	0
Strunk, cf.........	3	0	0	0	2	0	0
Whiteman, lf......	4	0	2	2	5	0	0
McInnis, 1b.......	2	0	1	1	10	0	0
Scott, ss...........	4	0	0	0	0	3	0
Thomas, 3b........	3	0	0	0	1	1	0
Agnew, c..........	3	0	0	0	5	0	0
Ruth, p...........	3	0	0	0	0	1	0
Totals	28	1	5	5	27	8	0

Chicago.	AB.	R.	H.	TB.	P.	A.	E.
Flack, rf...........	3	0	1	1	2	0	0
Hollocher, ss......	3	0	0	0	2	1	0
Mann, lf...........	4	0	1	1	0	0	0
Paskert, cf........	4	0	2	2	2	0	0
Merkle, 1b.........	3	0	1	1	9	2	0
Pick, 2b...........	3	0	0	0	1	1	0
Deal, 3b...........	4	0	1	1	1	3	0
Killefer, c........	4	0	0	0	7	2	0
Vaughn, p.........	3	0	0	0	3	5	0
*O'Farrell	1	0	0	0	0	0	0
†McCabe	0	0	0	0	0	0	0
Totals	32	0	6	6	27	14	0

*Batted for Pick in ninth. †Ran for Deal in ninth.

Boston	0	0	0	1	0	0	0	0	0—1
Chicago	0	0	0	0	0	0	0	0	0—0

Bases on balls—Off Ruth 1 (Merkle); off Vaughn 3 (Shean 2, McInnis). Left on bases—Chicago 8, Boston 6. Struck out—By Ruth 4 (Flack, Pick, Paskert, Vaughn); by Vaughn 6 (Thomas 2, Ruth 2, Shean, Whiteman). Hit by pitcher—By Ruth, Flack. Umpires—W. J. Klem at second, C. B. Owens at third, Henry O'Day at plate, George Hildebrand at first. Time—1h. 50m.

SECOND GAME—At Chicago, Friday, September 6.

Chicago.	AB.	R.	H.	TB.	P.	A.	E.
Flack, rf............	4	0	2	2	4	1	0
Hollocher, ss......	4	0	1	3	4	4	0
Mann, lf............	4	0	0	0	0	0	0
Paskert, cf........	4	0	0	0	2	0	0
Merkle, 1b.........	2	1	1	1	6	1	0
Pick, 2b............	2	1	1	1	5	4	0
Deal, 3b...........	2	0	0	0	1	1	1
Killefer, c.........	2	1	1	2	4	2	0
Tyler, p...........	3	0	1	1	1	2	0
Totals 27	27	3	7	10	27	15	1

Boston.	AB.	R.	H.	TB.	P.	A.	R.
Hooper, rf.........	3	0	1	1	1	0	0
Shean, 2b..........	4	0	1	1	5	2	0
Strunk, cf.........	4	1	1	3	1	2	0
Whiteman, lf......	3	0	1	3	3	0	1
McInnis, 1b........	4	0	1	1	7	0	0
Scott, ss..........	2	0	0	0	3	2	0
Thomas, 3b........	3	0	0	0	1	1	0
Agnew, c..........	2	0	0	0	2	4	0
Schang, c..........	2	0	1	1	1	0	0
Bush, p............	2	0	0	0	0	3	0
*Dubuc	1	0	0	0	0	0	0
Totals 30	30	1	6	10	24	14	1

*Batted for Thomas in ninth.

Chicago	0	3	0	0	0	0	0	x—3
Boston	0	0	0	0	0	0	0	0	1—1

Two-base hit—Killefer. Three-base hits—Hollocher, Strunk, Whiteman. Sacrifice bits—Scott, Deal. Bases on balls—Off Bush 3 (Merkle, Pick, Killefer); off Tyler 4 (Hooper, Whiteman, Scott, Bush). Left on bases—Chicago 7, Boston 4. Double plays—Killefer and Pick; Hollocher, Pick and Merkle. Struck out—By Tyler 2 (Shean, Dubuc). Umpires—George Hildebrand at plate, W. J. Klem at first, C. B. Owens at second, Henry O'Day at third. Time—1h. 58m.

THIRD GAME—At Chicago, Saturday, September 7.

Boston.	AB.	R.	H.	TB.	P.	A.	E.
Hooper, rf.........	3	0	1	1	3	0	0
Shean, 2b..........	4	0	0	0	1	2	0
Strunk, cf.........	4	0	0	0	1	0	0
Whiteman, lf......	3	1	1	1	3	0	0
McInnis, 1b........	4	1	1	1	12	0	0
Schang, c..........	4	0	2	2	6	3	0
Scott, ss..........	4	0	1	1	1	5	0
Thomas, 3b........	3	0	1	1	0	2	0
Mays, p............	3	0	0	0	0	2	0
Totals 32	32	2	7	7	27	14	0

Chicago.	AB.	R.	H.	TB.	P.	A.	E.
Flack, rf............	3	0	0	0	3	1	0
Hollocher, ss......	3	0	0	0	1	3	1
Paskert, cf........	4	0	1	1	1	0	0
Mann, lf...........	4	0	2	3	1	0	0
Merkle, 1b.........	4	0	0	0	9	2	0
Pick, 2b............	4	1	2	3	0	0	0
Deal, 3b...........	3	0	1	1	1	1	0
Killefer, c.........	3	0	1	1	8	0	0
Vaughn, p.........	3	0	0	0	3	3	0
*Barber	0	0	0	0	0	0	0
Totals 31	31	1	7	9	27	10	1

Boston	0	0	0	2	0	0	0	0	0—2
Chicago	0	0	0	0	1	0	0	0	0—1

Two-base hits—Mann, Pick. Stolen bases—Whiteman, Schang, Pick. Sacrifice hit—Hollocher. First base on errors—Boston 1. Bases on balls—Off Mays 1 (Flack); off Vaughn 1 (Hooper). Left on bases—Boston 5, Chicago 6. Double plays—Hollocher and Merkle; Vaughn and Merkle. Struck out—By Mays 4 (Paskert, Vaughn, Merkle, Hollocher); by Vaughn 7 (McInnis, Schang 2, Strunk 2, Hooper, Scott). Hit by pitcher—By Vaughn, Whiteman. Passed ball—Schang. Umpires—W. J. Klem at plate, C. B. Owens at first, Henry O'Day at second, George Hildebrand at third. Time—1h. 57m.

FOURTH GAME—At Boston, Monday, September 9.

Boston.	AB.	R.	H.	TB.	P.	A.	E.
Hooper, rf.........	3	0	0	0	1	0.	0
Shean, 2b..........	3	0	1	2	4	4	0
Strunk, cf..........	4	0	0	0	0	0	0
Whiteman, lf......	3	1	0	0	1	0	0
Bush, pitcher......	0	0	0	0	0	0	0
McInnis, 1b........	3	1	1	1	16	1	0
Ruth, p-lf..........	2	0	1	3	0	4	0
Scott, ss..........	3	0	0	0	3	8	0
Thomas, 3b........	3	0	0	0	2	3	0
Agnew, c..........	2	0	0	0	0	1	0
Schang, c..........	1	1	1	1	0	0	0
Totals	27	3	4	7	27	21	0

Chicago.	AB.	R.	H.	TB.	P.	A.	E.
Flack, rf...........	4	0	1	1	3	0	0
Hollocher, ss......	4	0	0	0	2	0	0
Mann, lf...........	4	0	1	1	2	0	0
Paskert, cf........	4	0	0	0	3	0	0
Merkle, 1b........	3	0	1	1	9	1	0
Pick, 2b..........	2	0	2	2	0	2	0
Zeider, 3b.........	0	0	0	0	1	2	0
Deal,, 3b..........	2	0	1	1	1	3	0
*O'Farrell	1	0	0	0	0	0	0
Wortman, 2b......	1	0	0	0	1	0	0
Killefer, c........	2	1	0	0	1	0	0
§Barber	1	0	0	0	0	0	0
Tyler, p..........	0	0	0	0	1	4	0
†Hendrix	1	0	1	1	0	0	0
‡McCabe	0	1	0	0	0	0	0
Douglas, p........	0	0	0	0	0	0	1
Totals	29	2	7	7	24	12	1

*Batted for Deal in seventh.
†Batted for Tyler in eighth.
‡Ran for Hendrix in eighth.
§Batted for Killefer in ninth.

Boston	....	0	0	0	2	0	0	0	1	x—3
Chicago	....	0	0	0	0	0	0	0	2	0—2

Hits—Off Tyler, 3 in 7 innings; off Douglas, 1 in 1 inning; off Ruth, 7 in 8 innings; off Bush, none in 1 inning. Two-base hit—Shean. Three-base hit—Ruth. Stolen base—Shean. Sacrifice hits—Ruth, Hooper. Bases on balls—Off Tyler 2 (Shean, Whiteman); off Ruth 6 (Tyler 2, Merkle, Zeider 2, Killefer). Left on bases—Chicago 6, Boston 4. Double plays—Ruth, Scott and McInnis; Scott, Shean and McInnis 2. Struck out—By Tyler 1 (Strunk). Wild pitch—Ruth. Passed balls—Killefer 2. Winning pitcher, Ruth. Losing pitcher, Douglas. Umpires—C. B. Owens at plate, Henry O'Day at first, George Hildebrand at second, W. J. Klem at third.

FIFTH GAME—At Boston, Tuesday, September 10.

Chicago.	AB.	R.	H.	TB.	P.	A.	E.
Flack, rf	2	1	0	0	1	0	0
Hollocher, ss	3	2	3	3	2	5	0
Mann, lf	3	0	1	2	2	0	0
Paskert, cf	3	0	1	2	3	0	0
Merkle, 1b	3	0	1	1	11	1	0
Pick, 2b	4	0	1	1	4	3	0
Deal, 3b	4	0	0	0	0	0	0
Killefer, c	4	0	0	4	0	0	0
Vaughn, p	4	0	0	0	0	3	0
Totals	30	3	7	9	27	12	0

Boston.	AB.	R.	H.	TB.	P.	A.	E.
Hooper, rf	4	0	1	1	1	0	0
Shean, 2b	3	0	1	1	3	2	0
Strunk, cf	4	0	1	2	4	0	0
Whiteman, lf	3	0	1	1	1	2	0
McInnis, 1b	3	0	0	0	9	0	0
Scott, ss	3	0	0	0	1	4	0
Thomas, 3b	3	0	1	1	1	1	0
Agnew, c	2	0	0	0	5	1	0
Schang, c	1	0	0	0	1	0	0
Jones, p	1	0	0	0	1	3	0
*Miller	1	0	0	0	0	0	0
Totals	28	0	5	6	27	13	0

*Batted for Jones in ninth.

Chicago	0	0	1	0	0	0	0	2	0—3
Boston	0	0	0	0	0	0	0	0	0—0

Two-base hits—Mann, Paskert, Strunk. Stolen base—Hollocher. Sacrifice hits—Mann, Shean. Bases on balls—Off Vaughn 1 (Jones), off Jones 5 (Flack 2, Merkle, Hollocher, Paskert). Left on bases—Chicago 3, Boston 3. Double plays—Merkle and Hollocher; Hollocher, Pick and Merkle 2; Whiteman and Shean. Struck out—By Vaughn 4 (Strunk 2, Hooper, Schang), by Jones 5 (Vaughn 3, Deal, Merkle). Umpires—Henry O'Day behind the plate, George Hildebrand at first, W. J. Klem at second, C. B. Owens at third. Time—1h. 42m.

SIXTH GAME—At Boston, Wednesday, September 11.

Boston.	AB.	R.	H.	TB.	P.	A.	E.
Hooper, rf	3	0	0	0	1	0	0
Shean, 2b	3	1	0	2	4	0
Strunk, cf	4	0	2	2	0	0	0
Whiteman, lf	4	0	0	0	2	0	0
Ruth, lf	0	0	0	0	1	0	0
McInnis, 1b	4	0	1	1	16	1	0
Scott, ss	4	0	1	1	3	3	0
Thomas, 3b	2	0	0	0	1	2	0
Schang, c	1	0	0	0	1	2	0
Mays, p	2	1	1	1	0	6	0
Totals	27	2	5	5	27	18	0

Chicago.	AB.	R.	H.	TB.	P.	A.	E.
Flack, rf	3	1	1	1	2	0	1
Hollocher, ss	4	0	0	0	4	0
Mann, lf	3	0	0	2	0	0
Paskert, cf	2	0	0	0	5	0	0
Merkle, 1b	3	0	1	1	8	2	0
Pick, 2b	3	0	1	1	3	1	0
Deal, 3b	2	0	0	0	2	1	0
*Barber	1	0	0	0	0	0	0
Zeider, 3b	0	0	0	0	0	0	0
Killefer, c	2	0	0	0	2	2	0
O'Farrell, c	1	0	0	0	0	0	0
Tyler, p	2	0	0	0	0	3	1
†McCabe	1	0	0	0	0	0	0
Hendrix, p	0	0	0	0	0	0	0
Totals	27	1	3	3	24	13	2

†Batted for Tyler in eighth.
*Batted for Deal in eighth.

Boston	0	0	2	0	0	0	0	0	*—2
Chicago	0	0	0	1	0	0	0	0	0—1

Hits—Off Tyler, 5 in 7 innings; off Hendrix, none in 1 inning. Stolen base—Flack. Sacrifice hits—Hooper, Thomas. Bases on balls—Off Tyler 5 (Thomas, Mays, Shean, Schang 2), off Mays 2 (Paskert, Flack). Left on bases—Chicago 2, Boston 3. Struck out—By Tyler 1 (Shean), by Mays 1 (Merkle). Hit by pitcher—By Mays, Mann. Losing pitcher—Tyler. Umpires—George Hildebrand at plate, W. J. Klem at first, C. B. Owens at second, Henry O'Day at third. Time—1h. 46m.

APPENDIX D

1918 World Series, Game Three
A Pitch-by-Pitch Account

The *Boston Sunday Advertiser and American* published a pitch-by-pitch account of Game Three (Boston 2, Chicago 1) on September 8, 1918. [Information in brackets was referred to in other newspaper accounts.]

First Inning

Boston:
Harry Hooper–Ball one, called strike one, foul strike two, single to left.
Dave Shean–Foul strike one, ball one, ball two, flyout to left.
Amos Strunk–Called strike one, line out to shortstop, Hooper doubled off first, shortstop to first base.

Chicago:
Max Flack–Ball one, called strike one, ball two, ball three, ball four/walk.
Charlie Hollocher–Called strike one, sacrifice bunt catcher to first base, Flack to second.
Les Mann–Flyout to right.
Dode Paskert–Called strike one, ball one, foul strike two, ball two, ball three, swinging strike three.

Second Inning

Boston:
George Whiteman–Called strike one, ball one, ball two, single to left.
Stuffy McInnis–Foul strike one, foul strike two, foul bunt/strike three.
Wally Schang–Called strike one, foul strike two, foul, foul, swinging strike three, Whiteman to second on stolen base.
Everett Scott–Ball one, called strike one, safe at first on shortstop error, Whiteman to third.
Fred Thomas–Called strike one, flyout to right.

Chicago:
Fred Merkle–Swinging strike one, ball one, ball two, ball three, called strike two, line out to right.
Charlie Pick–Ball one, called strike one, foul strike two, flyout to second base.
Charlie Deal–Called strike one, swinging strike two, groundout third base to first base.

Third Inning

Boston:
Carl Mays–Ball one, called strike one, foul strike two, groundout shortstop to first base.
Harry Hooper–Ball one, groundout first base to pitcher.
Dave Shean–Groundout pitcher to first base.

Chicago:
Bill Killefer–Swinging strike one, groundout second base to first base.
Jim Vaughn–Groundout second base to first base.
Max Flack–Called strike one, groundout to first base unassisted.

Fourth Inning

Boston:
Amos Strunk–Called strike one, called strike two, called strike three.
George Whiteman–Ball one, called strike one, hit by pitch.
Stuffy McInnis–Foul strike one, [ball two,] single to left, Whiteman to second.
Wally Schang–Ball one, single to center, Whiteman scored, McInnis to third.
Everett Scott–Single to pitcher, McInnis scored, Schang to second.
Fred Thomas–Called strike one, ball one, [ball two,] single to right, Schang out at home plate, right field to catcher, Scott to third, Thomas to second.
Carl Mays–Ball one, called strike one, swinging strike two, ball two, ball three, line out to center field.

Chicago:
Charlie Hollocher–Called strike one, ball one, flyout to right field.
Les Mann–Double to right field.
Dode Paskert–Ball one, flyout to left field.
Fred Merkle–Foul strike one, ball one, ball two, foul strike two, groundout shortstop to first base.

Fifth Inning

Boston:
Harry Hooper–Ball one, called strike one, foul strike two, foul, ball two, ball three, foul, ball four/walk.
Dave Shean–Swinging strike one, ball one, ball two, line out to pitcher, Hooper doubled off first base, pitcher to first base.
Amos Strunk–Called strike one, ball one, foul strike two, called strike three.

Chicago:
Charlie Pick–Ball one, ball two, called strike one, double to center field.
Charlie Deal–Ball one, called strike one, swinging strike two, flyout to left field.
Bill Killefer–Ball one, ball two, single to left, Pick scored.
Jim Vaughn–Ball one, called strike one, strike two, ball two, swinging strike three.
Max Flack–Ball one, ball two, called strike one, ball three, Killefer out at second base, catcher to shortstop.

Sixth Inning

Boston:
George Whiteman–Ball one, called strike one, ball two, line out to first base.
Stuffy McInnis–Swinging strike one, pop-up to third base.
Wally Schang–Foul strike one, [ball one,] swinging strike two, called strike three.

Chicago:
Max Flack–Ball one, called strike one, foul pop-up to catcher.
Charlie Hollocher–Ball one, groundout shortstop to first base.
Les Mann–Ball one, single to right field.
Dode Paskert–Called strike one, called strike two, single to center field, Mann to second.
Fred Merkle–Ball one, ball two, foul strike one, ball three, foul strike two, swinging strike three.

Seventh Inning

Boston:
Everett Scott–Foul strike one, ball one, foul flyout to right field.
Fred Thomas–Ball one, called strike one, called strike two, groundout first base to pitcher.
Carl Mays–Foul strike one, groundout pitcher to first base.

Chicago:
Charlie Pick–Called strike one, ball one, groundout shortstop to first base.
Charlie Deal–Called strike one, foul strike two, ball one, ball two, single to third base.
Bill Killefer–Foul strike one, groundout pitcher to first base, Deal to second.
Jim Vaughn–Called strike one, swinging strike two, flyout to left field.

Eighth Inning

Boston:
Harry Hooper–Ball one, ball two, strike one, ball three, swinging strike two, called strike three.
Dave Shean–Foul pop-up to first base.
Amos Strunk–[Swinging strike one, ball one,] Flyout to right field.

Chicago:
Max Flack–Foul strike one, ball one, flyout to center field.
Charlie Hollocher–Ball one, ball two, called strike one, swinging strike two, swinging strike three.
Les Mann–Ball one, foul strike one, ball two, groundout shortstop to first base.

Ninth Inning

Boston:
George Whiteman–Called strike one, ball one, swinging strike two, foul, groundout third base to first base.
Stuffy McInnis–Groundout shortstop to first base.
Wally Schang–Called strike one, single to right field.
Everett Scott–Ball one, Schang to second on stolen base, swinging strike one, foul strike two, ball two, swinging strike three.

Chicago:

Dode Paskert–Called strike one, called strike two, ball one, ball two, groundout shortstop to first base.

Fred Merkle–Called strike one, ball one, ball two, swinging strike two, groundout pitcher to first base.

Charlie Pick–Strike one, strike two, single to shortstop.

Turner Barber batted for Charlie Deal–Ball one, called strike one, Pick to second on stolen base, foul strike two, ball two, Pick to third on catcher's passed ball, Pick out at home plate, catcher to third base to catcher.

BIBLIOGRAPHY

Books

Adomites, Paul, and Saul Wisnia. *Babe Ruth: His Life and Times.* Publications International, Ltd., 1995.

Alexander, Charles. *Ty Cobb.* Oxford University, 1984.

Allen, Lee. *100 Years of Baseball.* Bartholomew House, 1950.

Asinof, Eliot. *Eight Men Out.* Holt, Rinehart and Winston, 1963.

Barrow, Ed, and Christy Walsh. *Adios to Ghosts.* 1937.

Barrow, Ed, and James Kahn. *My 50 Years In Baseball.* Coward-McCann, 1951.

Berry, Henry. *Baseball's Greatest Teams: Boston Red Sox.* Collier/Macmillian, 1975.

————. *Boston Red Sox: The Complete Record of Red Sox Baseball.* Macmillian, 1984.

Bowman, John S., and Joel Zoss. *Diamond in the Rough: The Untold History of Baseball.* Macmillian, 1989.

Burk, Robert F. *Never Just a Game: Players, Owners and American Baseball to 1920.* University of North Carolina, 1994.

Carter, Craig, ed. *The Sporting News Complete Baseball Record Book, 1996 Edition.* The Sporting News Publishing Co., 1995.

Chadwick, Bruce. *The Boston Red Sox: Memories and Mementoes of New England's Team.* Abbeville, 1992.

Clark, Ellery. *Boston Red Sox: 75th Anniversary History.* Exposition Press, 1975.

————. *Red Sox Forever.* Exposition Press, 1977.

————. *Red Sox Fever.* Exposition Press, 1979.

Clark, Tom. *One Last Round for the Shuffler.* Pomerica Press, 1979.

Cole, Milton. *Baseball's Greatest Dynasties: The Red Sox.* Gallery Books, 1990.

Connor, Anthony J. *Baseball for the Love of It: Hall of Famers Tell it Like it Was.* Macmillian, 1982.

Considine, Bob. *The Babe Ruth Story.* E. P. Dutton, 1948. Reprint, Penguin, 1992.

Creamer, Robert W. *Babe: The Legend Comes To Life.* Simon & Schuster, 1974.

Crepeau, Richard. *Baseball: America's Diamond Mind 1919-41.* University Presses of Florida, 1980.

Curran, William. *Strikeout: A Celebration of the Art of Pitching.* Crown, 1995.

Daniel, Dan. *The Real Babe Ruth.* C. C. Spink & Son, 1948.

Dewey, Donald, and Nicholas Acocella. *The Ball Clubs: Every Franchise, Past and Present, Officially Recognized by Major League Baseball.* Harper Collins, 1996.

Dickson, Paul. *The New Dickson Baseball Dictionary.* Harcourt Brace, 1999.

Duffy, John S. *World Series of 1937.* Dell, 1937.

Durso, Joseph. *The Days of McGraw.* Prentice Hall, 1969.

————. *Baseball and The American Dream.* The Sporting News, 1986.

Farrell, James T. *My Baseball Diary.* A. S. Barnes, 1957. Reprint, Southern Illinois University Press, 1998.

Frommer, Harvey. *Baseball's Greatest Rivalry: New York Yankees/Boston Red Sox.* Athenium, 1982.

————. *Shoeless Joe and Ragtime Baseball.* Taylor Publishing Co., 1992.

Gershman, Michael. *Diamonds: The Evolution of the Ballpark.* Houghton Mifflin, 1993.

Ginsberg, Daniel E. *The Fix Is In: A History of Baseball Gambling and Game Fixing Scandals.* Macfarland, 1995.

Gold, Eddie, and Art Ahrens. *The Golden Era Cubs: 1876–1940.* Bonus Books, 1985.

Goldstein, Richard. *Superstars and Screwballs: 100 Years of Brooklyn Baseball.* Dutton, 1991.

Golenbock, Peter. *Fenway: An Unexpurgated History of the Boston Red Sox.* Putnam, 1992.

Graham, Frank. *The New York Yankees: An Informal History.* Putnam, 1943.

Greene, Suzanne Ellery. *Baltimore: An Illustrated History.* Windsor Publications, 1980.

Gropman, Donald. *Say It Ain't So, Joe!: The True Story of Shoeless Joe Jackson.* Little, Brown, 1979.

Gutman, Dan. *Baseball Babylon: From the Black Sox to Pete Rose, the Real Stories Behind the Scandals that Rocked the Game.* Penguin, 1992.

Harries, Meiron, and Susie Harries. *The Last Days of Innocence: America at War, 1917–1918.* Random House, 1997.

Harris, Paul F. *Babe Ruth: The Dark Side.* Self-published, date unknown.

Heylar, John. *Lords of the Realm: The Real History of Baseball.* Ballantine, 1994.

Hirschberg, Al. *Baseball's Greatest Catchers.* Putnam, 1967.

Honig, Donald. *The American League Story: An Illustrated History.* Crown, 1983.

———. *Baseball America: The Heroes of the Game and the Times of Their Glory.* Macmillian, 1985.

———. *The Boston Red Sox: An Illustrated History.* Prentice Hall, 1990.

Hornsby, Rogers. *My Kind of Baseball.* McKay, 1953.

Hoyt, Waite. *Babe Ruth As I Knew Him.* Dell Publishing, 1948.

Humber, William. *Diamonds of the North: A Concise History of Baseball in Canada.* Oxford University, 1995.

James, Bill. *The Bill James Historical Baseball Abstract.* Villard, 1988.

———. *The Bill James Guide to Baseball Managers From 1870 to Today.* Scribner, 1997.

Kahn, James. *The Umpire's Story*. Putnam, 1953.

Keene, Kerry, Raymond Sinibaldi, and David Hickey. *The Babe in Red Stockings: An In-Depth Chronicle of Babe Ruth With the Boston Red Sox, 1914–1919*. Sagamore, 1997.

Kuklick, Bruce. *To Everything a Season: Shibe Park and Urban Philadelphia 1909–1976*. Princeton University Press, 1991.

Laird, A. W. *Ranking Baseball's Elite: An Analysis Derived From Player Statistics, 1893–1987*. Macfarland, 1990.

Lane, F. C. *Batting: One Thousand Expert Opinions on Every Conceivable Angle of Batting Science; The Secrets of Major League Batting and Useful Hints for Hitters of All Ranks and Ages, Collected over a Period of Fifteen Years from Nearly Three Hundred Famous Players*. Baseball Magazine, 1925.

Leisman, Louis J. *I Was With Babe Ruth At St. Mary's*. Self-published, 1956.

Lieb, Fred. *The Boston Red Sox*. Putnam, 1947.

———. *The Story of the World Series*. Putnam, 1949.

———. *The Baseball Story*. Putnam, 1950.

———. *The Baltimore Orioles: The History of a Colorful Team in Baltimore and St. Louis*. Putnam, 1955.

———. *Baseball As I Have Known It*. Coward McCann, 1977.

Linn, Ed, and Bill Veeck. *The Hustler's Handbook*. Putnam, 1965.

Linn, Ed. *The Great Rivalry: The New York Yankees and the Boston Red Sox, 1901–1990*. Ticknor & Fields, 1991.

Liss, Howard. *The Boston Red Sox: The Complete History*. Simon & Schuster, 1982.

Lowry, Philip. *Green Cathedrals*. Cooperstown-Society of American Baseball Research, 1986. Reprint, Addison-Wesley, 1992.

Luhrs, Victor. *The Great Baseball Mystery*. A. S. Barnes, 1966.

Mack, Connie. *My 66 Years in the Big Leagues*. Winston, 1950.

———. *From Sandlot to Big League: Connie Mack's Baseball Book*. Knopf, 1960.

McConnell, Bob, and David Vincent, eds. *SABR Presents The Home Run Encyclopedia: The Who, What, And Where Of Every Home Run Hit Since 1876*. Macmillan, 1996.

McGarigle, Bob. *Baseball's Greatest Tragedy: The Story of Carl Mays–Submarine Pitcher*. Exposition Press, 1972.

McGraw, John. *My 30 Years in Baseball*. Boni & Liveright, 1923. Reprint, University of Nebraska Press, 1995.

Meany, Tom. *Babe Ruth: The Big Moments of the Big Fellow*. A. S. Barnes, 1947.

———. *The Boston Red Sox*. A. S. Barnes, 1956.

Mercurio, John. *Chronology of Boston Red Sox Records*. Harper & Row, 1989.

Miller, Richard L. "The Old Ballparks of Massachusetts." *Sports in Massachusetts: Historical Essays*. Westfield State College, 1991.

Murdock, Eugene. *Ban Johnson: Czar of Baseball*. Greenwood, 1982.

———. *Baseball Players and Their Times: Oral Histories of the Game 1920–1940*. Meckler, 1991.

———. *Baseball Between The Wars: Memories of the Game by the Men who Played It*. Meckler, 1992.

Nicholson, Lois P. *Babe Ruth: Sultan of Swat*. Goodwood Press, 1994.

Okkonen, Mark. *Baseball Uniforms of the 20th Century*. Sterling Publishing, 1993.

———. *The Federal League of 1914–1915: Baseball's Third Major League*. Society of American Baseball Research, 1989.

Okrent, Dan and Harris Lewine. *The Ultimate Baseball Book*. Houghton Mifflin, 1979.

Oldstone, Michael B. A. *Viruses, Plagues, and History*. Oxford University, 1998.

Olson, Sherry H. *Baltimore: The Building of an American City*. John Hopkins University Press, 1997.

Paretchan, Harold. *The World Series: A Statistical Record*. A. S. Barnes, 1968.

Pirone, Dorothy Ruth. *My Dad, The Babe: Growing Up With An American Hero*. Quinlan Press, 1988.

Povich, Shirley. *The Washington Senators*. G. P. Putnam Sons, 1954.

Reach Official American League Guide, The. 1917–1922.

Rice, Grantland. *The Tumult and the Shouting*. Barnes, 1954.

Ritter, Lawrence. *The Glory Of Their Times: The Story of the Early Days of Baseball Told by the Men who Played It*. Macmillian, 1966. Reprint, Quill, 1992.

———. *Lost Ballparks: A Celebration of Baseball's Legendary Fields*. Viking, 1992.

Ritter, Lawrence, and Mark Rucker. *The Babe: A Life in Pictures*. Ticknor & Fields, 1988. Reprint, *The Babe: The Game That Ruth Built*. Total Sports, 1997.

Ritter, Lawrence, and Donald Honig. *The Image of Their Greatness: An Illustrated History of Baseball From 1900 to the Present*. Crown, 1979.

Rubin, Robert. *Ty Cobb: The Greatest*. G. P. Putnam's Sons, 1978.

Ruth, Babe. *Babe Ruth's Own Book Of Baseball*. G. P. Putnam's Sons, 1928. Reprint, University of Nebraska Press, 1992.

Ruth, Claire Merritt, and Bill Slocum. *The Babe and I*. Prentice Hall, 1959.

Scheinin, Richard. *Field of Screams: The Dark Underside of America's National Pastime*. Norton, 1994.

Seymour, Harold. *Baseball: The Early Years*. Oxford University, 1960.

———. *Baseball: The Golden Age*. Oxford University, 1971.

———. *Baseball: The People's Game*. Oxford University, 1990.

Shaughnessy, Dan. *The Curse of the Bambino*. Dutton, 1990.

Simon, Tom, ed. *Green Mountain Boys of Summer: Vermonters in the Major Leagues 1882–1993*. New England Press, 2000.

Smelser, Marshall. *The Life That Ruth Built*. Quadrangle, 1975. Reprint, University of Nebraska Press, 1993.

Smith, Robert. *Babe Ruth's America: A Warm and Rollicking Portrait of the Babe and his Times*. Crowell, 1974.

Sobol, Ken. *Babe Ruth and the American Dream*. Ballantine, 1974.

Solomon, Burt. *The Baseball Timeline: The Day-by-Day History of Baseball From Valley Forge to the Present Day.* Avon, 1997.

Sowell, Mike. *The Pitch That Killed: Carl Mays, Ray Chapman and the Pennant Race of 1920.* Macmillian, 1989.

Spaulding's Official Baseball Guide. 1917–1922.

Spink, J. G. Taylor. *Judge Landis and 25 Years of Baseball.* Crowell, 1947. Reprint, The Sporting News, 1974.

Starr, Bill. *Clearing the Bases: Baseball Then & Now.* Michael Kesend Publishing, 1989.

Stein, Irving. *The Ginger Kid: Buck Weaver.* Elysian Fields, 1992.

Stump, Al. *Ty Cobb: My Life in Baseball, The True Record.* Doubleday, 1961. Reprint, University of Nebraska Press, 1993.

———. *Cobb: A Biography.* Algonquin, 1994.

Sullivan, Mark. *Our Times: The United States, The War Begins 1909–1914.* Charles Scribner's, 1932.

———. *Our Times: The United States, 1914–1918.* Charles Scribner's, 1933.

Thomas, Henry W. *Walter Johnson: Baseball's Big Train.* Phenom Press, 1995.

Thorn, John, and Pete Palmer with Michael Gershman, eds. *Total Baseball, Fifth Edition: The Official Encyclopedia of Major League Baseball.* Viking, 1995.

Thorn, John, and John B. Holoway. *The Pitcher.* Prentice Hall, 1987.

Voigt, David. *American Baseball, Volume I: From Gentlemen's Sport to the Commissioner System.* University of Oklahoma Press, 1966. Reprint, Penn State, 1983.

———. *American Baseball, Volume II: From the Commissioners to Continental Expansion.* University of Oklahoma Press, 1970. Reprint, Penn State, 1983.

———. *America Through Baseball.* Nelson Hall, 1976.

Wagenheim, Kal. *Babe Ruth: His Life and Legend.* Praeger, 1974. Reprint, Holt, 1992.

Wallace, Joseph. *The Autobiography of Baseball: The Inside Story From the Stars Who Played the Game*. Harry N. Abrams, 1998.

Walton, Ed. *Day By Day in Red Sox History*. Stein & Day, 1978.

————. *Red Sox: Triumphs and Tragedies*. Stein & Day, 1980.

Ward, Geoffrey C., and Ken Burns. *Baseball: An Illustrated History*. Knopf, 1994.

Waterman, Ty, and Mel Springer. *The Year the Red Sox Won the Series*. Northeastern University Press, 1999.

Weldon, Martin. *Babe Ruth*. Crowell, 1948.

Wolff, Rick, ed. *The Baseball Encyclopedia: The Complete and Definitive Record of Major League Baseball, 9th ed.* Macmillian, 1993.

Zimbalist, Andrew. *Baseball and Billions*. Harper Collins, 1992.

Zingg, Paul. *Harry Hooper: An American Life*. University of Illinois, 1994.

Zinn, Howard. *A People's History of the United States: 1492–Present*. Harper Perennial, 1995.

Newspapers

Baltimore American, 1913–20.

Baltimore Sun, 1914–1919.

Boston American, 1918, 1947.

Boston Daily Advertiser, 1918.

Boston Evening Record, 1914–1920.

Boston Evening Transcript, 1914–1920.

Boston Globe, 1914–1920.

Boston Herald, 1947.

Boston Herald and Journal, 1914–1920.

Boston Post, 1914–1920.

Boston Sunday Advertiser, 1918.

Boston Traveler, 1917–1918.

Brooklyn Eagle, 1917–18.
Chicago American, 1918.
Chicago Daily Tribune, 1918.
Chicago Daily News, 1918.
Chicago Evening Post, 1918.
Chicago Herald and Examiner, 1918.
Detroit Free Press, 1918.
Cleveland Plain Dealer, 1918.
New Orleans Times-Picayune, 1918.
New York Evening World, 1918.
New York Herald, 1918.
New York Herald Tribune, 1948.
New York Sun, 1918.
New York Times, 1915–20.
New York Tribune, 1918.
Pawtucket (R.I.) Times, 1973.
Philadelphia Inquirer, 1918–21.
Riverside (Calif.) Daily Enterprise, 1959.
San Francisco Chronicle, 1918.
The Sporting Life, 1911–20.
The Sporting News, 1906–80.
Stars and Stripes, February 1918–June 1919 (Paris Edition).
St. Louis Globe-Democrat, 1918.
St. Louis Post-Dispatch, 1918, 1927.
Washington Post, 1918.
Washington Times, 1989.

Magazine Articles

Alabelli, A. A. "Babe Ruth's Home Run Secrets." *Popular Mechanics*, March 1928.

Barrow, Edward G. "When A Pennant Is Almost Won." *Baseball Magazine*, October 1918.

―――. "Why the Red Sox Won." *Baseball Magazine*, November 1918.

Belz, Rick. "A Potent Pitch for Ruth Registry." *Howard County (Md.) Sun*, February 1, 1989.

Brundidge, Harry T. "Quit Game in 1913 and Went Back to Grocery Job." *The Sporting News*, December 29, 1932.

Burnes, Bob and Carl Mays. "Death Pitch Still Plagues Carl Mays." *The Sporting News*, August 10, 1963.

Cashman, Joe. "Bill Carrigan Tells: My Days with the Red Sox; Lewis–Speaker–Hooper." *Boston Sunday Advertiser*, January 10, 1943.

―――. "Bill Carrigan Tells: My Days with the Red Sox; Fans Boycott Fenway in '12." *Boston Daily Record*, January 15, 1943.

―――. "Bill Carrigan Tells: My Days with the Red Sox; Wood-Johnson Hill Duel Revived." *Boston Daily Record*, January 16, 1943.

―――. "Bill Carrigan Tells: My Days with the Red Sox; Says Sox Lucky In Epic '12 Finale." *Boston Sunday Advertiser*, January 17, 1943.

―――. "Bill Carrigan Tells: My Days with the Red Sox; Job as Hose Manager Big Surprise." *Boston Daily Record*, January 18, 1943.

―――. "Bill Carrigan Tells: My Days with the Red Sox; Babe Sold to Hose in 'Panic' of '14." *Boston Daily Record*, January 19, 1943.

―――. "Bill Carrigan Tells: My Days with the Red Sox; Special Discipline Accorded Babe." *Boston Daily Record*, January 20, 1943.

―――. "Bill Carrigan Tells: My Days with the Red Sox; Old Master Talks on Pitching." *Boston Daily Record*, January 21, 1943.

―――. "Bill Carrigan Tells: My Days with the Red Sox; Duffy Lewis Hero of 1915 Series." *Boston Daily Record*, January 22, 1943.

————. "Bill Carrigan Tells: My Days with the Red Sox; Won '16 Flag With 4 Aces Missing." *Boston Daily Record*, January 23, 1943.

————. "Bill Carrigan Tells: My Days with the Red Sox; Ruth Pitches 29 Scoreless Innings." *Boston Daily Record*, January 25, 1943.

————. "Bill Carrigan Tells: My Days with the Red Sox; Quit Hose for Business Venture." *Boston Daily Record*, January 26, 1943.

————. "Feuds With Speaker Only Off-Field–Lewis." *Boston Daily Record*, January 15, 1951.

Conway, Jack. "Things Which I Believe Have Been Responsible For My Successful Batting." *Baseball Magazine*, April 1920.

Daniel, Dan. "From Peanuts to Pennants: The Story of Edward G. Barrow." *New York World-Telegram*, 1933.

Farrell, James T. "The King is Dead." *Sport*, May 1974.

Flack, Max. "The Muff that Lost the Series." *Baseball Magazine*, November 1918.

Frazee, Harry. "The Reasons Which Led Me to Sell 'Babe' Ruth." *Baseball Magazine*, April 1920.

Gallagher, Jack. "Bullet Joe Bush Remembers the Babe." *Baseball Magazine*, September 1972.

Hollocher, Charles, Babe Ruth, Everett Scott, Fred Mitchell and Stuffy McInnis. "Behind the Scenes." *Baseball Magazine*, November 1918.

Hooper, Harry. "The Secrets of Good Outfielding." *Baseball Magazine*, June 1917.

Johnson, Walter. "What I Pitch to Babe Ruth and Why." *Baseball Magazine*, September 1920.

Kieran, John. "Luck Helps Make Endurance Record Says Everett Scott." *The Sporting News*, April 6, 1922.

Killefer, William. "Bidding the Game Good Bye." *Baseball Magazine*, November 1918.

Lane, F. C. "The Slowball Wizard." *Baseball Magazine*, January 1913.

————. "'Dutch' Leonard's Three Ambitions." *Baseball Magazine*, November 1916.

————. "A Rising Menace to the National Game." *Baseball Magazine*, August 1918.

————. "The Season's Sensation." *Baseball Magazine*, October 1918.

————. "The Cubs Against the Field." *Baseball Magazine*, October 1918.

————. "The Hero of the Series." *Baseball Magazine*, November 1918.

————. "The Future Prospects of Major League Baseball." *Baseball Magazine*, November 1918.

————. "The Fire Brand of the American League." *Baseball Magazine*, March 1919.

————. "My Greatest Baseball Experience So Far." *Baseball Magazine*, November 1920.

————. "Ev. Scott, the Man Who Never Fails." *Baseball Magazine*, July 1922.

————. "The Yankees' Pitching Ace." *Baseball Magazine*, February 1923.

————. "Carl Mays' Cynical Definition of Pitching Efficiency." *Baseball Magazine*, August 1928.

Lanigan, Harold W. "Rated 'Too Light' at 125 Pounds, He Became Game's No. 2 Iron Man; Calls Red Sox Greatest." *The Sporting News*, October 29, 1942.

Lemke, Bob. "Canada Saved Dubuc From Landis' Wrath." *Sports Collectors Digest*, June 11, 1993.

Levin, Leonard. "Babe Ruth In Providence." *Providence Journal-Bulletin*, August 1995.

Mays, Carl. "A Good Ending." *Baseball Magazine*, November 1918.

————. "My Attitude Towards the Chapman Affair." *Baseball Magazine*, November 1920.

————. "What I Have Learned In Four World's Series." *Baseball Magazine*, November 1922.

McInnis, Stuffy. "My Fifth World's Series." *Baseball Magazine*, October 1918.

Mitchell, Fred. "The Strength of the Cub Machine." *Baseball Magazine*, October 1918.

Morris, Robert M. "Babe Ruth–Pitcher." *The New York Times Magazine*, August 10, 1958.

Paskert, Dode. "My Best Season." *Baseball Magazine*, October 1918.

Phelon, W. A. "Sensational Baseball Trades." *Baseball Magazine*, March 1918.

———. "Major League Baseball in the Balance." *Baseball Magazine*, September 1918.

———. "Who Will Win The World's Championship." *Baseball Magazine*, October 1918.

———. "How the World's Championship Was Lost and Won." *Baseball Magazine*, November 1918.

Piper, Pat. "World Series Hero Recalls the Great Stars." *Manatee (Wisconsin) Times*, April 4, 1976.

Ruppert, Col. Jacob and Ex-Governor Tener, etc. "Prominent Baseball Men and Their Opinions of Babe Ruth." *Baseball Magazine*, April 1920.

Sargent, Jim. "Walter 'Wally' Schang, The Greatest Forgotten Catcher: 1913–1931." *Oldtyme Baseball News*, Volume 6, Issue 2.

Schang, Wallie. "A Thumping, Clouting Backstop and His Picturesque Career." *Baseball Magazine*, October 1927.

Schwartz, Simon M. "1,307–Game Player Tells of Own Skein." *The Sporting News*, December 19, 1956.

Scott, Everett. "Everett Scott's Bid to Fame." *Baseball Magazine*, November 1924.

———. "Recollections of a Veteran Shortstop." *Baseball Magazine*, July 1926.

Scully, Matthew. "Remembering the Babe: His Younger Sister's Tale." *Washington Times*, August 29, 1989.

Sheridan, John B. "Sheridan Tells Why He Rates Babe Ruth An Ideal Hitter." *The Sporting News*, January 1, 1918.

Slick, Carroll S. with Joe Bush. "On the Mound." *The Saturday Evening Post*, June 8, 1929.

————. "At Bat." *The Saturday Evening Post*, June 22, 1929.

————. "Breaking In." *The Saturday Evening Post*, August 24, 1929.

————. "The Lost Arts in Baseball." *The Saturday Evening Post*, April 5, 1930.

Stout, Glenn. "1918." *Boston Magazine*, October 1987.

————. "The Last Champions." *New England Sport*, Summer 1993.

Thomas, Chet. "Babe Ruth the Super Player." *Baseball Magazine*, November 1920.

Trachtenberg, Leo. "The Durable Deacon." *Yankees Magazine*, December 17, 1992.

Vaughn, Jim. "One in Three." *Baseball Magazine*, November 1918.

Ward, John J. "The 'Pinch Pitcher' of the World's Champions." *Baseball Magazine*, December 1916.

————. "Hollocher, the Wizard Shortstop." *Baseball Magazine*, October 1918.

Wood, Allan. "Someone Can Recall Red Sox Title." *Baseball America*, March 6, 1997.

Baseball Magazine. "The Secret of a Rapid Rise." February 1919.

Literary Digest, The. "Babe Ruth Is Supernormal, Hence The 'Homers.'" October 1, 1921.

Sporting News, The. "School Mate Pitcher Was Enigma For Mighty Ruth." December 5, 1917.

Sporting News, The. "Mystery of Pinch-Hitter Bluhm Solved." December 15, 1962.

Sports Collectors Digest. "Ruth's 1918 World Series Watch Donated to Museum." April 26, 1991.

Toronto Blue Jays Scorebook. "The Unlikely Hero of 1918." 1977.

Telephone Interviews

Allen Agnew, February 22, 1995 and April 11, 1995.
Howard Ballard, May 20, 1996.
Elizabeth Mays Barker, May 30, 1995 and August 31, 1995.
Robert Bluthardt, July 24, 1995.
Maurice Dubuc, September 11, 1995.
Donald Duren, December 1995.
Jeanne Fahey, October 16, 1995.
Thomas Foley, July 22, 1995, October 30, 1995 and January 5, 1997.
Wes Goforth, July 17, 1995.
John Hooper, January 23, 1995.
Inez Klein, July 17, 1995.
Eileen Littlefield, August 7, 1995.
Ed Linn, November 19, 1995.
Frank McMillian, February 26, 1995.
Patrick Rock, September 12, 1995.
Jack Schang, September 11, 1995 and September 18, 1995.
Dave Shean Jr., February 28, 1995.
Ralph Sheridan, June 8, 1995.
Robert Smith, January 24, 1996.
Robert Thomas, April 12, 1995 and May 10, 1995.
Susan Constance Thomas, May 8, 1995 and July 18, 1995.
Warren Thomas, July 30, 1995.
Dick Thompson, September 8, 1995.
William Wagner, September 5, 1995.
Ed Walton, February 24, 1995 and April 18, 1995.

Personal Papers and Archival Material

Courtesy of Elizabeth Mays Barker, Carl Mays, audio cassette.

Courtesy of John Hooper, Harry Hooper, personal correspondence.

Courtesy of Robert Thomas, Fred Thomas, audio cassette and personal correspondence.

Courtesy of Cleveland Public Library, Cleveland, Ohio.

 Zinn Beck (interview by Eugene Murdock, audio cassette, December 31, 1979).

 Stan Coveleski (interview by Eugene Murdock, audio cassette, May 13, 1974).

 Red Faber (interview by Eugene Murdock, audio cassette, March 15, 1976).

 Fred Lieb (interview by Eugene Murdock, audio cassette, July 18–19, 1970).

 Bob O'Farrell (interview by Eugene Murdock, audio cassette, March 16, 1976).

 Elmer Smith (interview by Eugene Murdock, audio cassette, November 17, 1973).

Courtesy of National Baseball Hall of Fame Library, Cooperstown, New York, biographical information on each major league player.